The Great European Adventure

Visiting Forty-Nine Countries on a Budget

David Birkett

The Great European Adventure

Contents

Chapter	Page	
	4	Introduction
1	8	Rules of Engagement
2	15	France
3	20	The Balkans Part 1 - Greece, Macedonia, Serbia, Bulgaria
4	29	The Balkans Part 2 - Croatia, Montenegro, Kosovo, Bosnia
5	38	The Balkans Part 3 – Albania and Greece
6	45	The Balkans Part 4 – Slovenia and Italy
7	53	The Baltic States - Estonia, Latvia, Lithuania, and Finland
8	58	Romania and Moldova
9	67	Poland and Ukraine
10	74	Spain, Gibraltar, Ireland
11	85	Monaco, Italy, Austria, Liechtenstein, Switzerland, Germany
12	93	Andorra, France, Spain
13	102	The Czech Republic
14	108	Austria, Slovakia and Hungary
15	116	Belgium, The Netherlands, Luxembourg, France, Germany
16	125	Russia
17	135	Iceland
18	143	Norway, Sweden, Denmark
19	155	Portugal
20	167	Vatican City, Italy
21	178	San Marino, Italy
22	185	Malta
23	196	Belarus
24	211	Turkey, Cyprus
25	225	United Kingdom
26	235	Cyprus and The Turkish Republic of Northern Cyprus

Introduction

Travelling – it leaves you speechless, then turns you into a storyteller   **Ibn Battuta**

I haven't been everywhere, but it's on the list   **Susan Sontag**

This book is about a travel challenge. A challenge I set myself in 1997, and which I completed in 2017.

From my early teen years I have been addicted to travel. I love the planning. I love the journey as much as the destination. I love resolving problems when things go wrong. I love (most of) the people I meet. I love the surprises. I love the things I learn about the places I visit. And I love having a beer at a pavement cafe in the evening sunshine after a busy day's touring.

There are those who find a favourite destination and go there year after year. This is not for me. I rarely revisit a place, as to do so would mean missing out on other as yet unseen destinations. I do, however, regularly make an exception in the cases of Paris and Venice, two cities that I find irresistible.

There are those who will only travel on organised tours, be it by train, bus, or cruise liner. For them, travel is a pleasurable way of spending time abroad in which others decide on which places to visit and make all the necessary arrangements. Whilst superficially attractive, tours rarely allow participants to experience everyday life in the places they visit, and of course the itinerary is entirely in the gift of the tour operator. In addition, I calculate that the cost of a tour may be as much as double that of a similar itinerary assembled from home.

For couples with young children, as for the elderly, travel outwith the world of organised tours is, I am bound to admit, difficult, but not impossible. It may be that it best suits pre-marriage singles, or empty-nesters, but far be it for me to dissuade anyone who nurses the travel bug from doing their own thing.

For much of my working life I was able to travel as part of my job, giving me the opportunity to satisfy my addiction at someone-else's expense. However this changed in the late 1990s when I found myself desk-bound, on a modest wage, and obliged to settle for the usual four weeks' annual holiday. I was suddenly limited to perhaps four destinations per year, plus possibly two more at Christmas and Easter. And yet there were so many places I'd never visited, surprisingly many of which were on my own doorstep, so to speak.

I'm talking, of course, about the continent of Europe. Of the 49 countries in Europe, which may total only 47 depending on one's definition of a country, I'd only set foot in ten. Admittedly these ten had been visited many times, but I began to realise how little I knew of the others.

It was then that I decided on the challenge. I would attempt to visit every country in Europe during the coming years, making the best use possible of the few weeks available to me. In view of my financial situation, there would be no organised tours, which obliged me to organise the trips myself.

I devised a list of self-inflicted rules, all of which are listed in chapter 1, which are somewhat sinisterly titled "Rules of Engagement". These rules resulted in my spending widely varying periods of time in each country, with Andorra and Bosnia coming last in the "time spent" listing, at half an hour each. During the project I had no tablet or mobile phone, items that would undoubtedly make life easier should I repeat the exercise now, but I hope I can show that even today they are not essential.

As it transpired, in the 1990s and 2000s a number of disconnected events and changes conspired to make the project possible. The low-cost airlines were beginning to stretch their wings metaphorically; our membership of the European Union meant that no visas were required for all but one of the 49 countries; the Iron Curtain had been raised, opening up most of the ex-USSR countries to westerners, and ensuring that younger citizens learned English at school rather than Russian; the Internet was becoming invaluable for making hotel and travel bookings and getting detailed transport and country information; and as a bonus I found myself living reasonably close to the five "London" airports. I would go so far as to say that the project would have scarcely been possible twenty years earlier.

How many "countries" were involved? Surprisingly perhaps, the number varies, depending on one's definition of a country, and, indeed, Europe. There can be as many as 51, but this figure is the subject of debate. Russia, Azerbaijan, Kazakhstan, Turkey and Georgia are considered by the United Nations to be "Transcontinental", that is to say, both Asian and European. Armenia and Cyprus are considered as being located in what is defined as the "West Asia Territory". Cyprus has a further complication, being a member of the European Union but divided in two. The northern part, The Turkish Republic of Northern Cyprus, is self-designated as an independent country but is only recognised by Turkey.

The United Nations' definition of Europe lists 44 countries including Russia, but excluding Turkey, Cyprus (North and South) and Gibraltar (defined as a Dependency). My own conclusion was to include these four, together with Kosovo, which is currently recognised as a country by 110 UN member states and not recognised by 83 others. As a result, my final target was 49, of which Gibraltar is strictly speaking not a country but which I have arbitrarily decided to include as it possesses many attributes of a sovereign nation. The United Kingdom, my home country, did not require a "visit", but for completeness I have included an account of a single day's visit to some of the less well-known parts of London.

The full list of the countries I visited (in no particular order) is:

1	Russia	26	Norway
2	Germany	27	Ireland
3	UK	28	Croatia
4	France	29	Moldova
5	Italy	30	Bosnia and Herzegovina
6	Spain	31	Albania
7	Ukraine	32	Lithuania
8	Poland	33	Macedonia
9	Romania	34	Slovenia
10	Netherlands	35	Latvia
11	Belgium	36	Estonia
12	Greece	37	Montenegro
13	Czech Republic	38	Luxembourg
14	Portugal	39	Malta
15	Sweden	40	Iceland
16	Hungary	41	Andorra
17	Belarus	42	Liechtenstein
18	Serbia	43	Monaco
19	Austria	44	San Marino
20	Switzerland	45	Vatican City (Holy See)
21	Bulgaria	46	Turkey
22	Denmark	47	The Republic of Cyprus
23	Finland	48	The Turkish Republic of Northern Cyprus
24	Slovakia	49	Gibraltar
25	Kosovo		

Some 17 years after the project began I landed at Gatwick Airport, having returned from the last-remaining country on my list, Belarus, of which more later in this book. There were no press photographers at the arrivals hall, and no surprise parties back home, just a feeling of smug satisfaction that an ambitious goal had finally been achieved. Those who watched Michael Palin's television series "Around the World in Eighty Days" may remember his initial disappointment when he arrived back in London almost unnoticed after his epic journey. I can only say, and I'm sure he would concur, that a brief moment of disheartenment is quickly banished by an abiding feeling of achievement.

In writing this book I hope to persuade others to become a member of the "49" club, whether working full-time or not, and, most important of all, hope they will find it an enjoyable, educational, and memorable experience. This isn't a backpacker's guide, although backpackers may find parts of it useful, and it isn't a gap year project guide, as most of the visits, simple return journeys from England, lasted no more than a week or so. Nor is it a specifically a guide to museums, galleries and similar attractions, although inevitably these receive attention from time to time in the text. It simply describes some fascinating and occasionally remarkable travel experiences, almost exclusively using public transport, during my visits to every country in Europe.

Chapter 1

Rules of Engagement

In planning the project, I decided that there should be self-imposed (and therefore arbitrary) rules in order to keep costs down to a minimum. This cost-cutting did not, however, extend to sleeping rough or in hostels, or hitch-hiking, although I was obliged to do these things on a couple of occasions. It simply meant that I would be careful with money whilst still living reasonably comfortably. The project was completed from my home in the UK, but the rules could equally be applied by a traveller based in continental Europe, or indeed any other country. Finally, a reminder that the rules I created were intended to achieve the maximum enjoyment at the minimum cost.

From the outset I needed to define what would constitute a "visit" to a country. Some might argue that simply passing through on the train or bus is sufficient. Others might say that transiting in the airport is enough. Purists might insist that one must stay overnight. My own definition is somewhat different as outlined in "Travel Rules" below. As previously mentioned, organised tours were to be excluded in order to keep costs down, but, as will be revealed, I was obliged to break this rule twice, and it's no coincidence that this occurred in visits to two of the ex-Soviet Union countries.

Travel Rules

All air travel to the country concerned was to be by a scheduled airline. I am fortunate to live near the five London airports, so accept that this rule may be problematic for anyone using UK regional or foreign airports. I have to say that my project may never have left the ground (literally) without the availability of Easy Jet and Ryanair, both of whom have extensive lists of European destinations.

Rail Travel had to be by scheduled trains, and for UK travellers this naturally includes Eurostar trains from London to Paris, Brussels, and Lille. It occurred to me that it might be interesting to attempt the entire project by rail only, but this is for someone else to try! Boat travel had to be by scheduled ferries, and long-distance bus travel by scheduled buses.

Travel rules once I arrived at my destination were simple. No taxis were allowed – they are too expensive - particularly from the destination airport into town, but also for the duration of the visit, other than in exceptional circumstances. All airports run low-priced scheduled bus services into town or city centres for their employees and these had to be sought out and used. The cheapest I found was a fare of 49 Eurocents for a journey of 40 minutes from Bucharest airport to the city centre. Metro, tram, and train are of course also acceptable for this journey. Once installed in my hotel, I normally tried to spend the first evening familiarising myself with the local public transport system, usually over a beer at a nearby cafe, using my guide-book, often supplemented with whatever maps and leaflets were available at the hotel reception desk.

How does one define a "visit" to a country? After much deliberation I concluded that it is sufficient to set foot outside the perimeter of the airport, railway station, or bus station. Changing trains, planes or buses in a particular country does not constitute a visit unless one leaves the premises.

This inevitably sets me at odds with those who insist that an overnight stay is a more rigorous definition of a visit, but I believe my definition is at least adequate.

.In many European countries I've found that having English as a first language is vital. Most continental Europeans nowadays have learned English as a foreign language in school, thank goodness! The situation in ex-Soviet Union countries is, however, somewhat patchy. There, I always sought help from younger local people. Many of them have learned English in school, as opposed to the older generation who often only learned Russian as a foreign language.

These were the rules I set for myself. In Bosnia and Macedonia I was obliged to use taxis, and in Belarus I used the services of a tour operator, but for the remainder of the time I managed to obey them. By doing so I met people I would otherwise never have met, had experiences that would never have arisen on an organised tour, and at the same time I calculate that I spent on average half of what an organised tour would have cost.

Keeping Costs Down

The Flight

The budget airlines offer a wide range of fares to any particular destination, generally based on the time of departure, the day of the week, the month of the year, and the length of time between booking and travelling. I always tried to fly out midweek and return midweek, but if work dictated that I travel at the weekend, then I considered the possibility of taking an early-morning flight. However with two-hour check-in times this can mean arriving at the airport at 4am, which is never a pleasant experience. To take advantage of cheap early-morning fares I have sometimes travelled to the UK airport at 11pm the previous evening by bus or train and then slept fitfully in the departure hall till the flight is called at around 5am, an experience which is not for the faint-hearted. I always go to the airport by public transport if I can't persuade a friend to take me, and never drive there, as medium-stay car parking charges can sometimes be more than the cost of the flight.

I consider it my duty to go through an airport without making a single purchase. For food I take home-made sandwiches, but on those few occasions where I have found myself obliged to buy food whilst waiting for a flight I try to find a branch of Marks and Spencer or Boots as they charge high-street prices, usually much lower than the prices of sandwiches and rolls in the coffee shops. As for water, in my opinion there is never any excuse for buying water at the airport. Take a bottle of tap water with you to drink whilst you wait landside. When the flight is called empty whatever's left in the bottle down the landside toilet before you go through to airside, then refill it from the tap in the airside toilet. One airport I visited attempted to overcome this ploy, and thereby maintain the level of water sales in airside shops, by adding soap solution to the source of tap-water in the airside toilets, thus rendering it undrinkable. Thankfully they were persuaded of the error of their ways by the local health and safety department and the next time I visited that airport the taps were again dispensing pure water. With a little forethought you can join me in becoming one of that elite group of passengers that pass through any airport without spending a thing. As for purchasing inevitably expensive food on the aircraft, there is no need if you have brought your own sandwiches, and have water from the airside toilet washbasin.

Luggage

As for luggage, my own preference is for a single capacious shoulder bag that fits the standard airline dimensions for cabin baggage. I rarely take checked baggage as no check-in is required and I don't have to visit the carousel at the destination airport. At smaller airports I have found this invaluable as it has given me a head start in boarding the sometimes limited number of buses that have been laid on to meet the incoming flight. I am extremely ruthless when packing, and my bag carries sufficient changes of clothes for, say, 5 days' travelling without my becoming a health hazard to those around me. I never carry a spare pair of shoes because I have yet to find myself in a situation where one has been needed. A cabin-sized wheeled case can be a liability if you are travelling by tram or bus at your destination, but I do appreciate, however, that travelling so light may be easier for men than women.

Foreign Exchange

I am not a financial advisor so cannot advise on matters to do with foreign currency. All I would say is that in my experience exchange rates at the airport can be worse than those on your high street back home. I personally try to have a small amount of the destination's local currency with me when I leave home, and then use my debit or credit card on arrival in my destination city-centre to get cash. I always try to use cash-points at overseas high-street banks during their normal opening hours. That way, if the machine swallows my card, I can go into the bank and report it in person, and hopefully get them to do something about it on the spot.

Food and drink when you get there

At your destination you will find yourself tempted by local restaurants offering delicious local delicacies, but at a price. If sampling local cuisine is important to you, then go ahead, but be prepared to pay a high price. If not, then seek out other means of filling yourself up. There are many ways of avoiding expensive restaurant bills, thereby reducing costs considerably.

Your first action on arriving at your hotel, after obtaining details of local buses, trains, and trams, and a map of the locality from reception, should be to walk round the block and locate the nearest supermarket or convenience store. There you will find a wide range of food to satisfy the keenest of appetites, together with a variety of alcoholic and non-alcoholic drinks. If you buy wine, try to get something that is local and In a bottle with a screw cap. Buy plastic cutlery if you can find it, as you won't have been able to carry real cutlery onto the plane. Your hotel room may contain a minibar. On no account consume anything from it as the prices tend to be high, but it can be used to store canned or bottled drinks you have purchased that are best drunk chilled. Remove from it a few of the hotel's bottles and cans and place them on top, then use the space created for your own drinks. Remember to reverse this procedure each morning so as to avoid awkward questions from your chambermaid.

There should normally be no objection from the management to your eating in your room. Once in a rural hotel in France that operated a "No eating in Rooms" policy, I and my partner found a note pinned to the door of our room stating that crumbs had been found on the floor. They were in fact from the previous night's smuggled baguettes, as it happened. *Madame la patronne* reminded us curtly in the note that we weren't allowed to eat in the room. We decided she probably employed a tame mouse to check the floor for baguette crumbs and submit a daily report.

There is no need to partake of the hotel breakfast if it is not included in the price of the room, as long as you have bought wisely from the supermarket the night before. But, purely as a personal preference, I do allow myself the luxury of a cup of coffee at the hotel bar before leaving to sample the delights of whatever town or city I am visiting. Once, in Oslo, I had been obliged at short notice to check into a hotel that was way above my usual price range. I didn't realise breakfast was included in the price, and the following morning found me walking through the breakfast room casting envious glances at the delicious food on display, regretful that I was not allowed to touch it. Round the corner from the hotel, I found a McDonald's where I breakfasted contentedly on two Hamburgers and a coffee, at a total cost of the equivalent of three Euros. On returning to the hotel to check-out I was informed that breakfast had in fact been included in the price, but by then it was too late – I was full. The (rather obvious) moral of this tale is that when you check in to the hotel you should always ask if breakfast is included. If so, then during the meal next morning try surreptitiously to transfer items from the buffet into your bag whilst seated at your table. That way you can enjoy a pleasant picnic lunch later at no cost.

A special mention must be made of McDonald's. That much-maligned establishment is often a lifesaver in the more unexpected locations. Once, after struggling through the streets of Bucharest for several hours with my water bottle empty, and with the temperature hovering around 35 degrees, I spotted the McDonald's golden arches at Splaiul Indepentei with glee and there bought two chilled large Sprites which scarcely touched the sides as I gulped them down. I remember the joy to this day. As for eating at McDonald's at minimum cost, you can't do better than a hamburger. This is a simple burger bun containing a single burger, with a slice of gherkin and some tomato-type puree. It rarely appears in the tempting display above the counter, but is always listed in the legally-required table of prices at the side of the counter. Simply ask for "A Hamburger". The cheapest one I ever found cost 49 cents in Clermont-Ferrand in France, and at the time of writing I believe the price still to be around 1 Euro. With good coffee for around the same price it's a bargain.

A mention should be made of doner kebabs. Not everyone's cup of tea, I'm sure, but they can be a lifesaver after a hard day's touristing. Good fresh salad, tasty meat, and a topping of chilli sauce is served up in a pitta bread pouch. A delicious, affordable balanced meal and available in every city I've visited with the exception of The Vatican!

Another source of low-cost nourishment is street food. This can be wonderful, awful, or anywhere in between. Roast chestnuts in the autumn in Basel's streets smell and taste delicious, as does a Croque Monsieur in a Paris street fair. European street food is nowhere near as varied as that in Asia, but can certainly be as tasty. The next best thing to street food is any restaurant that serves predominantly local people. One such, just along the road from the bottom of the Ascensor da Gloria in Lisbon, and opposite the Pensao Monumental hotel, was more like a works canteen than a restaurant, selling meat and 2 vegetables at a remarkably low price. There were jugs of water on the tables at no extra charge.

Finally, in this low-cost food and drink section, mention must be made of universities and colleges. Every major town and city has at least one. Often reasonably central, they always have eating facilities for hungry students, and believe it or not most don't require you to produce proof of your student or lecturer status before they will serve you. Seville University is located in the centre of the city in the beautiful old tobacco factory that has associations with Carmen. Walk through the courtyard and just inside the entrance on the left is the student cafe, which serves great coffee and meals.

In general, food and drink can be found to suit any pocket in most European destinations. But you can pay surprisingly little for surprisingly good food if you're willing to shop around. Simply remember that eating abroad doesn't have to involve a sit-down meal at a restaurant every night! However, you shouldn't feel bad if you weaken on the final night and dine out at a restaurant, daringly choosing a local speciality. Care is advised however. When I was a student in Paris, I occasionally ate at a local restaurant and deliberately ordered anything on the menu with which I was unfamiliar, hoping to learn about French cuisine. When Boudin Blanc turned up, it consisted of two plump white sausage shapes that turned out to be boiled white black pudding, containing a gooey white sludge that oozed out when the sausage-skin was pierced. I managed to finish it, but only just.

Travel at your destination

All cities and large towns have public transport networks that may include any or all of buses, trolleybuses, trams, trains, and underground railways. Most hotels have excellent maps of these at reception and the receptionist will normally dispense advice on the best way to get into the centre or to any of the tourist attractions. However, ticketing and pricing is not always straightforward. Ticket options are usually shown on the relevant transport authority website, and, whatever the mode of transport, are usually offered as 1-day passes, 3-day passes, etc. Some tram systems, for example Basel, have a one-trip ticket that is valid for 30 minutes from the time of issue. Many cities offer combined tickets, for example tram, bus, and underground. What you buy depends on your requirements, as it is important to check the locations of the various tourist attractions you wish to see and establish if they are accessible by one or other of the tickets on offer. The Paris Visite Pass for example offers unlimited travel by bus, tram, metro, and RER (the local Paris rail system) on the inner three zones for 12.85 Euros for 1 day at today's price. However, you may be able to get by with a Paris Navigo card, costing 22.15 Euros for 5 days' travel, but with certain conditions attached. It has to be admitted that the options for travel by public-transport within European cities can be complex, and is best researched on the internet before you depart. One final note on trams and buses – if you buy a single ticket make sure you validate it in the machine on the tram or you may have to pay a penalty. Someone will show you how to do it if you ask nicely!

It goes without saying that car-hire at your destination is unlikely to be viable if you are on a budget and intend to stay in one location, but if you wish to travel further afield it may make sense. However, before making this decision, check the fares on the national railway system in the country (or countries) you're visiting – rail may be much cheaper than car hire and, speaking for myself, is usually more pleasurable. The enquiry office at the central station in your destination city will help you plan the journey. An example of such a rail trip was a journey I made that took in France, Monaco, Italy, Austria, Liechtenstein, Switzerland, and Germany in just 7 days. You may wish to do a similar trip, going out to a particular country, visiting others, and returning from another. In another case I flew to Austria and eventually returned to London by Eurostar train from Brussels. If you have a couple of months (and the money) to spare, I suppose you could take this to its logical conclusion and visit all 49 countries in the course of one trip by car and/or train (with a flight being necessary to Cyprus). But it might not be much fun!

Hotels

Throughout my travels I have tended to use budget hotels. Typically these may be part of a chain of hotels which offers "normal" and "budget" options. Two that I have used regularly are Hotel F1 (previously Formule 1) and Ibis Budget. Typically their budget prices are about half the "normal" equivalent. Such hotels are sometimes located away from the town or city centre so it's important to check their proximity to public transport - some tend to be better accessed by car. Rooms are always perfectly adequate with twin beds, shower, and TV, and there is usually a small bar downstairs for the obligatory morning coffee. Some do not have shopping close by.

As an example, the Ibis budget hotel in Seville is about five kilometres out of town and has been sited for its easy accessibility by car (It's actually on the edge of a small industrial estate). However there is a good local bus service into town from a bus stop around 200 metres from the hotel, and the walk to the stop does you good I'm told! The Hotel F1 at Basel airport is perhaps the most convenient of all as you can walk there from the arrivals hall in the airport in less than 10 minutes, using the grass verge of the airport road. From the hotel it's only a 5 minute walk to the railway station at Saint-Louis-la-Chaussee where you can get the train to Basel city centre.

In general, I would recommend checking out any budget hotel primarily for its proximity to public transport before making a reservation. This usually entails a simple internet search. A secondary consideration is the availability of shops nearby, particularly if you intend buying your evening meal from the local supermarket. *In extremis*, you can always buy from a supermarket in town whilst engaged in your touristing and take it back with you in the evening.

If you are in any doubt about staying at a budget hotel, then be aware that there are "normal" hotels in town and city centres that may offer good deals from time to time. The problem is that these "deals" may simply not be available for all or some of the dates you require. Six nights in a budget hotel will cost a total of around £180 at today's prices, or £90 each if there are two of you, and this is more or less the rate no matter when you go. Compare it with, say, £360.00 at a 2-star "normal" hotel for the same period.

Communication

My visits were made at a time when mobile phones and tablets were a rarity. I managed perfectly well without the benefit of these items, but now accept they are considered essential by most travellers. The only (intermittent) internet access available on my travels was through Internet cafes, which I used on a couple of occasions. Nowadays I carry my iPhone when I'm away, but mainly use it for taking photographs. Tablets do of course mean you don't have to spend ages searching for English-language channels on the TV in the hotel room, and they are convenient for emailing photographs of the day's exploits to relatives. For me, however, in order to save weight I restrict myself to taking my iPhone.

The remainder of the book describes my journeys to each of the 49 countries on my list. Generally I attempted where possible to visit two or more countries on each trip, purely to keep costs down. The most I ever managed in one week was seven, which sounds rather like a route-march but was, in fact, extremely enjoyable. I haven't listed the journeys in any particular chronological sequence, but have attempted where appropriate to group them loosely by region - the Balkans, Ex-USSR states, Northern Europe, Scandinavia, The Mediterranean, and the small principality-style states.

Chapter 2

France

"In what country on earth would I rather live? Certainly in my own, where are all my friends, my relations, and the earliest and sweetest affections and recollections of my life. But my second choice would be France."
Thomas Jefferson

> 1966 World Cup England v Mexico at Wembley. Hitch-hiking to France. Pick of the Pops on the cross-channel ferry. Thermodynamics and a camping disaster in Boulogne. French family hospitality.

I begin with the United Kingdom's closest neighbour, France. Its proximity, both physical and cultural, meant it was the obvious choice when I made the momentous decision in my late teens to go abroad for the first time. Since then I have visited it countless times and become a true francophile, leading me to live there for some time. I mentioned in the introduction to this book that when I decided to embark on the 49 country project I had already visited ten of them, of which one was France. I have written about all ten in the chapters that follow, and in the case of France I decided to record some of my earliest experiences there.

As a teenager I had of financial necessity been obliged to confine my travelling to England, Wales, and Scotland. I was conscious, however, of the lure of France, in large part due to my undying love, unspoken, and, of course, unrequited, for my attractive French teacher, Miss Symes, at school. It was she who engendered in me an abiding fascination with all things gallic, and patiently encouraged me in my attempts to learn the language. I was broken-hearted when she later announced her marriage to the English teacher, but this did nothing to curb my enthusiasm for all things French. I did well in my GCE French exam but was not destined to continue with the subject, finding laboratory work locally in the steelworks when I left school. It was not until I was 21 that I made my first foray across the channel.

In 1966, my friend Tony, a fellow steelworker, suggested we go abroad on holiday. It would be the first time for both of us, and France was the obvious choice. We decided to use a tour company, and found that Paris Travel Service offered a week in Paris at a price we could afford. The resulting trip by train and boat (there were no cheap airlines in 1966) included a stopover in London where we took the opportunity to go to Wembley to watch the England football team, on their way to winning the trophy, beat Mexico 2-0 in the World cup finals. It's difficult to believe nowadays, but we simply arrived at the stadium, paid cash at the turnstile, and went in. No prior booking of tickets, no security searches, and no sold-out games in those days!

The next day we took the train to Folkestone and boarded the Boulogne ferry. I still remember the feeling of quiet satisfaction when we disembarked on the quayside in Boulogne and walked over to the train in the platform at Gare Maritime. Tony and I subsequently spent an enjoyable week at the

Hotel Pretty in Montmartre, Paris, sampling that city's wonderful attractions for the first time. The hotel had no breakfast room of its own, so guests were obliged to eat in the cafe, open to the public and located on the ground floor of the hotel. Large cups of fresh coffee were served with warm milk in a jug, together with a selection of Bonne Mamam preserves, President butter, and crispy baguettes fresh from the bakery. Each morning, as we consumed this delicious meal, we noted the arrival of a delightful young lady dressed in a smart pink two-piece suit, who seated herself at one of the tables by the window and gazed out intently at the passing Parisians. After a while a man – a different one each time - would enter, have a whispered conversation with her, and they would leave together. She would then return half an hour or so later and resume her seat. It took us a while, but we eventually came to understand the nature of her business. She appeared to have an amicable relationship with the patron, a tall, balding middle-aged man with just a hint of Rene in "Allo Allo" about him. It wasn't clear if this was simply a financial arrangement, or if there was something more intimate.

My subsequent visit to France took place when I was studying at University. Although in poor financial health, I was determined to make the most of the 12-week summer break and in 1967 made the decision to cross the Channel and hitch-hike around the continent. It seemed to be the best way to achieve the maximum amount of travel at the lowest cost. The cheapest accommodation available at the time was in youth hostels, but I took the additional precaution of taking a tent, and to this end visited a local wheeler-dealer who worked full-time at the steelworks, but hired-out camping equipment as a sideline. The smallest tent he had was an ex-army "Bivvy" – short for Bivouac – which divided in two by means of buttons (yes, buttons – no tent zips in those days) along the ridge. It was originally designed for two soldiers to carry, half each, on route-marches, and was made from canvas, in those days the only tent material readily available, so it was heavy. There was no built-in groundsheet, meaning that a separate sheet of polythene would be required.

"The lightest tent you can get." he assured me.

"Are you sure it's watertight?"

"Yeah, no problem. Guaranteed."

Foolishly, as it turned out, I took him at his word.

And so it was that I headed for the open road in July 1967, carrying a rucksack with a Union Flag sewn prominently on the front, and with my bivvy strapped on top. A couple of lifts later I was heading south on the A1 in the company of two Hull University PhD philosophy students, in a Rover 90 sit-up-and-beg car. They attempted to involve me in a debate about the merits of the Platonic school of philosophy, but gave up when they realised I was a humble science geek, and we discussed football instead.

I eventually made it to Folkestone, and boarded the ferry to Boulogne. It was a Sunday afternoon of bright sunshine and inconsequential cumulus clouds, and I took a seat on deck with others of my age group to be entertained by "Pick of the Pops" on someone's transistor radio nearby. Alan "Fluff"

Freeman, the presenter of the show, was at his hyperbolic best, and to this day I recall the moment he played "A Whiter Shade of Pale", which I think was number one at the time. To this day, whenever I hear its opening chords, I'm immediately transported back to the sunbathed deck of that cross-channel ferry, the wind in my face and surrounded by excited holidaymakers. It was never better expressed than by Noel Coward in "Private Lives" when he wrote "Strange how potent cheap music is."

As the boat entered Boulogne Harbour, I spotted a campsite on the top of the cliffs to the east of the town, about three kilometres away. I set off to walk, and half an hour or so later found me booking in at the site office. I selected my pitch, and for the first time erected my tent. I had my doubts about its waterproof qualities as the buttoning along the ridge seemed less than robust, but I managed to set it up without mishap, finally crawling inside to spread out the loose groundsheet. As I worked I looked on enviously as my neighbours prepared a sumptuous al fresco dinner under the canopy of their huge multi-roomed tent. Hungry, and with no cooking equipment, I made for the site cafe and had a meal, then called in at the facilities block to wash. Walking back, I paused to view a breathtaking sunset over the English Channel, created in part by a darkening cloudscape, before finally crawling wearily into my tent.

I still had work to do – University work. As part of my course I had taken an exam in thermodynamics back in June and failed it. The resit was scheduled for September, which meant I had to revise during this holiday, so I had brought along the course book, "An Introduction to Chemical Thermodynamics" by Maurice Everdell, my tutor. I extracted it from my rucksack, switched on my torch, and began to read. Ten minutes passed, and suddenly there was a huge clap of thunder, followed by the sound of several very large drops of rain hitting the tent. Then more, and before I knew it my temporary home was being lashed by torrential rain. I bravely tried to continue reading, but the severity of the storm distracted me. Something close to panic set in as I saw the first drop of water penetrate the buttoned ridge and drip onto the groundsheet. Then there was another....and another. Water was soon gathering in pools on the groundsheet, obliging me to move to that half of the tent that was relatively dry. Still it rained, and seconds later I spotted a little rivulet of water running across the groundsheet from one side to the other, followed by another. At this point I decided to abandon the tent, head over to the facilities block, and hole up there until dawn, hoping the rain would stop for long enough to allow my tent to dry out in the morning sun.
As I exited the tent, my neighbour, standing out of the rain beneath his tent's capacious awning, removed the Gauloise from his lips and spoke.

"Ca va m'sieu?"

No, everything is far from alright, I thought.

"Non m'sieu"

"Je peux vous aider peut– etre?"

In vain I searched for the words from my limited French vocabulary that would enable me to ask exactly how he might help.

"I'm English. Do you have any English?"

"Mais oui. Un peu." He said, Then added, helpfully "A little."

And so it was that I failed my first real-life French exam. Mrs Symes would've been disappointed.

"You must stay with us. We have room". He said, generously. "Je m'appele Daniel."

"Je m'appele David."

Still the rain came down. I had no choice. He waved me into the communal area of the family tent and introduced me to his wife, young son, and daughter. A spare inflatable mattress was produced, on which I was invited to sleep, but not before joining them in what he called "Un p'tit rouge". The red wine was poured, and there followed a half-English half-French discussion on practically any subject that we could think of. My French seemed to improve as the wine flowed, and there was much laughter each time I made a mistake. Looking back, this single meeting had made all those hours spent conjugating French verbs worthwhile. I was actually communicating with French people in France!

The following morning I stepped outside and surveyed the scene. It was a bright and breezy day, perfect for drying out my tent and groundsheet. I arranged these as best as I could on the ground and went over to the facilities block to wash. When I returned, Daniel was on his way out of the tent, wearing shorts and flip-flops and carrying a bucket. I watched him scramble down to the shoreline and asked madame what he was doing.

"Ou va-t-il?" I asked

"Chercher des moules." She replied

Moules? Not a word I knew at the time, but half an hour later he returned with the bucket full of Mussels that he'd gathered in the rock pools. I added the word to my vocabulary.

Madame began preparing the vegetables for lunch. Daniel busied himself checking their tent for signs of leakage from the storm (the occasional "Merde!" emanated from inside) and the kids went off to play with friends. I busied myself with my tent, moving it around so that it might dry as quickly as possible. After all, I had to get down to the road and try to make Paris before nightfall.

"You eat with us?" said M. Hebert. It took me all of 2 seconds to respond.

"Mais oui! Bien sur!"

"Bon" said M. Hebert. "Mangeons".

And so it was that at midday I found myself seated at table outside in the warm sunshine, surrounded by the family, and tucking into *Moules Marinieres* and vegetables, washed down with red wine. I remember to this day the moment at the start of the meal when I took a mouthful of boiled potato followed by a sip of red wine. The combined taste, never experienced before, was simply delicious. No meal since then, regardless of cost, has ever provoked such a pleasurable reaction from my taste-buds.

During the course of the meal, and in very broken French and English, I told them I was heading for Paris. It transpired that they were heading home that day, and they offered me a lift to their home town, Mantes la Jolie, about half an hour outside Paris. I gratefully accepted. About 3 o'clock, installed in the family car, a roomy Peugeot 404, we bade farewell to the camp-site, and set off. In 1967 there were few short stretches of Autoroute in France, and none at all in the Nord region, so the journey was perforce via various towns and took around 3 hours. *En route* we stopped for a break in a small town. M Hebert went over to a *boulangerie* and returned with a few cakes. I'd expected the family to eat them in the car, but instead he took us into a cafe opposite and ordered drinks. To my surprise, he then unwrapped the cakes and began eating. I found later that this was perfectly normal in France at the time. I was happy to go along with it and returned to the car after consuming a delicious *mille feuille* and coffee. Before we left the children went to a shop over the road and returned with a brown paper bag that I thought contained sweets.

As we restarted our journey Pascal, the boy, offered the open bag to me. I stretched out my hand without seeing the contents, and, instead of the expected sweet, I pulled out an olive. Never before having eaten one, I took the plunge and put it into my mouth. It was not a particularly pleasant experience, but I feigned enjoyment. Pascal seemed delighted that I liked it, continuing to offer me more throughout the journey, and I was far too polite to refuse. Since that time I have come to love olives, particularly with ricotta cheese or hummus. Another stage in my culinary education in France had been completed.

The family lived in a flat not far from the Seine, which flows through Mantes-la-Jolie on its way from Paris to Le Havre. M Hebert parked the car and I helped them unload it. By now it was after 5 o'clock and I was anxious to get to Paris and find a Youth Hostel. Daniel would have none of it.

"Il est trop tard. You can stay here."

I didn't need to be asked twice, and slept well that night in the spare room. The following day they took me to visit a couple of local tourist sites, and then, with great sadness on my part, took me to the station to get the local train to Paris.

The experience had been the best possible introduction to daily life in France, and I still look back on it with great fondness. It didn't, however, end well. I kept in touch with the family for a couple of years afterwards and they even invited me to stay with them when they spent the 1968 summer holidays in the South of France. But it is to my great shame that I eventually lost contact with them. I have no excuse other than the fact that University and work meant that it was a busy period in my life. I regret to this day that I never got the chance to return their wonderful hospitality.

Chapter 3

The Balkans – Part 1 – Greece, Macedonia, Serbia, Bulgaria

"To Balkanize has come to be used in a derogatory sense meaning to violently fragment, disrupt or disorganize" **Antonia Young**

"The Balkans produce more history than they can consume" **Winston Churchill**

"There are some problems in the Balkans in the settlement of which the Bulgarians should also participate" **Todor Zhivkov**

Border police and deleted photographs. Duty-free at the railway station. Travelling with the tobacco smugglers. First-ever casino visit. Gate-crashing a funeral.

"The Balkans" refers to that group of nine countries in South-Eastern Europe bounded to the north by Hungary, Romania, and Italy, and to the South by the Mediterranean Sea. Two of these constituent countries, Bulgaria and Greece, have distinctly separate histories, but the remaining seven were originally part of a Kingdom which became the Socialist Federal Republic of Yugoslavia at the end of World War II in 1946. Yugoslavia's constitution was based on that of the Soviet Union, and in 1963 Josip Broz Tito was elected president for life. He remained in that post as a hard-line dictator until his death in 1980. On his death, underlying tensions that had simmered for many years between the member states now rose to the surface, leading ultimately to war between them which lasted until December 1996.

This particular visit to the Balkans took place 14 years after the fighting ended, but only 2 years after the new state of Kosovo, previously part of Serbia and Montenegro, finally declared its independence. By that time four of the Balkan countries had joined the European Union, and there was peace throughout the region. On this occasion I decided to start from Greece and work my way North, visiting Macedonia, Serbia, and Bulgaria.

And so it was that on a hot April evening, the heat tempered by a gentle Mediterranean breeze, I found myself exiting Thessaloniki airport in the North of Greece. I had last visited Greece 30 years previously, finding it a delightfully disorganised jewel in the Eastern Mediterranean, and was looking forward to seeing if membership of the European Union had produced any tangible improvements in the country's ability to govern itself. After taking the local bus to the city centre I checked into my hotel and picked up a photocopied map of the local area from reception. That evening I took a stroll to the railway station to check train times, and the walk suggested there had been little change in the intervening years. Pavements proved to be little more than obstacle courses to be negotiated, with holes, broken kerbstones, missing manhole covers, parked cars, and business wheelie bins all conspiring to persuade the pedestrian that it might be safer to walk in the road. Crossing to the other side of the road demanded a state of alertness normally needed by a gazelle surrounded by cheetahs in the veldt, a consequence of the apparent indifference of drivers to any sort of lane or pedestrian-crossing discipline. I was genuinely relieved to arrive at the station unharmed, and relived memories of my time in Cairo, many years before, a city where drivers saw a red traffic light as an invitation to accelerate.

The railway station, by contrast, was an oasis of calm, and I purchased my train ticket for the 6pm train to Skopje in Macedonia the following day. My plan was to travel via Skopje to Nis in Serbia, and thence to Sofia in Bulgaria, from where I would return direct to Thessaloniki, making it a round-trip of some 900 kilometres. After checking the timetable I renegotiated the route back to the hotel, stopping on the way at a cafe for a well-deserved beer and a tasty doner kebab with chilli sauce. I also called in at a convenience store to buy Greek lemon cake for breakfast in my room the next day, together with a bottle of iced tea. Back in my hotel room, I found the television schedules to be the all-too familiar mix of local-language channels, one of which was showing a badly-dubbed 1950s film and another the Greek version of "The X Factor". There were just two programmes in the English language, both rather boring news channels. I had no tablet at the time, and in any case I believe the hotel had no Wi-Fi, so I watched half an hour of news before turning in for the night.

After checking out of the hotel the following morning, I took a leisurely stroll of about a kilometre or so along the seafront in pleasant Mediterranean sunshine, and visited The White Tower at the end of the promenade. A cylindrical castellated brown stone tower 34 metres high, it overlooks the Mediterranean and was originally constructed for defence in the twelfth century, but became a notorious prison under Ottoman rule and was substantially rebuilt in 1912. Nowadays it is a museum showing Thessaloniki's history and has been adopted as the symbol of the city. From there I moved on to the Arch of Galerius. About half a kilometre inland, it is named after the Roman Emperor of that name and was erected as part of the city's Roman infrastructure. Constructed in brick, with a rubble masonry core, its central arch stands 12.5 metres high and there are two smaller lateral arches. The arch is best known for its roman carvings in marble, ant nearby is another Roman building, the Rotunda, a church also dating from the fourth century, originally of Greek Orthodox origin but converted to a Mosque in 1590 when Greece fell under the rule of the Ottoman Empire. Such conversions are to be found throughout the near-East, and there are particularly fine examples in Istanbul, Turkey, and Nicosia, Cyprus.

I walked back to the promenade in warm sunshine and found a cafe where I ordered beer and kebab with rice, and watched the silhouettes of distant ships coming and going in the sparkling blue Mediterranean waters. The port itself is the second-largest in Greece after Piraeus, containing both container and passenger terminals. Before long it was time to make my way to the station to get the 6pm departure for Skopje, and on the way I bought food for the journey. The train was almost full as I climbed aboard, but I managed to find a seat in a compartment and settled back for the ride. The first stop was scheduled to be at Gevjeliga, about ninety kilometres to the North, a small community of some 16,000 souls and with no particular claim to importance other than that it lies on the border between Greece and Macedonia. As we pulled into the station the sun was already low in the sky, and I was somewhat surprised to see all my fellow-travellers leave the compartment, without taking their luggage. The station is a small, pretty two-storey building the colour of Cotswold stone, and I took the opportunity to lean out of the corridor window and take a couple of atmospheric photos in the twilight. No sooner had I put the camera away but two burly uniformed border guards arrived, slid open the compartment door, and the older of the two demanded to see my passport. Seeing that I was English he told me sharply that photography was not allowed at the frontier. Thankfully he stopped short of arresting me, or even confiscating my camera, but insisted that I delete the pictures while he watched. His younger companion smiled politely.

"Your passport – you will need stamp!" the younger one said, helpfully

"Where do I go for it?" I asked, with the merest hint of panic in my voice.

"Over there. And hurry, Train will leave soon".

He pointed to a small office window on the opposite platform around which a number of fellow-passengers were gathered. Grateful that I wasn't destined to spend the night in a jail cell, I raced over to join the queue, and as I waited my attention was distracted by a large group of passengers queuing at the far end of the platform. I wondered if there was some additional piece of frontier bureaucracy of which I was unaware, and as soon as I'd received my passport, duly stamped, I rushed down the platform to join the queue. As it transpired, there was no cause for concern, as they were queuing outside a large duty-free shop! Travelling light, I sadly couldn't avail myself of the excellent spirit prices advertised in the window, and so made my way back over the tracks to my train. As I took my seat it occurred to me that in my years of travelling I had never before come across a Duty-Free shop at a railway station, and I speculated that Gevjeliga may be unique in the world in this respect. The clink of bottles in plastic bags carried by my fellow passengers as they rejoined the train suggested that the shop had done good business.

I settled down for the journey to Skopje, capital of Macedonia, a couple of hundred kilometres to the north, and around 11pm the train's brakes squealed as we slowed down in the outskirts of the city. I had failed to book a hotel in advance, assuming there would be one near the station, and searched the locality in vain. As I returned to the station a cab driver, dressed in the obligatory Balkan black leather jacket, approached me, introduced himself as Stefan, and spoke.

"You need taxi mister?"

"No." I said, always keen to avoid the expense of a taxi.

"You need hotel?"

"Er, yes. Is there one near here?"

" How much you can pay?"

"40 Euros? I have no denars."

"Hotels around here cost more. I can take you to one 30 Euros."

I weighed up my options. It was late, and I was tired. Public transport may not have been an option.

"OK."

I climbed into the warmth of the cab, and three hotels later Stefan found one with a vacancy. He was happy to accept Euros as payment for the ride, and insisted on helping me to book in, thereby no doubt enabling him to make whatever arrangement he could with the proprietor regarding his reward for taking me there. The hotel was a pleasant family-owned place, with a small bar in which a group of men were noisily playing cards. Before he left, Stefan had another question.

"How long you stay?"

"Just till tomorrow afternoon. Then I get the train to Nis in Serbia."

"I can give you tour of Skopje tomorrow. Take you to see the city. Twenty Euros."

I thought about it. There were things I wanted to see in Skopje, and I didn't have an alternative plan. I persuaded myself it wasn't too expensive.

"OK." I said. "Be here at 10 o'clock."

He smiled and left.

The following morning he arrived as promised. We first visited the old railway station, one of the few buildings still standing from the time of the huge earthquake that struck Skopje on July 26th 1963, resulting in 1,000 people being killed, 200,000 being made homeless, and 80% of the city's buildings being destroyed. Rebuilding eventually restored most of them, but the old railway station was left as a partial ruin. The front of the building still stands, with the large exterior clock above the entrance stopped forever at 5:17 am, the time when the quake struck. It is a truly emotional sight, much more powerful than any memorial statue or cenotaph could be.

Along the street from the station I spotted the office of the NKPJ, the New Communist Party of Yugoslavia. The party is committed to the rebirth of Yugoslavia as a Marxist-Leninist Communist State, an objective that surely could never see the light of day. Sadly the two members in the office had no English, so I was unable to discuss the current state of the party, but I was delighted when they sold me a red-flag hammer-and-sickle enamel lapel badge for a couple of Euros.

Stefan next drove out to mount Vodno, South-West of the city, and from which he was able to point out various items of interest, some of which dated from the time when the country was part of the Ottoman Empire. Down in the valley he pointed out the site of the Monopol tobacco factory, which was used as a transit base in 1943 for the 8,000 Macedonian Jews that were sent to the Treblinka concentration camp. The Vardar River, which divides the city of half a million inhabitants in two, was clearly visible. I reminded him of the impending departure of my train, and he dropped me back at the station. As I waited on the platform for the train I reflected on Macedonia's often unhappy history during the twentieth century. In addition to the major natural disaster that was the 1963 earthquake, the country was occupied by Bulgaria during World War II, and subsequently became part of the communist dictatorship of Yugoslavia, finally achieving independence in 1991. It is still not at peace with its newly-created neighbour, Kosovo, and is not currently considered suitable for membership of the European Union. As a result, its role in twenty-first century Europe remains undefined.

The 200-kilometre journey to Nis, Serbia's third largest city and a major industrial centre, was uneventful, if painfully slow. The border at Tabanovce, a tiny community of fewer than 1,000 souls, was thankfully passed without incident and my train pulled into Nis station at around 9pm, in murky darkness and persistent drizzle. The train to Sofia, capital of Bulgaria, was not due to leave until 1am, and the station cafe was serving drinks but no food, so I set out for the city centre, located a kilometre or so from the station, in search of food. On the way I passed a somewhat incongruous line of ancient rusting steam locomotives in a siding by the roadside and wondered if they might some-day be restored and moved to a museum. Soaked by the drizzle, and occasionally confused by the Serbian-language street signs, I found my way to the rather attractive, busy, city centre, and there found a cash machine close to a McDonald's. A meal of two hamburgers and a cup of coffee followed, and on the way back to the station I called into a cafe and had a beer. Thus refreshed, I checked the departure board at the station for details of the train to Sofia, and found a seat in the waiting-room.

When the time arrived a train entered my designated platform, and I walked over the tracks to climb aboard. Inside, I asked a passenger if it was for Sofia, and was told "No, Belgrade", resulting in a hurried exit only moments before it started its journey to Serbia's capital. The platform indicators were out of action as I looked around for some clue as to where I should go next. As I became increasingly worried, another train appeared and screeched to a halt in the far platform. I rushed over, clambered aboard and asked again, in English if it was for Sofia. "Yes. But you are in the wrong part. You must travel in the front half." said a youth. I rushed along the corridor and eventually found a seat in a nearly-full compartment in the right part of the train. I smiled politely at my fellow passengers, a youngish man, two late-teenage girls, and an older woman, all of whom had been on the train prior to its arrival in Nis. Each nursed a rucksack, three of which appeared to be empty. The man, clad in T-shirt, jeans, and the obligatory Balkans black leather jacket, confirmed that this was the Sofia portion, and I settled down for the journey.

About twenty minutes into the journey the man began searching in his rucksack, took out a longish screwdriver and proceeded to stand on the seat. Slightly alarmed by this, I was even more disconcerted when he began to undo the screws holding the oblong plastic cover in place over the neon-tube light fitting in the ceiling. For a moment I wondered whether to call the guard, or even pull the communication cord. The three women, who evidently knew him, showed no surprise. When all four screws were undone, he was able to lower the plastic cover and expose the still-illuminated neon tube inside. One of the girls then reached into her rucksack and from it extracted a large number of packs of 200 cigarettes. One by one, the packs were handed up to him so he could slip them into the space above the compartment's ceiling. Once the rucksack was empty he screwed the light cover back in place, and sat down. The train continued to rattle on through the darkness, and life returned to normal in the compartment.

I wondered again if I should notify the guard, as I was technically complicit in whatever they were doing, but I decided to sit it out and hope for the best. The others settled back and relaxed, but I was unable to do likewise. Eventually the train slowed, the brakes squealed, and we stopped at a deserted small station. All was quiet for ten minutes or so, but then the sound of footsteps and chatter emerged from the corridor. Three uniformed officials eventually appeared at the compartment door and one of them asked for passports, as it transpired that we were at the Bulgarian border station of Dragoman. Whilst one of them examined our documents, his colleagues proceeding to prise back part of the melamine lining of the carriage beneath the corridor windows at various points, checking the spaces behind. They then checked a hidden space behind the fire extinguisher at the end of the carriage and finally opened a small flap about three inches square in the ceiling of the corridor. One of them inserted a small camera into the slot and took a photograph, which, it seemed, was intended to show him if there was anything lurking in the corridor's false ceiling. He appeared satisfied with the picture, and after a brief muttered discussion the three of them thanked us for our time and proceeded down the train.

I heaved a silent sigh of relief. This was, however, short-lived, as the train's guard appeared moments later at the still-open compartment door. I was expecting further border-style action from him which could easily involve me. To my surprise, he seemed to know my fellow passengers and was particularly chatty with the older woman. It was as if they knew each other, and I even detected a hint of flirting between them. He finally left the compartment smiling broadly and, shortly afterwards, the train restarted. As a general rule in travelling I believe one should always attempt to get into conversation with fellow passengers on a train, no matter what language difficulties may exist. However this was one occasion where, as the Australians say, I decided to give it a swerve.

We had been inside Bulgaria for half an hour or so when suddenly, on instruction from the older lady, the two girls got up and left the compartment. Both returned a few minutes later carrying many cartons of cigarettes, which were then carefully packed into the rucksacks by the man. The older lady busied herself recording each carton in a small notebook and instructing him as to which rucksack it belonged. The impression I'd had earlier of her acting as mother hen to her chicks seemed ever more appropriate. The girls went back and forth several times, each time returning fully laden. I never found out where these additional cartons had been hidden, as they were retrieved from elsewhere in the carriage. When they'd finished the man turned his attention back to the light cover in the compartment, removed it, and extracted the cigarettes from the false roof. These were added to the third rucksack, carefully audited by the mother hen. There was now scarcely room to move on the opposite seat of the compartment as these were seriously large rucksacks which took up much of the available space.

At this point the mother hen seemed satisfied with the night's work, put away her notebook, and I soon drifted into fitful sleep. Eventually awoken by the light of dawn outside, I went into the corridor to stretch my legs. It was a chill, cloudless morning, and there was a hard frost on the fields. The train began to slow down, and soon drew to a halt at a tiny station in a small village of just a few houses and a church. A strange place to stop, I thought, given that this was an international train and we were only twenty minutes or so from Sofia. The only people to get off the train at this outpost were the man and two girls, each carrying one of the huge rucksacks. I watched them walk down the deserted village street and then they were gone. The mother hen stayed on the train until we reached our destination, Sofia, twenty minutes later, and then she was also gone.

This had been a fascinating, if unsettling journey. At the time I was unaware of the existence of tobacco smuggling from Serbia into Bulgaria, and I have since discovered that it is a major problem, given that Bulgaria is in the European Union and Serbia isn't. As an eye-witness to the process, I'm pleased I managed to steer clear of any involvement with the authorities, and as a law-abiding person, I couldn't condone what the team were doing, but was forced to admire them for their creative approach, and organisational skills..

I stepped outside Sofia Central station at 6:30am, cold and hungry, and asked a fellow passenger where I could buy Lev, the local currency.

"At this time of day", she said, "only in the Casino".

She pointed it out, a tall building just down the road from the station. In my less than immaculate travelling attire I approached the uniformed man on the door. He paused, looked me up and down, asked to look at my passport, and told me to check in at the reception desk. There I was directed to the casino's "bank" desk, and thankfully was able to change 50 Euros into Lev, secretly cursing that they gave me what could only be described as a usurous exchange rate. The casino was, amazingly, in full swing at that hour of the morning. Piped music competed with the restrained hubbub of the punters and the noise of slot machines. The roulette and blackjack tables appeared to be doing good business, and I was tempted for a moment to try my luck, but thought better of it. I did, however, get some small satisfaction in realising that it was the first time in my life that I'd set foot inside a casino.

On the way out, I asked the doorman if he could recommend a cheapish nearby hotel, and he gave me directions to a modern-looking place about half a kilometre away. And so it was that I pitched up at the reception desk of this pleasant little hotel at around 8:30 am and asked for a room. I was told firmly by the delightful blonde lady on reception that they had vacancies, but the room would not be available before midday. I pleaded fatigue after the overnight train journey and she finally relented and handed over a key. Once installed in the room, I was overtaken by the previous night's lack of proper rest, so I set my alarm for midday and went to sleep.

It was a cloudless but chilly day as I finally emerged refreshed from the hotel around 2pm and decided to get the tram to the city centre. After buying a day pass and obtaining a map at the travel office by the railway station, I boarded one that appeared to be going in the right direction, remembering to validate the ticket in the machine on board. I am a passionate advocate of tram travel, finding them a clean, efficient, and safe method of getting about any city. Their great advantage is that it's almost impossible to get lost in a city when you use the tram network, given that if you make a mistake you simply get off at the next stop, cross over to the other side, and return whence you came. Trams are also an excellent way of experiencing what the real city and its people are like once you get out to the (sometimes) less salubrious suburbs. In each city I visit I make a point of staying on at least one tram all the way to its terminus, for just this purpose. Time away from souvenir shops and tourist crowds can be a welcome and informative diversion.

Getting around ex-Soviet Union countries can often present a language problem for Westerners. Direction signs, street names, and station name-boards are normally written in Russia's Cyrillic text. For this reason I carry with me a small Russian dictionary, which in any case is useful for translation in an emergency, but which also lists the Cyrillic alphabet along with each letter's western equivalent. Thus armed, I was able to make use of the tram network for the remainder of the afternoon to explore the city. In the evening I ate a doner kebab at a small restaurant near the hotel, then called in at the sparsely-populated hotel bar and had a beer.

The following morning I headed first to the Russian Church, a classic green-roofed Eastern European orthodox design, easily spotted on account of its five gold onion-domes glinting in the sunlight. At the entrance a group of people, mostly clad in black, were standing around chatting, and I quickly concluded that there must be a funeral in progress. A hearse duly arrived, and as the coffin was carried into the church I attempted to follow the mourners, to be told politely told it was a private affair. I turned to leave, and to my surprise a mourner emerged carrying the coffin lid, which he propped against the wall by the door. This, I discovered, is the traditional way of showing that there is a funeral service in progress inside the church. The ceremony inside the church then presumably proceeded with the deceased on open display in the coffin.

I walked the short distance from there to Alexander Nevsky Cathedral, a major tourist attraction in the city despite the fact that it is barely a hundred years old. Named after the 12th century Russian Orthodox saint, it stands in the centre of a huge open area and looks something like the heavily-domed Suleymaniye Mosque in Istanbul, but without the minarets. I ventured up the broad flight of steps, entered, and watched as worshippers came and went. Each of the arrivals kissed an icon of the saint placed atop an ornate brass pedestal just inside the door, A lady, carrying a cloth and detergent spray, hovered nearby, and proceeded to wipe the icon clean after each kiss. I mused for a moment as to her employment status and job description, and then entered the main body of the cathedral. The ornamented interior was magnificent, and I noticed that, as is normal in Orthodox churches, there were no seats for worshippers.

Exiting the cathedral, I strolled over to the flea market in the car park. Much ex-soviet personal military memorabilia was on sale, with peaked caps a particular favourite. As I was travelling light, I could only find room in my bag for a red enamelled badge showing Lenin in typical pose gazing sternly towards the horizon. I subsequently sought out the nearest McDonald's by tram, ate a couple of burgers and drank a coffee, then returned to the Hotel with food and beer purchased at a corner-shop for a picnic in my room that evening. I needed to get to bed early as my train for Thessaloniki was due to leave at 7:30am the following day.

The next morning I checked out of the hotel and strolled over to the station. There were few people about, and the indicator in the departure hall showed the train time and destination but no platform number. I surveyed the platforms, conscious that the departure time was only ten minutes or so away. I could see two trains in the main part of the station and wondered which one might be mine.

There was no one to help who spoke English in the departure hall, so I dashed over to the train in the nearest platform and asked a passenger if it was bound for Thessaloniki. "No. Belgrade." he said, and then "You see that train at the end of the platform over there? I think that's it." I thanked him and rushed over to the three-carriage railcar he'd pointed out. He was correct – it was indeed the Thessaloniki train. I found a seat and settled back to enjoy my return to Greece.

There were no attempts at smuggling on this leg of the journey, and no complex and intimidating border formalities, as both Greece and Bulgaria were members of the European Union. It was an uneventful journey with nothing to do but read and gaze out at the relatively unexciting scenery. I returned to the same hotel in Thessaloniki, and the next day caught the service bus to the airport and flew home.

I glanced out of the window as the plane flew over the Balkans on the way to back to Stansted, musing on what I'd learned during the trip. I knew before I went that the Balkans certainly have a complex and troubled history, and even now, in 2010, it still seemed somewhat scarred by its past. I would have to make future forays into the area to get a more complete picture, and this journey had prepared me to expect the unexpected.

I was not to be disappointed.

Chapter 4

The Balkans – Part 2 - Croatia, Montenegro, Kosovo, Bosnia

"One of the main ways of understanding the war crimes committed in South-eastern Europe in the 1990s has been to say that the Balkans, after all, were never really part of Europe"   **Susan Sontag**

> Riot and teargas. Bosnian battlefield. United Nations occupation. Visiting the world's newest country. Spectacular journeys along the Adriatic and through the Balkan grand canyon. Second-worst bus journey ever.

About a year after my first Balkan foray, I decided it was about time to revisit this recently troubled area. A friend had spent a week in Dubrovnik, the walled city in Croatia on the Adriatic coast, and reported that it was a beautiful place. His holiday photographs confirmed this, and I was aware that tour operators thought likewise as it was becoming popular as a tourist destination. I decided it might be a suitable place to start and finish my next Balkans foray, being close to at least three other countries I needed to visit.

My visit was in late September, and as usual I flew with one of the budget airlines from London Stansted. After a two-hour flight I exited Dubrovnik airport on a balmy evening to seek out the service bus into town. I travelled on it as far as the stop just outside the city walls, and as I disembarked and looked around to get my bearings I spotted a couple of local men seated on a bench. Thinking they might be able to advise me on the subject of low-cost hotels, I walked over to them and, before I could speak, one of them, middle aged, balding, and wearing a short-sleeved shirt and jeans, spoke.

"You want somewhere to stay mister?"

Was it so obvious that I was a tourist? And English?

"Yes." I replied. "But not expensive. And not too far away. And only one night."

"I can let you have nice room. It is in my house. I live there with my mother. Good price."

Similar situations arise from time to time when travelling on a strict budget. A more or less instant judgement must be made as to whether it would be wise to accept, usually based on a bare minimum of information. The man looked honest, and when he said "30 Euros – cash in advance." I decided to take a chance. He smiled broadly as I accepted, introduced himself as Dominik, and led me through the nearby archway in the city wall and along a narrow street. About 100 metres further on we arrived at his small ground floor flat, and as he opened the door his mother, a tiny, smartly-dressed lady, greeted us. I was shown to my pleasantly-furnished room and afterwards he invited me for coffee in the kitchen, which I gratefully accepted.

Dubrovnik, a walled city of some 43,000 souls in the Republic of Croatia, lies on the Adriatic Sea about half-way along the west coast of the Balkan Peninsula and dates back to the seventh century. It is arguably the most beautiful Adriatic city after Venice, and has remained largely unchanged for centuries with its narrow streets, pantiled buildings, and rocky shoreline, overlooked by mountains to the East. At various times a vassal-state under the control of Venice, the Ottoman Empire, Austria-Hungary, and France, Dubrovnik became part of the Kingdom of Yugoslavia at its creation in 1918, which became the Republic of Yugoslavia following a military coup in 1945. Thereafter it remained subject to the communist dictatorship of Josep Tito until 1980, and eventually became part of the newly independent country of Croatia following the break-up of Yugoslavia in 1991. War in the area was, some would say, an inevitable consequence of the break-up, and as a result Dubrovnik was besieged by Serbian forces under the guise of the Yugoslav People's Army for a period of seven months, which resulted in the deaths of 417 citizens and damage to 56% of the city's buildings. The siege was conducted by the use of field artillery located in the mountains to the East of the city. In 2013 Croatia joined the European Union, a privilege granted to only one other ex-Yugoslavia state, Slovenia, at the time of writing. Dubrovnik is nowadays a major tourist destination, with over 800,000 people arriving by air and on cruise-ships in 2016.

I chatted to my hosts about the siege of the city, in which it transpired that they had not lost any family members, but knew of several families that were not so fortunate. Dominik eventually handed me a key and I slipped out into the streets to a nearby restaurant, where I ate a delicious wienerschnitzel and chips garnished with fresh lemon segments. Thus refreshed, I returned to the flat and retired for the night. The next morning I woke bright and early, to be served coffee and fresh bread with butter and homemade jam by Dominik's mother in the kitchen. Shortly afterwards I left for the bus station, located twenty minutes to the north close by the cruise-liner quayside. There I bought a ticket for the port of Bar, in Montenegro, about 120 miles south on the Adriatic coast, and took a seat on the right hand side of the bus to take advantage of the anticipated sea views *en route*. At the start of the journey the bus climbs high up a steep hill overlooking the city, providing a birds-eye view over its rocky shoreline, stone walls and pantiled roofs, an image beloved of those who produce holiday brochures of the region. As noon approached the sun moved round to my side of the bus, and I found myself in the bus passenger's equivalent of a greenhouse. Nevertheless, views of the glorious Adriatic coastline made it well worth any discomfort.

The journey was unique in that it took me along the world's second shortest coastline for a non-island state, a distance of some 20 kilometres on either side of the port of Neum in Bosnia. The reason for the 20 kilometres dates back to the break-up of Yugoslavia in 1991, when Bosnia, which lies inland from Croatia at this point, insisted on retaining access to the Adriatic Sea for strategic reasons, even though this meant splitting the state of Croatia in two. As a result, the drive from Dubrovnik to Bar first runs through Croatia, then 20 kilometres of Bosnia, then Croatia again, then finally Montenegro. Fortunately there were no border formalities on entry to, or exit from, Bosnia, as at the time of my visit Croatia had not yet joined the European Union.

At about three o'clock the bus drew into the bus station about half a kilometre from the port in Bar, Montenegro's principal port. A low-density low-rise community of some 18,000 souls, Bar suffered severe damage when it was occupied by the Italians in World War II, and was later devastated by an earthquake in 1979. As a result most of its buildings are less than fifty years old. On arrival in Bar it had originally been my intention to continue on to Albania, with the border being only a few kilometres further down the coast, but I had decided against it on this trip as the only transport over the border at the time was by an infrequent and untimetabled minibus service from Bar town centre. Passengers were dropped a couple of miles over the border in Albania and were expected to make their own way from there to the nearest town, many miles away. I now regret not having the courage to attempt it, and can offer no excuse other than that I was worried about the return journey. Instead I decided to travel to the Montenegro capital city, Podgorice, about 80 kilometres to the north.

I strolled the kilometre or so to Bar railway station, under clear skies and a pleasantly warm sun, and studied the timetable for Podgorice. I had half an hour to kill so took a leisurely look at the beautiful steam locomotive preserved on a plinth outside the station. The engine carries the nameplate "Sutorman" which I found out later is a river valley nearby. The nameplate was in fact written in Cyrillic lettering, looking like "Cytopnah" in latin lettering, thus requiring me to make use of the Cyrillic alphabet guide in my Russian dictionary.

My train arrived, outwardly smart in its sky-blue livery, looking every inch a typical European regional train. Alas, the interior failed to live up to expectations, with ripped seat upholstery, graffiti, and litter everywhere. The small number of fellow-passengers only served to heighten the general air of decay, but I was determined not to let this spoil my enjoyment of my first train journey in Montenegro. The line takes the train through the Skadarsko Jezero National Park, part of which is the Skadarsko Lake, 40 kilometres long and in places 20 kilometres wide, crossed by the railway by means of a road-rail bridge a kilometre long, providing glorious views along the way. I was soon to conclude that Montenegro is one of the most beautiful and underrated countries in Europe, every bit as spectacular as, say, Switzerland, and of course much less expensive.

An hour or so later my train shuddered to a halt in Podgorice, and outside the station I was briefly amused to find that the taxis were operated by a company named "Bum", the name being displayed prominently in large lettering on each vehicle. I wondered idly if the owners had ever considered opening an office in London. My "No taxi" rule in any case kicked in and I set off to walk to the city centre. It was by this time around 6pm, and I was struck by the large number of motorcycles and motor-scooters passing by, many of them carrying the Montenegro flag on a flagpole attached at the rear. There were also many pedestrians heading in the same direction, and I concluded they may be heading for some sort of national day rally, or possibly there was an evening football match scheduled.

Podgorice, capital of Montenegro, is a pleasant but unexciting city of approximately 190,000 souls. Founded in 1326, it has always been a centre of trade and communication, and was for over 400 years part of the Ottoman Empire. Montenegro joined the Kingdom of Yugoslavia following World War I, and Podgorice, along with Bar, was more or less destroyed during World War II. The city has since been almost completely rebuilt with broad boulevards and handsome stone buildings in the centre. After the war it was renamed Titograd, after Josep Tito, the Yugoslav dictator, but the name reverted to Podgorice in 1992 following the break-up of Yugoslavia. Fighting in other areas of ex-Yugoslavia in 1990 did not spread to Montenegro, leaving Podgorice unaffected by the conflict. The city is, perhaps surprisingly, twinned with London.

I approached one of the many policemen on the street, asked if he could recommend a low-cost hotel, and in reasonable English he gave me directions. The hotel turned out to be an imposing six storey stone edifice not far from a park, and reasonably close to the city centre. Inside, the spacious reception area exuded faded grandeur, and I could imagine that Josep Tito may well have stayed there in his day. Those days were long gone, however, and I headed upstairs to my high–ceilinged room on the third floor, which sported tall French windows opening onto a small balcony overlooking the rear of the building. The bathroom could best be described as "well-used".

As usual, after dropping off my bag in the room, I popped out to the local convenience store to buy food and drink. The trickle of flag-carrying people in the street had by now turned into a flood, resulting in a longish queue at the shop checkout. I was determined to see where these people were heading, so I made my purchases and continued on down the road to find a huge and noisy crowd in the adjacent park. On a stage some distance away a group of people – I could only assume they were politicians - surrounded a bank of microphones. As one of them stepped forward to speak, the assembled crowd roared in approval.   I surreptitiously took a couple of photos, aware that those around me seemed somewhat agitated, and eventually returned to the hotel.

Back in my room I switched on the television and searched for an English-language channel, then settled back to enjoy my beer, potato salad, ham, cheese, and cake. After maybe half an hour there was the sudden noise of an aircraft passing very low overhead. I reasoned that the hotel must be close to the flight-path to the airport. A minute or so later another came over, then another. Must be a busy period at the airport, I thought. After the tenth of these in a fifteen-minute period, followed by the sound of sirens from the street, I realised there must be another explanation. I put on my coat and opened the door. My eyes started to water as soon as I set foot in the corridor, and I knew instinctively it was my first-ever experience of teargas.

I made my way down to the lobby, my eyes watering copiously by then, where I found a group of men clad in what looked like tracksuits – all the same shade of red – chatting to the receptionist. At first I thought they were a sports team of some sort, but then noticed one of them giving medical assistance to a couple of youths seated at one of the tables in the nearby bar. The men in red were, in fact paramedics, presumably basing themselves at the hotel on standby. By this time the tear gas was severely irritating my eyes, but curiosity got the better of me and I went out into the street. At the end of the road, by the park and beneath the streetlights, I could see a line of policemen, with some firing teargas into what appeared to be a rioting crowd of flag-bearing youths. Above them, hovering low in the sky a helicopter shone its floodlights on the scene below. This was the "aircraft" I'd heard in my room, and I now realised it had been circling the area and was passing over the hotel every minute or so. Deciding that discretion was the better part of valour, and conscious that my eyes were now really suffering, I went back into the hotel and returned to my room, By 11pm the police sirens had stopped and peace seemed to have returned to the streets. Once the effects of the teargas had subsided I switched on the television to see if there was any local coverage. There was, but of course I didn't understand the language so was not much the wiser as to the cause of the conflict.

The following morning, as I checked out at reception, I assured the receptionist I had no lasting ill effects from the teargas, and was heading off to Kosovo. I asked her what had caused the riot. She said simply that the rally had been called by politicians to express the country's unhappiness with the recent granting of nation status to Kosovo, but it had got out of hand. The irony did not escape me. I was about to travel to the country that had been the unwitting cause of my being tear-gassed. As I headed for the bus station through the littered streets, the dustmen were making a start on clearing up the mess after the riot, and life was beginning to return to normal.

The bus station was crowded, with the inevitable early-morning queue at the ticket office, and after buying my ticket I sought out the stand where the Kosovo bus was loading. A large double-decker, with two sets of wheels at the rear, it boasted tables, each seating four people, in the downstairs section. I headed upstairs and settled in to a seat by the window, soon after which the engine coughed into life and we were on our way. Twenty minutes or so later we left the main road north of the city and began climbing towards the mountains on a fairly basic two-lane road which eventually levelled out half-way up the side of a precipitous gorge. The man beside to me explained.

"Moraca Gorge." he said, and added."Very beautiful."

It certainly was. Imagine driving along a narrow road located halfway up the side of the Grand Canyon in the USA, and following the same contour for thirty kilometres or more with spectacular views over the river's rapids three hundred metres or so below. At various points along the way the lack of Armco iron barriers gave credence to my companion's description of the highway as "Death Road", but in no way diminished my enjoyment of the journey. The mountain peaks on either side rise to around 2000 metres, and along the other side of the gorge the railway runs at almost the same elevation, making use of occasional skeletal bridges. It is, quite simply, the most spectacular road journey I have ever made. After some 40 kilometres it veers to the east, crosses the gorge on a spectacular bridge, and climbs into the mountains of the Moracke Planine.

We stopped at a wayside cafe just above the treeline which overlooked a pleasant little valley with mountain peaks in the distance. It was chilly, due to the altitude, and cloud drifted in from time to time. I ordered a double espresso and surveyed the scene in the crowded room. My fellow passengers, most of whom were male, appeared to be in their twenties and early thirties, and black leather jackets were *de rigeur*. I shared a table with two Kosovans, who proudly showed me their identity cards. The design of the Kosovo Passport had not yet been agreed, so its citizens were only able to travel using identity cards. Although these were evidently valid for travel to Montenegro, I wondered if they would be accepted by an immigration officer at London Heathrow Airport.

Back on the road, we continued to climb, and eventually reached the border. Here I queued to get my passport stamped, and was relieved not to be subjected to any interrogation about the purpose of my visit. Shortly afterwards we set off again and soon were climbing no longer. Then, suddenly, there lay before us the breathtaking sunlit view over the plain far below, surrounding the city of Pec, our destination. Seemingly unending hairpin bends lay ahead as we descended to sea-level, and as we approached the outskirts of the city I notice that many houses sported brand-new pantiled roofs, despite the fact that they looked to be distinctly old buildings. I realised that this was directly as a result of the war in Kosovo in 1999 when eighty percent of the city of Pec and surrounding villages was destroyed or damaged during the ethnic cleansing of Albanians by Serbs. The rebuilding had been going on ever since.

Kosovo, a land-locked state of some 2 million souls, of whom 88% are Albanian, is one of the world's newest countries, having been created in 2008 when it unilaterally declared its independence from Serbia, of which it was effectively a province during the years when Serbia was a part of Yugoslavia. This followed the end of a war waged in 1999 by Serbia to ethnically cleanse the predominantly Muslim Kosovo Albanians from the region. The United Nations Organisation entered the country soon after the end of the war and remains there today as a guarantors of peace and security. Since independence in 2008 the country has become recognised as an independent state by 115 countries out of 195 in the world, so to this day is unrecognised by substantial parts of the globe. The country is mainly mountainous, and covers an area of some 11,000 square kilometres, similar to that of the island of Cyprus and slightly less than neighbouring Montenegro. Its capital, Pristina, is 85 kilometres from Pec and accounts for 10% of the country's population and is the major driver of the economy, but there are few major industries other than construction and tourism. Pec, with a population of 100,000, is the third-largest city, and an important United Nations base.

I exited the bus station in Pec and walked along the main street in the evening sunshine looking for a hotel. There was a bookshop on the left, somewhere to buy a street map and guide, I thought. The owner looked up from his book as I entered. . .

"Do you speak English?" I said, hopefully

"A little."

"I'm looking for a street map of Pec." I said, being careful to pronounce the "c" as "ch", exactly as I'd heard it spoken in Podgorice.

"You mean Peje." He said, pronouncing it as you would say "payer" in English. "Pec is the Serbian version of the name of our city. Here we call it Peje. This is the correct version."

So saying, he offered me a rather basic street map.

"Can I pay you in Euros?"

"Of course. It is our currency. Ever since independence. "

"Is there a hotel nearby?"

"Yes. Continue down the street one hundred metres. Hotel Dukagjini. You cannot miss it."

I made a mental note to use Peje rather than Pec for the remainder of the visit. It seemed from his demeanour that the Serbian "Pec" might arouse hostility.

Thus armed, I found the hotel, a pleasant four-storey oldish building and checked in. That evening I had a beer on the hotel veranda overlooking the River Lumbardhi, and watched the sun go down. It had been an interesting day.

After breakfast the next day I walked around the city centre, unsurprised to see that there was still quite a lot of unrepaired war damage, but in general Peje seemed to be functioning quite normally. The Two mosques that I passed appeared undamaged and were already receiving worshippers for morning prayers, and the shops were busy. I walked the half kilometre or so to the railway station to see if it would be possible to get a train to Pristina, the capital. The station building and tracks were undamaged, but there were no trains – although I believe that since then the service has been restored.

At this time Kosovo was still a United Nations protectorate and there were UN non-combat vehicles everywhere – white, with "UN" in large black capital letters on the doors. A UN Landrover containing what looked like fairly senior uniformed UN officers pulled up alongside me, and I contemplated taking a photo, but decided it might not be wise in what was still a somewhat sensitive military area. A few blue-beret UN soldiers were to be seen on the streets, although it was a somewhat discreet presence. Cafes were open so there was no problem with food and drink, but I was unable to find any tourist souvenir shops - hardly surprising in the circumstances – which afterwards I realised must have made Peje a unique city in Europe. Hoping to find at the very least a fridge magnet as a souvenir, I was to be disappointed. However at an outdoor market I managed to buy a key fob showing the new flag – a blue field with a yellow silhouette map of Kosovo in its centre and an arc of six white stars above. This was to be the only material souvenir of my visit.

Early the following morning I made my way to the almost deserted bus station to get the bus back to Podgorice. As I sat outside in the sunshine, my fellow-passengers began to arrive in ones and twos. No matter how often I travel, I always feel slightly anxious at bus stations, constantly wondering if my bus will fail to show up, leaving me stranded. This time there was no problem. Climbing aboard, I headed for the top deck and settled back to enjoy that spectacular journey all over again. At the border high in the mountains an immigration officer boarded the bus and insisted we hand over passports and ID cards, then took them into his office. This practice, which I have come across at other roadside border posts, provokes anxiety every time. Would I ever get that precious document back? All was well, however, and we continued on our way.

My intention was to go from Podgorice back to Dubrovnik by bus. I had checked the timetable previously and knew there was a bus at 3pm. It was timetabled get me to Dubrovnik around 7:45pm which would give me ample time to find a hotel for the night, or even perhaps call on Dominik to see if the room was still vacant. Arriving in Podgorice in plenty of time, I bought food and drink for the journey from the bus-station shop. The timetable listed six stops en route, but as it turned out these were just the scheduled stops. Ten minutes after the first of these stops, the driver halted at a remote countryside crossroads where a man stood bearing a number of cardboard boxes. The driver opened the door, the man entered, loaded the boxes onto a seat, and left. This process was repeated several times throughout the journey, with packages being loaded and offloaded at various non-scheduled locations. I could see the likely arrival time in Dubrovnik getting later and later. Around 9pm the lights of the city appeared on the horizon, and I was looking forward to food and a beer. Not used to the geography of the city, I decided to stay on until we reached the bus station, from where I could walk the kilometre or so back to the city walls. As the bus halted for the final time I could see we were at the edge of a trading estate near the port, but nowhere near the bus station. I asked the driver how I was to get back to the city. He had no English so was unable to help, but he pointed towards a local bus parked just up the road. I walked over to it to find the driver checking his fare takings. Fortunately he had a little English.

"What time do you leave?" I asked

"No service." He said, curtly. "Finished for today."

"But I have to get into the city. How can I do it?"

"I go to garage now. You can come there if you wish."

"OK."

It had to be better than the trading estate. After ten minutes or so he stopped the bus.

"See that road? Hotel along there."

I thanked him profusely and alighted, just as It began to rain. The road was long, on a steadily rising slope, but mercifully soon led me through the city wall. It had been a long day, it was still raining, and I was beginning to lose heart, when suddenly I came upon a large and rather smart hotel, set back from the road. Feeling and looking like a refugee, I entered the reception area and enquired if they had a room. The man looked me up and down, paused for a moment, then said that they certainly had a room but I must pay in advance by card. The transaction completed, I headed for my room and there dried myself as well as possible. As it transpired, the hotel was almost empty, it being the end of the season, and I descended to the bar, a huge room that would normally seat hundreds. Apart from a small group of men playing cards in the far corner, I was the only customer. The barman looked up from his copy of the local paper and I asked for a beer. We chatted a while, then I took a seat and mused over the events of the previous few days.

The following morning I went down to the near-empty breakfast bar, ordered a coffee, and took a seat by the window. An elevated view of the old stone-walled port lay before me, with small boats bobbing at anchor. Beyond the port were the clear blue waters of the Adriatic, twinkling in the morning sun. It seemed a long way from teargas in the streets of Podgorice!

I spent the morning wandering around that beautiful city, and was particularly moved when I visited the museum devoted to the siege of 1991. One of the rooms contains nothing but photos, some in colour, some in black and white, of each of the 400 or so residents who were killed in the bombardment. A single red rose is placed beneath each rank of pictures. The visit reminded me I had yet to complete the final part of my trip, the deceptively simple matter of a visit to Bosnia, whose border runs no more than two or three kilometres inland from the city walls, a short distance into the mountain range that surround the city. Time was running out as I was scheduled to get the plane home that evening, so there were few options. J believed there was a bus service, but had no idea of departure times.

I rushed to the bus station, only to discover that there was no service that would allow a return visit in the couple of hours I had available. Opposite the bus station I spotted a taxi rank, and my "no taxis" rule suddenly seemed inappropriate. I spoke to the nearest driver, who was casually leaning against his Mercedes A class and smoking a cigarette. I told him I simply wanted to cross into Bosnia, stay there for a short while, then return. Possibly suspicious of my motives, he seemed reluctant to take me. But my offer of 20 Euros gave him pause for thought, and he finally said "OK for 25 Euros." Not in a position to barter, I climbed into the passenger seat and handed over the cash, at which he introduced himself as Ivan.

After three kilometres or so we arrived at the border. Ivan took my passport and handed it over to the border guard through the car's open window. They seemed to know each other and chatted awhile. I imagined that he was telling the guard that his passenger was a mad Englishman who, for some unfathomable reason, wanted to set foot in Bosnia. Whatever was actually said, we were waved through and continued until we stopped on a high plateau overlooking Dubrovnik. Ivan switched off the engine and I stepped out, thereby achieving my objective of actually setting foot in the country.

On the landward side I viewed a small village, where, just as in Kosovo, many obviously old buildings sported new pantiled roofs, presumably renovated after the military action during the siege. Before us was a glorious elevated view of Dubrovnik, with the Adriatic beyond. Ivan confirmed that the plateau had been the location for the heavy artillery used by the Yugoslav People's Army during the siege. I took a couple of photos, climbed back in the taxi, and we returned to the bus station. From there I took the bus to the airport.

It had been a memorable few days, combining journeys through spectacular natural scenery with regular reminders of the region's instability. One thing I was discovering is that the Balkan states are never dull. This was even more evident than in my next visit – to that most enigmatic of countries, Albania.

Chapter 5

The Balkans – Part 3 – Greece and Albania

I tried to visit Albania but I couldn't find it on the map. **Oscar Wilde**

Albanians are a nation of freedom fighters who know something about living under oppression.
Fatos Nano

Ejected from the National Bank of Greece. Severe currency problems. Worst-ever bus journey. Pursued by feral dogs at night. Beryl Cook. Taking a fall whilst running to catch a boat. Non-existent bus stations. Defence emplacements along the coast. Minimal tourist and transport information.

For many years I'd been intrigued by the modern history of the state of Albania (officially The Republic of Albania). A predominantly Muslim area since it was part of the Ottoman Empire, the country proclaimed its independence in 1912 at the end of the Balkan war. A turbulent period followed, culminating in the declaration of the first Albanian Republic in 1925. Further internal unrest led to it becoming a kingdom three years later, but this only lasted until the end of the Second World War, when communists seized power under Enver Hoxha, who declared the country to be a "Peoples Republic". He banned religious observance, nationalised land, and in 1967 declared his country to be the world's first atheist state. What was effectively a communist dictatorship began to crumble in the 1980s, largely due to the resentment by the devout Muslim population to the atheist dogma. Under a new president there was reform and the present-day Republic of Albania was created

Further unrest followed. A major economic crisis occurred in 1996 when up to a third of the population were persuaded to invest in a so-called "Ponzi " pyramid banking scheme which inevitably failed. Citizens were persuaded to invest in a scheme promising high rates of interest. The scheme continued to attract new investors as those that invested originally found themselves in receipt of very high levels of income. Little did they know that the source of that income was not from the intrinsic quality of the scheme, but In fact the payments the earlier investors were receiving were sourced from the monies paid in by the more recent investors, being those at the bottom of the "pyramid". There came the inevitable moment when no further investors were available to be signed up, at which point all "interest" payments dried up and all but those near the top of the "pyramid" lost their money. Following unrest on the streets caused by this fraud, the government were obliged to invite in a United Nations peacekeeping force to restore order. There were further problems in 1999 when Muslim refugees from the war in Kosovo arrived in the country. The twenty-first century has mercifully seen an unprecedented period of peace, with the country applying (unsuccessfully) to join the European Union, and with its borders being opened. But it fair to say that there are few countries in the world with a more turbulent recent history.

A friend of mine, a bit of a left-leaning firebrand in his day, decided to visit Albania in the early 1980s, at a time when the country was considered something of a model communist state by many socialists throughout the world. Unaccompanied tourists were not allowed into the country at the time, so he was obliged to join one of the organised tours that were arranged by the Albanian government for propaganda purposes. There were no scheduled flights from England, so he and his tour party were obliged to fly into Yugoslavia (possibly Podgorice) from where they were transferred over the border in Albanian state buses. After visiting hospitals, collective farms, schools, and the like over a period of a few days, carefully supervised by party apparatchiks, they returned to Yugoslavia and flew home. When contemplating visiting the country myself around thirty years later I found to my delight that tourists were now welcome.

I faced the usual dilemma – how to get there? At the time no budget airlines were flying to the capital, Tirana. However, I happened to come across a very cheap out-of-season package trip to the Greek Island of Corfu, which lies twenty miles or so off the coast of Albania. On finding that there is a daily ferry from there to Albania, I decided this was the way to go. As a bonus, Corfu appeared to be an interesting place in its own right, so what could be better than using it as a base?

Arriving at Corfu airport, I realised that, due to an oversight, I had no Euros with me. Normally I try to arrive with enough local currency to last a couple of days, but circumstances had prevented this, so I sought out a cash machine. There were no banks open in the arrivals hall, but I eventually found a free-standing cash machine outside an office. Breaking my golden rule – never use any cash machine that is not sited at a bank that is open for business - I put my credit card in the slot. The machine readily accepted it, and the screen immediately went blank. Panic set in. No matter what I did with the keyboard there was no response. I reported the incident to one of the airport managers, who responded with a simple Greek shrug of the shoulders and promised to report it to whoever owned the machine the next day. Thankfully, my other golden rule, which requires me always to have both a debit card and a credit card available on any journey, meant that I was able to survive the week with just one piece of plastic, my debit card. In the event, there were no further problems, other than a slight hiccup in Sarande, of which more later. I reported the loss of my card to the issuing company by phone when I got to the hotel, and was assured that all transactions would be stopped.

The hotel in Corfu was an unremarkable six-storey building constructed specifically to cater to the mass-tourist industry, located on the north-east coast of the island about half an hour's drive from the airport. My room on the third floor looked out over two pools, one of which was a rectangular 25 metre affair intended for the serious swimmers. Beyond the pools and the sea-shore lay the narrow strait that separates the island from the clearly-visible Albanian coast, my destination.

I spent a couple of days sprawled on a lounger by the pool, taking advantage of a spell of warm weather to catch up on my reading, and on the third day caught the bus into Corfu Town, more correctly known as Kerkyra, the island's capital and port, to book the ferry to Albania. Whilst there I took the opportunity to check out the town's few tourist attractions. The fortress didn't detain me long – for me, fortresses fall into the same category as castles and waterfalls – when you've seen one you've seen them all. Slightly more interesting, however, at least from an architectural point of view, is Mon Repos, a one-time holiday home for the Greek Royal Family which in 1921 was the birthplace of Prince Philip. The remainder of Kerkyra is small town Greece, attractive and interesting but rarely spectacular.

I was planning to take the ferry to Albania the following day, so needed to find a source of Lek, the Albanian currency. At a bank in the downtown area I was informed that the only place I could obtain Lek was at the Central Bank, just off the main square. I was rather surprised to learn that the Greek Central Bank has a branch in Corfu, which prompted me to speculate that the English equivalent might be a branch of the Bank of England on the Isle of Wight. By the square I found a handsome white three-storey pantiled building with shuttered windows and a classical staircase leading to a roman-arched entrance. The armed guard on the door was reluctant to let me pass, but eventually directed me to one of the tellers inside. There I was politely told that they were not a bureau de change, and in any case they did not keep Lek in cash. In retrospect, I can see it was the equivalent of calling in at the Bank of England in London and asking them if they would sell me Euros. I was escorted, rather too briskly for my liking, to the door. As a result it looked like I would be dependent on finding a source of Lek immediately on arrival in Albania, something of a gamble.

By now it was midday, and I needed to get a ticket for the ferry. In hot sunshine I walked the kilomrtre or so to the port. Commercial vessels of various sizes jostled with each other along the quayside, and opposite them on the port road were offices of the various shipping companies and ferry operators. It being lunchtime, most were closed, but I eventually tracked down one that was open and bought my ticket for Sarande, the port in Albania. Departure was at 8:30am the following day. Still without the requisite Lek, I walked back into town and had a beer at a restaurant in the main square, enjoying the sunshine whilst awaiting the reopening of the banks so that I might try my luck with Lek once again.

As it transpired, my luck was out, and I resigned myself to the prospect of arriving in Albania with no local currency. I took the bus back to the hotel, where later that evening the assembled guests were treated to an enjoyable Greek cultural show featuring a team of dancers and musicians in national costume. Towards the end we were invited to join the dancers to perform the obligatory "Zorba's Dance", but I declined on the basis that I have a medical condition known as "two left feet". Thankfully there was no plate-smashing afterwards.

At 7:15am the following day I exited the hotel and walked over to the bus stop. The bus duly arrived on time, but sadly I hadn't taken account of the fact that school starts early in Corfu. In consequence it was already full of boisterous schoolchildren, and the journey took 45 minutes instead the previous day's 25, with the result that I was running late. Nevertheless I foolishly spent longer than I should have in yet another bank on my way to the port, to find, inevitably, that they also carried no Lek. By now I realised I'd have to put a move on, and as I ran along the port road I tripped on a misplaced kerbstone and fell headlong. Thankfully the only damage was a graze to my right hand, and I arrived out of breath and dishevelled at the ferry just as she was boarding.

A member of the crew stood at the end of the rickety gang-plank. He viewed my ticket and asked for my passport. I handed it over, expecting it to be examined and returned, but he added it to a pile of passports beside him, presumably those of the passengers that had already boarded. I was unhappy at having to part with it, but there was nothing much I could do. He waved me aboard and I headed for the cafe on the lower deck of this small vessel, not much bigger than a good-sized fishing boat.

There I ordered a double espresso, which I thought was richly deserved given the morning's traumas.

As we left the harbour I took my coffee, went up on deck and found a seat. It was a cloudy, slightly chilly morning but the sea was calm. My fellow passengers, for the most part engaged in animated conversation, were a mixture of tourists and locals. The bridge was visible from my seat on the deck, and through its window I could see the captain at the wheel and beside him the passport man seated at a desk, in the process of painstakingly copying the details of each passport into a log. He was to emerge later as we passed the halfway-point in the journey to lower the Greek flag on the mast above the wheelhouse and replace it with the Albanian flag

Slowly the verdant coast of Albania drew nearer, until I could finally make out our destination, the port of Sarande, also known as Saranda, which, in the now-brightening sunlight, had the look of a typical small Mediterranean port. The passport man emerged from his makeshift office to return our passports, and half an hour later we were at the quayside and disembarking. Albanian Immigration control consisted of a lone uniformed man inside a small booth – I needed to ask him to stamp my passport – and before I knew it I was on the quayside road. Street-sellers were hawking their wares as I walked along, mainly seafood, and the market across the way was beginning to close after the morning's trading.

I'd taken the precaution back home of copying a few pages from the Lonely Planet guide, showing maps of the major Albanian towns and cities, and consulted the somewhat sketchy map of Sarande. It showed the bus station as being located part way up the hill, about half a kilometre away. Before that, however, there was the pressing matter of getting hold of some Lek. I walked past a couple of small pleasant-looking hotels overlooking the harbour, and eventually found a bank. There were no cash machines, so I entered and joined the queue. Progress was slow as stallholders from the market were paying-in the morning's takings, but I eventually reached the desk.

"Do you have a cash machine?"

Fortunately the young girl had some English

"No. There are none in Sarande."

"Then can you sell me Lek on my debit card?"

She looked perplexed.

"One moment please."

She turned and went into the office behind, and then, after a muffled discussion, returned accompanied by a man.

"My manager will help you."

He smiled, said hello, reached into a desk drawer under the counter, and took out a card swipe machine. With it was a user's manual, which he proceeded to leaf through. The girl, meanwhile, turned to serve the growing queue of impatient locals behind me.

"Sorry for the delay." He said. "We don't use the machine often. It is new"

Around five minutes later he seemed ready to proceed and asked for my card.

"How many Lek do you want?"

I hadn't realised that there may be problems paying by card in Albania so did a quick recalculation based on making all payments in the country by cash.

"About 15,000." I suggested, it being equivalent to £100.00

He keyed it in, offered me the machine for my PIN, and it worked! His evident surprise was matched by my evident relief, but we were not finished. The bank used the old paper-based double-entry accounting system, where each transaction must be recorded by hand on a multi-part form with carbon-paper. This was duly completed, and one part was torn off and handed to me, along with the Leks. I muttered my profuse thanks and left.

I could now seek out the bus station. The map showed it as being in the middle of a square. I soon located the square, which turned out to be a car-park bereft of any buildings, and there were a couple of buses parked In the far corner. I went over to the group of men chatting and smoking by the buses. One of them, evidently a driver, spoke English. My intention was to go to Vlore, some 125 kilometres up the coast. I asked him if there was a printed timetable. He smiled and said there wasn't. So how did I know which bus was going to Vlore? Simple – I must wait until I see a bus arrive with a Vlore destination board. How long would this take? Not sure, but should be soon. How do I buy a ticket? You pay the driver.

There being no seats (or for that matter anything else that constitutes a normal bus station), I went over the road to a cafe, ordered a double espresso, and sat outside to watch the buses come and go. Eventually one arrived with a plastic destination board placed on the dashboard stating "VLORE". I finished my coffee and wandered over. The driver had no English, but when I said "Vlore" he gave me a ticket, pointed to the price, and I paid him. With great relief, I boarded the bus, took a seat on the left side to ensure the best sea views, and we set off.

The road from Sarande to Vlore is one of the most spectacular coastal drives in Europe, arguably more dramatic than the journey from Dubrovnik to Bar, or the Amalfi Coast road in Italy. At the time of my visit it was unique in being free of tourist development for more or less its entire length of 125 kilometres, despite the fact that it runs alongside the Adriatic Sea from beginning to end. A long section of road- works just outside Sarande failed dampen my enthusiasm, and we were soon rattling along high up in the mountainside on a two-lane blacktop road with glorious views over the Strait of Otranto. The joy was, however, short-lived when we hit a further delay. There seemed to be no method of controlling traffic in the several miles of road-works that followed, and several times we were forced by oncoming traffic to leave the road altogether and drive on rubble. This was to be the pattern for the entire journey – great views whilst driving along spectacular sections of metalled road, alternating with long diversions onto unmade half-finished, and sometimes downright dangerous stretches.

It was at its worst about 50 miles out from Sarande when we arrived at Himara, a small town with a pleasant beach and a few small tourist hotels. The entire width of the road through the town had been dug up, but despite this, traffic was still being allowed along it. The resulting complete absence of lane discipline, traffic controls, and diversions meant it was a free-for-all in the narrow streets in both directions. From my vantage point behind the driver, and with mounting anxiety, I witnessed several near-collisions involving the bus, and have never been so relieved as when we finally got back on the open road.

The lack of tourists in Albania at the time meant that the beautiful beaches along the route were virtually empty. Many of them, however, were guarded by sinister silent sentinels in the form of dome-shaped Pillbox concrete bunkers. These were erected during the presidency of the country's one-time communist dictator, Enver Hoxha. For various reasons he had problems in his relations with both NATO and the Warsaw Pact at the time, and decided to go it alone in the defence of his country, it is reckoned that about 750,000 of these pillboxes were built throughout the country, but in particular along the coast, in expectation that any invasion force would most probably arrive by sea. These strange constructions, some of which look like giant concrete mushrooms, are now considered as monuments by some Albanians, and many have been painted by the locals in bright primary colours. I managed to get photographs of a couple of them, one red, yellow and green, and the other orange.

Not too far from Vlore we descended the mountainside and the driver pointed out what looked like a tunnel into the hillside on the far side of the bay.

"Submarine base." He said mysteriously.

It was apparently constructed by Enver Hoxha as part of the surrounding naval base, now-disused, possibly to conceal submarines.

The bus climbed again and then descended into Vlore, a large port with wide boulevards and a typically Mediterranean harbour with cafes and bars. The scheduled 3 ½ hour journey had taken 5 hours to complete. The driver dropped us all off at the roadside in the city centre, but again there was no bus station, nor even any bus stops, and it was clear the fourgon system was in operation. This system, incidentally in widespread use in Istanbul, is one where buses and minibuses effectively act as taxis, displaying a destination board and able to be hailed from the roadside. To this day I have been unable to decide if I had been on a scheduled bus service or a fourgon. I checked out where the bus station was supposed to be on my map, and was not surprised when the location turned out to be another featureless car park.

I crossed the road and entered the small hotel opposite, where I found a reception area somewhat bizarrely dominated by a two metre-square reproduction of a Beryl Cook painting. I wondered idly if she was aware her art had reached such distant outposts. I paid cash for my room, with no receipt sought or given, and after taking a shower I ate in the restaurant. I sought out the receptionist, a pretty blonde girl with adequate English, and mentioned that I might try to get to Tirana, the capital, by train the following day. She could give me no information on trains but suggested I pop along to the station. I asked if she had a map of the city, but she was only able to mark the station's approximate location on my very sketchy photocopied map, which sadly bore no street names. Nevertheless, I thought it worth trying. Whilst on the subject of transport I asked her about the bus station in Vlore. She said there was no central bus station as such, and confirmed there were no bus stops, thus confirming that the fourgon system applied.

It was dark by the time I set off across the road in the approximate direction of the railway station, intending to seek details of trains that would leave for Tirana the following day. Street lighting was poor, there were few people about, and in a narrow street I suddenly became aware of a pack of half a dozen feral dogs close behind me. I had no option but to continue walking as two of the larger ones in the pack came right up to me, their noses twitching as they checked out this intruder on their territory. For a few moments I wondered about the standard of accident and emergency healthcare in the city, and whether my travel insurance included repatriation of my body, but the pack eventually lost interest and dropped back. Ten minutes later I found the station, but was on the wrong side for the entrance and had to cross a building site in pitch darkness. Another feral dog appeared, approached me, barked, showed two ranks of fearsome teeth, and then thankfully disappeared into the night.

The tiny two-platform railway station was closed and locked up for the night. There were a couple of carriages in a siding but no sign of life. In the darkness I was unable to read the timetable which was posted high on the locked entrance door. There was nothing I could do but retrace my steps back to the hotel. On the way, the feral dogs reappeared, anxious to escort me from their patch, and occasionally responding to the howls of other unseen dogs along the way.

With much annoyance at my wasted journey, tempered with relief at getting back unmolested, I had a beer in the almost-empty hotel bar and contemplated my situation. What worried me most was the apparent lack of any organised and documented travel system in the country, together with the absence of maps and tourist information. I was sure that the locals understood perfectly well how to get about, but a visitor had little hope in the short-term of mastering such an *ad hoc* system.. As for my planned train trip to Tirana, the capital, I wondered about the reliability of a railway system that I already knew was somewhat neglected and with an infrequent service. Could it be relied upon to get me back to Vlore and thence back to Sarande by bus in reasonable time for the ferry to Corfu and ultimately the plane back to England?

I went back to the lady on reception, and told her of my worries. She attempted to reassure me by further explaining how the bus system worked, but admitted she'd never taken the train as there were often problems. As for the bus to Sarande, she happened to mention that one left from outside the hotel every day at 7:30am. I found myself, not for the first time, facing the traveller's dilemma – to continue with a somewhat bold plan that might fail somewhere along the way, or take the easy way out and quit whilst ahead. To my shame, I chose the latter. The knowledge that I could get the bus the following morning back to Sarande was persuasive, and the thought of a couple more days to explore Corfu – or simply to relax at the hotel -was a pleasant prospect. And I had, after all, succeeded in visiting Albania, which had been the main objective of the trip.

I resolved to get the next morning's Sarande bus. The lady couldn't guarantee an early-morning call so I went to my room and set my travel alarm. I slept fitfully, but woke at 6:30am and watched the news on CNN television news before heading downstairs to the car park, having little confidence that the bus would be there. It wasn't, but five minutes later it arrived and I paid my fare. I took a seat on the right hand side, which provided the best possible views of the Adriatic, but also allowed me to see how close we were to the vertiginous cliff edge every time we hit one of those confounded road-up sections.

Six hours later the bus pulled into the car-park at Sarande and I headed for the ferry terminal. After buying a ticket for the departure at 4pm I sought out a cafe on the seafront and sat outside in the warm afternoon sun consuming shish kebab with chips, washed down with a cold beer. As I watched the local fishermen go about their business it seemed a lifetime away from the feral dogs of Vlore!

The ferry journey back to Corfu passed without incident, effectively a mini-cruise in glorious sunshine on a flat-calm sea. As we arrived at Corfu harbour we passed a gigantic cruise-liner anchored offshore, and I genuinely felt pity for its passengers at that moment. After all, where's the enjoyment in a holiday where everything goes to plan?

The remaining days were spent enjoyably travelling in Corfu on the well-organised local buses, and, I have to admit, lounging around the hotel pool. I couldn't, however, feel satisfied with my failure to spend more time in Albania and in particular missing out on a visit to Tirana, the capital. It was an unwelcome reminder that I am far from the intrepid traveller I have occasionally thought myself to be. I'm sure those who travel regularly in third-world countries would probably look on me as a rank amateur, but at the end of the day it's a matter of character. Some of us are simply more adventurous than others.

Chapter 6

The Balkans - Part 4 – Slovenia and Italy

"From Stettin in the Baltic, to Trieste in the Adriatic, an iron curtain has descended across the continent" **Winston Churchill**

"You can do nothing about governments and winter." **Slovenian proverb**

> Worst-ever aeroplane landing. James Joyce. Tram closure. Arriving in the middle of nowhere with no currency. The finest view from the steps of a railway station anywhere.

Following my three visits to the Balkans, at times challenging, but always fascinating, there was just one country still to visit in that part of the world- Slovenia. Bordered by Italy to the East and Austria to the North, and with only forty-six kilometres or so of Adriatic coastline, it has enjoyed a much more peaceful modern history than the others. I consequently had high hopes of a pleasant holiday with no unexpected problems.

Invaded by Italy in World War II, during which some 8% of the population met their deaths, Slovenia rejoined Federal Yugoslavia at the end of the war, but in 1991 effectively seceded from that country and declared independence in what was to be labelled "The Slovenian Spring". Yugoslav troops invaded, but left after only ten days. The country was accepted as an independent state by the United Nations in 1992 and joined the European Union in 2004. Three years later it adopted the Euro as its national currency. A mainly Roman Catholic country, with a Muslim population of less than 3%, it had managed to avoid the racial tensions that have regularly blighted many of the other ex-Yugoslavian nations.

There being no budget flights to the capital, Ljubljana, at the time, I decided I would fly to Trieste in Italy, which conveniently lies some ten miles from the Slovenian border. It was mid-winter, and the landing at Trieste airport was possibly the worst I've ever experienced. The plane descended through a torrential rainstorm and was buffeted by high winds. I could only imagine the thoughts of the crew as the pilot struggled to keep the craft on an even keel. Children were crying, and for the first time ever on a flight I saw a couple of old ladies cross themselves. As we finally touched down I spotted standing water along the runway. The roar of the engines' reverse-thrust temporarily provided relief from the children's wailing, and we came to a shuddering halt. There was a brief silence, followed by spontaneous and prolonged applause from what seemed like the entire complement of passengers. I half-expected the pilot to emerge smiling from the cockpit to take a bow and be presented with a bouquet, The cabin crew were all smiles as usual as we disembarked at the terminal, but for a brief moment I recognised that they must occasionally find themselves fearing for their lives in what is considered by some as a glamorous profession.

It was still raining as I stepped out of the airport bus at the bus station in Trieste, handily sited next to the railway station. I took the opportunity to check the bus timetable for destinations in Slovenia, and in particular for Ljubljana, the capital, around 80 kilometres away and 2 1/2 hours by bus. There was also a local "international" timetable – a hand-written sheet pinned to a board by the ticket office. It was "international" in that it listed services to Slovenia, but only to destinations 20 or so kilometres away. I presumed it was intended mainly for workers who lived there and commuted to Trieste.

By this time the rain had stopped and I headed for the hotel, a small family-run place I'd found on the internet. Not a purpose-built building, it seemed to consist of two or three houses that had been knocked into one. The reason for the low price of a room soon became apparent – there were no en-suite facilities. I and the occupants of two other rooms on my landing were required to share a communal toilet/bathroom.

I slipped out to the local supermarket, bought food for the following day, and had a meal of pasta washed down with red wine in a small local cafe. Returning to my room, I considered the travel options. On the one hand a visit to the Slovenian capital would be enjoyable, but I had only four days on this trip, due to holiday availability at work. There was no direct rail connection with Ljubljana – you have to make a huge detour northwards to Vienna and then head south. I wanted to spend a little time in Trieste, and I was aware that I was only two hours or so from Venice, the most beautiful city in the world.

And so I made my decision. I would abandon thoughts of Ljubljana and take one of the local buses into Slovenia. All that was required was to choose a suitable destination, preferably not too far over the border. I would simply spend a few hours there, and get the bus back the same day. By so doing I would at least satisfy my requirement to set foot in this, my last, Balkan country. I didn't expect to find any cultural or visual surprises when I got there, but it would be a pleasant enough way to spend half a day or so. After some of my experiences elsewhere in the region it would be good simply to relax.

The following morning I could hear the inevitable game of musical chairs with the shared bathroom coming from the landing. I did as I always do, and waited until I was sure the others had left for breakfast before taking a leisurely shower. I breakfasted in my room courtesy of the previous night's shopping, and, suitably refreshed, exited the hotel to see what Trieste had to offer.

The city owes its importance to the fact that at the height of the Austro-Hungarian Empire in the nineteenth century it was the main port and shipbuilding centre for Vienna, even though the two cities are some 300 kilometres apart. Annexed by Italy at the end of the First World War, it remained so until the end of World War II when it was invaded by the Yugoslav People's Army, but shortly after that it was declared an independent city state by the Allies. In 1954 it was finally ceded to the Italians and has since grown to be a major Italian port.

There was a decided chill in the air as I made my way through the streets to the Canal Grande, built originally as an extension of the port with the aim of enabling ships to access the commercial centre of the city. Now used as moorings for pleasure craft, it boasts a pedestrian bridge about half-way along on which stands a life-size bronze statue of James Joyce, the Irish writer, striding purposefully across it. Wearing his trademark hat, bow-tie, jacket, and crumpled trousers, he looks every inch the casual visitor, but In fact he lived in Trieste with his wife and daughter for most of the period between 1905 and 1915 and is regarded as a local celebrity. The upper part of the statue is brightly polished as a result of the countless tourists that have had their photographs taken with their arms around the shoulders, but the legs by contrast had a bluish patina that suggested the statue was a favourite site for dogs in need of marking their territory. I wondered if they were making a subconscious comment on that most difficult of his novels, Ulysses.

I strolled the half a mile or so down to the old port and found a pleasantly warm bar in a side street that was in fact little more than an alleyway. The only other customers in the cafe were a couple of middle-aged men who were noisily indulging in a game of Backgammon. I often wonder why it is that no-one seems to be able to play that game quietly. I ordered a double espresso and glanced through a couple of tourist leaflets I'd picked up at the station. The result was not particularly encouraging, as there were no art galleries of note, and just couple of museums. The Cathedral looked worth a visit, so I finished my coffee and walked there, a distance of a kilometre or so. It turned out to be a rather unimposing building both inside and out, with surprisingly little in the way of the flamboyant Rococo decoration that I normally associate with Roman Catholic churches. More Calvinist than Catholic, I thought.

One particular attraction I was determined to sample was the Trieste-Opicina tramway, which links the city with Opicina, a small town high in the surrounding hills. It operates as a normal street tramway in Trieste, but the tram is then towed up a 1 in 4 gradient to around 330 metres above the city by means of a cable set between the tracks. Such a line is a rarity in that it combines street- tram and funicular systems on a single route. I decided it must be worth the trip if only for the views over the Adriatic. Half an hour later saw me arrive at the terminus station in Piazza Oberdan, to find that the line was closed for a week for maintenance.

This had not been the most productive of days. But there was a busy bar close by, which, in the chill wind, looked warm and inviting, and I reminded myself that I was, after all, here to relax after my Balkan exertions. I yielded to temptation and entered.

The following morning through drizzling rain I walked to the Bus station to seek out the options for travelling to Slovenia. This was not a straightforward matter, as I had no idea where to go. The handwritten timetable listed a number of stops for each of the services, and in the end I simply chose one at random – Kozina, which turned out to be a community of less than 600 souls. Making sure there was a suitably-timed return bus, I popped over to the station cafe for a coffee. An hour later I returned, searched out the bus, paid the driver, and took my seat.

The journey took us past the stacked containers and industrial units in the port. Slowly the drizzle began to ease off, and, sooner than expected, we arrived at the border. To my surprise, we were waved straight through by the border-guard –something of a contrast with my earlier experience at the border between Greece and Macedonia. After exiting the border post we started on a steep climb almost immediately, having to negotiate the odd hairpin bend in the road, and it was then that I began to notice drifts of snow on the rocky hillside. As we breasted the summit, some 500 metres above sea level, a snow-covered plain lay before us, white to the distant horizon. It was difficult to enjoy the undoubted beauty of this landscape, however, as I was obliged to keep an eye out for road signs bearing the magic word "Kozina".

Not long afterwards, the roadside sign announced we were there. The bus stop was located on the outskirts of what was little more than a village, opposite a filling station. Behind this was a small supermarket and, to the right of it a restaurant. I had two hours to kill, so negotiated the snow-covered pavements through the seemingly deserted village in a vain search for an open bank or at least a cash machine. I wanted to eat, but needed local currency to do it. Returning to the supermarket, I asked the lady at the checkout if she accepted Euros. "Ne". She said, shaking her head. I now knew that the Slovenian for "No" is "Ne" and was hoping at some stage I might learn the word for "yes".

The restaurant was my best hope. Steps outside it led to a bar, behind which lay a small dining room. Both were empty of customers. A young girl emerged from the kitchen, wiping her hands on a towel. Was she still serving lunch?

"No, but I have Slovenian pork soup. And bread. Oh, and beer."

Would she accept Euros?

"Yes, but I can't give you change."

I won't say it was the best meal I ever had, but given the circumstances it comes close. The deliciously thick soup was a meal in itself, the bread was beautifully fresh, and the beer so good I felt obliged to have another. To add to the pleasure, the clouds had parted outside, allowing light from a low winter sun to stream in through the dining-room windows. I was so comfortable that I was almost tempted to stay longer.

After settling the bill in Euros I trudged through the snow across to the bus stop and was pleased to see the bus arrive on time, almost empty. The front seat was vacant, so I took the opportunity to chat to the young driver and eventually turned the conversation from football – he was a Liverpool supporter - to politics. He saw his country's membership of the European Union as a positive move but said there were still many problems in the economy. What did he think about the old Tito dictatorship?

"He was a bad man. My family suffered in many ways and they were very pleased when he died. But still today my taxes are being used to feed his wife Jovanka. She is under house arrest in Belgrade."

I ventured to tell him about my experience of the riot in Podgorice. He laughed.

"Did you know that Tito renamed Podgorice when he came to power?" he asked. I had to admit I didn't.

"Yes. It became Titograd. It only became Podgorice again after he died. The airport's International code is still TGD" he added, with a wry smile.

Back in Trieste I decided to visit Venice the following day, simply because it was so easily reached by train. The journey is a pleasant 90-minute trip, with the Adriatic to the south, and endless vineyards backed by the distant Alps to the north. This was, however merely the curtain-raiser to the main event. As the train pulled into Venice Santa Lucia station, I was struck, as always, by its ordinariness. Built over a period of several years, it was finally completed in 1959 and is very much of that period. The building itself is basically a concrete box, and on exiting the train and negotiating the cluttered platform, any passenger may be forgiven for thinking they'd arrived in a third-world country. The feeling persists as you cross the entrance hall, but as you step outside, you are suddenly confronted by a breathtaking vista of the Grand Canal, stretching into the distance towards the Rialto Bridge, with gondolas and small boats busily plying their trade in the foreground. It is, in my opinion, quite simply the most magnificent exit from a railway station anywhere in the world, and I recommend that anyone who travels to Venice for the first time should do so by train. In Chapter eleven of this book I have described a separate visit to Venice in detail, so will spare you, dear reader, a detailed litany of this particular visit, but say merely that I purchased a *vaporetto* boat day ticket and spent a delightful day renewing my acquaintance with all my favourite haunts in this, the most beautiful city in the world.

My return journey, in darkness, was uneventful, and back in Trieste I ate two hamburgers, washed down by a coffee, at McDonald's, then had a beer at a nearby cafe before returning to the hotel, thereby avoiding the somewhat high food and drink prices in Venice. The next morning I checked again to see if the Opicina tramway had somehow come back to life, and was disappointed, but not surprised, to find that it hadn't. I vow one day to travel on it, which will necessitate a return to Trieste, which of course is the perfect excuse to combine it with yet another visit to Venice. Late that afternoon I took the bus to the airport, where my plane took off in calm, dry weather bound for London. Not a single child cried during the flight.

Chapter 7

The Baltic States – Estonia, Latvia, Lithuania, and Finland

I hope one day when I say I'm from Estonia people don't say "What? Where's that?" **Carmen Cass**

If you run from a wolf, you may run into a bear **Lithuanian Proverb**

> Hotel overbooked. Unpleasant crossing of the Baltic. Tram ticketing difficulties. Night-time border checks on the bus. No money for the toilet. Vodka and lemonade in the park. Bus cancellation problem.

Estonia, Latvia, and Lithuania are three small countries, each not much bigger than Wales, located at the northern end of the Baltic Sea on its eastern coast. The northernmost of them, Estonia, is separated from Finland by the Gulf of Finland, a stretch of water about 60 kilometres wide, through which shipping in the Baltic can access St. Petersburg in Russia, around 300 kilometres to the East.

Estonia's proximity to Finland means that many of its inhabitants regard themselves as Finnic or Nordic, whereas Latvians and Lithuanians tend to describe themselves as Baltic. The distinction has been the source of tension at various times during the area's history. The three countries spent much of the nineteenth century as part of the Russian Empire but following the First World War they achieved independence, each becoming what was effectively a communist dictatorship.

Following the outbreak of World War II the Soviet Red Army invaded all three countries and installed "Puppet" governments. The tens of thousands who resisted were sent to the Soviet Gulags or simply killed. The Germans invaded in 1941 and continued the process of expulsions and mass killings, albeit with different motives. Soviet rule was re-established at the end of the war and remained unchallenged until the late 1980s when the three countries combined to seek peaceful independence from the USSR. On August 23rd 1989, in order to give expression to this, the people came together to form a two-million strong human chain stretching from Tallinn in Estonia to Vilnius in Lithuania. The Soviets finally agreed to independence in 1991. In 2004 all three countries became NATO members and joined the European Union.

The only budget flights to the Baltic States at the time were to Riga, the capital of Latvia. Instead of making a simple return journey there, I opted to travel via Finland, where the only budget airline destination at the time was Tampere, a tiny regional airport about 160 kilometres from the capital, Helsinki. From Helsinki I would cross the Baltic by ferry to Tallinn in Estonia, visit Latvia and Lithuania, and return home from Riga.

I emerged from the terminal at Tampere on a clear, warm summer's evening and found just two buses waiting to take a planeful of passengers into the city. It was one of those situations where any stragglers could face the possibility of being left behind if there weren't sufficient seats available, as there was no regular bus service – the buses were simply provided to meet each of the infrequent incoming flights. Thanks to my policy of travelling with no checked baggage I smugly found myself at the front of the queue at the bus stop. Half an hour later we arrived at the railway station in Tampere city-centre and I headed for my hotel, five minutes' walk away. It was by now around 11pm and still daylight, due to the Northerly location, fewer than 400 kilometres from the Arctic Circle.

Tampere is Finland's second largest city and has been dubbed "The Manchester of Finland". An important industrial centre, but with wide boulevards and elegant buildings in the downtown area, I found it typically Nordic - clean, airy, and attractive. Arriving at the hotel, I was annoyed to find they'd overbooked, with the result that my room had been taken. After profuse apologies, the receptionist telephoned a nearby hotel that had vacancies, and offered to get a taxi to take me there. I declined, deciding instead to take a stroll in the balmy evening air. By now it was approaching midnight, but dwindling daylight persisted as I walked the eerily quiet streets. Half an hour later I was in my room and ready for a good night's sleep.

Nordic and Scandinavian countries invariably seem to include breakfast in the price of the room, and after breakfast the following morning I made my way to the station and took the train to Helsinki. It was to be a busy day as I was hoping to be in Tallinn, capital of Estonia, on the other side of the Gulf of Finland, by nightfall. The journey, in bright sunlight, took me through a pleasant but unremarkable landscape of fields and lakes, and a couple of hours later I emerged from Helsinki Central station into the busy streets of a bustling capital city.

After crossing the road, I glanced back to view the station and was astonished by its elegant and unique design. Constructed in light-brown Finnish granite, it is virtually impossible to describe using the normal architectural glossary. The best I can offer is "Art Nouveau crossed with Italian Rationalism from the Mussolini years". I was so taken aback that I decided to return to take a closer look at the interior, which turned out to be every bit as remarkable. It has to be one of the most beautiful railway stations in the world, and, for any visitor, certainly merits the detour, as the French say.

Time was passing, however, and I needed to get the ferry to Estonia, so was unable to do full justice to the city's many visitor attractions. Fortunately my route to the port passed by the Cathedral, situated on Senate Square and not far from the station. Built in the mid-nineteenth century, when Finland was part of the Russian empire, it is a domed design that was modelled on the neoclassical Saint Isaac's Cathedral in Saint Petersburg. With its white stonework and green domes, it dominates Helsinki, standing as it does at the top of a broad staircase high above the North side of the square. The interior is plain but dignified, as befits its Calvinist origins.

I walked the quarter-mile or so downhill to the port and studied the timetable for ferries to Tallinn. Had there been more time available I would have taken the normal ferry, which completes the journey in a leisurely three and a half hours. This would, I'm sure, have provided an enjoyable and relaxed sea crossing, giving time for regular strolls on deck to take in the mid-afternoon sun, alternating with visits to the restaurant and bar. Instead, I plumped for the two-hour catamaran service, bought the ticket, and went through to the departure area, to await the incoming boat's arrival, and buy Estonian currency. The catamaran turned out to be nothing more than a ruthlessly efficient people – carrier. There is no exterior deck, so passengers are herded into airline-style accommodation below decks in a large but strangely cramped cabin. As a result there was little reason to stir from my seat for the entire journey, other than to make a brief visit to a small but unsociable bar. About fifteen minutes into the journey the already-restricted view out of the cabin windows became completely obscured by spray rising from the hull as the vessel carved its way through the waves at high speed. The constant roar of the engines was not conducive to sleep, so I was thankful to have a book with me.

Disembarking at Tallinn, Estonia's capital city, I made my way to the road outside the port entrance and was delighted to find a tram stop handily placed for my journey to the city centre. To my dismay, there was no ticket machine. None of the people waiting at the stop had any English, so I was forced to sit and wait for a tram to arrive and try to work out how to obtain a ticket. Most of those waiting, presumably pass-holders, simply boarded the vehicle when it arrived and took a seat, but I noticed that one passenger, laden with shopping, made a bee-line for the glass partition immediately behind the driver and placed money in a pivoted container beneath. He then pushed the container through towards the driver, who turned, removed the money, replaced it with a ticket and pushed it back. The man picked up the ticket and found a seat. Nowadays, of course, most tram systems have ticket machines at each stop, but these were unusual at the time, particularly in ex-Soviet countries. The next tram, a particularly ageing graffiti-sprayed vehicle, arrived in minutes and I successfully followed the same procedure. Soon we were rattling through the city streets and I exited, along with most of the other passengers, at a stop near the Town Hall Square.

Away from the Soviet-style tower-blocks in the suburbs, Tallinn is a beautiful mediaeval city, with the area known as the old town listed as a UNESCO World Heritage site. A major tourist destination nowadays, it was slowly emerging from Soviet rule at the time of my visit. Estonia had been part of the Russian Empire in the nineteenth century, becoming an independent state following World War I, but was absorbed into the Soviet Union at the start of World War II. Subsequently occupied by the Germans from 1941 to 1944, it is estimated that 25% of the population were killed in that conflict. After the war, the Russians regained control, but in 1991 the country achieved independence once more, and in 2004 joined NATO and the European Union. The Russian and German occupations during the war were achieved without the use of heavy military force, with the result that the historic buildings at the centre of the city remain largely intact.

The Town Hall Square, paved with granite-setts and surrounded by tall ornate merchants' houses dating from centuries before, is nowadays home to numerous bars and cafes. I ordered a beer I and sat outside in the warm afternoon sun planning my visit, which would be somewhat compressed as I planned to get the midnight bus to Riga in Latvia that evening. My main objective was to see Toompea, the "High Town" an ancient area atop a limestone hill to the west. The steep climb, through narrow streets lined with pantile-roofed houses, was well worth the effort if only to see the "onion"-domed Alexander Nevski cathedral, and. further along, the castle. Tallinn Old Town is a district that, more than most, rewards the visitor who simply enjoys strolling along narrow streets lined with interesting houses, shops, and bars that seem to have stood unchanged for centuries.

Ideally I would have spent at least a couple of days in Tallinn, but I'd set myself a tight schedule. It was getting late, and there was a slight chill in the air as I took the tram to the bus station, a concrete and glass edifice located some way away from the city centre. Once there, I purchased a ticket for the midnight departure for the Latvian capital, Riga, and found a seat in the neon-lit waiting room. The sparsely occupied rows of chairs faced a television suspended from the ceiling, which was tuned to a non-stop pop-video channel. Depressed by the prospect of watching this for the next two hours, I went in search of food and found a pizza restaurant just across the road. The television there was a slight improvement, showing a football programme to the handful of male customers. An hour or so later, fully recharged after a pizza and a couple of beers, I wandered back to the bus station and took a seat by the stop for Riga.

It was by now around 11pm. My bus, not yet in the bay, was scheduled to be the last departure of the day, leaving at midnight. For a while all was quiet, but then, as I watched, cars began to arrive, and from each emerged parents and young teenagers. The ensuing excited chatter grew steadily to a crescendo as the group grew to 40 or 50-strong, and I cursed under my breath. It seemed there would be no sleep tonight on the Riga bus, but suddenly, like the cavalry appearing over the hill, a bus pulled in to the adjoining bay bearing the destination "St. Petersburg". Parental goodbyes were said, the kids boarded the bus, and peace returned as they were whisked off into the night, leaving just me and a few stragglers in the now almost deserted bus station. Twenty minutes later my bus arrived, already quite full, and I found a seat, settled back, and mercifully fell asleep as we hit the outskirts of the city.

The journey was uneventful save for the usual rigmarole at the border. Armed guards boarded the bus, waking all passengers who like me had been lucky enough to get to sleep. Passports were inspected and after few words with the driver they waved the bus through into Latvia. I must have gone back to sleep soon after, and was next awoken at around 6am by the warning bleeps as the driver reversed the bus into the bay at Riga bus station. I emerged blinking into the chill morning air. Over to the East the sun was rising in a clear blue sky. I was all too aware I needed three things urgently – the toilet, Latvian currency and coffee. The toilet was open, but seated at its entrance was a formidable-looking lady whose job it was to take the 20 santimu fee for using the facilities. A cash machine inside the waiting room offered hope, and duly supplied me with currency, but in large denomination notes. The cafe was closed, with the roll-shutter resolutely in the down position, and a quick glance outside showed there were no cafes nearby, but it was then that I spotted a coffee machine at the far end. Again the price was 20 Santimu but I had no coins. Desperate on two counts, I approached the lady at the toilet and offered her a twenty-latu note, equivalent to the cost of fifty visits to the toilet or the same number of coffees. She muttered under her breath, but slowly and deliberately counted out the change - 19 latu and 80 santini, all in coins. I handed back one latu as a tip and rushed past her. I had to admit she kept a very clean toilet!

With my new-found funds I bought a plastic cup-full of (very good) coffee from the machine, downed it almost immediately, and quickly bought another. Outside, I found a seat and surveyed the scene. Over the road, about 100 metres away, lay the distinctive buildings of Riga Central Market, considered Europe's largest market. The main part is unique, being made up of four huge arched concrete buildings, overlooking the Daugava River. These were constructed in part from four disused Zeppelin hangars bought from Vainode, a Latvian airbase, in 1924. Vainode had been the base in Latvia for the occupying German army and air force during World War I. The market is considered important enough historically to be included by UNESCO in the Riga World Heritage Site.

As I watched, traders were arriving to set up their stalls, whilst trams rumbled by carrying early-morning workers. It was not yet 7am, and I had five hours to kill before I could check into the hotel, so I crossed the tramlines, strolled over to the market, and mingled with the customers. Row upon row of outdoor stalls gave way to the four cavernous "Zeppelin" buildings where fish, meat, fruit and vegetables were on sale. Exiting from the far end of one these, I looked out over the broad Daugava River, shimmering in the reflected light of the rising sun, with its bridges and distant church domes downstream silhouetted against the sky. Back inside I located a stand-up cafe where I consumed a delicious egg and bacon bagel washed down by an Americano coffee. I couldn't help noticing that quite a few of my fellow-customers were already quenching their thirsts with beer. Suitably refreshed, I walked the short distance to the railway station.

Baltic train services at the time were at something of a low point in their history. There was no railway line directly linking the three capitals, Tallinn, Riga, and Vilnius in Lithuania. Much of the problem stemmed from political rivalry between the three states, and lack of investment. This had been evident during my visit to Tallinn station, where the majority of the run-down station buildings had been converted into a market. It was further highlighted when I had discovered that one could travel by train from Tallinn southwards towards Latvia, but the service terminated at the border city of Valga. There, the rail passenger was obliged to walk two miles across the border to a small country station in northern Latvia, and hope the infrequent service from there to Riga was operating.

As a result, it was no surprise on checking at Riga station to find that there was no service to Vilnius in Lithuania, unless one travelled via Minsk in Belarus, which would need the complication of a visa. There was, of course, a well-established bus service, which I planned to make use of, but not for a couple of days, as I needed to relax for a while. I walked the 200 metres or so to my hotel, where I was grateful to be allowed to occupy the room early. After a shower, I had a couple of hours' sleep.

Latvia's twentieth century history is similar to that of Estonia, in that it was independent between the two world wars but in World War II was invaded first by the Germans, then by the Russians, It became a member-state of the USSR after the war until independence in 1991 and joined the European Union and NATO in 2004. There was no major armed struggle in Riga, during the century, with the result that the historic centre, like Tallinn, was virtually undamaged and stands today beautifully preserved.

The hotel, a handsome five-storey nineteenth-century stone edifice, was located on the southern edge of what is known as the old town, and just round the corner from Central Park, which was to be my first port of call. It was a cloudless and by now very hot afternoon, and on my way to the park I found a small newsagent's shop, which, not unusually in ex-USSR countries, sold hot-dogs and cold drinks in addition to the usual newspapers and magazines. Whilst the assistant prepared my hot-dog, I checked out the drinks in the chilled cabinet. Amongst the usual ranks of half-litre plastic bottles of iced tea and the like I found several that at first glance looked like normal bottles of water. On closer inspection, however, these turned out to contain vodka and lemonade. At 14% proof, how could I resist?

Thus armed, I found a park-bench in a shady spot beneath a broad sycamore tree where I could eat, drink, and watch the dog-walkers and joggers come and go. Two hirsute tramps, each carrying a half-empty plastic bottle of what looked like a fearsome alcoholic brew, stopped by for a chat, but were disappointed to find that I was unable to speak Latvian, and shuffled away muttering. I returned my attention to the hot - dog, which was certainly tasty, and the accompanying vodka and lemonade, which was absolutely delicious. As I gently perspired under the afternoon sun, it was all too easy to persuade myself that the drink was an important source of rehydration, so I had no qualms about popping back to the shop to buy a second bottle. Returning to my seat, I continued the rehydration for a pleasurable half hour or so, and around mid-afternoon finally decided it was time to visit the Old Town. I have to admit that my exit from the park was slightly unsteady.

For the most part the old town is a maze of narrow streets, its houses and shops largely unchanged since mediaeval times. The star attraction is, however, the town square, a broad area paved with granite setts and surrounded by stunning buildings that reflect the city's wealthier times when it was a major Hanseatic League port. This trading alliance controlled a large number of ports in those countries having a coastline on the Baltic and North Seas between the fourteenth and seventeenth centuries, and It is interesting to note that King's Lynn in Norfolk and Boston in Lincolnshire were two of the English members.

Close by the town square is the cathedral, which I found surprisingly ornate inside, given its Evangelical Lutheran denomination. From there I took an early-evening stroll down by the river as the heat of the day began to subside, ending with a return to the crowded bus station to plan my visit to Lithuania. Needing to use the toilet facilities again, I this time handed the exact money to the lady, and was slightly miffed that she didn't seem to remember me. I also took the opportunity to renew my acquaintance with the coffee machine, and took a seat to study the timetable. A 9:00 am departure to Vilnius seemed to fit the bill.

The following morning I climbed aboard the bus for Vilnius and settled into my seat by the window, looking forward to my first-ever visit to Lithuania. The driver tuned in the radio to the obligatory easy-listening music channel and we headed off through Riga's busy streets. The urban sprawl eventually gave way to a landscape typical of rural Eastern Europe at the time. Every few miles we encountered a small village or hamlet consisting of little more than a line of houses either side of the road. Behind each house lay a strip of land, typically about 100 metres long by 10 metres wide, plainly under cultivation by the householder. I was reminded of history lessons at school when I'd learned about strip-farming in fourteenth-century England. Along the way we passed the occasional horse-drawn rubber-tyred farm wagon, laden with produce, and between villages the occasional flock of goats could be seen grazing contentedly in a roadside field. The border was passed with minimal formalities and we crossed into Lithuania. A couple of hours later we arrived at the outskirts of Vilnius, where unprepossessing blocks of flats erected during the USSR years finally gave way to older pantiled houses. The route to the city centre took us alongside the Neris River, on the far side of which, on a hill, stood St. Raphael church, its two baroque towers dominating the skyline.

The bus station departure board had a distinctive international flavour, listing destinations in Poland, Belarus, and the Russian *exclave* of Kaliningrad Oblatsk. (An exclave is defined as a part of a country which is surrounded by two or more other nations, giving it no direct land connection to the rest of its country). Kaliningrad Oblatsk, a part of Russia, is entirely surrounded by Poland and Lithuania. I mention it at this time as I had wondered if it might merit a visit as part of my quest to visit all 49 European nations, but concluded that, as I was already planning to visit St. Petersburg in Russia, a visit was not necessary. There is no doubt, however, that setting foot in Kaliningrad Oblatsk would qualify as a visit to Russia, thus avoiding the need to go to, say, Moscow or St. Petersburg. Incidentally, an *enclave,* as opposed to an *exclave,* is a country such as San Marino, surrounded by a single country rather than two or more.

I checked the departure board for my return bus at 6pm but it wasn't listed. I was told in the office that there was a problem and they couldn't be certain it would run. I was due to leave Riga for London the following afternoon, so with regret I decided to get the 3pm bus back, which of course meant I could spend only an hour or so checking out the city's attractions. After getting the minimum possible amount of local currency – Litas – from a cash machine, I took a walk down the road, found a bar, installed myself at one of their outside tables and spent the time eating kebabs, drinking a beer, and watching the world go by.

The return bus journey turned out to be unremarkable, and I found myself back at the hotel in Riga about four hours sooner than I'd planned when I'd set out that morning. So that, dear reader, is how I spent the third-shortest period of time in a single country – around 90 minutes – of all the 49 I visited. The shortest was, of course, Bosnia, where I spent all of 30 minutes, followed by Andorra, which consumed about an hour of my life. One day soon, however, I will return to Vilnius for a more leisurely visit, and, who knows, perhaps take the bus to Kaliningrad Oblatsk for a couple of days!

I spent the following morning relaxing in and around the hotel, but couldn't resist a further visit to the park at lunchtime for another hot-dog, but this time accompanied by peach-flavoured iced-tea. In mid-afternoon I caught the airport workers' bus which rattled along a tortuous route, making around 20 stops on the way. My flight left as scheduled, and as we headed out over the Baltic and emerged from the cloud base into a clear sun-drenched late-afternoon sky, I mused on the contrasts I'd encountered.

The beautifully preserved city centres, at the time ripe for development as tourist destinations, were at odds with the rural economy of the region, where modernisation seemed long overdue, and even more at odds with the cities' suburbs, with their preponderance of crumbling soviet-era apartment blocks. Nowadays, as members of the European Union, the countries are benefitting from widespread investment, which must ultimately improve their prospects. And, best of all, Tallinn, Riga, and Vilnius are now busy tourist destinations!

Chapter 8

Romania and Moldova

The foetus is the property of the entire society. Anyone having children who abandons the laws of national continuity is a deserter
                                                                                        Nicolae Ceaucescu

Stealing from capitalism is not like stealing out of our own pockets. Marx and Lenin have taught us that anything is ethical, so long as it is in the interest of the proletarian class and its world revolution

                                                                                        Nicolae Ceaucescu

The people on the other side of the Prut river in Romania are our blood brothers, so I think their help is sincere, but the overwhelming majority of the population support the continuing statehood of Moldova.
                                                                                        Vasile Braghis

---

More feral dogs, and some humping. The heaviest building in the world. The place a dictator realised the game was up. McDonald's the life-saver. Journey in a police-car. Border check in the middle of a field. Two Eiffel constructions. Possibly the world's worst train.

I had long harboured thoughts of visiting Romania, ever since I'd watched television footage of its revolution in 1989 which led to the overthrow and execution of its dictator, Nicolai Ceaucescu, together with his wife, Elena, who was considered by some to be the power behind the throne. At their deaths, the Ceausecus had ruled the country with a rod of iron for 24 years, maintaining power through the Securitate secret police, an internal state security organisation employing 11,000 agents and half a million informers. There are striking parallels with the dictatorship of East Germany's dictator Erich Honecker, whose Stasi secret police performed a similar function and kept him in power until the Berlin wall fell.

A supporter of Germany's Nazis during most of World War II, Romania changed sides in 1944 and fought alongside the Russians until the armistice. At the time a kingdom, the country declared itself a Communist People's Republic in 1948, and the king abdicated. Royal supporters were either killed or sent to Russian Gulags. Post-Ceausescu, Romania became a democratic republic, joining NATO in 2004 and the European Union in 2007.

I have to admit that my decision to visit the capital, Bucharest, was motivated more by my fascination with the recent history of the country than a wish to see historic places. Many modern-day tours take in Transylvania and the Danube River, pleasant enough excursions I'm sure, but not high on my list of priorities. I therefore decided to stay in Bucharest, as I had in any case planned a visit to Moldova, located around 450 kilometres to the North – West.

Budget airline policy at the time was to land at any airport reasonably close to the destination city, as long as the landing fees were much lower than those at the principal international airport. Step forward Baneasa airport, located some eight kilometres from Bucharest city centre, and very much the poor relation of the city's principal international airport at Otopeni. Not until I arrived did I realise that this was to be a rare treat. The airport, opened in 1909, has the distinction of being visited at the time by Louis Bleriot, the aviation pioneer. His statue outside the terminal bears witness to this historic event. Not only unique in its history, the terminal is architecturally unique in that it resembles a very large reinforced –concrete flying saucer, with the inside waiting area located under a large dome. It is believed to be the oldest continuously operating airport in Eastern Europe, and amongst the oldest five airports in the world. I recommend it to anyone travelling to Bucharest , as in my experience there are few other airports that offer both an interesting history and rare architectural style.

The journey into the city was something of a trial, however. Sticking to my policy of taking the normal public bus, I could see the bus-stop on the far side of an extremely busy dual carriageway a couple of hundred metres from the terminal. Under a clear sky and in stifling heat and humidity, I took the largely unmade footpath from the terminal via the Bleriot memorial to the roadside. The crossing-point was a further 100 metres or so away, necessitating a dust-blown walk alongside the road and, after a somewhat perilous crossing, a walk back to the stop. Local kids played football in an adjacent car-park as I waited, drawing applause from my soon-to –be fellow passengers when a fine volleyed shot produced an acrobatic save from the goalkeeper. As the teams took up position for the resulting corner I was slightly disappointed to see the bus arrive. Taking the empty seat immediately behind the driver, I watched as we passed by the serried ranks of concrete high-rise apartments on the outskirts which eventually gave way to the older, mainly stone-built offices, hotels, and public buildings in the city centre. At the bus terminus I consulted the map I'd obtained at the airport and walked the short distance to my hotel.

After a much-needed shower I sought out the nearest convenience store and bought food and drink which I would eat in my room later. The heat of the day seemed to be easing, and in the deepening twilight I could think of no better way to spend the next hour or so than enjoying a double espresso at a pavement cafe.

I've often found something almost magical about a city centre on warm summer's evenings. The incessant day-time traffic is reduced to a mere trickle, and families emerge from their homes to take leisurely post-prandial strolls in the fading light. The pleasant hubbub of cafe conversation fills the air and, at least for a few short hours, all seems well with the world. This particular evening proved to be no exception, and I simply relaxed and watched the world go by.

The following day was to be devoted to the tourist attractions of the city. There is a metro system, adequate for reaching most of these, so I bought a day-ticket at the station near my hotel. Top of my list was The Palace of The Parliament, a monument to the vanity of Nicolai Ceaucescu, the country's former dictator. It has the distinction of being the second-largest administrative building on the planet, after the Pentagon in the USA. Weighing in at just over four billion kilos, it is the heaviest building in the world. It was commissioned after an earthquake in 1977 which resulted in damage to buildings in an area of 7 square kilometres near the city centre. Instead of rebuilding this densely-populated neighbourhood, Ceaucescu decided to clear the area, bulldozing houses, churches, monasteries, and factories, The parliament building was erected in the centre of the resulting vast open space, along with a number of government offices on either side of a boulevard leading to the city centre. Today only 400 of its 1100 rooms are occupied, as most of the remainder are unfinished internally. History does not record the fate of the thousands of citizens that were displaced from their homes.

. Emerging from the metro station, which stands a few hundred metres from the main entrance to the Palace of the Parliament, I could already feel the heat of the sun on my back, and the humidity level meant that walking any sort of distance was uncomfortable. The building is surrounded by a road, on the inside of which is a metre-high concrete "tank trap"-style wall and of course inside that is a high boundary fence. I eventually located the guarded entrance gate, smiled at the guard as I walked through, and strolled the hundred or so metres across the car-park to the building's entrance. Inside, a tour group was already gathering by the cash desk, but I was told I couldn't join them as tours had to be pre-booked and they could only take bookings for the following day. After buying a fridge magnet and a couple of postcards from the shop I departed. At least I could say I'd been inside the heaviest building in the world, but I have to admit that a tour would have been a bonus.

From there I set off down Unirii Boulevard, which in layout and grandeur is much like the Champs Elysees in Paris, but without the shops and cafes. My water-bottle now empty, I sought in vain a shop selling bottled water, to the point where dehydration was beckoning in the heat and humidity of the day. I reached Piata Uniri, a large open city square, where, on the far side, I could just about discern the golden arches logo of a McDonald's. I hurried over and there purchased two large Sprites, with Ice, one of which, as they say, scarcely touched the sides as I drank it, and followed up with a couple of hamburgers. Half an hour later I declared myself ready to take on the world again, and headed for Piata Revolutiei, "Revolution Square", and specifically the old Communist Party Headquarters, about a mile away, where the final act of the Ceausescu years was played out in 1989.

On the way there I bought water, and, still in need of rehydration, perched on a low wall whilst I refreshed myself. As I drank, a group of half a dozen feral dogs arrived and for a brief moment interested themselves in whatever odour I was giving off. Evidently satisfied that I was not a threat, they settled down on the grassy area slightly to the right and behind me. As I continued drinking, a couple of passers-by stopped, looked my way, and laughed. Another man joined them, and from their laughter I wondered if I was showing something I shouldn't. I quickly checked my clothing and all seemed to be in order. Then one of them, grinning, poked me with his finger, and used the same finger to point at the dogs. I turned to see two of them locked together in carnal passion, with the male looking as if he could go on all day. The bitch, I have to say, looked bored, and I found myself checking the others in the pack. As far as I could see she was the only bitch. No wonder she was bored.

Revolution Square is home to important buildings – the old Royal Palace, the University Library, and the Athenaeum. All classical buildings, they are part of the city's architectural heritage. In the centre of the square stands an obelisk and bronze statue, memorials to those who were killed in the 1989 revolution. But the prize for the most important building must surely go to a rather unprepossessing six-storey block on the south side, namely the old Communist Party and Securitate headquarters. The building's ground-floor entrance projects outwards from the main part, such that its roof may be accessed by a door leading out from the first floor, effectively making it a balcony. It was from here that Nicolei Ceaucescu and his wife Elena addressed the people of Bucharest on 22nd December 1989, in a last-ditch attempt to stave off their overthrow. When rocks began to be thrown at them they fled inside the building and took the lift to the top floor. The crowd broke down the door and entered the building, but by then the Ceaucescus were on the roof and were rescued by helicopter. Some way into the flight, and heading for one of their country residences, the helicopter pilot was radioed by the army and ordered to land, with the ultimatum that otherwise the aircraft would be shot down. The pilot obeyed and landed in a field, from where local police took the Ceaucescus to a local agricultural institute to await the arrival of an army detachment. Three days later, on Christmas Day 1989, they were subjected to a show trial in which they were accused of crimes of genocide and illegal gathering of wealth. Found guilty, they were taken outside to a wall at the rear of the building and shot dead by firing squad.

I stood for a while, imagining the scene. The Ceaucescus had stood on this very balcony, with Nikolei attempting unsuccessfully to make himself heard over the noise of the baying crowd, all of whom were demanding an end to the years of poverty, corruption, and Securitate surveillance. Elena tried to speak and, like her husband, was shouted down, both being regarded with equal contempt. It was common knowledge that the building contained Securitate files on many of those present in the crowd, so it was no surprise when they surged forward and broke open the door to the building. The Ceaucescus, realising that the game was up, fled from the balcony and into the room behind. Anger must have turned to dismay moments later when the protesters saw the helicopter arrive on the roof and whisk away the fugitives.

I walked around the square and examined the memorial in the centre, a somewhat nondescript obelisk commemorating the 3,352 lives lost in the uprising. There being little else to detain me, I headed for Lipscani, the old town, to be greeted on the way by another pack of feral dogs. I was now getting the hang of it, and this time successfully ignored them. Lipscani is a typical "old town" area, with narrow streets paved with granite setts and containing the usual mix of cafes, small shops, and restaurants. Mititei is the typical street food there – rolled minced beef with spices – best dipped into Dijon mustard and eaten with fresh bread. I enjoyed one of these at a stand-up cafe then sought the sanctuary of a bar for a very welcome beer.

The following morning I headed for the railway station, again running the gauntlet of a pack of dogs. Were these the same lot? Were they secretly following me? Was I becoming paranoid? Whatever, I bade them farewell at the entrance to the ticket office and bought my ticket to Iasi, a city located about 400 kilometres North-West of Bucharest, and not usually a must-see stop on the tourist trail. Its advantage, however, is that it is located a mere 20 kilometres or so from Ungheni, a community of some 35,000 souls, lying just over the border in neighbouring Moldova. I knew from the Thomas Cook European Railway Timetable – a must for all who travel in Europe – that there was just one daily train each way on the line from Iasi to Ungheni, which would allow me to spend a mere two hours in Moldova. This would certainly not be sufficient for an in-depth study of what that country might offer to the day-tripper, but it was better than nothing,

The railway line from Bucharest runs over a relatively featureless plain for the first half of the journey, thereafter skirting the foothills of the majestic Carpathian Mountains to the West. The scheduled journey time was to be around seven hours, a bit of a challenge, but at least the train carriages turned out to be double-deckers, the upstairs deck being so much better for viewing the world outside. Suitably armed with food, drink, and a book, I climbed the stairs, installed myself in a window seat, and settled back for the journey. Once clear of the soviet-style tower-blocks and general urban sprawl of the suburbs, we were soon passing the type of small village and farm that typified rural Eastern Europe at the time. Horse-drawn farm carts would come into view from time to time, usually charged with mountainous loads of hay or straw and trundling sedately along largely unmade roads. In common with many ex-communist bloc countries, strip-farming still persisted in the land behind village houses, and those working there would often pause for a moment to watch the train as it thundered by.

After about three hours' travelling we pulled into Focsani station, a nondescript reinforced concrete construction that for some reason necessitated a stop of 20 minutes or so. The town is not far from Odobesti, one of Romania's most important wine-producing regions, but other than that doesn't appear to have a lot to offer the casual visitor. As I sat idly gazing out across the platform I was nudged by a newly arrived passenger, a middle-aged man clad in the almost obligatory black leather jacket, who proceeded to let me know, without needing a word of English, and with a gold-toothed grin, that I was in fact sitting in his reserved seat. I apologised, without needing a word of Romanian, and found another seat.

The journey thereafter offered tempting views westward towards the Carpathian Mountains in the far distance, albeit under an increasingly cloudy sky, and from time to time the nearby South-facing slopes would reveal serried ranks of vines. As the afternoon wore on I dozed fitfully in my seat, eventually to be roused by the squeal of brakes as the train shuddered to a halt in Iasi station. I hurriedly got my things together, descended onto the platform, and exited onto the station's forecourt.

Built in 1870, the design of the station building is claimed to have been based on the Doge's Palace in Venice. To be honest, I couldn't really see the resemblance, but as a result it is listed in the Romanian Register of Historic Monuments and is undoubtedly a handsome place. Sadly, substantial construction work was being carried out, which was to affect my plans for the following day. Armed with a map from the tourist office I contemplated taking a tram to my hotel but decided instead to walk. Ten minutes later I found myself at the reception desk of the Grand Hotel Traian, which I mention by name as it is probably the most prestigious hotel in the city and a place I would normally avoid on simple grounds of cost. I had, however, been offered a very low price at the time I booked, which I discovered was because they'd only just reopened after a lengthy renovation, and were trying to rebuild the client base. Furnishing and decor in rooms, restaurants and bars was very much along the lines of the Ritz hotel in London, and I have to admit to feeling somewhat out of place.

Of neoclassical style, the hotel was designed, perhaps surprisingly, by Gustav Eiffel in 1882, two years before he built the Statue of Liberty and seven years prior to the construction of the Eiffel Tower. Amongst its many claims to fame, it became the seat of government for Romania during the First World War, and in 1934 boasted Greta Garbo amongst its long-term residents. After checking into my room I strolled around the block to search out a convenience store, guiltily concealing my food and drink purchases in my travelling bag as I returned through the reception area.

The following morning I took my seat for breakfast in the elegant restaurant. This high-ceilinged room is located on the first floor at the front of the building overlooking Piata Unini, a square with a busy tram interchange station at the far end. The previous day's thick cloud had been replaced by wind-blown cumulus, and the sun was making ever more frequent appearances. Watching the trams come and go, I felt relaxed and ready for whatever the day had to offer. My aim was to get the train to Ungheni in Moldova, but there was no hurry, as it was not timetabled to leave until midday.

Arriving at the station, I found that due to the extensive building works the scheduled platform for the Ungheni train was out of use. Worse, the train details failed to show on any of the departure boards and I began to panic. Surely I hadn't made a mistake? I quickly consulted my photocopy of the appropriate page of the Cooks European Timetable and there it was, clearly listed. There being no-one around who spoke English, I looked around the forecourt and saw a young policeman in uniform leaning against his police car and smoking a cigarette.

"Do you speak English?"

"A little."

"I want to go to Ungheni but I can't find the train."

He smiled.

"You have wrong station. Trains start from Jassy in North Iasi during building work."

"How far is it? Can I get a taxi?"

"Not necessary." He said. "I will take you."

And so it was that I found myself in the passenger seat of a police car, chatting to my Romanian policeman-driver about English football teams, whilst speeding through the streets of the city. Thankfully he decided against activating the car's blues and twos, and when we arrived at the somewhat decrepit suburban station he refused to accept any payment. He pointed out the ticket office building, a small brick shed located around 100 metres away, then bade me farewell and drove off to resume his duties. The wind had by now dropped and it had turned out to be a very warm day, so I was sweating by the time I got to the ticket office.

After purchasing my ticket I walked back to the main station building. The entrance door was locked, but lounging around on the steps outside were what I assumed to be my fellow passengers, forming a disorderly queue. They were mainly poorly dressed middle-aged women, many wearing headscarves, and most of them carrying large, unmarked plastic bags full of shopping. It was impossible to tell if they were Romanians or Moldovans, but either way I concluded that the shopping must have been better in Iasi than in Ungheni. One of them was nursing a large shallow cardboard tray containing about 30 uncooked chicken legs and thighs, covered with a sheet of newspaper. I wondered how the meat was coping with the heat of that late-morning sun.

About 11:45 am the door at the top of the steps opened and a man stepped out. In faltering English he announced that foreign passport holders should come forward first, so I got to my feet and threaded my way through those sitting on the steps, feeling somewhat embarrassed at taking precedence for no reason other than that I was a foreigner. He waved me to a makeshift passport control desk, where I insisted on getting my passport stamped, and accompanied me to the door that led out to the platform. I took a seat and waited for the train to arrive.

I expected a smart branch-line diesel railcar. What I got was a graffiti-covered diesel locomotive, lazily spewing out diesel fumes as it trundled into the platform, coupled to a single carriage that, judging by its dents and peeling paintwork, had seen much better days. The inside was no better. Laid out exactly like a bus, the low-backed seats boasted thinly-padded red plastic upholstery. At the far end were a toilet and a tiny recess for the guard. When all passengers had boarded, an asthmatic hoot from the locomotive signified that we were about to depart, and soon we were trundling through fields towards the River Prut, a natural border between the two countries. Gustav Eiffel, previously mentioned as the designer of the Traian Hotel, was invited by the Russians in 1876 to design the railway bridge over the river at this point, and three days after it opened in 1877 it was used to transport Russian troops into Romania in furtherance of their war with the Ottoman Empire. It remains strategically important to this day, and is still in its original condition.

Once over the bridge the train screeched to a halt in the middle of an open field, and we sat for a while, the only sounds being the song of a blackbird in a nearby tree, accompanied by the gentle throb of the locomotive. Then, across the far side of the field, three military-uniformed men appeared, striding purposely towards the train. Climbing aboard, they checked passports using a portable electronic device, pausing occasionally to interrogate one or other of the women. After sharing a joke or two with the guard they climbed down into the field and were gone. The locomotive coughed back into life and we soon pulled into a small branch-line platform at the south end of Ungheni station in Moldova. Here, in a tiny office not much bigger than the average kitchen, full immigration and customs checks were carried out, during which I was obliged to reveal whatever foreign currency I was carrying. Going through, I exited onto the main station platform and noted the exit up a flight of stairs.

I had just two hours to do justice to Ungheni, and, by proxy, to Moldova. It was not going to be easy. A town of some 35,000 souls, most of whom are Russian Orthodox Christians, it has no tourist landmarks other than the Eiffel Bridge, and is part of a largely agricultural community. Moldova, one of the smallest countries in Europe, with an area less than half that of Scotland, declared independence from the Russians in 1992 and since then has been a Parliamentary Republic. Its earlier history is bound up with the history of Bessarabia, a province of the Russian Empire, which included most of the present-day country and part of Romania. Since independence, there have been frequent political and economic crises, during which a request to join the European Union has been turned down. The country is the least-visited in Europe, receiving an average of 11,000 visitors a year, making me quite a rarity, particularly in Ungheni. The East of the country, an area known as Transnistria, has for many years been locked in a drive for independence, and has attempted to gain recognition as a separate state. In general, Moldova's twentieth-century political and economic history has been, to say the least, chaotic, resulting in a level of poverty that means life-expectancy for men is 67.5 years, the lowest in Europe.

As I sat on the platform, the daily train from Moscow to Bucharest, an astonishing journey taking around 40 hours, drew into the station. From each dust-covered carriage emerged bleary-eyed passengers, taking the opportunity of the lengthy stop to stretch their legs and perhaps have a cigarette or two in the open air. Others gazed out of curtain-lined carriage windows, perhaps checking how much further they had to go. Sadly, during all this time I would dearly have loved to take photographs, but was reluctant to do so at such a militarily sensitive location. I didn't want to repeat my previous problems in Greece. Aware time was tight, I climbed the exit stairs and went exploring.

The road from the station passed a small onion-domed Greek Orthodox Church, so I took the opportunity to look inside. I found a typically mosaic-decorated interior, but in the central area were piles of black plastic bags containing clothes. I never did find out why they were there, but there is, believe it or not, a large Salvation Army presence in the town so perhaps there was some sort of connection. Turning right into Strada Nationala, a wide tree-lined boulevard, I came across a huge wedding party heading for the Sala di Ninti Patria, which I suppose is the equivalent of a British registry office. All present sang in unison as they lined up to enter the building, a rather pleasing tradition I thought.

Strada Nationale was strangely quiet, there being little in the way of traffic, just the occasional minibus picking up passengers at the bus stop half-way along. A little further along, to the right, I crossed a small park to examine a huge green-painted preserved Russian steam locomotive, marooned on a plinth at a point overlooking the station. Here I managed a couple of surreptitious photographs, but as time was getting on I decided to head back to the station. I didn't want to miss my train back to Iasi, the only one of the day.

And that, dear reader, is the story of my visit to Moldova. Longer by ninety minutes or so than my earlier visit to Bosnia, I can't in all honesty say I did the country justice. One day I may return to the capital, Chisinau, which undoubtedly offers more in the way of tourist attractions, but for the time being I have to settle for having spent two unremarkable but pleasant enough hours in Ungheni. On the plus side, I'd had the unique experience of breakfasting that morning in a hotel designed by Gustav Eiffel and, four hours later, crossing a bridge also designed by him. I couldn't avoid a feeling of smug satisfaction.

The return journey in an almost empty carriage was uneventful, with similar security checks being made but without my being required to declare any foreign currency. I happened to notice that at the Romanian end of the Eiffel Bridge there was a small wooden hut, outside which a soldier stood on duty. I wondered idly if he ever thought about the meaning of life during those long empty hours on guard. Back at Jassy station in Iasi I managed to track down a tram which, with a couple of changes, got me back to the tram station in the square outside the hotel.

The following day I decided there was a tram network to be explored. My train back to Bucharest was due to leave at 3pm, giving me around five hours to see what the city had to offer. The highlight was the Palace of Culture, a huge Neo-Gothic edifice built as recently as 1925 and set amongst beautiful gardens. With its high central clock tower it somewhat unexpectedly put me in mind of a much larger version of the Hotel de Ville in Calais. There are many historical connections between France and Romania, probably stemming from the role of Napoleon III in establishing the state in 1858. During my stay I often found myself able to understand written words in Romanian, a Romance language having many similarities with French.

My journey back to Bucharest was uneventful, but as I exited the station at around 10pm I was briefly reacquainted with the pack of feral dogs. Swiftly, and with scarcely any hint of panic, I headed off to the hotel. The next day saw me back at Baneasi airport, seated under the dome in the circular departure lounge in contemplation of the events of the past few days. My first-ever visit to these two countries had been both informative and enjoyable, but there was more to it than that. Travel is seen by many as a pastime that rewards careful planning and predictable outcomes. That is why organised tours are so popular, minimising, as they do, uncertainty and fear of possible problems. But individual travel has something more to offer, in that there is the ever-present possibility that something may go wrong. When it does, the traveller has to think on his or her feet and reorganise. The resolution of such problems almost invariably results in unexpected encounters with both people and places, and in my experience this adds piquancy to what might otherwise be considered relatively bland fare. And there is the added feeling of smug satisfaction when difficulties are overcome and the trip is back on track. It's far more rewarding than simply being able to complain to a tour guide!

Chapter 9

Poland and Ukraine

Ukraine announced plans to open Chernobyl, their nuclear disaster site, to the public. They say it's just like Disneyland, except that the six-foot mouse is real   **Conan O'Brien**

I married a German. Every night I dress up as Poland and he invades me   **Bette Midler**

Squirrels at the airport. Changing the wheels on the train. Vodka binge on the train with two strangers. Currency from the hole-in-the-wall. Socialist-realist architecture. Border fence and Alsatian dogs on the station platform. Fisticuffs and police checks in the waiting room from hell.

My home town boasts a Polish Club, set up after the war by Polish airmen who had serviced and flown Lancaster bombers based at the surrounding Lincolnshire airfields during the conflict. They had decided to stay on in the county when hostilities ended, and settled in the area, becoming well-established members of the community. From time to time in my early twenties I went along to the club, usually invited by my ex-father-in-law who enjoyed the convivial atmosphere almost as much as the low-priced beer. The Poles I met were invariably friendly, gregarious types and there was always a laugh or two during the course of an evening. There was also a small Ukranian club nearby, which I regret to say I never visited.

With this in mind, I was keen to visit both countries in a single trip. It made sense geographically, as they share a common border, with good travel connections between them. Due to work commitments I had a mere four days available, so of necessity it would be a somewhat superficial visit. I decided to base myself in Krakow, the second-largest and arguably most attractive city in Poland, which I already knew well from previous visits. Alternative bases could have been Warsaw, the Polish capital, or Lviv, the nearest Ukranian city, but neither of these had a good budget airline service at the time.

Poland, nowadays a parliamentary republic, has survived many turbulent periods in its recent history, sometimes a result of to its often-fractious relationship with Russia. The ninth-largest European nation, with a population of around 38 million, Poland has borders with no less than seven neighbours, and its modern history is largely defined by the invasion by Nazi Germany in 1939 which led to the outbreak of the Second World War and the subsequent deaths of 5.7 million Poles, almost one fifth of the population. Warsaw's most traumatic period began in 1940 when its Jewish inhabitants, making up 30% of the total population of the city, were systematically killed by the Nazis over the following three years. In 1944 the Russians arrived to liberate the country, in response to which Adolf Hitler ordered the destruction of Warsaw, resulting in 85% of the city being reduced to rubble. After the war the country was effectively annexed by Russia and became a communist state, albeit without actually becoming a member of the Soviet Union. As a result the post-war rebuilding of the country was largely controlled and financed from Moscow. This alliance crumbled in 1989 as the USSR began to break up, and Poland subsequently joined NATO in 1999, followed four years later by its accession to the European Union.

As I emerged from Krakow airport on a cold, rainy evening, I noticed many improvements had been made both inside and outside the terminal since my previous visit, undoubtedly due to the continuing substantial increase in budget airline traffic. On my first visit, two years previously, I sought the bus to the city centre and had been directed to a poorly-signposted, unprotected bus-stop on the far side of the terminal's car-park. Behind, and separated from the pavement by a high chicken-wire fence, stood a dense group of tall pine trees, silhouetted against the early evening sunshine. Whilst waiting for the bus to arrive, I and my fellow passengers were entertained by a hyperactive group of squirrels busily foraging for food. Never before or since have squirrels been part of my airport experience. This time, however, there had been a major change. The trees, (and squirrels) were still evident, but a hastily-erected sign directed the traveller to a newly-constructed single-platform railway station, located about 100 metres away down a narrow lane. There, a two-car diesel railcar waited impatiently for passengers to board, and no more than thirty minutes later I found myself at the main railway station in Krakov city centre. Outside the station I boarded a tram at the adjacent terminus and twenty minutes later was checking into my hotel. Krakow's extensive, efficient and cheap tram network is one of many hundreds in continental Europe, and, as frequently happens, I found myself wondering why there were not more such networks back home in the UK.

The following morning, under cloudy but rain-free skies, I took the tram back to the station and bought a ticket to Warsaw. Conscious that I had no Hyrvnia, the Ukranian currency required for my forthcoming visit, I sought out a foreign exchange shop. The first two I approached were unable to provide any, but then, in the underpass, I spotted what can only be described as a hole in the wall with the magic word "Change" above it. Inside, a callow youth, perched on a stool, was busy scribbling figures in a small well-worn notebook

"Do you have Hryvnia?" I said, aware that my pronunciation of the currency was probably less than perfect.

"What?"

"Hryvnia."

"I don't understand."

I tried a couple more ways of pronouncing it. The second of these produced a grin of recognition.

"You go to Ukraine?"

"Yes, that's it. Ukraine."

"I have. How much you want?"

I told him the amount. He had a number of supermarket bags on the floor. Selecting one of them, he took from it Hryvnia notes, counted them out, and took my Euros, which were then dispatched to one of the other bags.

"Thank you sir." He said, with a toothsome smile. "Have a nice day!"

I couldn't help thinking that, over the years, countless books have been written about foreign exchange, with mathematicians being paid huge sums to create complex algorithms that will predict currency-market movements, thereby giving one dealer the edge over his competitors. The man in the hole in the wall had little to learn from these experts, I concluded. Thus armed with what I hoped was genuine currency, I took the train to Warsaw.

My plan was to take the train from Warsaw to Lviv, in Ukraine, that afternoon , which gave me a couple of hours to spare in the capital, so I took the opportunity to visit the Palace of Culture and Science, Poland's tallest building and a monument to the Soviet influence during the post-war rebuilding of the city. Originally named the Josef Stalin Palace of Culture and Science, it stands 237 metres high and dominates the skyline. For those who have visited Moscow, it bears a striking resemblance to a couple of the old post-revolutionary socialist-realist skyscrapers there, and is still regarded by many Poles as a symbol of hated Soviet oppression. Amongst its more inconsequential claims to fame is the fact that the communist regime boldly allowed it to be used to host a Rolling Stones concert at the height of the cold-war in 1967, and in 2006 the Miss World contest was held there. The building now contains Theatres, a cinema, offices, and a museum, but was for many years a venue for party conferences and home of much of the apparatus of government.

I passed through the unguarded entrance and lobby, looking in vain for any stonework showing evidence of the removal of Stalin's name. My initial aim was to visit the Congress Hall, a circular 3000-seat arena originally intended for government meetings and political rallies. A cleaner looked up from her mop and bucket and smiled a greeting as I passed her in the marble corridor, and I soon found myself in the hall, which in basic layout could be described as a much smaller and less-decorative version of London's Royal Albert Hall. The "audience" area consisted of semi-circular rows of red-upholstered seats, facing a "stage" which boasted a large wooden table behind which was a row of similarly red-upholstered chairs. As I viewed the scene from the back of the hall, I was reminded of black-and-white television news programmes in the nineteen-sixties, which at the time regularly reported on Communist Party conferences taking place in one or other of the iron-curtain countries. Grainy footage would show ranks of dark-suited delegates, almost invariably men - few women seem to have ventured into communist politics at the time - listening intently to their leaders' pronouncements, dutifully applauding during pre-advised pauses in the oratory. I couldn't resist walking across to the stage to sit for a moment in the seat of power.

There is a lift up to the terrace on the 30th floor, and from there I took in the view of the city, sunless as the clouds sped by in an increasingly chilly easterly wind. Conscious that time was short, I headed back to the station. My plan was to spend the coming night in Lviv, the seventh-largest Ukranian city situated about 90 kilometres from the Polish Border. There were a couple of international trains from Warsaw which went all the way through, but not at a time that was convenient, so I was obliged to go via Przemysl, a small city located on the Polish side of the border, and change there onto the Lviv train.

The lengthy journey to Przemysl was uneventful, and I exited the station there at around 7pm, anxious to find a cafe or restaurant. This would not normally have been difficult in a community of some 66,000 souls, especially one boasting a small but interesting city-centre of narrow lanes and alleyways, but I hadn't reckoned with the fact that it was Sunday evening in rural Poland, and the streets were almost deserted. In the gathering twilight I found restaurant after restaurant closed, and at times half-expected to see tumbleweed drift by along the street. Just as I was about to give up my search, I came across a crowded pizza restaurant and grabbed one of the few tables available. Twenty minutes later, despite repeated requests, I hadn't been able to place my order with either of the busy waitresses, so I decided to cut and run. A final search back in the streets immediately around the station revealed a Polish version of what is known in the UK as a greasy spoon cafe. The only customers in the murky interior were a couple of middle-aged men playing cards, and as I took a seat the owner wiped his hands on his non-too-clean apron and came over with a menu. I had no Polish and he no English, but we managed to communicate to the extent that I left, an hour later, having eaten a hearty meal of ham, egg, and chips, washed down with a couple of beers.

The border procedure at Przemysl station is similar to that at many railway border-crossings. A separate and militarily secure part of the main building, including a secure dedicated platform, is set aside for passengers travelling to or from Ukraine. Passport checks and customs inspections are carried out here, and, once through onto the train, passengers are not required to undergo any further checks at the border. In effect, the system avoids the need for immigration officials to travel on the train or board it when it crosses the border.

I walked through the underpass to this, the most distant part of the station, and joined the queue of hopeful emigrants outside the locked door marked "International Departures". An hour before the train was due to leave, the door was opened and we began to file through, first getting passports checked and then undergoing cursory bag-searches. I mentioned in the book's introduction that the removal of visa requirements by most of the 49 countries had stimulated me to undertake the project in the first place. Ukraine had at one time been an exception to this, requiring all European Union nationals to purchase a visa. However, in 2005, the Eurovision Song contest was held in Kiev, the capital, and as a gesture of goodwill to participants and fans the government temporarily abolished visa requirements for the two-week period either side of the contest date. Afterwards, in the hope of stimulating tourism, they decided to make the ruling permanent, with the effect that my visit was visa-free and around £30.00 cheaper than if I'd made the trip in 2004. I have no interest in the Eurovision Song Contest, but I'm grateful for the £30.00. I mentioned this to the immigration officer who smiled without comment as he stamped my passport and waved me through onto the platform. Access to trains was, however, still denied by the presence of a wire fence, around three metres high, stretching the entire length of the platform. The gap of around two metres between the fence and the platform edge was patrolled by three armed guards, each with a German Shepherd dog on a lead. On the arrival of the train, which was already carrying international passengers, two gates in the fence were opened by the guards and we all trooped through and climbed aboard.

The train was entirely made up of sleeping cars, meaning that I had been allocated a numbered three-berth compartment, which I eventually located, hoping to have it to myself for the journey. I opened the door and instead found two balding middle-aged men tucking into food and drinking Vodka at the small fold-down table. I smiled and said hello, and they smiled back and replied in Polish, a language of which I know little apart from the words for "Hello", "Yes" and "No". I could see that conversation was destined to be a bit of a problem, particularly as I was not intending to sleep during the two-hour journey. They both had only very basic English, but as I sat down on the lower bunk the chubby one said "You like drink?" Without waiting for a response he reached into his bag and brought out a third glass. And so began a couple of hours of largely monosyllabic discussion of football, politics, and women, interspersed with occasional attempts at jokes, and lubricated by regular top-ups of Vodka. As a modest drinker, I was soon beginning to feel the effects of the alcohol and was quite pleased when the bearded one shared out the last of the bottle's contents. My relief was short-lived, however, when he produced a full bottle from his bag, opened it, and without ceremony topped up all three glasses yet again. I was also offered cheese, fresh bread, and gherkins, which I was too polite to refuse and which in any case I very much enjoyed. The convivial journey came to an end, however, around midnight when the train shuddered to a halt in Lviv station. Saying my farewells, I thanked them both profusely, and walked, slightly unsteadily on account of the vodka, to the end of the corridor and out onto the dimly-lit platform.

The location of the border between Ukraine and Poland has changed several times during the region's turbulent history, with the result that Lviv, like Przemysl, has at one time or another belonged to both countries, the last change occurring when it was ceded to Ukraine at the end of World War II. Ukraine, as currently constituted, dates from the establishment of the Ukraine People's Republic in 1917, a theoretically independent country but dominated by the Soviet Union. This dominance continued through the inter-war years, but ended when the Germans invaded in 1941. It became a member of the USSR following the defeat of the Germans in 1944, achieved independence in 1991 during the break-up of the Soviet Union, and is currently constituted as a parliamentary democracy which has recently sought membership of the European Union. In light of its current difficulties with Russia, however, over that country's claims on Ukranian territories in the South and East, there can be no formal application to join. Lviv is the country's seventh-largest city, with a population of around 730,000. Roman Catholicism is the city's principal religion, possibly due to the part Poland has played in the city's history, and the written language uses a variation of the Russian Cyrillic alphabet, always a challenge for the western visitor.

By now it was nearly midnight, and I needed to take a tram to the city centre in search of a hotel, but outside the station, chilled by a biting wind, I found only a building site where the tram terminus was supposed to be. Deciding to walk, I first had to negotiate the 100 metres or so along the unlit Chernivetska Street towards the main road into the city centre. The entire length of the street was effectively a continuation of the building-site, resulting in an obstacle course that would be difficult enough to negotiate on foot in daylight, let alone at night and without street lights. Snow began to fall as I passed a huddled figure sleeping on a park bench under trees to my left. At the end of the street I searched up and down the main road and in the surrounding area for any sign of a hotel, but in vain. There wasn't even a cafe where I might get information. The only signs of life were the occasional car speeding by, and a few pedestrians, clad in the obligatory fur hats and coats, hurrying home. I sought refuge from the snow in a shop doorway and considered my options.

It had always been my intention to get the 6am train back to Warsaw, as it was one of the few that underwent a wheel -change at Przemysl . A short explanation may be called for. Ukranian trains operate on a track width of 5 feet, whilst Polish railways have a width of 4 feet 8 ½ inches. The historic reason for the difference (and the imperial measurements) need not detain us here, but it means that in normal circumstances Ukranian locomotives and carriages can only travel as far as the border, where passengers must then disembark and cross over to the Polish train. This is somewhat inconvenient for those on long-distance international sleeping-car trains, who rightly expect to occupy their sleeping compartment for the entire journey. So at Przemysl the train is shunted into a yard, and the carriages are lifted on jacks to allow the Ukranian wheels – known as "bogies" - to be removed. Polish bogies are then slid under the carriage and bolted in place when the carriage is lowered. All this takes place with the passengers remaining inside the train, often still asleep, and it was a process I dearly wanted to witness. The 6am train, a sleeping car train, originated in Moscow and was destined to run through to Warsaw, thereby requiring the bogie change at Przemysl.

By now it was almost 1am and I reasoned that there was little point in taking a taxi to a hotel where I would probably get no more than four hours sleep, So, as the snow started to settle I renegotiated Chernivetska Street and sought out the station waiting room.

There were, in fact, two waiting rooms, located on either side of a corridor. The one on the left was almost full, but I was delighted to see that the one on the right was completely empty, I found out why as soon as I pushed open the door. There was no heating inside and the room was icy-cold. The other room, by contrast, was well-heated and inside I managed to find a seat on the periphery and surveyed the scene. About 20 metres square, the room possessed a high ceiling, with tall windows at the far end offered glimpses of the falling snow in the light of a street-lamp outside. My fellow travellers, as I soon discovered, were, in the main, not travellers at all, but members of Lviv's homeless community, huddled together in what was presumably for them the only available refuge from the cold. Seated along the opposite wall, a number of bag-ladies chatted quietly, each of them guarding a bulging battered shopping-trolley. To the left, a row of dishevelled old men, most sporting unkempt and greying beards, argued sporadically and occasionally aggressively amongst themselves. Their worldly goods were contained in a selection of grimy sports-bags and rucksacks, with a couple of them clutching aluminium crutches. Amongst those on the benches in the centre of the room, the few bona fide passengers could be seen dozing behind wheeled suitcases.

I settled down and was beginning to doze when a couple of policemen entered. A hush descended as they slowly walked round, pausing at one point to half-heartedly examine the contents of a bag - lady's shopping trolley. Every half-hour thereafter they returned and selected someone, seemingly at random, for more bag searching. After about an hour of this I found myself unable to sleep and in need of a coffee. On my way to the machine on the concourse I remembered that I had to pay for my sleeping-car reservation, without which I could not travel, at the ticket office. There being no cash machine available, or foreign exchange shop open, I was pleased I'd had the foresight to buy the hryvnia from the man in the hole in the wall at Krakow station. The reservation obtained, and bearing a cup of coffee, I returned to the waiting room, and as I was settling down I saw out of the corner of my eye a bag lady surreptitiously trying to open the rucksack of the old man sleeping in the next seat. He suddenly woke, uttered what was presumably a Ukranian oath, and punched her in the face. Fortunately for him this happened in between police patrols, but there followed a noisy argument in which one of the woman's friends became involved. Eventually peace returned, only to be disturbed by the reappearance the police, who for no obvious reason frogmarched one of the other rucksack men out of the room.

Peace prevailed thereafter, and eventually it was time to head for the platform and board the train. I'd again hoped for an empty sleeping compartment, but this time found its upper bunk occupied by Agnieszka, a young girl in her mid-twenties, who, it transpired, lived in Warsaw and was returning from a visit to her grandparents in Kiev. She had reasonable English, and told me she intended changing trains at Przemysl, so I asked her to wake me when we got there. As we were chatting, a knock on the door signalled the arrival of the carriage attendant, a woman of formidable stature and voice, who firmly insisted that I had over my passport for the duration of the journey. I knew this was common practise on international sleeping-car trains, but I can never be comfortable whilst I'm separated from my proof of identity, if only for a few hours. That done, I removed my shoes, cleaned my teeth, and wearily climbed onto the lower bunk where I quickly drifted off to sleep.

Agnieszksa woke me, as requested, as the train was threading its way through the outskirts of Przemysl, and suggested I follow her example and change onto a Polish train for the ongoing journey. "It will be much quicker." she assured me. "Everyone does it." I thanked her but told her I preferred to stay where I was, and after she departed I opened the compartment curtains to see her crossing to the platform opposite in the morning sunshine.

Aware that it was bogie-change time, when the 5ft gauge wheel sets would be replaced by bogies of 4ft 8½ inches, I was determined not to miss this rare experience. Ten minutes or so later the train lurched into life and began reversing into a goods yard nearby. On arrival in the yard the carriages were carefully positioned between two lines of yellow-painted hydraulic jacks, each about as high as the lower edge of the carriage window. At this point I popped into the corridor and drew back the curtains. On the adjacent line the new bogies awaited being called into action, and half-a dozen men busied themselves walking up and down the track, checking the positions of the Jacks against each carriage, They then left the scene, but ten minutes or so later two of them reappeared in the corridor of my carriage and entered the end compartment, As I looked on, they pushed aside the compartment's floor covering, opened a trapdoor in the floor, and undid the steel nuts holding the bogie in place. Once satisfied that all was well, they repeated the exercise in the compartment at the other end before moving on to the next carriage. Twenty minutes passed as they tackled the rest of the train, and then, without warning, the carriage shuddered and began to rise. Soon the train was entirely separated from its bogies, held in mid-air by the jacks. Noises underneath signified the removal of the 5ft bogies, linked together and dragged away along the dual-gauge rail-line beneath, shortly to be followed by the sound of the arrival of the 4ft 8½ inch versions. Once all bogies were lined up under the appropriate points of the train, the order was given to lower the carriage bodies and it was a relatively simple matter to reattach them via further visits by the men to the end compartments. The train then moved off, this time heading for the Polish part of the station rather than the Ukranian platform, and we were soon rattling along through South-East Poland on the way back to Warsaw. I took the opportunity to catch up on much-needed sleep.

Back in Warsaw I made a brief and disquieting visit to the last-remaining section of the perimeter wall of the Ghetto, built by the Nazis during World War II to contain the city's Jewish population prior to them being sent to the extermination camp at Treblinka . A simple brick construction, the wall is located in an unremarkable area of low-rise apartment blocks and cannot hope to convey any sense of the horrors that occurred behind it, with 300,000 Jews being killed over a three-year period. I couldn't help thinking of that small group of Poles back in my home town's Polish Club, who, along with many of their countrymen, had managed to make it to England during the war to join the Royal Air Force. Their contribution to the war effort had, albeit indirectly, led to my being free to visit this place, for which I will always be grateful.

Chapter 10

Spain, Gibraltar, and Ireland

There is no night-life in Spain. They get up late and they go to bed late. That is not night-life. That is delaying the day.
Ernest Hemingway

The last time I was in Spain I got through six Jeffrey Archer novels. I must remember to take enough toilet paper next time.
Bob Monkhouse

Well, Gibraltar is a place which you either love or hate. I quite like it. It's a rock, that is essentially what it is. It's a British colony.
Nigel Short, chess champion

When I told the people of Ireland that I was an atheist, a woman in the audience stood up and said "Yes, but is it the God of the Catholics or the God of the Protestants in whom you don't believe?"
Quentin Crisp

Poetic reminiscences at the airport. A paddle in the Mediterranean on the Costa del Sol. Crossing an international airport runway on foot. Thieving apes. Marks and Spencer 1,700 kilometres from home. Lost hotel. University canteen. Hen-night capers. Dublin without spending a single Eurocent.

I must begin this chapter by conceding that Gibraltar is not, as currently defined by the United Nations, a country. In its 1945 restatement of the definition of a country, previously coined by the League of Nations, the UN stated simply that "A resident of a **country** is subject to the independent exercise of legal jurisdiction. " Gibraltar is defined as a British Overseas Territory, its head of state being Queen Elizabeth II, and therefore does not possess independent legal jurisdiction. However in many other respects it acts independently, having its own parliament, and through this has almost complete internal democratic self-government. To my mind, Gibraltar is at least half-definable as a country, and certainly worth including in my list of 49. In any case I'd always wanted to visit it, ever since the stamp collecting days of my youth, when it produced highly attractive landscape-style stamps, showing romantic panoramas of the rock and the views across the Straits of Gibraltar towards Africa. Incidentally, I've never been able to understand why, in those days, postage stamps from British colonies and protectorates were always so much more colourful and attractive than those of the home country.

The closest Spanish city to Gibraltar is the port of Algeciras, about 22 kilometres away by road and even closer by ferry, but at the time of my journey there were no low-cost flights there or, indeed, to Gibraltar itself. However, budget airlines were already flying to holiday destinations on the Costa del Sol, the southernmost of the Spanish "Costas", and the best-served of these was Malaga, which I decided to use as a base for exploring the area. Malaga, an important port, is perhaps best-known as the birthplace and childhood home of Pablo Picasso, the artist. With a population of around 750,000 it is the sixth-largest Spanish city, as well as being the oldest, originally established by the Phoenicians in 770BC. Tourism is its chief industry, with six million visitors arriving each year to spend holidays in the city and along the adjacent coastline at resorts such as Fuengirola, Marbella, and Torremolinos.

Emerging from the customs hall at Malaga airport, I was unimpressed by the signage in the arrivals area. I'd intended taking the train to the city centre from the airport railway station, but was unable to find either the station or any indication of how to get to it. Eventually a helpful policeman guided me across the fume-filled ground-floor of the multi-storey car park on the North-East side of the airport, and out onto a gravel path that led to the tiny unmanned two-platform station, beyond which lay green fields and distant hills. Consulting the makeshift timetable posted on a board outside, I took a seat on the platform in the heat of the midday sun, finding the surroundings unexpectedly tranquil so close to such a busy airport. The peace and quiet was occasionally disturbed by birdsong, and I was reminded of that wonderful poem "Adelstrop" by Edward Thomas, written about a train's unscheduled stop at a remote railway station in Gloucestershire. The first eight lines seemed particularly appropriate.

> Yes, I remember Adelstrop –
> The name, because one afternoon
> Of heat the express train drew up there
> Unwontedly. It was late June.
> The steam hissed. Someone cleared his throat.
> No one left and no one came
> On the bare platform. What I saw
> Was Adelstrop- only the name

A handful of passengers eventually joined me on the platform, and the train duly arrived. As we reached the outskirts of Malaga the line plunged underground, and the train called first at the main station, Malaga Maria Zambrano, and finally Malaga Alameda, a small station having the advantage of being nearer the city centre and, more important, close to the Ibis hotel, my choice as a base for the next few days. The road from there to the hotel runs alongside the canalised River Guadalmedina, empty of water at that time of year and simply operating as a storm drain. Its concrete floor was the perfect surface for local youths who were variously using it as a football pitch, skateboard park, and roller-skate arena.

Later that evening I headed for the Plaza de la Merced, a large square in the city centre, and found a seat outside a cafe from which to watch the world go by. It was after 9pm, a time when the Spanish traditionally emerge from their homes and take to the streets. Smartly-dressed groups of friends and families appeared, some with dogs and children in tow, possibly heading for a favourite cafe, or simply strolling around the area and talking animatedly about this and that. For people watchers, late evenings in Spain are always a fascinating experience.

An hour or so later, feeling suitably relaxed, I set off back to the hotel. On the way I paused at a stand-up cafe to consume a large doner kebab, then bought food and drink for breakfast and beyond from the adjacent convenience store. On the bridge over the Guadalmedina, just along from the hotel, I paused for a few minutes to watch a noisy game of football taking place on the concrete pitch down below, the street lights offering patchy but adequate floodlighting. The encounter reminded me that there was a football match coming up on the forthcoming Saturday between Malaga and Granada in La Liga, the Spanish first division, which I was determined to attend if possible.

The following day was to be devoted to Gibraltar, around 140 kilometres from Malaga southwestwards along the Costa del Sol. The route passes through Fuengirola, Torremolinos, and Marbella, names I only knew courtesy of television holiday programmes. Never having been on a sea, sun, and sand holiday, I was anxious to find out what the fuss was all about, so decided to stop off at one of them en-route to check it out. The choice was narrowed down when I realised I could get the train to Fuengirola, and from there pick up the bus to Gibraltar.

Bright and early the following morning, under a blue cumulus-flecked sky, I boarded the train at Alameda station and half an hour later alighted at Fuengirola, an undistinguished town of some 72,000 souls outside the holiday season, but catering for possibly four times that number at the height of summer. I was determined to check out the beach, about half a kilometre away, and set off down a steep, narrow street. It soon became clear that the British are well represented both as residents and visitors in the town. "A" boards outside restaurants and cafes invariably offered the uniquely British alternatives of fish and chips or all-day English breakfast, with custard getting an honourable mention as an accompaniment to many of the desserts. The drinks menus offered draught English beer in pints rather than litres. One of the boards claimed that its restaurant had a connection with an East-Enders actress, and many others offered "all-day" BBC and ITV television programmes. At this time of year, however, there were few holidaymakers around, and it was reassuring to pass by a restaurant in a small open square which appeared to be hosting a boisterous Spanish family gathering.

Fuengirola beach, a broad expanse of sand stretching for an impressive eight kilometres or so in either direction, and overlooked by an uninterrupted line of high-rise hotels, would I'm sure normally boast hundreds, if not thousands, of sun loungers, but as this was out of season there were just a few scattered groups of holidaymakers relaxing on the sand in the spring sunshine. One or two brave souls splashed about in the sea, whilst a young couple were attempting to show a young child how to fly a kite, a difficult enough exercise at the best of times, but almost impossible in the light onshore breeze. The clear blue Mediterranean, almost flat-calm, stretched hazily to the horizon, beckoning me to go for a paddle, and I was unable to resist. Paddling is something of a ritual for me on those few occasions when I find myself on a beach and I guess the compulsion must hark back to childhood visits to the seaside.

Time was passing, and I was still a good way from Gibraltar. There is no rail connection onwards from Fuengirola, but an adequate bus service connects the two, and I located the bus stop just round the corner from the railway station. Once on board the bus, I found a seat on the left-hand side, hoping for spectacular views of the Mediterranean and the beaches of the Costa del Sol during the journey. I needn't have bothered. There were very few delightful sea vistas, just a succession of building sites, almost entirely uninterrupted by Mother Nature. I discovered later that this ribbon of housing development – almost 100 kilometres long -was considered the largest of its kind in the

Europe, and was partially responsible for the severe banking collapse in Spain around 2008. My mind went back briefly to my journey from Sarande to Vlore in Albania, a similar distance, also overlooking the Mediterranean, but with virtually no hotels or housing along its entire length.

Only in the final 10 kilometres or so before Gibraltar did nature reassert itself by way of fields, woods, olive groves, and stands of palm trees. These, however, quickly gave way to the built-up outskirts of La Linea de Concepcion, a small town just to the north of the border with Gibraltar, and the end of my journey. From there it was but a short walk through the streets to the border, offering along the way a first breathtaking glimpse of the rock itself. After the usual passport and customs checks I stepped outside the checkpoint and into Gibraltar.

Gibraltar's name comes from the Arabic, Jabal Tariq ("Mountain of Tariq"), named after an Arab general who invaded the peninsula in the year 713. Moorish rule ended in the 13th century and the area changed hands many times thereafter, it finally becoming a British possession after the war of the Spanish succession in 1713. Its strategic military location, overlooking the 13-kilometre wide entrance to the Mediterranean Sea, has led to continuing pressure from Spain, which asserts a claim to the territory. The peninsula is a mere 6.8 square kilometres in size, making it no larger than a small English town, and with a population of around 30,000 it is one of the most densely-populated areas in Europe. The rock itself is 425 metres high, and the summit can be reached by cable-car. The major contributors to the economy are the British military, financial services, on-line gambling, shipping, and tourism.

From the border, a road leads southwards for about a kilometre and a half to the downtown area. As time was short I took the nearby bus, a double-decker, one of the many reminders of the fact that I was on British territory. The brief journey terminated at what might be described as the town centre, and I alighted almost opposite Marks and Spencer, the British clothes and food store. As it was by now past lunch-time I popped in there to buy sandwiches and a screw-capped half-bottle of Rioja wine. It remains the only shop I have ever patronised where the tills are programmed for payment in either Pounds Sterling or Euros. I chose to pay in pounds, and have the till receipt to prove it. Outside, I found a bench by the bus-stop and, as I ate my lunch, observed the quintessentially English high-street scene. The principal language is, of course, English, but many residents also have Spanish, and there is also a small number of Arabic-speaking Moroccans. Bars and restaurants display menus in English, and our old friends, fish and chips and the full English breakfast make frequent appearances.

After lunch I strolled down to the Botanic Gardens, and in bright sunshine took the cable-car to the summit of the rock. The views on the way up were impressive, but at the top were simply breathtaking. To the South, Tangier and the Moroccan coast were clearly visible through the heat-haze, whilst the port of Algeciras dominated the bay to the North. At the base of the rock to the West I could see the naval and port facilities, and to the East lay Gibraltar's only beach, by this time in the shadow of the rock. As I walked around, the apes, traditional symbols of the rock, kept a watching brief, presumably checking me out as a potential food-donor. More correctly known as Barbary Macaque monkeys rather than apes, they currently number several hundred, and are protected by law. They are genetically similar to the Macaque troupes in the Atlas Mountains of Morocco, from where their ancestors are believed to have originated.

In need of a rest, I took a seat on a bench outside the visitor centre, whilst over on the wall opposite a couple of the apes lazily preened each other. As I prepared to photograph them, out of the corner of my eye I saw one of their colleagues raiding a supermarket bag, placed on the ground by an unsuspecting fellow-photographer. I shouted, causing the ape to look up, startled, and this provided the split-second necessary for the owner to snatch back his property. The antics of the apes reminded me of a friend from my youth, Alan, who'd joined the Merchant Navy at the tender age of sixteen. Each time he returned from a lengthy voyage he would regale us with tales of the exotic places he'd visited, and Gibraltar was a regular port of call for merchant seamen at the time. It seems it was common parlance for them, and consequently Alan, to refer to anyone who was not too bright as a "Rock Ape". After all these years, I'd finally encountered real "Rock Apes"!

Back in the busy downtown area I decided to walk the couple of kilometres back to the frontier rather than get the bus, and the route took me past the Trafalgar Cemetery, a peaceful green space set back from the busy main road. Here are to be found the graves of two men who died of wounds sustained in the battle of Trafalgar in 1805. It was, tradition at the time for those who died in naval action to be buried at sea, but those who were wounded in that epic battle were afterwards brought the short distance to Gibraltar to receive hospital treatment. Many of these survived, and subsequently rejoined the fleet, but Captain Thomas Norman and Lieutenant William Forster died in the hospital. The cemetery also has graves of men who died in the hospital following injuries sustained in the three other sea battles that took place in the Western Mediterranean during the Napoleonic campaign.

Back on the road to the frontier, I looked forward to the unique experience, for me, of walking across an international airport's main runway. Gibraltar airport lies at the northern end of the narrow peninsula, with its main runway running East-West across almost the entire width of the isthmus at that point. As a result, half-way along the runway is the point at which it intersects with the main road that runs South-North towards the border. During take-offs and landings, barriers are lowered across the road, thereby stopping all traffic until the plane is either airborne or on its way to the terminal. When all is clear the barriers are then lifted and street life returns to normal. Imagine, if you will, having to sit in your car at the barrier of a railway level crossing waiting for a train to speed by. In Gibraltar it will be an aeroplane rather than a train, so drivers may be treated to the sight of an Airbus A320 passenger jet crossing the road in front of them. Unfortunately, on this occasion, there was no flight in or out, so I couldn't witness the system in operation, but I at least achieved my aim of crossing an international airport runway on foot.

The border checks took longer than I'd anticipated, as many of the Spanish workers who worked in Gibraltar were on their way home, it being late afternoon by now. However I caught the bus as planned, returning via Fuengirola to Malaga, and even found time to have a beer at a bar in the city centre before going back to the hotel. Attached to the wall above the door of this particular bar was a small cage, not much bigger than a shoebox, inside which were two canaries, each surveying the scene from their perches and occasionally bursting into melodious song. I have to admit they both looked (and sounded) well cared for, but I couldn't help feeling guilty by association.

I planned to spend the next couple of days in Seville, the capital of the region of Andalusia, that huge area of South-West Spain which happens to include Malaga and the Costa del Sol. New high-speed trains had just been introduced by RENFE, the Spanish railway company, and I couldn't wait to try one out. Arriving at Malaga station to catch the early-morning train, I was surprised to find baggage x-ray machines at the platform entrances, something I'd only previously encountered at stations served by Eurostar services via the Channel Tunnel. The train had that unique "new" smell as I boarded, and I settled down in a window seat for a restful journey through rural Spain. Before long we were speeding past kilometre after kilometre of sun-drenched orange groves, their trees laden with fruit, alternating with fields of gnarled and twisted olive trees. Otherwise the landscape was mostly featureless, a flat agricultural plain, wherein, according to George Bernard Shaw, the rain stays mainly. Cordoba, a beautiful sometime Roman city is the only settlement of any size *en route*, and I was to return there some years later to view its amazing Mosque-Cathedral, originally constructed as a mosque by Moorish invaders in the eighth century, but taken over by the Roman Catholic Church in the thirteenth century after the Moors were defeated and largely unchanged thereafter.

The city of Seville is the fourth-largest Spanish city, with a population of around 1.5 million. It is the city from which Magellan started out when he made the first circumnavigation of the world, and Christopher Columbus is generally thought to be interred in the cathedral, although there has always been controversy over the identity of the body contained in the tomb. Seville Santa Justa station lies close to the strangely-named Avenida de Kansas City, a main road heading eastwards out of the city, and along which I needed to travel to get to the Ibis Budget hotel where I was to spend the night. Having found and boarded the bus, I consulted the hastily-scribbled map of the route I'd made back home, trying to make sure I alighted at the right stop, located around four kilometres away and not far from the ring-road. On any bus journey it can often be a bit of a gamble trying to alight at exactly the right stop, and I wasn't sure that the Hotel was visible from the road. No one on the bus knew of the Ibis, so I was forced to take a chance and, as it transpired, alighted one stop short. With no map of the immediate area, I boldly decided to take the road to the left which soon led into a trading estate. A man working in the forecourt of a garage directed me further along it, but at the end there was still no sign of the hotel. Another road led back through the estate, past warehouses and small factories. With no-one nearby to ask, I decided to give it a try, and at the far end, through a gap between two industrial units, I finally caught a glimpse of the Ibis sign. I mention this simply to highlight the point that travel on local buses can have its problems, as I'd previously found in Croatia, and a scribbled map copied from the internet is rarely adequate!

The hotel, it transpired, had been opened only recently, and, despite its proximity to the trading estate, stood in a pleasantly landscaped area. After checking in and finding my room I walked the short distance to the nearby bus stop on the main road, and returned to the city centre. There, I bought a one-day travel-card and hopped onto the tram to San Bernardino, where stands one of the city's iconic buildings, the Royal Tobacco Factory, now occupied by the University. A three-storey stone building, dating from 1728, it covers almost three hectares and its frontage of 150 metres is decorated with multi-coloured ceramic tiles. Originally, as the name suggests, it was a tobacco factory employing as many as 5,000 women, some of whom were considered, rightly or wrongly, to be ladies of easy virtue. It was this all-female workforce that Inspired French novelist Prosper Merimee to write his book Carmen in 1845. This was the basis for Georges Bizet's opera of 1875. In the story Carmen met her maker in the Seville Bull-Ring, of which more later.

As it was lunchtime, I was pleased to find that the students' union, located just inside the colonnaded entrance, was open for business, so I queued up for subsidised sandwiches and coffee, and found a seat at a table occupied by half a dozen students. One of those at the table, a young man in jeans and, implausibly, wearing a Che Guevara T-shirt, introduced himself. When I told him I was from the London area his eyes lit up. He asked if I knew Brixton. I told him I wasn't too familiar with that particular part of the capital.

"My brother has just moved there." He said. "He is studying at Imperial College. Civil engineering. I will visit him in the summer. Is there good night life in Brixton?"

I had to admit I was no expert on the subject.

"From what I hear," I ventured cautiously, "it is a place with a very relaxed atmosphere. "

He laughed.

"Ah, you mean ganja! That's what my brother said. He said it is legal!"

I hastened to correct him.

"No. I don't think so. But maybe in Brixton they're not strict."

By now somewhat out of my depth, I decided a change of topic was called for.

"I've just been to Gibraltar."

His eyes lit up again.

There followed a prolonged and at times quite heated debate with him and the others about the Spanish claim on that territory. Outnumbered, I was always destined to lose the argument, but I like to think I scored the occasional hit, to the extent that I was a little disappointed when they had to leave to attend a lecture. The event, trivial in its own way, reminded me how much I used to enjoy that sort of informal debate in my student days.

Back outside, in the heat of the afternoon sun, I walked over to the cathedral, undoubtedly a beautifully constructed flying-buttressed building, but largely unrewarding from a strictly aesthetic point of view. It is claimed to be the second-largest cathedral in the world. My main reason for visiting it was to take a look at the tomb of Christopher Columbus, supposedly the explorer's last resting-place. I won't go into the debate in detail, but there are those who claim it may in fact be his brother's remains in the tomb rather than those of Columbus himself. The bones arrived in Seville in 1898, almost 400 years after the explorer's death in 1506, having being moved from place to place at least five times during that 400-year period. For a time they were held in the Dominican Republic, alongside those of his brother, which is why that country is currently claiming to hold the true remains, stating that the remains eventually transferred to Seville were those of the brother. I was reminded for a moment of saintly relics, usually body parts, held by churches around the world. if the claims of The Cetinje Monastery in Montenegro, The Topkapi Palace in Istanbul, and the Forerunner on Mount Athos are to be believed, St John the Baptist had three right arms.

Much more interesting is the Alcazar, or Royal Palace, which is situated adjacent to the cathedral and consists of beautifully decorated rooms, corridors, and colonnades surrounding magnificent gardens, all in the Moorish style of the twelfth and thirteenth centuries. Kings and Queens have lived here since the beginning, and its history is the history of Spain as a country. For me, the palace outshines even the Alhambra and Generalife palaces of Granada in terms of the quality of its Moorish ceramic tilework, ubiquitous stone carving, and decorative furnishings. The gardens are hidden deep within the confines of the palace, and therefore not visible from outside the building. They boast tall palm trees, ornamental ponds, and a multitude of flowering creepers and shrubs. I came across them almost by accident as I exited one of the palace rooms, and the beauty of the scene caused me to stop dead in my tracks. Glorious natural colours, shapes and reflections were lit by the yellowing afternoon sunlight under a clear blue sky. That moment was to be the most memorable of all in my visit to Seville, and, along with my first sight of Tangier from the rock in Gibraltar, would rank as the most unforgettable experience of the entire journey.

I spent far longer than I should have in the Alcazar, but eventually made my way back to the tram stop as I had to go shopping for a T-shirt. I'd only brought two of them on the trip, not expecting the weather to be so warm, so needed a third. The tram took me along Avenida de La Constitucion, a wide boulevard, where a few boarded-up shops suggested all was not well with the Spanish economy. A couple of bargain clothes outlets appeared to fit the bill. Sadly, neither had plain white T-shirts, which meant I had to select both a colour and a design, something I'd managed to avoid doing for many years. After examining what seemed like hundreds, I finally found one that was my size, in white, and which wasn't proclaiming the merits of this or that song, film or TV series on the front. It simply bore a photograph of a woman's face with the words "I know" above and "Specially for you" beneath. I wore it the next day, but after several amused glances by passers-by, I knew my attempt at being down with the kids had failed. Needless to say, I haven't since worn it in public.

Finally, there was to be another "first" for me, a visit to the bull-ring, located a short distance away down towards the river. As I arrived, the last tour of the day was just starting, and the uniformed lady guide said I was welcome to join them. My fellow tourists were mainly Japanese, along with an American husband-and-wife couple and a smattering of Spaniards, and we were first of all directed up the stairs into the (empty) 12,000-seat arena where we took seats just below the Royal Box to hear about the history of the place. Below us lay the immaculate circular sand surface of the arena, surrounded by a red boundary fence, with ranks of seating soaring upwards towards a glorious clear blue sky, all contributing to a glorious portrayal of symmetry and colour. All was fine on the tour until we went backstage to view the museum, and I could tell by her comments that the American lady was not too happy when we visited the chapel where the bullfighters pray before the fight, and was even less happy when shown the mini-hospital where injured participants are treated for their wounds. She finally told her husband firmly that she hadn't wanted to come in the first place and was leaving, with or without him. He duly left with her. As for me, I glanced round the museum, full of Toreador costumes, stuffed bull's heads, and general bullfighting memorabilia, but found little of interest. Bullfighting remains a politically contentious activity in Spain, as it does in Southern France where it is also practised, and my visit simply confirmed my view that the world would be a better place if it didn't exist.

As I walked back to get the bus, the light was beginning to fade, and by the time I got back to the hotel – this time alighting at the right stop – it was almost dark. It had been a busy day, and I slept well that night, safe in the knowledge that I'd be able to wear my new T-shirt the next day.

The following morning I checked out of the hotel and took the bus, then tram, to visit the Plaza de Espana, a large semicircular area along the perimeter of which lies a decorated three-storey brick building constructed in a curve, and in front of which lies a canal on which small boats are available for hire. Built for the Seville Expo in 1929, the building now houses government offices. Much of the facade, and the bridges across the canal, are faced with multi-coloured ceramic tiles, celebrating the various regions of Spain. There have been many attempts over the years to define its architectural style – my favourite is "Renaissance revival with Art Deco and Neo-Mujedar" - but in all honesty I can only describe it as "George Gilbert Scott meets Disneyland." Even so, I was pleased to have seen it, unarguably a spectacular sight in the morning sunshine.

The train journey back to Malaga was uneventful, and I arrived there early enough to allow me to visit Picasso's birthplace and museum. And yes, the following day I managed to fit in a visit to La Rosaleda stadium to watch Malaga FC play Granada in the Spanish football first division. I was intrigued to find that passageways inside the stadium bore the label "Vomitorio", a word used by the ancient Romans to indicate the exit routes underneath an amphitheatre. I searched afterwards to find out if there was any etymological connection with the act of vomiting, and was somewhat relieved to find there is none.

At the airport check-in that evening I was entertained by a group of young women, evidently returning to Ireland after a hen-weekend. They had been informed that several of them exceeded their baggage allowance and wouldn't be allowed to board the plane. The check-in lady suggested they move clothing from the overweight suitcases to those that were underweight. As I stood in the queue, I was thus treated to the sight of ten opened suitcases on the terminal floor, with girly contents being transferred from one case to another, accompanied by a sometimes heated debate as to what should go where. I still wonder if they all made their flight.

My final destination on this trip was to be Dublin, capital of the Irish Republic, and served by regular flights from Malaga. My intention was to spend a few hours there before returning home to England. This, however, presented me with a major personal problem. As a student, I lived in Birmingham in the late 1960s where, unbeknownst to all at the time, an Irish Republican Army cell was operating in Ladywood, an area of the city not too far from my flat. In common with many fellow-students, I would often meet up with friends in one or other of the many city-centre pubs, often choosing the Mulberry Bush, but occasionally opting for the Tavern in the Town, where the beer was better. On the evening of November 21st 1974, thankfully a few years after I'd moved away from the city, the IRA detonated bombs in each of these pubs, killing 21 people and injuring 182, some of whom were almost certainly my successor students. Since then I'd vowed never to visit Ireland, fearing that some of the money I would necessarily spend may find its way to the IRA, by then a spent force militarily, but believed by many to be continuing to control mafia-style criminal activity across the country. My decision to visit all 49 European countries meant that Ireland could not be excluded from the list, but presented me with a dilemma. After much thought, I had decided to compromise by visiting Dublin but spending nothing whilst I was there, something I had already achieved, albeit unintentionally, in Bosnia and Moldova.

The flight from Malaga was unexceptional, save for a larger than usual number of highly vocal children on board, and I found myself exiting the customs area at Dublin Airport and wondering how I would achieve my "no spend" objective, as I intended visiting a few of the city's tourist attractions in the four hours or so before my flight to England. As I entered the arrivals hall I was confronted, somewhat ironically given the political nature of my problem, by a television showing an interview with Ian Paisley, the IRA's arch-enemy. Outside the terminal, in pleasant sunshine, I located the stand for the number 41 city-centre bus, an unexceptional double-decker in yellow and blue, its engine ticking over and the entrance door open. The driver looked up from his copy of the "Sun" newspaper and informed me that a return ticket to the city centre was six Euros, which I duly handed over. This was to be the only time that my hand troubled my pocket in the entire visit, and I reasoned, or rather hoped, that it was unlikely that any part of it would find its way to the IRA.

And so it was that I found myself on the top deck of a Dublin double-decker bus, rattling through rather drab suburbs towards O'Connell Street, a broad boulevard running North-South through the city centre. There I alighted opposite the neo-classical frontage of the post-office, a mundane-sounding but critically important building in the Republic's history. It was here, over a six-day period in Easter of 1916 that the building was commandeered by the Irish Nationalists and served as their headquarters during a military uprising against the British, which saw almost 500 people killed. The failed insurgency eventually led to the partition of the island in 1922, with the southern part becoming an independent republic, known as the Irish Free State, whilst counties in the north, previously part of the territory that had since 1800 been known as The United Kingdom of Great Britain and Ireland, now became part of The United Kingdom of Great Britain and Northern Ireland.

Dublin, a city of around 1.4 million souls, almost one-third of the total Irish population, lies on Dublin Bay on the country's East coast. Geographically it is divided by the River Liffey, which rises in the Wicklow mountains to the South, and by the time it reaches the city is a broad, straight waterway around 50 metres wide and crossed by fifteen bridges within the city boundary. The most famous of these is the Ha'penny Bridge, a pedestrians-only cast-iron structure half a kilometre South of O'Connell Street .The bridge sections were cast in 1816 in Coalbrookdale, England, the location and place of manufacture of the world's first iron bridge built thirty five years previously. Crossing over it, I headed for Trinity College, Ireland's top university, which covers around 20 hectares of prime land in the city centre. Its many buildings, some neoclassical and dating from the eighteenth century, surround grass-covered open spaces. The Old Library, a huge five-storey block built between 1712 and 1732, has special status under the British Legal Deposit Libraries Act which means it receives a copy of every book published in the UK and Ireland, currently running at around 100,000 volumes every year.

From the University I walked the half-kilometre or so southwards to the Shelbourne Hotel, fulfilling a promise I'd made to my partner, whose grandfather had worked there many years ago. A six-story corner brick building overlooking St Stephen's Green, an attractive park, the hotel has hosted many famous visitors over the years, including Michael Collins and his team when they drafted the Irish constitution in 1922. Less historically significant, but worthy of note, is the fact that in the early 1900s, Alois Hitler, Adolf Hitler's half-brother, worked there. Inside, the hotel combines Regency elegance with a hint of Art Nouveau, particularly evident in the attractive, predominantly blue, glass dome over the reception area. Conscious that time was passing, I set off northwards back towards the Liffey, passing cafes and bars *en route*, but of course unable to call in for a drink in fulfilment of my no-spend vow. I have to admit the temptation to drink a pint of Guinness in its home city was almost too powerful to withstand.

Back on the North side of the Liffey, I took a walk to Earl Street, a pedestrianised area adjacent to O'Connell Street, boasting a simple life-size bronze statue of the writer, James Joyce, in characteristic floppy hat and raincoat, apparently pausing during a walk along the street as he leans on his walking stick. I was reminded of my recent trip to Trieste, Italy, where I'd viewed a similar life-size statue of Joyce, on the canal bridge, again pausing as he walked along, Returning to O'Connell Street, I caught the bus back to the airport and was soon checking in for my flight to London. It was only when I got airside in Terminal 1 that I found out that my departure gate was the one furthest away from the terminal, at the end of a dreary ten-minute walk with no travelators. I arrived exhausted to find no facilities of any sort by the gate, just a scattering of seats. For a moment I wondered if this may be some sort of reprisal by the city of Dublin for my not having spent a single Eurocent there, other than the cost of the airport bus. I couldn't, however, contain a feeling of smug satisfaction at the thought that I was probably the lowest-spending tourist that Dublin had ever seen.

Chapter 11

France, Monaco, Italy, Austria, Liechtenstein, Switzerland, Germany

Liechtenstein is the world's largest producer of sausage casings and false teeth **Anonymous**

The story goes that I first had the idea for The Hitchhiker's Guide to the Galaxy while lying drunk in a field in Innsbruck **Richard Adams**

It is always assumed that Venice is the ideal place for a honeymoon. This is a grave error. To live in Venice, or even to visit it, means that you fall in love with the city itself. There is nothing left over in your heart for anyone else **Peggy Guggenheim**

Driving in Monte Carlo is like riding a bike in your house **Nelson Piquet**

> Seven countries in seven days. Train journey from hell. Millionaire's yacht marina. Venice, the most beautiful city on earth. Watching gondolas being built. Birth of renaissance art by Giotto. Visit to Francesco da Mosta, that bloke off the telly. Birthplace of Zeppelin airships.

Let us briefly consider the subject of Europe's "tax havens". These are countries or regions boasting low levels of personal and/or corporation taxation, offering confidential financial services to those, often wealthy, individuals who wish to reduce or avoid paying tax in their country of residence. There is much debate as to whether any particular place constitutes a tax haven, and, for example, I have excluded Luxembourg and Switzerland from my list as they only partly fulfil the criteria. According to my own arguable definition there are seven that can truly be considered as members of this exclusive club. Two, or possibly three of the seven are not independent countries. The Channel Islands and the Isle of Man are Crown Dependencies of the UK, and subject to UK law, so cannot be considered as countries. Gibraltar, as discussed elsewhere in this book, has its own special status as a British Overseas Territory, and whilst it is not recognised as a country by the United Nations it has many of the characteristics of a country.

That leaves just four. Of these, Monaco, Liechtenstein, and Andorra are principalities, meaning that they are ruled by princes, and are defined as Sovereign City States, making them independent countries. Interestingly, Andorra is in fact a co-principality, whose ruling princes are the President of France and the Spanish Bishop of Urgell. San Marino, however, is an independent republic, the smallest member of the European Union, and as such is very much a country. These four have therefore been included in my list of 49 European countries. All are enclaves, so may be susceptible to political influence by their neighbours, but to all intents and purposes are independent. They are widely scattered geographically across the continent, so it seemed to make sense to visit each one individually as part of a tour of their adjacent countries. In the case of Monaco and Liechtenstein, Although 450 kilometres apart as the crow flies, I decided both could be included in an ambitious single trip which also included visits, however brief, to the intervening five countries over the course of a week. The distance between the two by rail, using the route I selected, was about 1,300 kilometres.

The outward flight was to be to Nice, on the French Riviera, the nearest budget-airline airport to Monaco, with the return flight planned to be from Friedrichshafen, in Germany, the nearest budget-airline airport to Liechtenstein. I planned an ambitious route between the two, which was to take my partner and me through Italy, Austria and Switzerland in addition to France, Germany, and the two tax-havens countries. Travelling was to be over the Christmas period, notorious in the UK for a lack of public transport, but with normal daily timetables in continental Europe. Seven countries in seven days sounds much like a route-march, but as it transpired was highly enjoyable.

The flight path into Nice airport on the French Riviera, at low altitude and parallel to the seafront, provided a spectacular and reassuring panorama of Mediterranean beaches, pantiled city roofs, and the green hills of Provence in the distance to the North. There was a palpable air of relief amongst all passengers as we touched down, evidenced by a smattering of applause, as we'd experienced severe turbulence during the flight over the snow-capped Alps. The airport bus took me and my partner to the railway station, and our adjacent hotel. Once installed in the room, we took the tram to the busy Christmas market in Place Massena, close to the seafront, where we warmed our hands round cups of mulled wine in the chilly evening air. I've always been somewhat ambivalent on the subject of Christmas markets. On the one hand they're a chance to mingle with local people, buy regional speciality foodstuffs, and learn about traditional and contemporary local crafts. On the other hand they are invariably high-priced and there are usually a great many stalls selling what can only be described as tat. Our only purchase on this occasion, other than the mulled wine, was a bag of delicious roast chestnuts. We toured the adjacent funfair, its music adding to the carnival atmosphere, and after some discussion decided against a ride on the Ferris wheel. On the way back to the hotel we found a Lebanese-owned restaurant where we had doner kebabs and chips.

The following morning we walked over to the station to get the train to Monaco, and in particular its capital, Monte Carlo, effectively the downtown area of the principality. From there we intended to cross Italy and reach Venice, 570 kilometres away, that evening. We had been warned by the lady working on reception at the hotel to expect what the French refer to as "perturbations" on the railway – in English, delays and cancellations – and sure enough the train we'd hoped to get had been cancelled. Half an hour or so later a crowded train pulled into the platform and we managed to force our way on board. It took less than fifteen minutes to reach our destination station, Monaco-Monte Carlo, almost certainly the only railway station in the world that is named after both a country and a district within that country.

Monaco is tiny, having an area of 2 square kilometres, which makes it the second smallest country in the world, as well as being the most densely populated. Incidentally, it boasts the world's shortest coastline of all coastal countries, at around 4 kilometres. There is no income tax, and 30% of its population are reputed to be millionaires. The country has little of cultural interest to offer, with the best-known building being the casino, built in 1863 and typical of French municipal architecture from that period. The capital, Monte Carlo occupies little more than a cliff-top and harbour area, with the two being connected by lifts and walkways carved out of the rock.

Outside the station, located high on the cliff-top, we took the lift down to the harbour, wherein were moored dozens of huge ocean-going private yachts. From there we walked through the road tunnel, well-known to fans of Formula 1 racing as part of the Grand-Prix circuit. No visit to Monte Carlo would be complete without checking out the Casino, a pleasant enough building standing in carefully-manicured grounds with leggy palm trees lining the road leading to the entrance. After taking a couple of photographs we headed back to the lift and returned to the station. And that, dear reader, is the story of our brief visit to Monaco, which lasted only an hour or so longer than previous visits to Bosnia and Moldova.

In truth, we were anxious to get a train out of there as soon as possible, given the delay encountered earlier. The Milan train arrived more than half an hour late, and when we crossed the border into Italy at Ventimiglia we were mightily relieved to have left the French railway troubles behind us. The Thomas Cook European Timetable was consulted, showing that we would almost certainly miss the connection to our destination, Venice, when we eventually reached Milan, but there was an alternative departure not long afterwards which would get us there. Little did we know that this was only the start of our travel problems. By now it was dark, and at Milan station we waited in vain on the concourse for the alternative train to arrive. It was shown on the indicator, but with no platform number, and the information desk had no idea as to when it might arrive. We decided to take a slower train that would at least get us to Venice, even though much later than we'd planned, and were promptly fined a penalty fare of 8 Euros by the ticket inspector on the train for not having booked in advance. Still in hope of getting to Venice in reasonable time, our hearts sank when the train shuddered to a halt in the middle of nowhere, and we were eventually informed that the preceding train had broken down. Eventually our train limped into Chiari, still 200 kilometres from Venice, where we changed onto a local train that was only going as far as Mestre, technically part of the city of Venice but located on the mainland some nine kilometres from the island.

Arriving at a cold, damp, foggy Mestre at 1am, we found the streets more or less deserted, with the last train to Venice long gone. There were a couple of buses outside the station, which for a moment gave us hope that they might be heading for Venice, but enquiries revealed both were going to Slovakia. The only possible solution to the problem of covering the final short distance to Venice was to break the habit of a lifetime and spend 21 Euros on a taxi. The journey was worth every Eurocent of the fare, however, not least because as we crossed the four kilometre causeway the fog thickened considerably, making driving conditions very difficult. Fortunately our driver knew the exact location of our hotel, and we finally stumbled into reception there at around 1:30 am, some five hours later than originally planned.

I have described in some detail the problems encountered on this journey to highlight the fact that that public transport is not always reliable, and this particular day was one of the worst I'd experienced in many years of travelling. It's important to stress, however, that such a concatenation of problems is rare, and the two countries involved, France and Italy, normally boast two of the best and most reliable rail networks in Europe. In any case, if the destination is Venice, *la Serenissima*, then to arrive there is worth any amount of difficulties on the way.

The following morning, after a breakfast of fresh-baked rolls and coffee, we stepped outside and viewed the area around the hotel for the first time in daylight. The dense fog had given way to a thin mist, which shrouded distant buildings and added an air of mystery to the rather mundane surroundings. For those who know Venice, the hotel is close to Piazzale Roma, the main coach park for the city, located not far from the railway station. We were at the western end of the Grand Canal, anything but grand at this point as it is largely fronted by commercial premises save for a small adjacent church. We set off over the nearby bridge and soon found ourselves by the steps in front of the railway station, where we bought travel-cards at the canal-side vaporetto ticket office. The vaporetti are boats which take passengers along numbered routes to various parts of the city, and are the Venetian equivalent of buses. They are effectively the only way to explore the city other than on foot.

Venice's history, geography, architecture, and abiding beauty make it for me one of the world's greatest cities. Made up of 118 islands of varying sizes, it dates back to the tenth century BC when what amounted to an offshore swamp was settled by the local tribe, the Venetii. Over the ensuing years it was conquered and reconquered, becoming an independent republic and City state in the eighth century AD, and part of modern-day Italy in 1866. In the period from the thirteenth to the seventeenth centuries Its location at the head of the Adriatic Sea was a major factor in facilitating the creation of a substantial political and trading empire that covered most of the present-day Balkans, together with areas around the Mediterranean and Black Seas, including Constantinople, (Istanbul), and swathes of present-day Northern Italy. The empire was to fail, however, when Napoleon invaded in 1796, ending centuries of growth funded by the riches of empire. Many of the present-day buildings, lapped by the waters of 177 canals, date from the empire period, beautifully decorated merchants' palaces built, surprisingly, on wooden foundations. The largest of the canals, the Grand Canal, is the main thoroughfare through the islands, and many of the most important buildings are located along it. For a first-time visitor, a vaporetto ride along the Grand Canal provides an unforgettable introduction to the glories of the city.

It being the Christmas holidays, there were few tourists on board our vaporetto as it chugged through the mist at the regulation seven nautical miles per hour eastwards along the Grand Canal to our first destination, San Giorgio Maggiore, an island located on the south-east side. The church and monastery on the Island are thought by many to be Palladio's greatest architectural creation, and I cannot disagree. There we took the lift to the top of the church's bell tower, which would normally afford a magnificent panorama of Piazza San Marco opposite and the rooftops of the city beyond, but on this occasion the view was somewhat obscured by the lingering mist. I confess that I was beginning to like this foggy, damp version of Venice, not encountered in previous sun-drenched visits, with the lack of visitors contributing to a feeling of isolation and, dare I say it, mystery.

From there it was a short Journey by vaporetto, past moored gondolas, to Piazzetta San Marco, through which we walked to Piazza San Marco, better known as St. Mark's Square, the beating heart of the city. There we sought a table at the richly-decorated Caffe Florian, established in 1720, and Venice's most famous cafe, patronised at one time or another by Casanova, Charles Dickens, Lord Byron, and Marcel Proust amongst others. It gained notoriety in the eighteenth century as the only cafe in Venice to allow women to enter, and is thought to have become a high-class bordello at the time.

A short walk across the square took us to the Doge's Palace, where, in contrast to our previous visits, there was no queue at the entrance. Taking advantage, we enjoyed a relaxed stroll around its magnificent interior, which dates back to the fifteenth century, and walked over the Bridge of Sighs to the prison in which Casanova was held, and from which he escaped. There followed an evening visit to the Christmas Market at Campo Saint Stephano, where we again had a glass or two of mulled wine, then had dinner at a very reasonably-priced self-service restaurant near the railway station.

The following morning again dawned damp and misty, and we caught the train to Padua, around 40 kilometres to the East, and there paid a visit to The Scrovegni Chapel, a short bus journey from the railway station. The chapel itself, erected in 1305, has no great architectural significance, being not much more than a simple box-structure similar in size to a typical small-town Welsh Wesleyan chapel. That, however, is where the similarity ends. Entry is via an air-lock, with the visitor being held in an outer chamber for 15 minutes or so before being allowed to enter the chapel itself, in order to minimise disturbances to the air within, vital for conservation of the artworks. The chapel is considered to be one of the most important locations in the history of Western art, as its walls and ceiling are covered by a series of 38 frescoes by the artist Giotto di Bondone, showing various aspects of the bible story. The significance of these 700-year old frescoes is that they are amongst the earliest-known examples of art showing emotion on the faces of the people being depicted, with one of the panels including what is believed to be the first-ever kiss to appear in a painting. Church art hitherto had tended to show stylised people in a flat, unrealistic, excessively holy byzantine manner, and Giotto's revolutionary style is believed to have been the foundation of the Renaissance art movement that blossomed one hundred years later.

On arriving back in Venice the mist had gone, and in pleasant sunshine we had an unannounced visit to make. There had recently been a highly enjoyable British television series called "Francesco's Venice" in which Francesco da Mosto, an architect, born and raised in Venice, took the viewer through a chronological history of the city, often going off the tourist trail to visit little-known locations. We enjoyed the programme so much that we decided to try to visit him at his home unannounced the next time we were in Venice, in the hope that he would at least say hello and perhaps allow us to take a photo or two. That morning we'd consulted the telephone directory in the hotel and found his address. There are few streets in the city, as most of its buildings are surrounded by canals, so most addresses are simply shown as a house number, coupled with an area of the city. We therefore knew only that the house was located somewhere in the maze of canals on the South side of the Rialto Bridge. Most houses are part of a block, surrounded on all four sides by water. Each block contains a consecutive series of numbers, each of which identifies a particular house. The problem for the visitor is that there seems to be little relationship between the numerical sequence of any particular block and that of its neighbouring block. The only way to find a particular house is to search out a couple of house numbers on a block, usually visible above front doors, and guess whether they are likely to be within a sequence that would include the number you're seeking. If so, then walk round the block and if you're lucky you'll find the house you're looking for. If not, then it's on to the next block to repeat the exercise. And that, dear reader, is why we spent almost an hour wandering around the canals to the South of the Rialto Bridge, and eventually – bingo! – found a block with the right sequence of numbers. At the far end we found Francesco's distinctive front door, which we recognised from the television series, and round the corner we spotted his blue motor-boat, the Venice equivalent of the family car, tied up on the canal alongside.

I pressed the entry-phone button and a lady answered. I explained why we were there, to which she replied, surprisingly, "Come upstairs" and buzzed us in, Francesco, smiling, greeted us on the landing, ushered us into his somewhat chaotic office, and introduced us to his young son, who had also been featured, albeit briefly, in the television series. For ten minutes or so we chatted, during which he mentioned that he was preparing to leave for Cortina that afternoon, as he always tried to fit in a few days' snowboarding during the Christmas holidays. After taking a couple of photographs - there were no "selfies" at that time – we thanked him for his hospitality and left.

Back at the Rialto Bridge we made a longish journey by Vaporetto that took us via the Eastern end of the Grand Canal to a stop on the South side of the island on the Zattere promenade, from which we took a short walk to the Squero di San Trovaso, an ancient industrial unit on a narrow branch of the canal where traditional Gondolas are still made and repaired. "Squero" means "boatyard" in Italian. The Gondola, a one-man operated passenger boat, has been a Venetian icon for centuries. Tourists pay around 2 Euros per minute to hire one of these craft and be taken on tours of the various canals. Passengers are seated on a forward-facing upholstered transverse bench, whilst the gondolier stands at the rear, skilfully propelling the vessel by means of a single oar. All gondolas are of similar design, around ten metres long and one and a half metres wide, with the front and rear ends clear of the water due to the banana-shape of the hull. A weighted ornament known as a Ferro adorns the prow of each boat and helps to counterbalance the weight of the gondolier at the stern. By tradition all are painted black. In the days when they were used for moving goods around the city, there were several thousand in service, but nowadays the number has dwindled to four hundred or so, entirely devoted to carrying tourists. As a result of the decline, many boatyards closed, and Squero di San Trovaso is one of the few remaining. A group of four low-rise wood and stone buildings are located around three sides of a square, with the canal constituting the fourth side. The yard is a genuine relic of the seventeenth century and is still building and repairing gondolas. Our unannounced visit seemed to be scarcely noticed by the two or three men who were busy working on repairs to a couple of gondolas that stood out of the water on the forecourt. Inside the shed on the south side we found the skeletal structure of a new boat under construction, part-assembled and not yet painted. The yard was heavy with the smell of paint and freshly-cut timber, adding to the artisanal atmosphere, and, as the French say, Squero di San Trovaso certainly merited the detour.

Back by the Grand Canal, we took a vaporetto to the Pieta musical instrument museum, only to find it closed, then returned to the hotel via the local Co-op supermarket.

Venice has never been the sort of city that you can "do" in a couple of days. There is so much more to see than we managed on this brief visit – the glass-making island of Murano, the Rialto Bridge, the Lido, and St Mark's Church, to name but a few. But I find that even a short time in Venice lifts the spirit in a way that no other city can, particularly in winter when there are few tourists around. We'd arrived at dead of night in thick fog after a train journey from hell, and had every right to be unhappy with life. However a journey along the misty but beautiful Grand Canal the following morning had seen any lingering annoyance dissolve like sugar in an espresso coffee. It has long been my belief that doctors could do worse than prescribe a few days in Venice as an alternative to psychotherapy.

The following day we checked out of the hotel and walked in bright sunshine to the railway station, where we boarded the train to Verona, about 120 kilometres to the West. Verona, like dozens of other towns and cities in Italy, merits a lengthy visit to explore its attractions, but all we could do on this occasion was change trains, heading now northwards to Innsbruck in Austria. The railway runs through the Brenner Pass, one of the half-dozen or so major crossing points over the Alps and arguably the most spectacular. The motorway that occasionally runs parallel to the railway is Europe's third-highest, regularly subject to heavy snowfalls and constructed on sometimes impossibly high viaducts and bridges. Our faith in the Italian railway system was completely restored as we sat in the warmth of our compartment, eating a picnic lunch, purchased at the Venice Co-op. Along the way we enjoyed spectacular sunlit views of snow-capped peaks surrounded by forests and fields, all under an impossibly blue sky. At one point I calculated that we were only fifty kilometres or so from Cortina, and I wondered if Francesco and his family were already out on the slopes. At the end of the three-hour journey we exited the train at Innsbruck and headed through occasional snow flurries to our hotel, about half a kilometre away on the far side of the river Inn. The hotel was located at a junction of two busy roads, and access to its entrance was along a worryingly narrow pavement less than a metre wide.

Innsbruck, the capital of the Tyrol area of Austria, is a pleasant enough city of some 130,000 souls, with an economy heavily influenced by its alpine location which makes it an important winter sports centre. It had no involvement in the First World War, but was annexed by the Nazis in World War II and heavily damaged by allied air raids between 1943 and 1945.

There was little time to tour the city that evening, it being dark by 5pm, so after an appropriate dinner of wienerschnitzel and chips at a nearby restaurant we decided to have an early night. The following morning we did, however, have time to take the Hungerburgbahnen funicular-railway up to the tiny village of Hungerburg. At a relatively modest altitude of 860 metres, it is scarcely one of the high points of the Tyrol, but nevertheless provided us with a breathtaking snowscape down towards Innsbruck, and beyond the city to the craggy peaks on the horizon. On our return, we called in at the cathedral, a relatively undistinguished eighteenth century catholic church with excessive, some might even say vulgar, baroque decoration throughout, particularly around the high altar. A service was just ending, so we lingered to catch the final hymn, "In Dulci Jubilo", a pleasant reminder that this was, after all, Christmas time.

The plan for the remainder of the day was somewhat daunting, as we intended to visit a further three countries before dark – Liechtenstein, Switzerland, and Germany, making a total of four in one day. There are no direct trains from Innsbruck to Liechtenstein, so the route to Vaduz, its capital, required a little creative thinking. Back at Innsbruck station we caught a westbound train to Feldkirch, which lies on the Austrian border with Liechtenstein. From there we caught a train going westwards to Buchs in Switzerland, twenty kilometres away, along a railway that actually runs through Liechtenstein but offers only a couple of stops each day at the pricipality's sole station, a small village located North of the capital. The line at one point crosses the upper reaches of the River Rhine, which forms the border between Liechtenstein and Switzerland. From Buchs station it was but a short bus ride to Vaduz. And so it was that we arrived in Liechtenstein on a chilly but bright boxing-day afternoon, thereby achieving our aim of visiting two tax-haven countries in one trip.

Liechtenstein, it has to be said, is not the most exciting place on earth, culturally or politically, but Its alpine location makes it one of the most attractive countries on the Continent. With an area of 160 square kilometres and a population of some 37,000, it is the largest of the four European "tax havens". Originally part of Lower Austria, and later the Holy Roman Empire, Liechtenstein became an independent sovereign state in 1713, but subsequently has always depended to some extent on the various powers ruling the continent from time to time, including the Austro-Hungarian Empire and France under Napoleon. It became a partner in neutrality with Switzerland during the Second World War, and is not a member of the European Union, but is closely linked to it as a member of the Schengen group of countries having no border controls within the Union. Currently closely tied economically to Switzerland, it uses the Swiss Franc as its currency. Vaduz, the capital, is pretty enough, dominated by the Castle wherein the royal family resides, but its population of just over 5,000 souls scarcely make it a bustling metropolis. It has the distinction of being the only European capital without an airport or railway station, and is designated a town rather than a city.

We stayed for an undistinguished hour or so before heading for the small bus station to catch the bus back to Feldkirch, in Austria. There we caught the train to Lindau, in Germany, located some 50 kilometres to the North on the shore of Lake Constance, a popular tourist destination and Central Europe's third-largest lake. Lindau is a small island on the north side of the lake, reached by a joint railway-road causeway, and would have merited further exploration had it not been for the fact that we were heading for our hotel in Friedrichshafen, some 20 kilometres further along the north shore of the lake. It was in any case dark as we boarded this, our final train of the day.

Attached to the modest two-star hotel in Priedrichshafen was a Greek restaurant, at which we again ate Wienerschnitzel and chips, washed down with good German beer, our final meal of the week before heading back to England. The following morning, however, we had one last diversion – a visit to the city's Airship Museum.

Friedrichshafen was the location of the world's first airship factory, established by Ferdinand von Zeppelin at the end of the nineteenth century, in which were produced large numbers of airships for military and civilian use. The most famous was the Hindenberg, whose end was captured on newsreel film when it arrived in New Jersey in 1937 after one of its many crossings of the Atlantic, when it burst into flames as it was mooring. The museum contains a remarkable cut-down replica of the Hindenberg, 33 metres long, showing a section of the balloon, and beneath it the two-storey passenger cabin, complete with bedrooms and dining areas. We were later to climb aboard the twenty-first century successor to the Hindenberg, an Airbus 320 jet aircraft, at Friedrichshafen Airport, for the journey home.

It had been an interesting week, to be sure. We'd visited seven countries, eight if you count England, including two of Europe's four tax havens. We'd visited or travelled through beautiful places, including France's Cote d'Azur, Venice, the Brenner Pass, the Austrian Tyrol, and Lake Constance. We'd met a Television star in his home, and seen the frescoes that gave the world Renaissance Art. It had been surprisingly relaxing, considering we'd travelled a total of over 1,300 kilometres by train and bus, rising to 3,200 kilometres if the flights are included. I recommend it!

Chapter 12

Andorra, France, Spain

In his first three years as a professional golfer, Arnold Palmer's "army" was about as multitudinous as the Andorran Navy **Herbert Warren Wind**

We have the most beautiful planet – the Rockies, the purple fields of the United States, the Lake District, the Pyrenees, the turquoise seas of the tropics **Dan Ackroyd**

Watching A380 airliners being built. Christmas–day walk along the *Canal du Midi*. Peeing in a *pissoir*. The world's largest brick-built cathedral. Racy stuff at the Toulouse-Lautrec museum. Frites and mulled wine for Christmas dinner. Shortest ever visit to a country – Andorra.

Andorra, one of the four "tax havens" in Europe, is perhaps the most inaccessible by public transport, and arguably the least interesting culturally. It is, however, located high in the snow-capped Pyrenees, that natural granite barrier between Spain and France, which gives it the edge over the other three for anyone seeking magnificent scenery. As the French say, it certainly does merit the detour. However, if you are not a winter sports enthusiast, or a summer walker along *Grand Randonnee 10* in France, the 866 kilometre footpath running the full length of the Pyrenees, you will probably be happy to settle for a few hours, or at most a day or so, in the capital, Andorra la Vella. Away from Andorra there are interesting places to visit on both sides of this natural border between France and Spain, but the French side, for me, seems to offer more in the way of culture and history. I have to admit, however, to being biased, having lived and worked in France. The aim of the trip, therefore, was to visit some of the French towns and cities in the region, and allocate a day or two to visit Andorra. This was to be over yet another Christmas-holiday period, as I was then working full-time and needed to make the most of my Christmas leave.

After checking suitable budget airline destinations, my partner and I decided to head for Girona, in Spain, at the foot of the Pyrenees and about 80 kilometres from the border with France, A pleasant enough place and a major Catalan city, it boasts a magnificent cathedral which we were to visit on our return later in the week. On arrival there, however, we simply settled into a hotel for the night and the following morning took a short walk to the railway station in the pale winter sunshine, and headed for Toulouse in France. At Cerbere station, just over the border in France, we were obliged to change trains, due to the change of track gauge. French trains run on tracks 4 feet 8 ½ inches apart, some 9 ½ inches narrower than those in Spain, which at the time meant there were no through trains between the two countries.. More recently, however, the French-gauge line has been extended all the way through to Girona and ultimately Barcelona, rendering the change of trains at Cerbere unnecessary and thereby probably greatly reducing the level of business at the cafe on the platform! The line continues to be a vital rail link, particularly for freight, between Spain and the rest of Europe.

By mid afternoon we'd arrived in Toulouse, the capital city of the French *Departement* of Haut-Garonne, and the fourth-largest city in France after Paris, Lyon, and Marseille. Whilst it would prove a convenient place from which to explore the region, we were aware that it was still 180 mountainous kilometres away from our principal destination, Andorra. Toulouse is situated on the Garonne River, and the city is bisected by the Canal du Midi which links Bordeaux on the Atlantic Ocean with the town of Sete on the Mediterranean Sea. It is perhaps best known nowadays as the centre of the European aerospace industry, with the local *Airbus Industrie* factory employing over 21,000 workers. Later in the week we were to visit the site to see A380 airliners being assembled, at the same location that saw the first Concorde supersonic airliner make its maiden flight in March 1969. Architecturally, the older parts of the city are largely constructed from pinkish terracotta bricks, earning it the nickname "La Ville en Rose". It is perhaps best known artistically for its links with Henri de Toulouse-Lautrec, the post-impressionist artist, whose father, Count Alfonse Charles de Toulouse-Lautrec, headed one of the city's best-known aristocratic families.

Once installed in our fifth-floor hotel room we took in the view from the window across the moored boats on the Canal du Midi, beyond which stood the magnificent station building, built in 1905 and typical of the grandiose railway architecture of the period. Rather less imposing were the couple of tramps on the bench immediately below, apparently arguing over the ownership of a half-full wine bottle, the action being viewed with disinterested boredom by a couple of feral dogs.

Taking a stroll around the neighbourhood, just inside the city centre, we were delighted to come across a Lidl supermarket, where we bought food for a picnic dinner in the room that evening, and breakfast the following morning. We then briefly popped into Galeries Lafayette, a somewhat provincial and much-reduced version of the famous store on Boulevard Haussman in Paris, but still a handsome art nouveau building for all that. On the way back I called in at the club shop of Stade Toulousain, better known as Toulouse Rugby, arguably the most successful Rugby-Union club in the world and involved in some close encounters with my own club, Saracens, over the years. Later, back at the hotel, we watched "The Lion, the Witch, and the Wardrobe" on the TV in our room, in English with French subtitles. Not exactly first-choice viewing as far as I was concerned, but in continental European hotel rooms you have to take whatever you can get TV-wise.

The following morning we were booked in for a tour of the Airbus factory, located outside the main part of the city and not far from the airport, at 10:20am. Our plan was to take the bus to the airport, located to the north of the city, then take a taxi for the short ride from there to the Airbus visitor centre. A mistake in timing, however, meant we ended up taking a taxi all the way from the hotel to the factory, at a cost of 20 Euros, which was not a great start to the day. At the time, Airbus Industrie had four different aircraft types under construction, but we were specifically heading for the assembly shop for the Airbus A380, at the time a brand-new and in many ways revolutionary double-deck aircraft able to take up to 540 passengers on any existing long-haul route. Following the prototype plane's maiden flight in April 2005 there had been major production problems during the four succeeding years, meaning that we were to see some of the very earliest to be built.

After meeting up with the other tour participants at the visitor centre, which adjoined a small souvenir shop selling high-priced Airbus and Concorde memorabilia, we attended an interesting video presentation on the A380's history, followed by a visit to a flight simulator room to see video footage of the first A380's maiden flight. We then followed our guide over to the huge assembly building, which we were informed covers an area the size of 300 tennis courts within the 55 hectares devoted exclusively to the A380. Once inside, we took a lift up to a high walkway, from which we were able to view the entire assembly area. Side by side below us on the shop floor were three planes, two for Air France and one for Lufthansa, in the final stages of construction, the nearest looking more or less ready to fly. I was particularly struck by the cathedral-like silence in the building, broken occasionally by the sound of this or that power tool, and mentioned to the guide that I was somewhat surprised by the relatively small number of workers around the place. "C'est normal." he said, smiling. The statistics for the A380 (nicknamed the "Super Jumbo") are mind-boggling. With a wingspan of 80 metres, the length of a football pitch, a fuel capacity of 720,000 litres, and a maximum take-off weight of 575 tonnes, it is the largest airliner ever built, needing a 22-wheel undercarriage. Three hundred miles of cabling are used in its double-decker construction. Our guide explained that the wings are manufactured in England and flown in using specially adapted freight aircraft, pointing out one of these on the airfield outside. Known as "Belugas" (a kind of whale) in France, they are somewhat irreverently referred to as "Pregnant Guppies" in England. They look like any normal freight aircraft but with a fuselage twice the usual height. Other major structural parts of the plane are built in Spain, Germany, and elsewhere in France, making the Toulouse plant very much an assembly operation rather than building from scratch. Outside the plant were four completed aircraft, identifiable from the tailplanes as being destined for Emirates, Air France, and Quantas airlines. Back in the office we were taken to a large indoor area containing a two-storey mock-up of seat layouts, giving us the rare opportunity to try out some very comfortable first-class sleeper-seats. At the end of what had been a fascinating tour, we reduced the return cost by sharing a taxi back into town with another couple. As an aside, the City has since opened a tram line which links the city centre with a point just over a kilometre's walk from the visitor centre, the fare for which is not much more than a tenth of the cost of our taxi ride.

Back at the busy station ticket office we were obliged to join a long queue to get tickets for Albi, a small city of some 50,000 souls around 85 kilometres North West of Toulouse. There were two reasons for visiting this relatively obscure little corner of South-West France. The city is dominated by its imposing thirteenth-century cathedral, located on a hill, which, along with the cluster of buildings surrounding it, is constructed from that most unclerical of building materials, red brick. It is claimed to be the largest brick building in the world, and its design is perfectly defined by that rarest of architectural styles, "Brick Gothic". Adjacent to it is the old Bishop's Palace, also built in the thirteenth century out of brick, and home to the Museum dedicated to the works of Henri de Toulouse-Lautrec, who was born nearby. Many of his most famous post-impressionist paintings, often depicting the seamier side of life in late-nineteenth century Paris, are to be found there.

Walking northwards from Albi station, along a gently rising road, the horizon was dominated by the huge cathedral and its surrounding buildings, a brown-pink extravaganza, lit by a yellow afternoon sun and set against a pale blue sky. For a moment I was reminded of the cathedrals at Lincoln or Ely in England, which similarly dominate their surroundings, but by contrast are constructed from dour, discoloured grey stone. Originally built as a fortress, Albi cathedral is also unique in that there is scarcely a right-angle to be seen externally, all vertical edges and buttresses being curved. Inside we found the usual baroque extravagance in the decoration, albeit slightly less overpowering than in many Roman Catholic cathedrals. We spent several minutes inside studying a wonderful mural of the Last Judgement, sixteen Metres square and dating from around 1480. It was painted by Flemish contemporaries of Hieronymus Bosch, and there is much in it that is reminiscent of his weird and often disturbing works. On the right hand side of it are graphic scenes of the hellish fate that awaits non-believers, whilst on the left side blessed believers are shown entering the gates of heaven. I wondered for a moment if this was some sort of allegorical reference to political allegiance. If so, I must happily conclude that paradise awaits me on the other side.

Time was passing and we headed for the Toulouse-Lautrec Museum, with a brief diversion to the windswept gardens overlooking the broad sweep of the river Tarn, which runs through the city and past the Cathedral's West end. Inside the museum we found some of the master's best-known works, most of which were donated by his mother after his death in 1901. Fin de Siecle Montmartre paintings, many showing scenes in clubs, bars, and bordellos, are displayed alongside posters for Parisian events of the period, and there are fine examples of his early less well-known studies. Galleries around the world pay particular homage to the Impressionists and Post-Impressionists, but few collections capture the authentic atmosphere of late nineteenth century life in Paris better than the Toulouse-Lautrec Museum.

Outside, in the fading daylight, and chilled by the easterly wind, we walked down to an open-air ice-rink and then on to a nearby square offering a small Christmas market. The highlight here was seeing Father Christmas on walkabout amongst the stalls, greeting often-apprehensive children with a smile and a hug. His credibility was somewhat marred, however, by the fact that Santa's Little Helper, clad in a traditional green costume, and sporting a Robin Hood hat, looked to be at least fifty years old. No purchases having been made, and with no gifts from Santa, we headed back to the station and boarded the train back to Toulouse.

The following day was meant to be the climax to the week, a couple of days in Andorra, one of Europe's four independent tax-haven states and a major winter sports venue. Sadly it has no railway, but we initially looked at getting there by taking the train to L'Hospitalet Pres l'Andorre, high in the Pyrenees but with a very restricted service, and from there onwards by bus for the final 40 kilometres or so to the capital, Andorra la Vella. Timetable complexities, however, meant that it would be difficult to get there and back at times that suited us, so we opted for the simpler but far less interesting option of going by road, a distance of 180 kilometres, direct from Toulouse.

The day dawned chilly but bright, a good omen for a road journey into the high Pyrenees. Over at the bus station we bought tickets and headed to bay 15, expecting to find a touring-style coach waiting, but instead there was a 20-seat minibus, its door open and the driver ready to depart. The journey through the Toulouse suburbs was unexceptional, save for a glimpse of the recently renovated Stade Ernest-Wallon, home ground of the Toulouse rugby team, as we headed east down the motorway towards Narbonne and the Mediterranean. After 20 kilometres or so we turned South, and half an hour later entered the foothills of the Pyrenees, stopping at Pamiers, a small town best known as the birthplace of Gabriel Faure, the composer. Thereafter, occasional evidence of local sympathy with Basque nationalism began to appear, in the form of the red, green and white Basque flag, displayed outside houses that also traditionally boast red window shutters, the householder's way of showing solidarity with the cause. Whilst not a major Basque area – generally defined as being further north on the French side of the Pyrenees, and of course over in Northern Spain – there is sympathy with the separatists throughout much of the Pyrenees region.

We now entered the foothills and began the long climb to L'Hospitalet Pres l'Andorre, effectively the border post, located around 40 kilometres from the capital, Andorra la Vella. Almost immediately the driver was obliged to switch on the windscreen wipers as spots of rain began to appear, and by the time we'd crossed the border we were travelling through what could only be described as a cloudburst. Recent deep snow by the roadside was being instantly transformed into muddy slush, and at times the spray from overtaking cars and trucks made the journey seem like a white-water rafting expedition. On either side of the road, through the rain-spattered windows we could make out little more than duty-free shops, ski lifts and hotels, evidence of the country's popularity as a winter sports venue. The capital, Andorra la Vella, appeared unremarkable as the driver navigated us through streets running with torrents of water, and it was with some relief that we finally pulled into the tiny bus station.

Needing to find lunch, I left my partner in the bus station and walked in the driving rain down to the busy main road to seek out takeaway food. Burger King beckoned on the far side, but at that point the road had become a small lake and i was obliged to wait until there was a long gap in the traffic both ways to avoid being drenched by the spray from any passing car. It being lunch-time, there was the usual queue at the counter, but I eventually got back to the bus station and we took a seat whilst we ate and discussed our options. We'd booked a hotel, but the prospect of tramping the streets searching for it didn't fill us with joy. It was then that we discovered that the bus service back to Toulouse was cancelled for the following day, Christmas day. Having achieved the principal objective of actually getting to Andorra, we quickly came to the conclusion that without an improvement in the weather we might just as well go back to Toulouse straight away. A quick check of the timetable suggested the next bus, due to depart in ten minutes, was a possibility, and it turned out to be the same bus on which we'd arrived. We quickly bought tickets and climbed aboard,

The return journey proved uneventful other than the fact that we had a cat in a basket as a fellow-passenger. Its owner set it down on the seat beside her, and politely asked us and the half-dozen or so other passengers if we minded travelling with a cat, which, of course, we didn't. I wondered idly if it had been charged the full adult fare. Once we'd left the mountains behind, the rain ceased and the sun emerged. Back at the hotel we found our room had been taken, as we'd checked out that morning, but we were directed to another hotel further along the road which proved acceptable.

And so it was that Andorra claimed that coveted first place in the list of my shortest-ever visits to a European country, beating the likes of Bosnia, Monaco, and Liechtenstein. Looking back on it, I'm not sure that it would have been the most interesting place in which to spend a couple of days, but I would very much like to return for a day or so, preferably during the summer, as the majestic Pyrenees, snow capped all the year round, are as spectacular as the Alps, and the lower slopes have the advantage of a Mediterranean climate.

The following day, Christmas-day, we discussed how to best to spend this unexpected bonus of a "free" day over a breakfast of coffee and Madeleine cakes at the hotel. No more than 50 meters away lay the Canal du Midi, inviting us to take a Christmas-day canal-side walk in the bright but chilly morning air. Crossing over to it, we passed the tramps on the bench, who appeared to be sleeping off what had presumably been the previous night's excesses. Turning left along the towpath, we headed in a generally westward direction, the canal at that point running between tree-lined streets on either side.

The Canal du Midi, 241 kilometres long and constructed between 1666 and 1681, is one of Europe's oldest, predating the Grand Union Canal (or, more accurately, the Grand Junction Canal) in England by some 115 years. It is in fact made up of three sections, one of which is the navigable part of the river Garonne, west of Toulouse, and strictly speaking the name "Canal du Midi" refers only to the section from Toulouse Eastwards to the Mediterranean. No matter how it may be defined, it is a navigable waterway linking Bordeaux on the Atlantic Ocean with the Etang de Thau, a seawater lake on the Mediterranean Sea. Fans of Rick Stein, the celebrity chef, may have seen his series of British television programmes showing his voyage by canal boat from one end to the other, sampling and cooking local food along the way.

The three-kilometre walk took us as far as the broad basin that is the junction with the canalised portion of the Garonne River, on which dozens of houseboats were moored. The basin has historic significance as it is effectively the start of the original canal, and at one time boasted a lock at the far end giving direct access to the Garonne. Sadly, this was closed when the city's ring-road was built, and access to the river is now via a lock some 80 kilometres North via the aforementioned Garonne Canal. Returning towards the city centre, and feeling smugly satisfied that we'd walked at least 1% of the entire length of the canal, we found the metro station aptly named "Canal du Midi" and took the train to the city centre in order to look around the Cathedral, but were astonished to find it firmly locked, something of a shock given that it was Christmas day. Our disappointment was somewhat alleviated when we found a stall in the nearby Christmas market that sold delicious *frites*. As a Christmas dinner it wasn't quite what they were having back home, but at least there were no Brussels sprouts.

After a brief walk round the crowded market, during which we were again unable to resist the mulled wine, we walked over to the Capitol, a handsome neoclassical edifice in pink brick, uncannily similar in design to Buckingham Palace in London. Originally the administrative centre of the city, it is nowadays open to the public, and houses spectacular murals, covering almost every wall inside, relating to events in the city's history,. From there we walked the half-kilometre or so down to the bridge over the Garonne River, on the way to which we happened upon a rare example of that most nostalgic of French street furniture, a *pissoir,* constructed according to the traditional design, but built of concrete rather than the more common green-painted steel. I decided it would be sacrilege not to make use of it, and as I stood inside, looking out over the wall at the busy street scene beyond, I remembered the first one I'd ever patronised some 40 years previously in Boulevard de Clichy in Paris.

The elegant Garonne, almost 100 metres wide at this point, is bordered by walkways and grassy areas down at river level, backed by high brick walls, beyond which ranks of plane trees at road level conceal all but the roofs of the buildings behind. It is evidently a favourite place for an afternoon stroll, judging by the number of people out enjoying the late sun, and after crossing the bridge we found a crowded metro station where we took the train back to the hotel

And so ended a Christmas day that had been anything but traditional. Whilst those back home had been enjoying roast turkey and Christmas pudding, we'd enjoyed frites and mulled wine. We'd avoided the questionable delights of the Queen's message to the nation followed by endless pre-recorded "TV specials" that were anything but special. Yes, of course, we'd missed not seeing our families, bit on the whole I think it was a good day and wouldn't hesitate to do it again.

The following morning, Boxing Day, we checked out of the hotel early as we intended to go on to Perpignan, 200 kilometres to the South-East and close to the shores of the Mediterranean. However we had yet to visit Toulouse's main art gallery, the Musee des Augustines, so we left our bags with the hotel reception and paid it a visit. A pleasant cloistered brick building, constructed in the fourteenth century, and with aspects of its design reminiscent of the Cathedral at Albi, it was originally a convent, but was seized after the revolution and converted to a museum specialising in French art. Very much a second-division collection, it does however contains an interesting group of paintings from the impressionist school, the highlight of which is a work by Berthe Morisot, one of the three female member of that group. The inevitable Henri de Toulouse-Lautrec is also well-represented. On the way back to the hotel we called in at the cathedral and yet again found it locked, so we collected our luggage and boarded the train for Narbonne, where we were to change for Perpignan.

The rain began soon after we left the Toulouse suburbs behind, and it was still raining when we booked into the hotel in Perpignan. As we were in urgent need of food and drink, we took a brief walk around the block, chilled by a freshening wind that was thankfully serving to disperse the rain clouds, revealing a clear, starlit sky. We returned to our room laden with cheese, ham, potato salad, bread, Madeleine cakes, and beer from the local convenience store and settled down in front of the television to enjoy Nick Park's "Chicken Run", thankfully broadcast in English with French subtitles.

The next day we were to return to Spain by train, but at the station that morning we were told there was a rail strike, meaning that the earliest train we could get to the border at Cerbere was due to leave just before six o'clock that evening. There was, however, a bus leaving at 2:30, which would take us direct to Girona Airport in Spain, and from there we could get to the hotel in Girona that we'd reserved for the night. We therefore returned to the hotel, left our cases at reception and set out in bright sunshine to explore the delights of Perpignan. A pleasant but unremarkable city of 120,000 souls, it was established in Roman times, and in the fourteenth century was ruled from Aragon, in what is present-day Spain. it was eventually ceded to France in 1659, and is a major city in the Catalan region, which straddles the border between both countries. Many of its street signs are in both French and Catalan languages, and the city still celebrates historical links with Mallorca in Spain.

Not far from the hotel we found La Bassa, a pretty canalised stream with broad walkways on either side leading to a park, through the centre of which ran a long footpath path between heavily pollarded plane trees. I must admit I am yet to understand the French obsession for pollarding, particularly in hot Mediterranean regions where shade afforded by such trees in their natural state must surely be desirable. Towards the end the trees gave way to an open area, wherein lay the Fontaine de Perpignan, a circular area about ten metres across, within which were multiple water-jets located inside stainless-steel metal sculptures of flowers. Inactive when we arrived, the fountain suddenly burst into life and for five minutes or so went on to provide a complex display using ever-changing groups of jets, then just as suddenly lapsed back into inactivity. We took a seat nearby and watched the delighted reaction of children when they were suddenly confronted with the start of the show.

We were not in an immediate hurry to get anywhere in particular, and the sun was shining, so we spent quite a while there, eating our picnic lunch and watching the world go by. Eventually we headed back to the hotel, picked up our luggage, and returned to the station to get the Girona Airport bus. At 4pm we disembarked at Gerona Airport, took the bus into the city, and by 5pm were installed in our hotel.

Girona, a fascinating city of 100,000 souls, is much more than a simple budget-airline destination, but inevitably gets overlooked by most of those who simply pass through the airport on their way to the fleshpots of nearby Barcelona. Bisected by the River Onyar, running North-South through the centre, and less than 100 kilometres from the Pyrenees and the French border, Girona's location has led to it being invaded many times in its 1,300-year history. After being seized during the Napoleonic wars it even became a French city between 1809 and 1813, but was returned to Spain thereafter. Given that we had little time to check it out, we left the hotel whilst it was still daylight and headed for the Cathedral, about a kilometre away but up a very steep hill. The walk required us to pass by the river, which at that point flows between terraces of ancient five-storey apartment blocks that front directly onto it, there being no space between them and the river. This unusual arrangement is similar to that in Venice, except that in this case the foundations are concrete rather than wood. Many of these buildings are attractively painted in pink or orange, giving a pleasing panorama from the bridge at the southern end. We walked along the parallel road, and found our way through to the second of five bridges in that section of the river. This particular bridge, made of iron and for pedestrian use only, has the distinction having been designed by Gustav Eiffel, designer of the Eiffel Tower and builder of the Statue of Liberty. Having already come across examples of his work a couple of times in my travels, in Romania and Moldova, I concluded that Monsieur Eiffel had obviously been a well-travelled man during his lifetime!

In a freshening chill wind, as darkness began to descend, our walk continued upwards through the narrow cobbled streets of the old city, taking us past a church in which a service, attended by a meagre congregation of no more than half-a-dozen worshippers, was in progress. Eventually we arrived at the broad and daunting flight of ninety or so steps leading to the Cathedral entrance, and wearily tackled the climb, wondering how the weak and disabled could ever attend services there. As we climbed, the Cathedral doors opened and crowds of people emerged, most dressed in what could only be described as their Sunday best, the men in suits and many of the women sporting fur coats. Inside there were hundreds more worshippers, some chatting to the many assembled church dignitaries by the altar, others standing around in groups, possibly discussing what had presumably been an important church event . Unfazed by this, we boldly entered and walked around.

The vast Gothic nave is the widest of its kind in the world, and the second widest nave of all styles after St Peter's Basilica in Rome. The relative lack of baroque frippery gives the interior a somewhat Anglican feel, with clean vertical lines leading the eye upwards towards Gothic arches and rib-vaulted ceilings. Some of the side-chapels, however, more than make up for this, with the Chapel of Saint Andrew being possibly the worst, displaying wall-to-wall gilt statues, plaster mouldings, and paintings. By the time we'd finished our tour most of the congregation had departed, and we retraced our steps back down to the hotel, determined to return the following morning to see the building and its surroundings in daylight. On the way back we called in at the crowded craft market in the main square, but failed to make any significant purchases. The relatively rare sight of an Indian restaurant abroad always gladdens the heart, and the one just down the road from the hotel was no exception. There we shared a hot chicken madras and a medium chicken biryani in what was our valedictory meal at the end of what had been an unexpectedly busy week of travel.

Back at the hotel we made the best of our second-floor room, trying to ignore the traffic noise from the busy street below, and the worrying musty smell emanating from the bathroom. The following morning we checked out and left our luggage at reception, aiming to return to the Cathedral and its ninety steps via the Eiffel Bridge. On the way we visited the Arab Baths, dating from the 11th century and a relic of Spain's Moorish past, and then spent half an hour or so, under a cloudy sky, taking in the spectacular views from the cathedral grounds, as far as the distant Mediterranean. The Pyrenees, sadly, were too remote to be clearly seen. Back in the main shopping street we ate a picnic lunch of baguettes and satsumas, sitting on a bench, surrounded by mendicant pigeons, and afterwards we retrieved our luggage from the hotel and were soon on the bus to the airport to catch our 5pm flight home.

It had been a strange sort of week. Originally principally intended as a visit to Andorra, that objective was scarcely achieved, but on the plus side we'd seen A380 aircraft being built, visited a couple of unique European cathedrals, and toured fascinating cities that are to some extent off the tourist trail on either side of the Pyrenees. I was left hoping that a planned visit to San Marino, the last of the tax havens, would be equally enjoyable.

Chapter 13

The Czech Republic

The ancient splendour and beauty of Prague, a city beyond compare, left an impression on my imagination that will never fade **Richard Wagner**

Tesco store 1,000 kilometres from home. Fried carp for Christmas dinner. Visit to home of Kafka. Dvorak museum, and Mozart's non-home. Palindromic number on the bridge.

The Czech Republic was born on January 1st, 1993, following the division of Czechoslovakia into two independent countries, the other being Slovakia. Czechoslovakia was originally created in 1918 following the demise of the Austro-Hungarian Empire, and after being occupied by the Germans during the Second World War became a communist state under the control of the Soviet Union. It joined the European Union in 2004, as did Slovakia, and has open borders under the EU Schengen agreement. The country has yet to satisfy EU requirements necessary for it to join the Eurozone, and continues to use the Koruna as its currency.

Prague, the capital, is the fourteenth largest city in the European Union, with a population of around 1.3 million, and is the fifth most-visited European city after London, Paris, Istanbul, and Rome. At one time or another the home of Mozart, Janacek, Kafka, Dvorak, and Smetana, the city gained world attention in spring 1968 when the then leader, Alexander Dubcek, backed by huge numbers of peaceful protesters, attempted to loosen the ties of Soviet domination. There followed a coordinated and uncompromising invasion by other Warsaw-pact countries which saw the attempt fail.

My visit to Prague, again with my partner, took place over the Christmas period, shortly after the country had joined the European Union. On this occasion we decided to stay in one place for the duration of the holiday, rather than travel around the country, thus avoiding the sometimes irksome moves from one hotel to another, and the resulting dependence on train and bus timetables.

The flight from London Stansted airport was uneventful, and at Prague Airport we obtained currency from a cash machine, then purchased seven-day passes for buses, trams, and the Metro, a bargain at 250 koruna, equivalent to about £7.50 at today's exchange rate. From the airport we took the 119 bus which serves the city centre, changed onto the Metro, and alighted at Vitavska, just north of the city centre. The hotel, a chilly five minute walk from the station, occupies the upper floors of a substantial five-storey block, with a couple of public restaurants at street level. We quickly checked in and installed ourselves in the somewhat cramped but peaceful fourth-floor room, then headed back out to the Metro station and travelled to the unimaginatively-named Municipal House in the city centre.

One of the city's Art Nouveau architectural gems, The Municipal House was built in 1912 and consists of a symphony concert hall with attached restaurant and cafe. Imagine if you will a substantial three-storey corner building in light-coloured stone, with tall arched windows on the first floor fronted by balconies of classic Nouveau ironwork. The entrance doors, set at an angle across the corner of the building, are guarded by two ornate freestanding columns, reaching as high as the top of the first-floor windows, and topped with illuminated glass globes. Elaborate ironwork surrounds this part of the frontage, paying homage to Guimard's metro-station entrances in Paris, and at third floor level the ironwork gives way to a broad stone arch which frames a large mural, the whole being topped by a green-painted dome. The Municipal House is a remarkable building which in my opinion is alone almost worth the price of the airfare to Prague.

We'd hoped we could get seats for a concert that evening in the concert hall, but sadly the only ones available cost 800 Koruna, too much for our budget, so we instead installed ourselves in the restaurant and ordered goulash, beer, and Ice cream in what, in my opinion, is one of the most attractive places to dine anywhere in Europe. The Art Nouveau theme is maintained here, but with the occasional hint of Eastern Europe and even a little bit of Art Deco, and for a moment I imagined how the place must have appeared when frequented by the city's gentry during the latter days of the Austro-Hungarian Empire. The present-day clientele, well- dressed and impeccably behaved, suggested that the place was still one of the must-eat places for the Prague elite. It was a perfect introduction to the city on our first night, and we were only sorry to have missed out on the concert.

The following day dawned bright but cold, and by way of contrast with the previous evening we decided to see how life compared in the less salubrious parts of the city, taking the train out to a small suburb chosen at random. We arrived at an industrial area, dotted with sometimes derelict industrial buildings, interspersed with small nineteenth century cottages and the occasional high-rise Soviet-style block of flats. It was a reminder that, fifteen years on from the country's independence, the Czech economy was still recovering from the years of under-investment when subjected to Soviet control. We called in at a small family-run cafe with Formica-topped tables and had coffee costing 26 Koruna, not much more than 50p. Workmen were eating breakfast, some already having their first beer of the day.

Back at the main railway station, Praha Hlavni Nadrazi, we took time to view some of its magnificent Art Nouveau decoration. It is perhaps known in the UK as the starting point from which Sir Nicholas Winton, later to be named by the press as the "British Schindler", arranged the transportation by rail of large numbers of children, mainly Jewish, to England on the eve of World War II. One of those rescued was a six year-old Alf Dubs, who became a Labour MP and was ennobled in 1994 as Baron Dubs. He continues to promote the cause of migrant children into the UK from his position as a member of the House of Lords.

From the station we walked the few hundred metres to one of the first Tesco supermarkets to be built outside the UK, and were surprised to find it full of familiar own-brand products identical to those in our local store back home. Today there are seventeen Tesco shops in the city.

It was Christmas Eve, for the Czechs the most important day of the holiday period, and the day when they traditionally eat Christmas dinner, usually as an evening meal. Anxious to participate in this, we returned to the hotel and later headed out by metro to The Old Town Square, a classic eastern European square paved with granite setts and surrounded by elaborately ornamented houses, once owned by the city's wealthy merchants. Its principal attraction, however, is the astronomical clock on the wall of the old town hall, installed in 1410 and the oldest still working in the world. Consisting of two circular dials, one above the other, and each around three metres in diameter, it shows at any one time the current positions of the sun, moon, and zodiacal stars. Little was known about the movements of the visible planets at the time it was constructed, so these were excluded. Above the dials are animated figures, the best known of which is a skeleton, that emerge and move every hour on the hour.

As we arrived, the Christmas market was in full swing, so we took the opportunity to sample mulled wine and mingle in the chilly night air with the locals, Afterwards we sought the warmth and comfort of The Franz Kafka restaurant nearby, which was serving a traditional Czech Christmas dinner. Located in the converted ground floor of one of the houses on the square, it was already busy even though it was still relatively early in the evening, but we found a table and enjoyed fish soup, followed by fried carp, accompanied by a salad containing potatoes, hard-boiled egg, pickled gherkins, carrots, and onions. To follow we were served a plate of Czech sweetmeats, all washed down with the Czech Republic's best-known export, Budweiser beer. Compared with other Christmas dinners I'd had on my travels – frites, McDonald's hamburgers, and doner kebabs, to name but a few – I concluded that a proper meal at Christmas-time has a lot going for it.

Back outside, under a clear sky and almost full moon, a choir was performing the haunting 1796 Czech Christmas Mass by the Czech composer Jacub Jan Ryba, providing a fitting end to what had been a memorable Christmas Eve. Trains on the Metro were by then crowded, and few and far between, but we eventually got back to the hotel around eleven-thirty after a thoroughly enjoyable day.

Christmas day dawned sunny but cold, and after breakfast we took the tram westwards over the river Vitava for a kilometre or so towards the suburb of Ujezd, situated on the edge of parkland, from where we took the funicular railway up the steep hill to the Petrin lookout tower, a well-known landmark visible from most vantage points in Prague and reminiscent of the Eiffel Tower in Paris. The resemblance is no coincidence, it being constructed after a visit by the members of the Czech tourist club to the 1889 Paris World Expo. On their return, they decided to erect something similar in Prague. The resulting tower is, however, one-fifth the height of the Eiffel Tower and octagonal rather than square in cross-section. It has always fulfilled its purpose in providing a wonderful platform from which to take in the view over the city, and on this particularly clear day we could see beyond the surrounding countryside as far as the distant extinct volcanoes that stand like sentinels on the horizon. At the base of the tower we drank Nescafe at a small wooden cafe, and joined the other half-dozen or so well-clad visitors in the outdoor seating area. After the bustle of the city-centre, it made a pleasant change to be able to sit in the pale winter sunlight and simply enjoy the silence. A blackbird arrived and, from its perch on the birch tree not twenty metres away, went through an extensive repertoire of birdsong before moving on.

Rather than returning by the funicular railway, we decided instead that a stroll down the winding path through the wooded slopes would be rather pleasant, and back at the main road we took the tram along the West side of the river to St. Vitus Cathedral, more correctly known as The Metropolitan Cathedral of Saints Vitus, Wenceslaus and Adalbert. Classically gothic with splendid flying buttresses, its construction began in 1344 but it stood half-finished for almost 600 years or so due to a number of problems, and was finally completed in 1929. Inside, it wears its baroque decoration lightly, but in common with many Eastern European Roman Catholic churches this is more than made up for by the gilt excesses of some of the chapels.

The Cathedral is located within the walls of Prague Castle, a huge fortress dominating the North-West skyline of the city, and a major stop on the tourist trail. In the Guinness Book of World Records it is listed as the largest ancient castle in the world, covering 70,000 square metres. I'm afraid, however, that I feel about castles much the same way I feel about waterfalls – once you've seen one you've pretty well seen them all. As a result, we didn't linger to do the full tour, but were pleased to find a pleasant cafe serving mulled wine which we drank outside in the sun. Wispy cirrus clouds were gathering, normally a sign of an impending change in the weather, but it was still very pleasant sitting and watching the world go by. As we were leaving, we passed by Golden Lane, an interesting and brightly-coloured row of artisans' cottages situated within the castle complex. Whilst of ancient appearance, the cottages were heavily restored in the mid-twentieth century, and it is difficult to be precise about the proportion of each that is truly ancient. Franz Kafka, the writer, lived at number 22 during 1916 and 1917, and number 20 is believed to be largely unchanged since the sixteenth century. After calling in at the castle's toy museum we left and took the tram back to the hotel .

As it was Christmas day evening we decided to return to the Old Town Square in the hope there were festive activities going on, and found a small choir, mainly girls, in national dress singing Christmas carols, and further on couple of itinerant musicians. A stand-up cafe provided a meal of a frankfurter-style hot-dog and chicken with noodles, after which we decided to return to the Municipal House for coffee and dessert. Not quite a traditional Christmas day menu, but any day that ends with a visit to Prague's Municipal House Restaurant is guaranteed to be memorable.

The following day, Boxing day, started with delicious scrambled egg on toast in the breakfast bar at the hotel, and, thus fortified, we walked the three hundred metres or so in pouring rain that had been presaged by the previous day's cirrus clouds, to the National Gallery at Veletrzini Palace, to be confronted by a somewhat unexciting 1928 building, architecturally categorised as "Functionalist", and looking like nothing more than a seven-storey office block, anything but a palace in the regal sense of the word. Inside, however, it is stunning, with a magnificent central atrium rising to rooftop level and overlooked by balconies on each floor that provide access to the exhibits. Those who think atria are an invention of late-twentieth century office and hotel architects should think again! The art collection was always interesting, concentrating as it does on international modern art, with all the acknowledged masters of the period represented, including a section devoted to modern and contemporary Czech artists. The impressionists and Post-Impressionists were reasonably well catered for, but in a slightly second-division sort of way. Sadly the bookshop had no guidebooks relating to Czech art, so there was no possibility of learning more after the visit.

Outside we took the number twelve tram to the Mozart museum, known as Bertramka, a beautiful two-storey pantiled villa set in pleasant parkland over on the West side of the river Vitava and supposedly where the great man lived during two or three of his five brief visits to Prague over the period 1787 to 1791. Sadly, there is little hard evidence that he did actually live there, although there is some evidence that he visited the owners from time to time. Some who visit the museum will, however, return home and tell their families, authoritatively, that they "visited the house where Mozart lived". I was reminded of the case of Tintagel, in Cornwall, England, whose entire tourist industry is based on two historical creations, King Arthur and Merlin the Magician. The truth is that they are simply the stuff of legends created centuries ago, and almost certainly never existed, but I'd wager this isn't always made clear to Tintagel's tourist throng. In the case of Mozart, we are told that at the very least he regularly called at Bertramka, but there is no reliable evidence of even this, let alone that he actually stayed there as alleged by some sources. The villa is located well outside the eighteenth-century city walls, which would have required him to commute daily to his work in the city centre, an irksome and possibly dangerous journey in those days. There is, however ample evidence that he lived in at least two locations *within* the city walls.

Controversy aside, however, Bertramka does contain a pleasant enough museum with some artefacts connected with the master, and there is a cafe where we enjoyed acceptable beer and cake. After a brief tour we headed back in pouring rain to the tram to continue the musical theme with a visit to the Dvorak museum, located on a quiet street near the city centre, and backing onto parkland. The museum is a handsome converted detached two-storey town house, with a baroque facade in pink and cream. Dvorak is known not to have lived there, but it is an important repository for manuscripts and correspondence, and contains his viola and piano.

We spent an enjoyable half-hour or so looking around, afterwards taking the tram in pouring rain to Wenceslas Square, arguably the Prague equivalent of Trafalgar Square in London, having been a focal point for political protest and national celebration over the years. It is in fact a wide tree-lined boulevard rather than a square, and is named after Saint Wenceslas, patron saint of Bohemia, who is the subject of the Christmas carol "Good King Wenceslas". The square was famously the location of peaceful protests during the 1968 "Prague Spring" when the city was invaded by Warsaw Pact allies to neutralise growing anti – USSR sentiment at the time. There were further protests in the square in1989 which led to the "Velvet Revolution". This time, the USSR felt unable or unwilling to act, leading to the break-up of the Soviet Union, and, ultimately, the creation of the Czech Republic within the European Union.

Back at the hotel we dried out, having been rained on for most of the day, and had a glass of rather fiery inexpensive Cabernet Moravia red wine bought from the supermarket. It is, i know, sacrilege to do it, but we added a little sugar, transforming it into a half-decent beverage. Suitably revived we headed under clearing skies for the city centre, past the busy open-air ice-skating rink, and alighted by the Estates Theatre, the rather prosaically named venue for grand opera in the city. Sadly, we arrived too late to tour the building, an imposing eighteenth century neoclassical pile where, amongst others, composers such as Weber and Mahler conducted their own works. The theatre is, however, most famous throughout the musical world for hosting the world premiere of the opera Don Giovanni, conducted by its composer, the 31 year-old Wolfgang Amadeus Mozart, in 1787. It remains the only theatre in the world still standing where Mozart performed, and explains much about the city's desire to claim him as an adopted son.

Just over the road, probably less than one hundred metres from where the great man had stood on the podium that October evening 217 years earlier, we found a cellar restaurant and tucked into goulash soup, tenderloin of pork with sauté potatoes and sauerkraut, washed down by good old Budweiser beer, the real thing from the Czech republic rather than the unsatisfactory but much better-known United States version.

And so ended a day dominated by Prague's musical history. As a footnote, Mozart's Symphony No. 38, written whilst he was staying in the city, is known the world over as the "Prague" symphony, which I'm sure is a matter of great pride to the people. He composed it in late 1786, when he was thirty years old, and it was premiered in the city. I'm listening to it as I write this, and as usual I'm thinking, as I so often do, about the great achievements that might have lain ahead of him, had he survived for more than the meagre five years that remained of his life.

The following day, under leaden but rainless skies we made our first visit to the Charles Bridge over the Vitava River. Those who know the city may be surprised we'd waited four days before we went there, as the impression gained from tour brochures is that all visitors should make it a point of pilgrimage the moment they step off the plane. It is undoubtedly a star attraction, linking as it does the Castle on the West side of the river with the Old City on the East side. Built of stone in 1537, it is six hundred metres long and ten metres wide, and is nowadays pedestrianised, with hawkers selling souvenirs and antiques along its length. Protected by a huge soot-blackened gothic tower at one end, and guarded by baroque statues along both sides, its foundation stone is believed to have been laid by King Charles IV on the ninth of July 1357 at 5:31am. The story goes, and who are we to deny it, that his numerologist, a court favourite at the time, told him that the resulting palindromic number, 1357 9 7 5 31, would ensure the bridge's long life. And he was right!

On the far side lies Kampka Island, a delightful area of the city separated from the West bank of the river by a canal known as The Devil's Stream, bordered by pantiled houses and apartment blocks. Water flowing along the canal drove watermills, none of which is still operating, but two restored waterwheels are visible, one of which is linked to a factory that has been converted to a modern art gallery. From there we took the number 18 tram to its terminus, for no other reason than to sample the less-touristy parts of the city, and there found a restaurant serving very tasty potato and vegetable omelettes.

Back in the city centre, we visited the location of the old Jewish ghetto, viewed its cemetery, then tried one last time to take the tour of the Estates Theatre, and failed – it was closed. As compensation we returned to the Municipal House, where we found the main restaurant full. There is however, an American bar to the rear, with unique decor that can only be described as Nouveau with the occasional hint of Deco. There we each ordered a delicious Cafe Americano amongst clientele much younger than those in the restaurant. That evening we ate at a local Chinese restaurant, which was to be our final dinner in Prague as we were to return home the next day. We couldn't resist, however, visiting the Municipal House one more time the following day before heading off to the Airport.

Prague, when part of the Soviet Union, was an unlikely tourist destination. During, say, the nineteen-sixties, and In common with most Soviet cities, any visitor would have been part of an organised and closely monitored group and obliged to spend at least part of the holiday visiting schools and hospitals as well as the usual tourist attractions. He or she would be required to stay in a government-run hotel where babushkas – older women located on each floor – were employed simply to monitor visitor activity and report anything they considered unusual to the local members of the ruling Communist Party. The speed with which Prague has thrown off this shroud of Communism is remarkable. Our visit was a mere 15 years after the end of the Soviet Union, but the city has so thoroughly embraced western capitalism that its Communist years are but a distant memory. In that short period of time one of Europe's most inaccessible cities has become a major tourist destination, and rightly so, as it is for me one of the most attractive–and interesting – cities on the continent.

Chapter 14

Austria, Slovakia and Hungary

Vienna is a handsome, lively city and pleases me exceedingly **Frederic Chopin**

If you walked into a coffee shop in 1903 in Vienna, you might find at the same table Gustav Klimt, Leon Trotsky, Sigmund Freud, and possibly Adolf Hitler, who lived in the city at the same time.

Eric Weiner

Budapest is a prime site for dreams: the East's exuberant vision of the West, the West's uneasy hallucination of the East. It is a dreamed-up city; a city almost completely faked; a city invented out of other cities, out of Paris by way of Vienna — the imitation, as Claudio Magris has it, of an imitation

M John Harrison

Most of the time I'm working in places I'm not familiar with. Sometimes it's Slovakia, and sometimes it's Hawaii. Not to bash on Slovakia, but I really did enjoy Hawaii **George Clooney**

Shooting gallery with real guns in the railway station. Tower of Babel and Hunters in the Snow by Pieter Bruegel the Elder. Gasholders as desirable residences. Mozart and Strauss concert. Loss of watch and an afternoon spent at the police station.

Austria and Hungary are historically much more than European neighbours, in that they jointly affected the political direction of a large swathe of the continent during the nineteenth and early twentieth centuries, being in part responsible for events which led to the outbreak of the First World War. In 1867 the two countries created a union known correctly as Austria-Hungary, but usually referred to as the Austro-Hungarian Empire, an alliance of two separate nation states, both of them monarchies, under the control of a single royal family, the Habsburgs. It could be argued that in some ways the resulting empire was the precursor to the European Union, in that both countries retained their own parliaments and capital cities, and wielded huge influence elsewhere on the continent, particularly in the northern Balkan states. The Habsburg family's heir presumptive, Archduke Franz Ferdinand, was assassinated on a visit to Sarajevo in Serbia in 1914, his death leading to the outbreak of the First World War and the eventual collapse of the empire.

Since that time the two countries' troubled political journeys through the twentieth century could not have been more different. Austria eventually aligned itself with the ultimately doomed ultra right-wing Nazis in Germany, whilst Hungary espoused the ultra left-wing, and equally doomed, Communists in Russia. The wheel has now turned full circle in that both countries, almost a hundred years later, are again part of a union of nation states, the European Union. With this in mind it seemed appropriate to visit the two capitals, Vienna and Budapest, in a single trip, and the Christmas period of 2007 presented an ideal opportunity. Between the two countries lies Slovakia, with its capital Bratislava conveniently located on the railway line between Vienna and Budapest.

These cities have the distinction of being three of the four European capital cities on the Danube River, the other being Belgrade in Serbia.

My partner and I decided to start the holiday in Vienna and return from Budapest, taking advantage of living within range of both Stansted and Luton Airports, allowing us to fly out from one and return to the other. Getting to Stansted has always been a source of annoyance, requiring as it does a journey by London Overground, then London Underground, and finally National Rail. I have long wondered why there is no outer-London circular railway line linking Gatwick, Heathrow, Luton and Stansted airports, thus greatly reducing traffic on the M25 London orbital motorway, but am not hopeful of it ever being built.

At Vienna airport we bought weekly travel passes at 14 Euros each and took the S-Bahn train, short for Stadtschnellbahn, meaning "rapid city railway", changing at Landstrasse onto the underground, and alighting at Pilgramsgasse in the west of the city, where, under threatening rainclouds and in a chill wind, we had a longer walk than anticipated to the hotel. The sixth-floor room was kitted out with a kettle, and after making a welcome cup of tea we idly searched the TV channels for something worth watching, only able to come up with an episode of "The Simpsons", annoyingly dubbed in German, so not exactly entertaining viewing. In need of Euros, and, more important, a meal, we went out for a late-afternoon stroll and soon found a cash machine close by a small but busy local restaurant. There, in deference to our surroundings, we ate wienerschnitzel and potato salad, and planned the next day's itinerary.

The next morning, mindful of the previous day's long walk to the hotel, we opted to take the bus to the metro station at Pilgramsgasse and travelled to the Museumsquartier, a grouping of galleries and museums adjacent to Ringstrasse, a broad boulevard encircling much of what could be described as the historic city centre. The Ringstrasse is by no means completely circular, starting as it does by the Danube River and ending again by the river but at a point about a kilometre downstream. Along it lie grandiose nineteenth century buildings such as the Town Hall and the Opera House. Our destination was the National Art Gallery, the rather forbiddingly named Kunsthistorichesmuseum, a substantial five-storey sandstone edifice set well back from the road in topiaried gardens. Built in 1891 to house the art collections of various members of the Habsburg royal family, it is undoubtedly a first-division gallery and concentrates on art in the period between the fifteenth and nineteenth centuries. Works that are well-known include an entire room devoted to Pieter Bruegel the Elder featuring "The Tower of Babel" and "Hunters in the Snow". Several portraits of the Spanish Royal Family by Diego Velazquez are highlighted, painted in Madrid but presented to the Austrian Royal Family as they were relatives of the Spanish Royals.

Outside, in a biting wind and occasional snow flurry, we made our way back to the metro to visit what we anticipated would be quite a contrast to the gallery, the four gas-holders located about four kilometres South-East of Ringstrasse. The metro station is, unsurprisingly, named "Gasometer". The gas-holders were built in the 1890s by a British company and used to store coal-gas from the adjacent gasworks. Similar in size to gas-holders that were once present in almost every town in the UK, these are strikingly different in appearance. Instead of being simple green-painted telescopic steel cylinders, supported externally by latticed steel frames, the Viennese gasholders were erected within full-height circular decorative brick walls, sporting windows at all levels round the entire structure. The walls supported shallow-domed structural steel roofs, giving them the appearance of cylindrical high-rise blocks of flats, seventy metres tall and sixty metres in diameter. When natural gas replaced coal-gas in 1984 they became redundant, and the decision was made to convert them into living spaces. In 2001 the conversions were completed and they were opened as apartment blocks, with the ground floors being devoted to retail space, a cinema, and a theatre.

As we approached from the metro station, the nearest of the four erstwhile gas-holders, standing atop a small hill, looked like nothing so much as a residential version of Clifford's Tower, the preserved thirteenth—century castle keep in York. The snow was by now settling, turning the surrounding lawns white, and we hurried inside and found a restaurant, located beneath the vast glass-dome of the atrium, where we ate delicious gulash and seeded bread. From our table we looked across to the apartments around the perimeter, on six floors and rising to the very top of the building. Their internal windows gave their occupants a view over the activity down below in the atrium, whilst their outer windows, particularly those of the upper apartments, would no doubt provide pleasant vistas of Vienna. There was something of a village atmosphere about the place, housing as it does some 1600 people over the four buildings, with seventy of the eight hundred apartments being used as student accommodation. Back outside the snow was now settling, and on the way back to the hotel we called in at a Billa supermarket and stocked up on food and drink for the room. In reception at the hotel we found a flyer for a symphony concert that evening, and after a short, civilised debate we decided to go.

Anyone who spends more than a few hours in Vienna city centre cannot avoid the many stickers and hoardings advertising symphony concerts. There seems to be at least one every night of the week, with performers in "period costume" performing a programme that almost always consists of works by Mozart and Johann Strauss. I must confess I have usually been somewhat wary of these events, using, as they do, session musicians, playing "popular" pieces to a mainly tourist audience. However we were determined to experience Mozart's music in Vienna, the city where, at the tender age of six years he gave a piano recital before Maria Theresa, Queen of Austria, and where he lived from 1784 to 1787.

After a snack in the hotel room we headed over to the concert hall at Beethovenplatz, just off Ringstrasse, and inside the entrance mounted a steep flight of stairs, emerging into a large wood-panelled auditorium beneath a very impressive hammer-beam roof. There we encountered a mainly middle-aged audience and joined in the polite applause when the period-costumed orchestra members, fifteen in number, emerged from backstage and took their seats, followed by the conductor. As it turned out, the concert was rather good, starting with a selection of Strauss waltzes, followed by four of Mozart's German Dances and, finally, his Symphony Number 40. Back outside, in a flurry of snow, we walked to the Metro and ate a welcome meal in the warmth of a nearby restaurant.

The following day dawned bright but bitterly cold, and we took a tram to the Musikverein, the city's major concert hall, only to find the main building closed. Fortunately the separate box-office was open, and, rather optimistically, I collected a copy of the brochure listing coming seasons' concerts. The nearby Schubert Cafe beckoned, where we had Minestrone soup and bread, less for the need of food than the need of a place to escape the biting wind. There followed a visit to Mozart's House, a somewhat nondescript four-storey stone building in Domgasse in the old town, where he rented rooms from 1784 to 1787 and during which time he wrote the opera "The Marriage of Figaro". In a recent attempt to raise visitor numbers, much renovation work has been carried out, including the installation of a lift, with the result that the building is now more of a museum and study centre. His six-room first-floor apartment, somewhat grandiose for a struggling musician at the time, remains intact and contains memorabilia relating to him and his family. The basement has been converted into a small concert room, whilst on the ground-floor there is the inevitable shop, selling, amongst the usual memorabilia, Mozartkugel, a delicious chocolate-covered spherical bon-bon of pistachio marzipan and nougat, wrapped in tinfoil decorated with a picture of the great man. It is almost impossible to find any small general shop in Vienna that doesn't sell Mozartkugel, and I wonder what his view might be of such exploitation of his image. From what we know of his character, it's fairly certain he'd love it, as long as he was getting a percentage of sales income!

It was by now getting dark, but finding ourselves close to the Old Town Hall we couldn't leave without visiting the huge Christmas market in its grounds. There we bought Beerenpunsch, a hot concoction of the juice of various berries mixed with red wine. A traditional drink at many European Christmas markets, it is served in a commemorative blue ceramic mug costing two Euros in addition to the cost of the drink. I still have my mug, which I use for coffee from time to time here at home. Despite the festive atmosphere, we left after only half an hour or so, having scarcely visited half of the hundred or so stalls, due in part to the intense cold.

The following day we took the metro to the Sudbahnhof station and boarded the train to Bratislava, capital of Slovakia, and a mere sixty kilometres to the East. Slovakia has at various times been host to large populations of Austrians, Germans, Serbs, Hungarians, and Slovaks, so has arguably been one of the most cosmopolitan of all European states. Ruled by Hungary from the year 1000 until 1867, and then by the Austria-Hungary union until 1918, it then joined forces with Bohemia, Moravia, and other adjoining states following the collapse of that union to create Czechoslovakia. After World War II Czechoslovakia came under the control of the Soviet Union and remained so until 1989 when communist rule ended and the nation split into two independent republics, The Czech Republic and Slovakia, known as the "Velvet Divorce". Bratislava was chosen as Slovakia's capital city, and the country joined the European Union in 2004, adopting the Euro as its currency in 2009.

The city of Bratislava, on the banks of the Danube, is typically Eastern European, but sadly we had little time to sample its tourist delights, as we had only an hour or so to wait until the next train arrived to take us onwards to Budapest that afternoon. On the way through the station, and amongst a clutch of the usual railway-station shops, I noticed down a side-entrance what appeared to be a shooting gallery, with a couple of leather-jacketed customers shooting at well-dented metal targets with what looked like .22 rifles. Despite myself, I was unable to resist a "well done" when one of the targets fell, at the same time wondering if this surreal scene could ever be repeated at any other railway station in the world.

Outside the station we were surprised (and delighted) to see trolley-buses waiting at the stop opposite. Trolley-buses last ran in the UK in the 1960s and early 1970s – I remember travelling on one in Walsall in 1970 – but this was a reminder that there are plenty of trolley-bus systems still operating efficiently and pollution-free in Eastern Europe. Alongside the station stood the Penzion Antic Cafe, a wood-framed, slightly run-down transport cafe-style building from which the delicious aroma of lunch-time cooking emanated. I decided we must make the best of what time we had and at least visit part of the town. Looking upwards, I noticed a monument, overlooking the city high on a hill, and suggested we check it out. My partner sensibly preferred to wait in the warmth of the cafe so I found myself walking alone up the steep hill through an attractive middle-class snow-covered suburb, eventually reaching the Slavin War Memorial, about half a kilometre south of the station. The site is a graveyard and a memorial to the 7,000 Russian soldiers killed whilst fighting the Nazis at the end of World War II. Covering a broad hilltop area of a hectare or more, its central point is dominated by an open temple-like structure consisting of eight plain columns surmounted by a roof on which stands the memorial, a stone column of around 40 metres high topped by a statue of a Russian soldier. Tombstones, set low in the ground amidst the settled snow, and each inscribed in Cyrillic script, surround the monument. I concluded that any visitor surely could not fail to be impressed by such a dramatic yet peaceful location with its extensive views over the city in every direction. It yet again proved to me that when travelling, any climb, no matter how hard, is always worth the effort.

Back at the railway station, I rejoined my partner inside the busy, hot, steamy station cafe, its windows wet with condensation, to find her deep in conversation with Norman, a youngish Scot from Paisley, a lecturer on the Teaching English as a Foreign Language Programme, who was passing through on his way to Vienna. I ordered bean soup and beer, and joined in the chat until he had to leave to get his train. Fifteen minutes later we boarded our own train to Budapest and said farewell to Slovakia. Thus I concluded yet another country visit of less than two hours, to add to those to Liechtenstein, Bosnia, Andorra, and Monaco.

The journey to Hungary's capital, Budapest, some 200 kilometres distant, passed without incident, and in the early evening we arrived at Keleti, the main Budapest railway station. Built in 1881 as the terminus of lines from Transylvania and the Balkans, it is one of many grandiose Eastern European railway stations exhibiting a gloriously eclectic mish-mash of architectural styles. From the platform, sheltered by a the broad single-span arched roof, we found the main exit hall, within which are huge religious frescos painted by Karoly Lotz, a famous Hungarian artist whose work adorns many major buildings in the city. Such frescos would not be out of place in any cathedral. Outside, in the station forecourt, we looked up at the statues of George Stephenson of England and James Watt of Scotland, the two railway pioneers, gazing down from high recesses on either side of the building's facade and capable of evoking a brief moment of national pride in this English visitor. From there we threaded our way carefully through the snow-covered building-site in front of the station, where construction work on the new Metro Line 4 was in progress, and soon reached the hotel opposite. Once checked in, a visit to McDonald's followed, and we were soon early to bed after what had been a busy day.

Hungary, a nation state since the late ninth century, became a kingdom in 1000, and in 1867 was able to persuade the ruling Habsburg Monarchy to become rulers over the union of Austria-Hungary, otherwise known as the Austro-Hungarian Empire. The collapse of that union after World-War I led to the country losing 71% of its land area and 58% of its population, and the inter-war period saw two failed attempts at re-establishing a constitutional monarchy. Political and economic instability followed, and resulted in the country aligning itself with the fascists of Germany and Italy in 1936. This alliance became known as the "Axis", a word coined by Gyula Gombos, Prime Minister of Hungary at the time, leading to the creation of the Red Arrow Party, Hungary's equivalent of the German Nazi Party. The country suffered a chaotic World War II, first declaring war on Russia and, when this failed, attempting to withdraw from the conflict altogether. German occupation followed, which ended when the Russians invaded in 1944. After the war the Russians continued to wield control through a period of instability, leading to Hungary's failed revolution in 1956.Thereafter the country became a Soviet Satellite until the fall of the Iron Curtain in 1989. Since then there has been relative stability under NATO, joined in 1999, and The European Union, Joined in 2004. The country has yet to join the Eurozone, continuing to use the Forint as currency. In summary, it is probably true to say that Hungary's twentieth century was more politically and economically chaotic than that of any other European state.

The capital, Budapest originally consisted of two separate cities, Buda and Pest, located on either side of the Danube River. Much debate continues over the origin of these names, with one theory intriguingly suggesting that Buda was named after Bleda, the brother of Attila the Hun. The two cities were united, together with a third, Obuda, in 1873 and the resulting city of Budapest acted with Vienna as joint capital of Austria-Hungary under the Habsburg monarchy until 1918, when it reverted to being the Hungarian capital. A city of 1.8 million souls, it boasts an excellent transport network involving a four-line Metro system, Trams, Trolley-Buses, and Buses. The River Danube, almost half a kilometre wide at some points in the city, offers boat trips locally and until a year ago there was a daily hydrofoil service to Bratislava and Vienna, a service sadly now believed to have ceased. The city suffered heavy damage in World War II during which around 75,000 of its Jews were sent to labour camps and killed. When the fall of the Iron Curtain took place in 1989 42 statues glorifying communism and its leaders were removed from their pedestals around the city and transferred to Memento Park, a short bus ride from the city centre, where they can be viewed on payment of a small entrance fee.

Our first full day in Budapest, Christmas Eve, dawned cold, with a biting wind, and after buying travel passes we headed west to the Danube with the aim of taking the tram over the Szabadsag suspension-bridge which crosses the River. On the South side it is close to the Gellert Hotel, a huge six-storey secession art-nouveau stone edifice famous for its indoor and outdoor thermal baths, swimming pools, and spa treatment rooms. The bridge, however, was undergoing substantial rebuilding, obliging us to walk over, and once at the hotel we quickly sought refuge from the weather in the chandeliered espresso cafe. We found a table by a window facing the Danube, and soon relaxed in maroon-upholstered Queen Anne-style dining chairs, eventually lunching on gulash soup and beer. Sporadic snow flurries outside almost persuaded us to spend the rest of the afternoon there, but we had other places to see, and after an hour or so returned by tram to the hotel and then took the Metro to St Stephen's Basilica, the city's Roman Catholic cathedral, best described as neo-classical with Eastern European influences.

St. Stephens is a relatively new building, being completed in 1905, fifty-four years after the foundation stone was laid. Its elevated location allows it to dominate the city's skyline, and external features include the two high dome-topped towers flanking its frontage. Internally, it is pleasantly free of gilt baroque decoration and sports unusual internal square-section support pillars in maroon and white marble. In general, though, it is an unremarkable place, save for it being my first-ever experience of the church espousing twenty-first century technology in the form of electric candles. Activated by a coin-in-the-slot mechanism, they light up, presumably for a fixed period of time – I didn't have the nerve to ask how long – and look like nothing so much as the control panel of a 1980s Hollywood computer. I'm aware of the case against real candles in church – they are messy to deal with and produce smoke that stains masonry and artworks – but to me this is a modernising step too far.

Back at the hotel we ate a Christmas Eve dinner of Cheese, crisps, apples, biscuits and cake purchased at modest cost from the local convenience store and then popped over to the station for coffee. We passed by one of those coin-in-the-slot machines dispensing clear plastic spheres containing a random children's toy, an ideal opportunity to buy souvenir presents for each other. In mine was an Andy Pandy doll, whose current whereabouts are unknown, and my partner received a slightly more interesting alphabet puzzle. The spheres contain a slot, with the intention of their being used by children as piggy banks. Mine is still in use as a repository for non-Euro coins left over after each trip abroad, and serves as a constant reminder of that exceptionally cold day in Budapest.

The following day, Christmas Day, we noticed at breakfast that the number of hotel guests had dwindled substantially, and once outside, under leaden skies and the occasional snow shower, we found the streets similarly half- deserted. Determined to make something of the day, we caught the metro to Ferenc Puskas Stadium and there changed onto one of the vintage angular yellow trams still operating on line 1 in the city. In the leading car there is a recessed area containing an elevated seat and small counter, from which, in the Communist era, a conductress would sell and check tickets, no doubt also keeping a watchful eye on passengers at the same time. The line took us across the Rakoczi Bridge over the Danube, giving us a fine view upstream towards the Gellert Hotel, but, more important, in the distance, the Hungarian Parliament building, completed in 1904, a wonderful gothic-revival pile overlooking the river and undoubtedly the city's most spectacular building. With its lengthy riverside frontage it has much in common with another gothic-revival masterpiece, the Houses of Parliament in London.

Back at the strangely deserted Keleti Railway Station we walked the half-kilometre or so to the Kunsthalle Art Gallery, and were unsurprised to find it closed. The gallery is located on the edge of Varosligeti To, a long, narrow lake, frozen over at this time of year, and located within a snow-covered park. Skaters were out in their droves, creating a scene reminiscent of Breugel's "The Hunters in the Snow", a similar largely monochrome scene under a leaden sky, which we'd seen a few days earlier at the Kunsthistoriches Museum In Vienna. From there we paused by a small pond in the north of the park, presumably fed by hot springs as there was mist over the water, the apparently warm temperature attracting large numbers of waterfowl.

In the biting wind we headed back to the hotel, and back in the room I realised my Rotary watch was missing. An expensive twenty-first birthday present from my parents, it had great sentimental value and its loss would be a bitter blow. There was no sign of it on the bedside table, and I concluded it was either taken from the room or had somehow fallen from my wrist during our morning walk. Hotel staff claimed to know nothing about it, so the only thing we could do was to retrace our steps around the park. This involved a hand-search through the snow around the pond, which proved fruitless, and we eventually asked a passer-by to direct us to the nearest police station. There, we found little sign of activity, it being, after all, Christmas day, but in any case nothing could be done for us until the desk sergeant had summoned a translator from her home. After a long interview we were obliged to wait for a report to be drawn up, in both English and Hungarian, which I duly signed. Copies were made and handed over, the entire process taking more than three hours to complete. To this day I'm unsure as to how the watch came to be lost.

As an attempt to lighten what had been a thoroughly depressing day, we booked dinner at the only restaurant that was open, the Hotel Hungaria, just down the road. Beef stew, stewed veal, and stodgy apple pudding with meringue lightened the mood somewhat, but as we walked back to our hotel along the by now almost deserted street and in yet another snow flurry it was difficult to look back on our first visit to Hungary as a complete success. We had only glimpsed Budapest's crowning glory, the wonderful parliament building, from the windows of a tram, and had viewed the Chain Bridge, the city's historic bridge over the Danube, from a distance. Back at the hotel we packed our bags in preparation for a 6:30am departure to the airport, a journey that was to require taking two different metro trains and a bus to complete, the most difficult city-centre to airport transfer I've experienced. The return flight was uneventful, and when we exited the arrivals hall at Luton Airport the sun was shining, there was no chill Easterly wind, and not a flake of snow to be seen!

Looking back on the week, it had been a mixed bag. Vienna never disappoints, whatever the weather. Bratislava was just a stopover, and I'd like to return some day to explore the city properly. Budapest will, however, always be remembered for its relentless cold weather and an afternoon spent at the police station. To this day I have heard nothing more about my watch, and only hope whoever's wearing it appreciates its history and value. It is the only serious loss I have suffered in many years of travelling, so I suppose I shouldn't complain, and I'm sure many travellers have suffered something similar over the years.

Chapter 15

Belgium, The Netherlands, Luxembourg, France, Germany

Belgium is a country invented by the British to annoy the French   **Charles de Gaulle**

I was shocked to discover that homeschooling is not allowed in the Netherlands. I could only imagine that after legalizing pot, prostitution and gambling, they had to outlaw something.   **Quinn Cummings**

When the going gets tough, you have to lie   **Jean-Claude Juncker**

Overrun by kids at St. Pancras International station. Hotel in red light district. Visit to home of Karl Marx. The city where the Eurozone was created. The bookshop that was a church and bike-shed. Location of Andre Rieu open-air concerts. A walk through the Finance Ministry's front garden.

Belgium, The Netherlands, and Luxembourg, often referred to as the Low Countries, are located in that part of Northern Europe bounded by the North Sea to the North, and France and Germany to the South. Belgium shares a border with both the Netherlands and Luxembourg, and land travel between all three by train and road is simple and convenient, no two towns being more than 300 or so kilometres apart. As a bonus, the three countries are easily reached by rail from London, with Eurostar trains from St. Pancras station running to the Belgian capital, Brussels, where connections are available to any of the other major towns and cities. For this reason my partner and I decided to avoid the sometimes irksome human processing that is *de rigeur* at today's airports, and for once travel by train. Our first destination, Luxembourg, required us to take the Eurostar to Brussels where we would change onto a Belgian Railways train direct to the capital, Luxembourg City. We would in effect make a round trip of the region from there, visiting France, Holland, and Germany *en route*, and then return to Brussels and home.

The Eurostar departure lounge at St. Pancras station is normally a peaceful and civilised place to wait, but on this occasion the peace was shattered by the presence of dozens of small, excited children who, with parents, were booked on the train going to the geographically misnamed "Disneyland Paris", a theme park, not located in Paris but at Marne la Vallee, a good 30 kilometres from the French capital. Excitement amongst the kids grew to fever pitch with the appearance of a couple dressed for the occasion as Disney characters, but peace soon returned after the impending departure of their train was announced, with the kids rushing off to the platform. The occasion evinced images of the train-borne hockey-stick wielding pupils of St. Trinian's school in the film "The Great St. Trinian's Train Robbery".

Eurostar trains are normally a pleasure to ride, being clean, fast, and quiet, and they have the additional benefit of rarely being patronised by groups of drunken football supporters or hen-nighters. This one proved no exception, although we both experienced a slight *frisson* of anxiety when the train slowed to a crawl halfway through the Channel Tunnel. All was well, however, and the 2 ½ hour journey passed without further incident, arriving exactly on time at Brussels Midi station, where we were to change onto a Belgian Railways train bound for Luxembourg City, the capital of Luxembourg. Those with a penchant for irrelevant facts may wish to know that Brussels was the birthplace of one of Hollywood's greatest stars, Audrey Hepburn.

With half an hour to spare before our departure, we took a stroll around the station's *environs*, an inelegant mish-mash of offices, hotels, and small shops, and served by a crumbling, litter-strewn tram station. The Parc de Hal, a short walk to the East, offered a brief but welcome parkland break before we returned to the station and boarded our train. The journey of 220 kilometres to Luxembourg City is mainly through unremarkable countryside, justifying the soubriquet "Low Country", but arrival at the city of Namur at the half-way point provided interest. There, the train runs between rocky hills before crossing the broad River Meuse, affording a view upstream of the confluence with the River Sambre. The area was once an important centre of the Sambre-Meuse Coalfield, situated on either side of the two rivers for almost their entire lengths and often dubbed the "Backbone of Belgium". Nowadays all but defunct, the coalfield during much of the nineteenth and twentieth centuries provided Belgium with its only indigenous source of domestic and industrial energy.

Luxembourg City station proved to be something of an anticlimax. We expected a large, bustling city centre transport hub, but instead found ourselves inside a modest station served by a mere half-dozen or so platforms. Outside, in fading light and with rainclouds gathering, we walked over to our hotel, a nondescript five-storey building on the corner of a long narrow street that to our horror seemed to be entirely devoted to the sex industry in all its various manifestations. On both sides, as far as the eye could see, were flashing neon signs outside strip clubs, "hostess" bars, and the like, with doormen soliciting business from the few potential punters idly walking up and down. We hurriedly discussed looking for a different hotel, but decided that at this late hour we would take a chance and spend our first-ever night in a hotel in a red-light district. Just inside the hotel door we were greeted by a man seated in what can only be described as a sentry box. He looked up from his newspaper and gestured idly that we should continue down a long corridor, at the end of which was the reception area. To this day I'm still not sure why he was there, but guess that it had something to do with the fact that we were in the red light district. Our room, on the fourth floor at the rear of the building, had no toilet, necessitating a trip to a communal toilet at the end of the corridor. Other than that it was acceptable, not least because there was no street noise.

Luxembourg is unique in European countries in that it is the only remaining Grand Duchy. The title was common in previous centuries when certain states were under the control of, or influenced by, an adjoining monarchy. Finland and Lithuania both enjoyed this status at certain times in their history. Luxembourg, having been absorbed into the French Empire soon after Napoleon came to power, became a Grand Duchy after his defeat in 1815, but was only fully recognised as a sovereign state in 1839. The ruler, currently Henri, bears the inherited title of Grand Duke, rather than King, and is addressed as "Your Royal Highness". The country currently has a population of just under 600,000 souls, and is one of Europe's smallest states, covering an area less than twice that of Greater London. Surrounded by France, Germany, and Belgium, its history is heavily linked to those countries, in particular during the first and second world wars when, on both occasions, though a neutral country, it was occupied by the Germans. It was a founder-member of the European Union, is a member of NATO, and forms part of the Benelux group of countries, together with Belgium and The Netherlands, all to be visited on this trip. The principal language is French. The capital, Luxembourg City, is, somewhat surprisingly, twinned with the London Borough of Camden, a fact of which I was blissfully unaware during the several years I lived in that part of London.

After depositing our belongings in the room we decided there was time for a brief visit to the city centre, located about a kilometre or so away and atop a 70 metre cliff overlooking the River Petrusse. Outside, In drizzling rain, we followed the road over the stone Adolphe Bridge which straddles the river, and on the far side, at the top of the cliff, we encountered a maze of narrow streets lined with modest slate-roofed buildings, each not much larger than a good-sized terraced town-house. To our surprise we found that many of these were seemingly important government offices of one sort or another, with the area apparently unprotected by security personnel. At one point we found ourselves in front of the Ministry of Finance, an unremarkable building, fronted by a small, well-kept garden. Unable to resist the temptation, we walked through the garden along a narrow path between the flowers and shrubs, feeling strangely elated at this, our first-ever stroll through a Ministerial garden. Back on the main road, we found a McDonald's and enjoyed burgers and coffee, and finally returned to Rue Joseph Junck to find that the rain seemed to have deterred all but the most determined sex-industry punters. The man in the hotel sentry-box scarcely looked up from his newspaper as we entered.

Luxembourg City, with a population of 115,000, roughly equivalent to that of Watford in England, has been important since Roman times due to its militarily strategic cliff-top location overlooking the Petrusse river and attendant (originally Roman) roads. The castle, fortress, and substantial city walls, have at various times protected the city from invasions by the French, Spanish, Austrians, Prussians, and Germans, and the city was described by the French military engineer, Lazare Carnot, as "The best fortress in the world, except Gibraltar." The Germans were, however, not to be denied in either of the two world wars, and after their invasion in 1941 all street names were changed, with "Avenue de la Liberte", the road we'd taken into the city centre the previous evening, becoming "Adolf Hitler Strasse". The country was liberated by the Americans in September 1944, during which action the famous general George S Patton was killed. He is interred in the city's US military cemetery along with over 5000 of his compatriots. The country's post-war history is inextricably intertwined with that of the European Union, being one of the six founder-members of the European Coal and Steel Community in 1951, the predecessor of the European Economic Community which later became the European Union. As a result, Luxembourg City has become deeply involved in the administrative operation of the European Union, playing host to the European Court of Justice, The Secretariat of the European Parliament, and the European Investment Bank.

The next morning dawned dry and bright, and after a delicious hotel breakfast of fresh-baked rolls, butter, jam, cheese, and very good coffee, we popped over to the station to visit the tourist office and buy all-day bus tickets, rather expensive at five Euros each. We first visited the cathedral, a pleasant enough grey-stone Gothic pile with a simple slate roof and three elegant spires, originally built as a Jesuit church in the seventeenth century and elevated to the status of a cathedral by Pope Pius IX in 1890. It stands at the far end of a broad paved square which is lined on one side by trees, and on the other by a pleasant terrace of three-storey office buildings. The location, sadly, suffers from the incessant traffic noise from the nearby Boulevard Franklin Delano Roosevelt. Inside the Cathedral stand ten huge grey columns, each two metres or more in diameter, reaching up on either side of the nave to the high rib-vaulted ceiling. The building for the most part speaks to the Gothic-Calvinist style, there being little in the way of baroque decoration, arguably appropriate for a cathedral located in a region that had been eager to espouse the Protestant Reformation.

From the Cathedral we walked the hundred metres or so to the Grand Ducal Palace, the official residence of Grand Duke Henri, Luxembourg's ruler. Located in a narrow street, the palace resembles nothing so much as a low-rise nineteenth century stone-built bank building, examples of which may still be found in the City of London. A crowd of tourists had gathered opposite the central arched vehicle entrance, which has blue sentry-boxes one on either side. As we arrived, a noisy military band, around 40-strong, entered the street at the far end and marched past us. Immediately behind them a phalanx of around 50 soldiers, clad in fawn shirts and khaki trousers, and each clutching an automatic rifle, took up position directly in front of the palace, and the band fell silent. On command, a single bugler sounded, marking the start of, to me, unnecessarily complex manoeuvres to effect the changing of the guard. The process, lasting no more than ten minutes, ended when the band struck up again and led the men away down the street. It had been an interesting diversion, but didn't quite emulate the entertainment value of the changing of the guard ceremony in Athens.

Luxembourg City is one of the few European capitals that possesses no tram network, although a new tramline, under construction by a British company, is due to open in 2017, linking the railway station, city centre, and airport. The last tramway in the city closed in 1964, but fortunately someone at the time had the foresight to preserve what was left of the rolling stock and equipment, now located in a museum about three kilometres from the city centre. We took the bus there and spent an hour or so checking out the exhibits, which range from horse-drawn trams to ancient buses and workshop equipment. Outside, we consumed a picnic of cheese rolls and iced tea, then headed for the railway station from where we planned a brief visit to the nearest French town, Longwy, located a few kilometres the other side of the Luxembourg-France border.

A town of some 10,000 souls, Longwy has for years struggled to recover from the loss of its major industry, the manufacture of decorative enamelled pottery, in the 1950s. In its heyday it was a celebrated producer of this high-value product, and Longwy pottery is still known the world over and considered highly collectable. Our journey westward took less than half an hour, and we emerged from the station with only an hour or so to see what the town could offer. A stroll in the early-evening sunshine through the drab, unexceptional town centre, where we passed fly-posted boarded-up shops, walls sprayed with graffiti, and vandalised street furniture, suggested there had yet to be anything in the way of a tangible economic recovery. We called in at a rather run-down supermarket where we bought food to eat back at the hotel that evening, then headed back to the station. Longwy, we concluded, was a town far-removed from the romantic images of France as portrayed in the holiday brochures, and was still struggling to recover from the loss of its major employer, much like many British communities after the demise of coal-mining. I understand that since our visit the enamelled pottery business has returned to the town, as yet on a very small scale, but at least this means the Longwy pottery mark is again appearing on high-quality items. Perhaps the town benefited from the media exposure it received when it hosted stage three of the 2017 Tour de France cycle race. We returned on the train to what was, by contrast, a vibrant and wealthy Luxembourg City, its red light district already busy as we walked over to the hotel.

The following day we checked out of the hotel, left our luggage with the reception desk, and in glorious sunshine took a train to Trier, in Germany, another border settlement, some 5 kilometres from the Luxembourg border and 50 kilometres West of Luxembourg City. Located on the Moselle River, and ten times the size of Longwy, Trier was first settled by the Romans over 2000 years ago and became part of the German Empire in 1871. In June 1940, during World War II it became the staging post for 50,000 British and French soldiers, captured during the Dunkerque defeat, who were *en route* to German prisoner-of-war camps. Heavily bombed by the Allies in 1944, the city emerged from the war to regain its position as one of the largest German wine-producers, with engineering and textiles as its other major industries. There is much for the tourist to see in Trier, but, needing to return to Luxembourg City to catch an afternoon train, we decided we should concentrate on its major attraction, the birthplace of the founder of Communism, Karl Marx.

His house, a three-storey green-shuttered town-house dating from 1727, is sandwiched within a terrace of shops and apartments on a busy street about a kilometre from the station. Here, in 1818, Karl Marx was born into a middle-class family of Jewish ancestry, his maternal grandfather having been a Rabbi. His father, Heinrich, a lawyer with business interests in a number of Moselle Vineyards, had recently converted from Judaism to Lutheranism, and his mother, Henriette, A Dutch Jew, came from the family that was eventually to create the Philips Electronics company. Karl was the third of nine children, and finally left home in the late 1830s after spells at Bonn and Berlin Universities. He completed his Doctoral thesis at Jena University in 1841, and then spent periods in Paris, Brussels, and Cologne before his final move to London in 1850, where he spent much of his time in the British Museum Reading room developing his political philosophy. In the early 1860s he published the first volume of "Das Kapital", a book which offered a blueprint for political change and eventually led to Communism in its various forms being adopted in many parts of the world. He died stateless in London in 1883, and was buried in Highgate Cemetery, with only 11 mourners present at the graveside. The grave, always immaculately maintained whenever I've visited it, is marked by a huge black-marble bust of Marx, gazing out enigmatically over the surrounding sometimes unkempt graves and vegetation.

Not simply a Museum to Marx, the house also explores the effect of "Das Kapital" on political philosophy, and in particular its part in the rise of Communism across the world in the twentieth century. In all, it is a fascinating and enlightening place, and certainly "merits the detour" as the French would say. It is somewhat ironic that when Germany was partitioned after the Second World War, Trier found itself in what became known as West Germany, a fervently capitalist country. Equally Ironic is the fact that its Communist counterpart, East Germany, found itself being bailed out financially by West Germany when the Berlin wall fell.

Back at Trier station we returned to Luxembourg City, collected our luggage from the hotel, bade farewell to the man in the sentry-box, and took one last look at the red-light district, before walking over to the station to get the train to Liege, 160 kilometres to the North, in Belgium. Under bright afternoon sunshine the train whisked us past farms, villages, and rolling hills on the way to the somewhat unprepossessing urban outskirts of the one-time industrial city of Liege. The guard announced that we were about to arrive at Liege Guillemins station, and a minute or so later we found ourselves on the platform of what appeared to be a huge building-site. The station was, in fact, in the throes of being completely rebuilt to take the new ICE and Thalys high-speed trains, and we discovered that we had alighted one stop too soon, the city centre stop being Liege Palais, seven minutes further down the line. Although annoyed at the time for making such an elementary mistake, in the following couple of years I was able from home, via the internet, to enjoy monitoring progress on the station's rebuilding. The finished station, opened in 2009, is a glorious curved symphony of steel, glass, and white concrete, looking like a huge flying saucer fabricated in net. It is surely one of the most attractive railway stations in the modern world, and offers hope to those who have justifiably criticised railway architecture, and architecture in general, over the past fifty years.

We took the next available train to Liege Palais station, an altogether depressing subterranean station, found our hotel, and installed ourselves in a room on the fifth floor. A brief walk around the block in the rain revealed a convenience store where we bought food for a picnic in the room, including – and I make no apologies for this – a perfectly acceptable bottle of red wine costing one Euro.

Liege, situated on the broad reaches of the Meuse River, is a city of some 200,000 souls and is the third-largest Belgian city. Previously part of France, and later Holland, the city became part of the newly independent Belgium in 1830. Occupied by the Germans in the Second World War, it was liberated by the Allies in September 1944, but thereafter was bombarded by around 1500 German V1 and V2 rockets, more than the number that struck the whole of England during the war. After the war the city regained its importance as a major centre of the Belgian coal and steel industries, but since the 1970s these have both suffered steep declines in demand. Nowadays the city's major industries are information technology, engineering, including the manufacture of parts for the A380 airbus, and production of water, beer, and chocolate.

The following day, cloudy but thankfully rain-free, saw us taking the train back to Guillemins station, changing platforms there amidst the building chaos, and taking the train to Maastricht in The Netherlands, or Holland if you prefer it, about 35 kilometres to the North. "Netherlands" means "Low Countries", and relates to the fact that only 50% of the country's land mass is higher than one metre above sea level. In all, 17% of its landmass has been reclaimed from the sea. Created In its present form in the sixteenth century, The Netherlands became a powerful world and colonial power, colonising Manhattan Island on North America's East coast, naming it New Amsterdam, the precursor of present-day New York. Other colonies were established in Indonesia, Africa, South America, The West Indies, Japan, and Taiwan. In 1606 Willem Janszoon discovered Australia, 164 years before that country's supposed "discovery" by the British explorer James Cook. Established as a Constitutional Monarchy in 1815 after the defeat of Napoleon Bonaparte, The Netherlands grew steadily wealthy from that time, largely on the back of its involvement in the slave trade, and its exploitation of Indonesia. In World War II it was occupied by the Germans, and in 1951 became a founder-member of the European Coal and Steel Community, the precursor of the European Union.

Maastricht, in the extreme South-East of the country, was already known to both of us, but for just two reasons. The first was the fact that it lent its name to the European Treaty signed by Prime-Minister Thatcher in 1992, a document that effectively gave birth to the Euro currency and European Citizenship. From a UK point of view the treaty is sadly about to be consigned to the dustbin of history. The second reason is rather less weighty. Maastricht is the home of Andre Rieu, a violinist and orchestral conductor, who travels the world with his orchestra, dancers, and soloists, playing music that sits firmly on the fence between classical and pop. Some may refer to it as "light orchestral", covering as it does items such as "Ave Maria" and the Johann Strauss waltzes. The ladies of the orchestra, clad in multi-coloured Disney-princess ball-gowns, appear to have been instructed that they must always give the impression that they're having fun. The shows invariably take place in the evening beneath starry skies on huge stages in beautiful city squares, or in parkland, or in the grounds of a stately-home. Audiences contain more than the usual quota of mature couples and ladies of a certain age, who sing along where appropriate or simply sway in their seats to the rhythm of the music. I mention this because we had recently watched ten minutes or so (it's difficult to keep watching for longer) of a recording of one of Mr. Rieu's evening concerts in his home town, Maastricht, played before a huge audience in front of the Basilica in the Vrijthof square, our destination as we strolled through the city-centre.

Occupied since Roman times, the city of 120,000 souls lays claim to being the oldest in Holland, although this is disputed by Nijmegen. Originally a major centre for pottery, with 7,000 employed in the industry at its peak, it now boasts a diverse, mainly service, economy. Its many tourist attractions are principally linked to its Roman past, but its fortifications from the middle-ages are also as important as they are imposing. Its twentieth-century history is, like the rest of Holland, defined by the two world wars, and in World War II it was the first Dutch city to be liberated from German occupation, in September 1944.

Arriving at Vrijthof Square, the scene of Andre Rieu's many triumphant concerts on his home soil, we first walked across to Sint Janskirk, a fourteenth-century gothic church in grey marlstone, sporting, uniquely, a red-painted bell-tower, making it the most distinctive building in the Square, or, indeed, the city. We took the opportunity to climb the 220 steps to the wooden belfry, from which we enjoyed panoramic sunlit views over the city and its surrounding countryside. I couldn't help thinking that this Protestant church must sit slightly uneasily alongside its immediate neighbour, the Basiliek van Sint Servaas, a Roman Catholic Romanesque building, again in grey marlstone, which incidentally we declined to visit as there was an entrance charge. By now in need of sustenance, we selected one of the many cafes on the East side of the square and passed a pleasant half-hour or so watching the world go by and being entertained by a stilt-walker whose stilts must have been all of three metres high. From there we walked to the Market Square to admire the Town Hall, a four-storey seventeenth-century edifice, also in grey marlstone, and described as being in the Dutch Baroque style. We had, however, left the best almost till last.

The elegant Gothic Dominican Church in Helmstraat, constructed in the fourteenth century, fell into disuse when Napoleon invaded the city and evicted the monks in 1794. Afterwards it was used variously as a warehouse, an archive, and, more recently, a bicycle store. In the early part of this century a proposal was approved to convert it into a bookshop. The resulting conversion boasts a number of tall metal bookshelves running the full length of the nave, with their upper levels accessible by stairs and a lift, leading to walkways. In the Choir there is a cross-shaped "altar" surrounded by seats, enabling it to be used as a reading desk. The beautiful rib-vaulted ceiling and murals have been perfectly preserved, and the "Guardian" newspaper is quoted as saying it is "The best bookshop in the world". Outside, under gathering clouds, we walked the kilometre or so to the Bisschopsmollen, a working watermill situated on a small stream running into the River Meuse. The wooden wheel still operates, providing power for the milling of grain in the bakery alongside. A final pause was necessary at a cafe by the Sintservaasbrug bridge over the Meuse, from where, as the sun briefly emerged from behind its blanket of cloud, we watched the huge numbers of cyclists entering and leaving the city centre. Back at the station, we boarded the Liege train and during the short journey ate delicious almond slices, purchased earlier from a bakery in the city centre. That evening, as a rare treat, we decided to eat in the hotel dining room, and were not disappointed by the Wienerschnitzel, chips, and beer.

The following day we resolved to learn more about Liege's industrial past. In the late nineteenth century the city had been one of continental Europe's most important manufacturers of steel, largely due to the efforts of John Cockerill, from Haslingden in Lancashire, England, who established the area's first iron-making plant in 1817. He continued to expand his activities into engineering and manufacturing, becoming the area's biggest employer, but his business failed in 1840. He travelled to St Petersburg in Russia to try to raise funds from Tsar Nicholas 1st, but on his return contracted Typhoid and died in Warsaw in June of that year, at the age of 50, leaving no heirs. The company, however, survived, and around 1860 began making high-volume steel, eventually becoming for a while the world's largest steelmaker. However the 1970s saw falls in world demand and greater output from developing countries, leading to closures in Liege and a deep recession in the industry which matched similar recessions in many other European towns and cities that were heavily dependent on the steel and coal industries.

We decided on a visit to Maison de Metallurgie et de l'Industrie, the city's museum for the iron and steel and related industries, about a kilometre and a half from the hotel, the walk taking us past the cathedral in the city centre and through the Parc d'Avroy, a pleasant green space sporting a lake with fountains. From there we struck out Eastwards to first cross the fast-flowing River Meuse then the parallel Meuse Canal, finally arriving at the museum, a small row of two-storey brick buildings with arched windows and pitched roofs, fronting directly onto the pavement. The buildings date from 1848 and were originally a sheet-metal factory. Expecting something larger, we bought tickets and checked out the modest collection of exhibits. The star attraction is an original charcoal-fired blastfurnace, which produced iron but not steel, dating back to 1693, a time well before the technology had advanced far enough to use coke as a fuel in smelting iron. There are disappointingly few exhibits relating to high-volume steel production, which began in England in around 1855 with the invention of the Bessemer Converter. Steel production was undoubtedly the city's major commercial activity over a period of a century or more, and I felt it should have been more central to the museum's exhibits. There is photographic display explaining the development of the steelmaking process, which was helpful, but other than this there was only a forge, and a helpful room devoted to John Cockerill's pioneering work in establishing the industry in the City. Other rooms are devoted to topics such as the computer and energy industries, presumably there to interest the school-age visitor. For me the most intriguing exhibit was a Zinc-coated metal bathtub, purporting to have belonged to Napoleon I.

Outside we recrossed the canal and walked through the nearby Parc Bovarie in warm sunshine, heading for Liege's main art gallery, La Bovarie, a handsome domed stone building with a hint of the Belle Epoque about it. Its collection is not without merit, with a reasonable selection of 20th century work by such as Picasso, Chagall, and Leger, in addition to earlier works. The parkland location is delightful, and we were happy to relax in the cafe and simply enjoy the day.

Back at the hotel we collected our luggage, returned to the building-site at Guillemins Station, and caught the train to Brussels, a pleasant one-hour journey in the sunshine. At Brussels we crossed over to the Eurostar side of the station and some 2 ½ hours later were disembarking at London St

Pancras station. It had been a busy five days during which, excluding The UK, we'd visited five countries and discovered some interesting and entertaining towns and cities that are rarely on the tourist trail. As a bonus, we'd managed to do this without setting foot inside an airport. As we travelled home from St Pancras we discussed channel-hopping on the TV, and agreed that, in future, if we happened to light on an Andre Rieu concert from the Vrijthof Square in Maastricht, we would be honour bound to watch it all the way through.

Chapter 16

Russia

The secret of politics? Make a good treaty with Russia — **Otto von Bismarck**

Russia is a riddle wrapped in a mystery inside an enigma — **Winston Churchill**

I took a speed-reading course and read War and Peace in twenty minutes. It involves Russia — **Woody Allen**

Homosexuality in Russia is a crime and the punishment is seven years in prison, locked up with the other men. There is a three-year waiting list — **Yakov Smirnoff**

The Fuhrer has decided to raze the city of St. Petersburg from the face of the earth. After the defeat of Soviet Russia there will be not the slightest reason for the future existence of this large city — **Walter Warlimont**

Vladimir Ilyich Lenin hailing a taxi. Problems with the Cyrillic alphabet. Caviar and vodka supper. Bump and rob attempt on the metro. Possibly the world's greatest museum. Two of the sixteen oil paintings by Leonardo da Vinci known to exist. 125-metre escalator. Bus journey without paying. Amber stolen by Nazis. Gold box containing beauty-spots. Revolution locations.

Russia, more correctly known as the Russian Federation, is the largest country on earth by area, accounting for one eighth of the planet's land-mass. Stretching from eastern Europe to central and eastern Asia, there has long been a debate as to whether it should be considered a European nation. Pragmatically, any country on the continent of Europe that lies to the west of the Ural Mountains and to the North of Kazakhstan is normally deemed to be European, and whilst only 22% of the Russian land mass is so defined, this area contains 77% of the country's population, and includes its two largest cities, Moscow and St. Petersburg, with the result that the country is generally classified as "European".

The Russian language presents more than the usual problems to visitors from overseas, in that it is written in the Cyrillic script, which has only a passing resemblance to the Western European Latin alphabet. It requires the visitor to have phonetic knowledge of the 49 individual letters in Cyrillic before he or she can even attempt anything but the most basic verbal translation. For example, in the word that looks like "Mockba" in Cyrillic script, the "Mo" is unchanged in Latin Script, but the "c" is pronounces as "s" in Latin. The "k" remains as the Latin "k", the "b" is equivalent to "v" in Latin, and the "a" is identical to the Latin "a". The word in Latin script can therefore be written and spoken as "Moskva", the name of the Russian capital, Moscow. I found it is useful to carry with me a copy of the Cyrillic alphabet, with phonetic Latin equivalents, to help in pronunciation of place-names, particularly when travelling by train, tram, and underground.

Russia's twentieth-century history is largely defined by its Revolution in 1917 when the population rose against and eventually overthrew the ruling imperial Romanov family. A year later an outbreak of civil war saw the deposed Emperor, Tsar Nicholas II, his wife Alexandra, and their five children evacuated to Yekaterinburg in the Ural Mountains, where they were later shot dead by the revolutionary Bolsheviks. The country thus became the world's first Communist State, its system of government being based on the political philosophy promoted by Karl Marx in his book "Das Kapital". In the early 1920s the country's first Communist leader, Vladimir Ilyich Ulyanov, better known as Lenin, was instrumental in creating a wider Communist bloc known as the Soviet Union, a grouping of nominally independent East European states that were subservient to Russia and to all intents and purposes ruled from Moscow. Lenin died in 1924 and was succeeded by Joseph Stalin, a ruthless dictator who subsequently led his country and the wider Soviet Union in the defeat of Germany in World War II. A major event in that conflict was the Siege of Leningrad, later to become St. Petersburg, when German forces laid siege to the city over a period of 872 days, during which around a million residents died, mainly from starvation. After the war, the strict authoritarian Communist regime resumed under Stalin until his death in 1953, and subsequently continued under his successors. In 1991, following a long period of economic and social unrest, the party leadership decided to abandon Socialist principles and become a fully-fledged Capitalist state. As a consequence the Soviet Union was disbanded, with most of its member-states joining the European Union. Symbolically, most of the statues of Joseph Stalin were subsequently removed from public places and destroyed when it emerged that his peacetime economic policies may have led to the deaths of up to six million citizens. His predecessor, Lenin, who was held responsible for only a small number of peacetime deaths by comparison, was spared such ignominy.

My partner and I took the opportunity this time to fly as non-package tour passengers on a five-day package-holiday flight from London Gatwick. We'd found this convenient on previous occasions, taking advantage of a low-cost flight but avoiding the expense of obligatory involvement in guided tours at the destination. The month was October, chilly in England but likely to be colder still in St Petersburg, a city on a similar latitude to that of Anchorage in Alaska. At the time Russia is one of only two European countries that require visas, the other being Belarus, so we were duly documented as we landed at Pulkovo International Airport, about 20 kilometres South of the city.

On arrival at the airport the tour leader kindly allowed us to travel into the city on one of the tour's coaches, despite the fact that we were two of the half-dozen or so "flight-only" passengers, and we therefore benefitted from her helpful running commentary *en route*. As we bowled along the broad boulevard of Moskovsky Avenue towards the city centre we passed the awe-inspiring, not to say intimidating, House of Soviets, a huge stone edifice in the Stalinist style originally built as the administration headquarters for the entire Soviet Union. Construction was completed in 1941, just before the invasion of Russia by the Germans, and as a result the building was never used for its intended purpose. Ironically, it now houses businesses who live and presumably thrive in the capitalist world. As if to emphasise the recent political changes, on the far side of the Square opposite I spotted the unmistakeable golden arches of a McDonald's burger restaurant. By contrast, In front of the House of Soviets, and right by the roadside, stands a ten-metre high plinthed statue of Lenin, his right arm outstretched, seemingly pointing towards some far-off ideological destination for his people. Our young Russian tour guide, Natasha, couldn't resist sharing a little joke.

"And on your left, ladies and gentlemen, you will see a statue of Vladimir Ilyich Lenin, hailing a taxi!"

Twenty years previously, had she uttered such words to a group of tourists, she would have risked arrest by the secret police, interrogation, then exile to a Gulag labour camp where she would have been obliged to spend the next few years being "re-educated". In one short sentence Natasha had managed to encapsulate her country's recent seismic political changes.

About half a dozen of us exited the bus at the Angleterre Hotel , a handsome six-storey building on the South-West side of St Isaac's Square in the city centre, close by the Neva River and directly opposite St. Isaac's Cathedral, a domed neoclassical building that had been deconsecrated during the Soviet era. The hotel, opened as recently as 1991, replaced a previous building on the site, Hotel Leningradskaya, and under the ownership of Rocco Forte & Family PLC of England was one of the earliest to take advantage of the country's capitalist transformation. After checking in and depositing our luggage in our third-floor room, my partner and I made the short windswept walk under cloudy skies to Nevsky Prospekt, the city's main shopping boulevard. There we found a pleasant restaurant, and joined its youthful clientele to eat borscht soup with potatoes, followed by meringue, and accompanied by a couple of beers. Thus fortified, we returned to the hotel and planned the week ahead.

St Petersburg was created in 1703 by the Russian Emperor, or Tsar, Peter the Great, who at the time was conscious of his country's need for a major port on the Baltic Sea. The city was constructed on the malaria-infested River Neva delta, in the eastern arm of the Baltic, known nowadays as the Gulf of Finland. From 1732 to 1918 it was the capital of Russia and home to the country's royal family. In 1918 Vladimir Ilyich Lenin came to power as the country's first communist leader and, fearing possible sea-borne invasion, decided to move the capital to Moscow, some 650 kilometres to the South. Arguably the most important port on the Baltic Sea, St. Petersburg is also a major centre of manufacturing, being involved in steelmaking, aerospace, shipbuilding, and motor vehicle manufacture amongst other industrial activities. During its turbulent history the city has undergone various changes of name. From 1703 to 1914 it was named Saint Petersburg, then became Petrograd from 1914 to 1924, in order to remove the German word "burg" from the name, then Leningrad in 1924 following the death of Vladimir Ilyich Lenin, and finally back to St. Petersburg in 1991 after the fall of Communism.

The following morning we headed over to the Hermitage Museum and Art Gallery, undoubtedly St. Petersburg's star attraction, being one of the largest museums in the world, attracting three million visitors annually. The Hermitage collection was started by Catherine II, also known as Catherine the Great, Empress of Russia for 34 years from 1762, and was originally displayed by her privately in one of the five adjoining buildings that currently make up the museum. At the time the buildings constituted what was known as the Winter Palace, dating from 1711 and the home of the ruling family. They make up what is effectively a neoclassical terrace almost 200 metres long, approached from the south over the huge expanse of Palace Square, a paved space where today's visitor can hire a horse-drawn carriage to tour the city.

It is impossible to do justice to the Hermitage collection in a few short paragraphs, just as it is impossible to view it in its entirety in less than, say, two full days. The building covers an area of 220,000 square metres and the collection totals over three million items, including 18,000 paintings, amongst which it boasts two of the thirteen completed paintings by Leonardo da Vinci known to exist in the world. There are 750,000 archaeological items, 13,000 sculptures, and 620,000 graphic items. Paintings alone occupy 120 rooms and cover all movements, styles, and artists from the twelfth century to the mid-1900s. A separate section, known as the Treasury, contains what is possibly the greatest collection of gold, silver, and precious-stone items on public display anywhere in the world. Two treasury tours are on offer, one named Gold" and the other "Diamond". We chose "Gold", which covers five rooms mainly devoted to gold artefacts from around the world, usually jewel-encrusted, and many of which were in Catherine the Great's original collection. Some of the more ancient items have important archaeological significance in that they originate from tribes that once inhabited the Russian landmass, but many of those from the eighteenth century Royal collection are little more than opulent, or, in some cases, just plain vulgar, trinkets.

A typical example is a small, gold, diamond-encrusted beauty-spot box. This was designed to contain small circular black pieces of taffeta or velvet, one of which would be applied to the face or neck of a woman (in this case Catherine the Great), its position conforming to a code which indicated her emotional state at the time to members of the court. Inside the box a mirror would assist her in discreetly changing the spot's location during a ball or similar grand occasion if she underwent a change of mood. The most opulent, or vulgar if you prefer it, item in the collection is surely the horse attire presented to Nicolas I by Mahmud, The Sultan of the Ottoman Empire. Its metre-square saddle cloth bears gold fittings and is encrusted with more than 16,000 diamonds.

For the remainder of the day, and with frequent stops to rest, we toured as much as we could of the art collection's 120 rooms, taking more time than we could afford in the magnificent Impressionist section. It was here that we came across Monet's "Woman in a Garden" a breathtaking study in light and colour that for me outshines almost all his considerable *oeuvre*. Painted when he was a mere 27 years old, it simply depicts a lady in a plain white dress standing in a sunlit garden. For me, this painting alone justified the visit, but In the time available it soon became clear that we couldn't possibly see the whole collection, thereby missing many of its important works. Hoping to return later in the week, we left at closing-time and under leaden skies headed back to the hotel.

On the far side of Palace Square we encountered the somewhat unusual sight of a flat-bed lorry parked in the street, its trailer bearing half a dozen cut-down public-style telephones along either side. Customers, standing on the pavement or in the road, were busy using them to make calls, in much the same way that they would if they were calling from a phone-box on the street. At the time mobile phones were unavailable to anyone but the very rich in Russia, so it seems we were witness to the first attempts by local entrepreneurs to provide a mobile service in their city. Nearby we paused for a coffee in an internet cafe, then found a convenience store where we picked up food and drink for snacks in our room, including a bottle of vodka costing the equivalent of £2.00. Back at the hotel we had time to make use of the swimming-pool, situated on the fourth floor with its windows looking out over to the floodlit St. Isaac's Cathedral across the square. As I swam I pondered as to how many swimming-pools there are in the world that offer the swimmer a cathedral view.

That evening we returned to the restaurant on Nevsky Prospekt, where we ate fried Perch with cheese and mushroom sauce. Perch is regularly eaten throughout Eastern Europe, along with Carp, which is also commonly found on restaurant menus in France. For me it has always been something of a mystery as to why both fish, equally delicious, seem for some reason to be considered inferior to sea-fish by the British. After the meal we walked over to the somewhat indelicately-named but spectacular Church of Our Saviour on Spilled Blood, its floodlit baroque frontage reflected in the waters of the adjacent Groboedov Canal. Arguably the most exotic of St. Petersburg's buildings, its exterior is a riot of baroque ornamentation topped by five differently-coloured onion domes of varying sizes and designs. The church was erected on the site where Tsar Alexander II was assassinated in a bomb explosion in 1881, hence its name. His son, Alexander III, ordered it to be built in memory of his father, and construction was completed in 1907, fewer than a hundred years prior to our visit. After the revolution it was deconsecrated and was used variously as a mortuary for some of the million or so who died in the city's siege in World War Two, and then as a vegetable warehouse. Today it is restored to its former glory but has never been reconsecrated.

For the first time we took a ride on the Metro, starting at Nevsky Prospekt station, whose escalator is one of the longest in the world at around 125 metres, taking close to two minutes to reach platform level. It was here that I suffered an attempted "Bump and Pickpocket" attack. As the train arrived and the doors opened, I was heavily jostled by surrounding passengers, and when I finally extricated myself from the crowd I noticed that the zip on my coat had been opened to more than half-way down. Fortunately my wallet was still in place in its inside pocket, but it had been a close-run thing.

The following morning, in glorious winter sunshine, we walked the half-kilometre or so across the Trinity Bridge over the sparkling River Neva to the island on which stands the Peter and Paul Fortress. Discarded vodka bottles littered the pavement, making this something of an obstacle course, and at the far end of the bridge we encountered a street trader selling traditional Russian-style fur hats, *de rigeur* at that time of year amongst the city's citizens. The efficacy of these hats has always been something of a mystery to me, as logic dictates that the fur should be on the inside rather than the outside for maximum benefit. Foregoing the opportunity to buy, we crossed the short pedestrian bridge onto the island and entered the fortress, the original Citadel of St. Petersburg, effectively the city's birthplace. For much of its time it served as a high-security prison, incarcerating at various times in its history Fyodor Dostoevsky, Maxim Gorky, Leon Trotsky, and even Josep Broz Tito, the dictator of Yugoslavia. Known as the "Russian Bastille", the fortress was stormed by the Bolsheviks during the 1917 revolution, where they found only seventeen prisoners in the cells. This bears ironic comparison with the storming of the Bastille prison in Paris during the French Revolution in 1789, where a mere seven prisoners were liberated. In both cases, the action has historic national symbolism that far outweighs its practical benefit to the revolutionaries at the time.

The most attractive building on the island is undoubtedly the Peter and Paul Cathedral, an elegant domeless Russian Orthodox edifice in pale yellow stone boasting a high bell-tower topped by a gloriously slender central spire 123 metres high, allowing the city to lay claim to possessing the world's tallest Russian Orthodox cathedral. The bell-tower contains a carillon of 51 bells, made in The Netherlands in 2001 as a replacement for a previous set that was unserviceable. The building contains the tombs of all but two of the Russian Tsars, and in 1998 finally became the last resting place of Nicholas II, whose remains, and those of his wife and five children, had been discovered buried in woodland close to where they had been executed in Yekaterinburg eighty years earlier in 1918.

The Island proved a pleasantly peaceful contrast to the hustle and bustle of the city centre, and as we strolled around we were able to enjoy the view of the distant Hermitage Museum across the placid Neva River, some five hundred metres wide at this point. From the Island we walked westwards along the Neva embankment in search of the Aurora, a three-funnelled navy cruiser moored on the river and now a museum. Built in 1900, the vessel took part in the Russo-Japanese war in 1904-5, before being sent to patrol the Baltic during World War I, during which time she happened to be anchored in St Petersburg awaiting major repairs in February 1917 when the revolution began. The crew immediately joined forces with the Bolsheviks, shot dead their captain, and set up their own revolutionary committee. The vessel became forever a symbol of the revolution when, by agreement with the Bolshevik leaders, its forecastle gun was used to fire the first (blank) shot of the revolution on 25th October 1917. It had been agreed that this signal would precipitate the storming of the Winter Palace opposite, thus setting the revolution in motion. Subsequently converted into a museum, the vessel underwent a refit in 1987 when, it is claimed, some of its armour plating was found to have originated in Britain. On board we found memorabilia associated with the revolution, with visits to the crew's quarters and engine-room giving a fascinating insight into life at sea at the time.

From there we walked the half-kilometre or so to the Finland Railway Station, a somewhat uninspiring rectilinear soviet-style building rebuilt in 1960 after suffering damage during World War II. Fronted by a pedestalled statue of Lenin, once again appearing to be hailing a taxi, the station has its place in history assured, being the location of Lenin's arrival in April 1917 on his return from exile in Switzerland. Greeted by a huge crowd of cheering fellow-Bolsheviks, he was hoisted onto the roof of an armoured car and driven through the streets to the revolution headquarters. The steam locomotive that hauled his train is preserved inside the station, and inside the concourse are typical soviet-style sculptures glorifying the revolution.

We continued the railway theme with a metro ride to the Warsaw Station, disused at the time and part-converted into a largely-outdoor railway museum. I understand the main station building has since been converted into a shopping mall. The museum is an excellent collection of ancient locomotives, rolling stock, and railway artefacts, but the prize for best exhibit must go to the huge rail-mounted MK-3-12 gun, almost fifteen metres long and with a bore of 305 millimetres. Originally intended for use on a battleship, the gun's design was adapted during World War II to enable it to be used as a land weapon mounted on a railway truck. Three of these trucks were built, their guns being rescued from the battleship Inperatritsa Marya, which had sunk off Sevastopol during the First World War. The gun had a range of 29 kilometres, and even today, in a museum setting, it looks terrifying.

Our final visit was by tram to Vitebsky station, another historic railway landmark, being the first railway station in Russia. Originally opened in 1837 by Tsar Nicholas I, the station was built to link the city with Tsarskoe Seloe, also known as Pushkin, the location of the Royal Summer Palace. Completely rebuilt in 1904, the station is one of St. Petersburg's best kept secrets, a glorious art deco building, with Jugendstil decoration, more like a royal palace than a railway station. Tsar Nicholas II was of course a regular user on his way to the summer palace, and the royal retiring rooms have recently been opened to the public.

On the concourse we found the station almost deserted, with just a single platform occupied by the green and white rolling-stock of the evening train to Minsk, capital of Belarus, which stood ready to depart. The 800 kilometre journey requires an all sleeping-car train, and the presence of smoke rising lazily from a small chimney at the end of each carriage indicated that the train attendants, one to each coach, had already fired-up the solid-fuel stoves which would enable them to provide hot water to their passengers. In the gathering twilight, and beneath the cavernous arched train shed, we lingered at the end of the dimly-lit platform, waiting for the train to depart. As we waited, savouring the delicious scent of wood-smoke that filled the chill evening air, the eerie silence was finally broken when the train began to move, imperceptibly at first, and set off on the fifteen-hour journey to Belarus. Although these ten or so minutes were little more than a brief and inconsequential part of what had thus far been a busy holiday, the experience nevertheless has become one of those rare, almost mystical moments in life, the tiniest details of which remain inexplicably lodged in the memory.

Back at the hotel we put on extra layers of clothing before venturing out in a snowstorm to the restaurant on Nevsky Prospekt. On the way back we called in at a busy, elegant, wood-panelled delicatessen with the intention of buying caviar. The window display suggested that the delicacy was available at a bargain price, and, never having tried it, I was determined to grasp the opportunity. The shop was, I believe, one of the last in the city to still operate the old Communist system for retailing, which seems to have been designed to maximise employment and minimise customer convenience. After queuing at the counter and identifying which small tin of Caviar I wished to buy, I was handed a slip of paper by the assistant, on which she'd written the product name and price. She gestured that I should take it to an elevated cash-desk at the far end of the counter, where I joined another queue. There, I handed the slip of paper to the cash-lady, who rubber-stamped it and handed it back after I'd paid the requisite amount of cash. I then returned to the original counter where I joined a third queue, eventually handing the piece of paper to the assistant who smiled as she gave me my tin of Caviar.

Outside, in snow that was beginning to settle, we called in at a convenience store to buy savoury biscuits and the smallest-available of bottle of Vodka. Opposite the store stood a busy branch of McDonald's sporting a gaily-coloured, slightly intimidating life-size plastic figure of Ronald McDonald seated by the window. For a moment I wondered what Vladimir Ilyich Lenin would have made of this quintessentially capitalist invader of his beloved city, ninety years or so after his arrival at the Finland Station to lead the revolution. Back at the hotel a supper of caviar, biscuits, and vodka provided a fitting ending to what had d been a busy and fascinating day.

The following morning in bright sunlight, but with snow on the ground, we walked to New Holland Island, a triangular piece of land surrounded by canals. Although not a major tourist venue, we were interested to visit it simply because in the eighteenth and nineteenth centuries it was a shipbuilding centre for the city, with its entrance guarded by a magnificent eighteenth-century neo-classical brick arch some thirty metres high and flanked by red granite columns. For those who know Rome, it bears some similarity to the Arch of Septimus Severus in the forum. At the time of our visit most of the island's buildings were disused or derelict, and in any case the pathway over the narrow canal bridge leading to the arch was blocked, so we could see little from the outside. I understand the island stayed closed to the public until 2010, but has now been developed as a park and cultural centre, financed by Roman Abramovich, the owner of Chelsea Football Club in London, who has expressed the intention to open a gallery in the cultural centre in which he will display his own extensive art collection.

From the Island it was but a short walk to the Mariinsky theatre, opened in 1860 and where composers such as Tchaikovsky, Mussorgsky, and Rimsky-Korsakov premiered many of their works. Named after the wife of Tsar Alexander II, the name's link to Russia's imperial past was deemed unacceptable during the Communist era, leading to it being renamed the Kirov Theatre. Its ballet company became world famous, responsible for nurturing the careers of the likes of Anna Pavlova, Vaslav Nijinsky, and Rudolf Nureyev. The building's neo-classical exterior fronts a spectacular and highly ornate "U" shaped auditorium, which sadly we were unable to view, the box-office being the only part that was open at the time. A beautiful scale model of the auditorium can, however, be examined just inside the entrance, serving only to remind us that we should have found time to attend a concert there whilst in the city.

Outside we took a tram back to Vitebsky railway station, the scene of the previous evening's visit, as we planned to take the train to the Tsar's Summer Palace, known as the Catherine Palace, at Tsarskoye Selo, a town about thirty kilometres to the South. In the station buffet we consumed pancakes drenched in condensed milk, not necessarily a meal that the Tsar might have enjoyed, I thought, but nevertheless delicious and surely worthy of being considered as a menu item by restaurateurs in the West. This time there was no scent of wood-smoke as we boarded the train, a somewhat run-down suburban unit, consisting of open carriages with low-backed wood-slatted seats, half-full at best and in desperate need of a window cleaner. The half-hour ride through the sunlit suburbs was pleasant enough, however, and we exited the station at Tsarskoye Selo to find a world devoid of Latin-script signs, thereby obliging us to resort to our copy of the Cyrillic alphabet in an attempt to get directions. The Palace is more than two kilometres from the station, so we needed to take a bus, which meant identifying the bus number, the location of the bus stop, and the procedure for buying a ticket.

Those who visited Eastern Europe in the late twentieth century may be familiar with the booths outside railway stations that sold sweets, tobacco, snacks, and newspapers. These differ from similar pavement-booths in the West in that all transactions are conducted through a small opening at the front, situated at waist height and not more than thirty centimetres square, thus obliging the purchaser to stoop if he or she wishes to engage the owner in conversation. After two stooping attempts to get information about the buses, it became clear that this was not to be a fruitful line of enquiry, so I turned instead to a nearby youth, clad, despite the chill weather, in what seemed to be the almost obligatory black leather jacket, T-shirt and blue jeans. In very basic English he told us we were to take bus number 376 and helpfully pointed out the bus stop. Unable to find a ticket office, we took a chance and climbed aboard the crowded bus when it arrived, obliging us to stand for the entire journey. Unable to see through the steamed-up windows, we were prevented from identifying any landmark en route that might be useful should we be required to return on foot. Eventually, however, we managed to catch a glimpse of the palace, its three gilded onion domes glinting in the late afternoon sun beneath a clear blue sky. With great relief we exited the bus at what appeared to be its terminus, relieved to have reached our objective without suffering an embarrassing confrontation with a ticket inspector. From there it was a walk of a hundred metres or so along the road to the Palace's entrance.

The Catherine Palace, often referred to as the Summer Palace, is arguably second only to the Hermitage in St Petersburg in the pantheon of Russia's greatest monuments. Its rococo neoclassical frontage, painted sky-blue and white with gold decoration, is more than 300 metres long and is surmounted by the three golden onion-domes. The building is surrounded on three sides by huge formal gardens with lakes and fountains, and its grand scale and layout has much in common with the Palace of Versailles in France, which had been extended to its final size in 1715, only some 37 years before the design for the Catherine Palace was approved by Empress Elizabeth in 1752. There is no record of Elizabeth having visited Versailles, although it is known that she had strong francophile views at the time. The Palace was completed four years later, six years before Elizabeth's successor, Catherine II, known as Catherine the Great, ascended to the throne. It is said that Catherine and her successors used this country retreat as a sanctuary from the burdens of state in St. Petersburg, but it is equally possible that summers in that city, built as it was on what was effectively a river delta swamp, were sometimes made unbearable due to mosquito infestation.

The interior of the palace, still being restored after having been looted by the Nazis as they fled following their unsuccessful siege of Leningrad (St Petersburg) in 1944, is never less than spectacular, with a couple of rooms particularly worthy of mention. Pride of place must go to the Amber Room, some 10 metres high and covering an area about the size of half a tennis court, whose walls were originally covered from ceiling to floor with huge murals assembled from carved pieces of amber, the precious stone which washes ashore on Baltic Sea beaches. Amber possesses the rare property of changing colour if heat is applied, with the final shade being dependent on the duration of the heating and the temperature used. This technique provided the craftsmen with a palette of some 350 colours, including shades of yellow, red, brown, and black. When completed, this incredible room was often referred to as the eighth wonder of the world. Sadly, as the Nazis retreated they took with them all the amber panels, which have never since been recovered. Debate continues regarding their possible location, and theories have come and gone, but it is fair to say that after seventy years the trail has run cold.

In 1979 a decision was taken to restore the room, a task employing 40 Russian and German carvers, and reputedly requiring six hundred kilos of amber. The work was completed by 2003, partly due to a donation of £3.5 million dollars from the German energy company E.ON as a gesture of wartime reparation. Vladimir Putin of Russia and Gerhardt Schroeder of Germany performed the opening ceremony at completion, symbolically on the 300th anniversary of the founding of St. Petersburg. At the date of our visit the restoration had only recently been completed and I must say that the astonishing finished product justifies every bit of effort and money that has been expended. The design and quality of the carving is breathtaking, and outside the room is a fascinating display explaining the technical problems encountered, particularly in creating the many colours required..

From there we visited the palace ballroom, also known as the Great Hall, 1,000 square metres in area and spanning the full width of the building, thereby affording views over the extensive snow-covered gardens to the front and rear through high, arched windows. Gilded stucco decorates the entire interior, and a huge mural named simply "Russia" covers the ceiling. As visitors, we were issued with soft slippers to wear over our shoes to prevent damage to the intricately patterned wooden floor. Catherine, presumably sporting one of her beauty-spots, received high-ranking guests in this room prior to enjoying sumptuous feasts in the nearby dining room, at a time when the peasants in the surrounding fields perhaps wondered where the next meal was coming from.

On the way back to the bus we took a route through the garden, and were pleased to be asked by a class of twenty or so Russian schoolchildren if we would take a group photograph of them, using their own cameras, with the Palace in the background. These were the days before mobile phones and selfies, and the complex operation required them to hand over half a dozen or so of their cameras at a time, allowing me to take one picture with each, hand them back, then take the next half-dozen, and so on until they each had a picture on their own camera. At the end we were honoured to be asked to join the group whilst one of them took a picture. I wonder if that photograph is still to be found in a photograph album somewhere in deepest Russia, perhaps occasionally being shown to a son or daughter as a reminder of how photography used to be. Nowadays, when I see the plethora of selfies being taken at tourist sites, I often find myself wistfully thinking back to the Catherine Palace.

It was by now getting late, and after checking out the souvenir shop we headed back to the bus terminus and this time travelled back to the railway station legally, having been able to buy a ticket. The train ride back to St Petersburg took us past ranks of Soviet-built tenements and high-rise blocks of flats, now somehow rendered slightly less menacing by the light covering of snow and the reddening light from the setting sun. The Metro at Vitebsky Station took us back to the hotel and from there we walked over to the usual restaurant on Nevsky Prospekt for our final meal in St. Petersburg.

We had spent a fascinating and rewarding time in one of the world's great cities. Everything had gone according to plan, despite the occasional panic whilst travelling by train, metro, and tram, usually caused by nothing more than problems with the Cyrillic alphabet. The freedom we enjoyed is worth comparing with what might have happened on a similar visit fewer than twenty years previously. At that time we would only have been granted a visa as part of an organised party, and on arrival our every move would have been monitored by the State. All tourist travel before 1992 was controlled by an organisation called Intourist, which was run by the KGB, the Russian secret service. Intourist owned the half-dozen or so hotels in St. Petersburg where tourists were allowed to stay, and it controlled all travel by tourist groups to places of interest. At the time it was said that "Intourist is to tourism as indigestion is to digestion." Thankfully the organisation was privatised in 1992, along with much of the Russian state-owned assets, and today it operates as a respectable capitalist business in joint venture with Thomas Cook PLC. A visitor can now travel freely more or less anywhere in the country, and St. Petersburg, once Vladimir Ilyich Lenin's beloved capital city, is now a major tourist destination. I wonder what he would have made of it all....

Chapter 17

Iceland

Depression hangs over me as if I were Iceland   **Philip Larkin**

Iceland is a living geological masterpiece, a peerless volcanic land of dramatic skies, bubbling earth, thundering waterfalls and thermal lagoons. If you want an insight into how the planet was sculpted by the forces of Mother Nature, exploring the golden circle will provide many answers   **Clare Jones**

Touching the Eurasian and North American tectonic plates. Sulphur smell from domestic hot water. Health scare in the cold. Whaling ships. Strokkur geyser. The world's first parliament. Algae and mud from the Blue Lagoon at 95 Euros per tube.

For much of the late twentieth century Iceland was an expensive destination for the traveller. Prior to the liberalisation of the global airline industry, which began in Europe in December 1987, air travel was heavily regulated in terms of prices, entry and routes. Inter-country air transportation was governed by a maze of bilateral and multilateral agreements between governments and air carriers, meaning that since 1970 Icelandair had enjoyed a monopoly on flights in and out of the island and was able to charge whatever (often high) prices they chose to impose. By 1993 the European Union had swept away all such agreements and as a member of the European Economic Area, with access to the single market of the European Union, Iceland, and hence Icelandair, was for the first time obliged to allow competition from low-cost carriers such as Easyjet and Ryanair. As a result Iceland has seen a huge expansion in its tourist industry, with nearly two million arrivals in 2016 compared with fewer than 100,000 in 1980. Easyjet have played no small part in this, and I was happy to give then my business, given that their return fare to Iceland was less than the price of a train ticket from London to Glasgow.

A November flight meant that its low cost would be offset by the possibility of less than ideal weather, coupled with the fact that daylight would last for no more than seven hours, with sunrise as late as 10:30am. This is due to the island's latitude, immediately to the South of the Arctic Circle and more northerly than much of Alaska. The inhabited Island of Grimsey, forty kilometres from Iceland's northern coastline and around four hundred kilometres from the capital, Reyjkavik, is bisected by the Arctic Circle, and the more intrepid visitor can take the three-hour boat-trip from the northern mainland to this island and have a photograph taken beside the post which marks the circle's location. My visit of three days' duration meant that there would sadly be no time for this, and in any case there would be plenty to do in and around the capital.

Keflavik, the Island's international airport, located around forty kilometres from the capital, Reykjavik, was anything but busy as I emerged from airside into the arrivals hall and obtained Icelandic Krona from a cash machine, before seeking guidance as to the best way to reach the capital. Most of my fellow-passengers were collected by friends and relatives by car, leaving me and a few stragglers to board the only bus parked outside. Whilst costing more than I would normally pay for a transfer, the bus provided a service that is probably unique in Europe in that the driver took note of each passenger's hotel name and told us we would be delivered to the door. In darkness, and beset by the occasional snow flurry, we set off along the unremarkable two-lane blacktop road westwards to Reykjavik. True to his word, the driver toured the streets of the city and deposited each of us in turn outside the appropriate hotel. Mine was a small family-run establishment in the west of the city, and once I'd checked in I had a beer in the small downstairs bar before turning in for the night.

Iceland's recorded history goes back to 874 AD when Norwegian settlers first arrived on the Island. In the sixteenth century it fell under Danish rule, becoming a colonial territory with the Danish King as Head of State. This arrangement continued until 1944 when a plebiscite was held, resulting in a 97% vote for abolition of the Monarchy and the establishment of a Republic. In 1946 the country joined NATO, becoming the only member of that organisation without a standing army. In 1994 it joined the European Economic Area, giving its businesses unfettered access to trade within the European Union in exchange for free movement of EU nationals who wish to live and work there. In the past few years there has been talk of applying for full EU membership, but this is still under debate.

Geographically, the Island's nearest landmasses are Greenland, just 290 kilometres to the West, Great Britain, 750 kilometres to the South, and Norway, just under 1,000 kilometres to the East. It is Europe's second largest Island after Great Britain, with 67% of its surface being tundra. Lakes and glaciers cover a further 14%. The island sits astride the junction of the Eurasian and North American tectonic plates, rendering it constantly susceptible to seismic and volcanic activity. This activity has resulted in the almost limitless availability of geothermal hot water and steam for electricity generation and heating. It is I believe the only country in the world where water for the domestic "Cold" tap must be routinely cooled on its way to consumer. Of the country's population of approximately 330,000, similar in number to that of the city of Cardiff in Wales, more than two thirds live in the region around Reykjavik. Around 40% of the country's economy is derived from the fishing industry, with a further 35% being from the manufacture of aluminium-related products. The process for smelting aluminium from ore consumes large quantities of electricity, and the country's three large smelters take full advantage of the almost limitless availability of low-cost electricity available. Iceland is in consequence the world's eleventh largest producer of Aluminium metal.

Before leaving the UK I'd checked the internet for local bus services to each of the major tourist destinations on the island, with little success. Their remoteness means there is little demand from the Icelanders for a regular bus service, with the result that these routes have effectively been abandoned by the local authority and handed over to tour operators. When travelling, I always try to avoid organised tours wherever possible, but I knew that Iceland would be one of the few European countries where a guided tour would be necessary on at least the first day.

Taking a shower in my room the following morning, I noticed a slight sulphurous smell seemingly emanating from the hot water, something I hadn't experienced when cleaning my teeth using cold tap water. When asked about this, the lady on reception told me it was perfectly normal, as the hot water is geothermal in origin, whereas the cold water is sourced from reservoirs. Thus, at least partly reassured, I joined a scattering of fellow-guests in the breakfast room and tucked into cold meat, cheese, bread, and yoghurt, washed down with two cups of very good coffee. During the meal I studied the street map kindly provided by the hotel receptionist and on it located the Golden Circle tour-bus garage, about a kilometre away. It was scarcely daylight when, chilled by a bitter northerly wind, I set out from the hotel, and as I negotiated the uneven covering of snow on the pavement I was grateful for the lingering illumination provided by the street-lamps. Directly ahead on the Eastern horizon the brightening but cloud-covered sky suggested the sun was rising, but there seemed little hope that the tour would take place under a clear blue sky. At the tour office I joined fellow-tourists queuing for tickets for any of the half-dozen or so tours on offer, my choice being the "Golden Circle". This appellation is given to a six-hour tour covering South-West Iceland's most popular tourist sites – the Gulfoss Waterfall, the Strokkur Geyser, and Thingvellir National Park, all located on the edge of the country's South-Western uplands. After a short wait the coach emerged from the garage and I climbed aboard, managing to grab a window-seat near the front.

Reykjavik is a compact city, and within minutes we had escaped its suburbs and were speeding along a windswept road and heading for the Thingvellir National Park, a World Heritage Site and arguably the most spectacular location on the tour. Soon we were travelling along a snow-covered two-lane road through a flat treeless plain, with red-tipped posts indicating the roadside snow depth to drivers. Alongside the road ran a substantial pipeline, perhaps a metre in diameter, that I later discovered carries hot-spring water from a distant source to the citizens of Reykjavik. The road eventually began to skirt a range of precipitous hills, the bases of which were strewn with huge boulders, the result of ancient earthquakes or volcanic activity. Mamy of the small farmsteads on the plain boasted an outbuilding from which steam rose, indicating that the farmer could be using steam from his own hot spring to drive an electrical generator, or perhaps heat his greenhouses.

Thingvellir National Park, an area of just under 100 square kilometres, lies in a rift valley marking the crest of the Mid-Atlantic Ridge, with the North Atlantic tectonic plate to the West and the Eurasian tectonic plate to the East. The visitor centre overlooks a canyon which is the meeting point of the two plates, perhaps thirty metres deep and ten metres wide, stretching out into the distance. We were encouraged by our tour guide to descend to the path at the bottom and walk along for a few hundred metres. Once there I took the opportunity to walk across the canyon from one vertical side to the other, enabling me later to claim that I had walked from North America to Europe in a matter of a few paces. Viewed from the top of the canyon, the park is a vast snow-dappled green, brown, and yellow tundra plain stretching out northwards towards the distant mountainous horizon, whilst to the South lies Iceland's largest fresh water lake, Pingvallavatn. The area is truly one of Europe's greatest natural wonders, not only providing a spectacular panorama, but also prompting a moment's pause to contemplate the potential impermanence of the planet on which we live.

A couple of kilometres or so to the North-East of the visitor centre, and visible below us on the plain, stood a terrace of five white -painted pitched-roof houses in a clearing by a small lake, with a small white steepled church close by. Surrounded by trees, relatively uncommon in Iceland, the buildings sit somewhat incongruously in the barren landscape. However the location has great historical significance for the Icelanders in that it is the site of the Althingi, the country's first parliament, established in 930AD to resolve problems between tribal chiefs, and claimed to be the world's oldest parliament. Despite its remote location the site remained in use as the country's legislative assembly until 1800, when it was moved to Reykjavik.

Back on the bus we headed for Gulfoss, a spectacular waterfall where the broad river Hvita descends what is effectively a huge three-step staircase, 32 metres high, then runs into a 70 metre-deep

Canyon. Arriving at the visitor centre, I was sorely tempted to head straight into the welcoming arms of the cafe, but instead decided to go to the viewing area on the basis that the already deteriorating weather might get even worse. A snow shower, blown by the bitter north wind, did nothing to ease my fears, but I made my way there along a narrow ice-covered path with only rickety handrails for support. The waterfall is certainly a cut above many I've seen, a violent and unchecked flow of water, and the freezing conditions had led to the formation of huge icicles on either side, some as much as ten metres long. I came away, however, more convinced than ever that for me, waterfalls are like castles – see one and you've seen them all. In addition, the bitter wind in this highly exposed setting was beginning to chill me to the bone, and I urgently needed the sanctuary of the cafe. On the way back up the path, still clutching the rickety handrails, I suddenly found myself scarcely able to get my breath, with the result that the final hundred metres or so took what seemed like an age to complete. Once inside the cafe I simply grabbed the nearest seat and sat, motionless, for all of fifteen minutes as my body slowly recovered from whatever had afflicted me. Eventually I was able to get up and go over to the counter, and after two cups of coffee and a sandwich I felt once again able to look the world in the eye. This had been my only health scare in all the years I'd been travelling, and fortunately there were no long-lasting effects. On the way out through the souvenir shop I forwent the opportunity to buy a soft-toy puffin, and back in the warmth of the bus I settled down for the final leg of the journey, a visit to the geyser Strokkur in the Haukadalar Valley, about twenty kilometres to the South.

The English word "Geyser" is derived from the Icelandic word Geysir, the name of a specific erupting hot spring in Iceland rather than a generic term for all such phenomena. Geysir was the first of these to be to be seen by modern Europeans, and means "Gusher" in Icelandic. Incidentally, the English word "Geezer", meaning "Man" or "Bloke" is etymologically different, being derived from the word "Guiser", meaning a mummer, an actor or someone who wore a disguise, Geysir itself has had long periods of inactivity in its history, and since 2003 has virtually ceased to erupt. Its activity is affected by the geological instability of the area, where even slight seismological activity can affect the underground water-course necessary for it to work. In 1981, after it had entered an inactive phase, the authorities began adding soap solution to the water-course, which for a while prompted eruptions of up to 70 metres high, but this practice was stopped on environmental grounds, leaving Geysir dormant. Fortunately, fifty metres to the South, lies Strokkur, which currently erupts every six to ten minutes up to a height of around twenty metres, providing a spectacular display, but not quite in the league of Geysir at its best.

At the visitor-centre car-park we dutifully filed out of the bus and walked over to the site, an unremarkable area of flat rock surrounded by the inevitable low mounds of lava. We were first taken to inspect the inactive hole in the ground that is Geysir, helpfully identified by a small plate bearing its name, and then directed to join other visitors behind the rope on the upwind side of Strokkur. We'd been told by that there was an eruption every ten minutes or so, and were informed by an onlooker that the next one was due in about five minutes. Strokkur consists of a shallow circular basin some three metres in diameter with a sink- hole approximately half a metre across at its centre. About a minute before the eruption, water began to bubble up through the central hole and gradually fill the basin. When full, the whole body of water suddenly rose to become, for a second, a liquid hemisphere, which immediately disintegrated as the eruption occurred. Those who had foolishly stood downwind got a soaking, and one or two of our number were moved to applaud both the eruption and the soaking. We stayed for a second eruption, then a third, and would no doubt have stayed for more had we not been reminded that the bus was due to leave.

The return journey was uneventful, and back in Reykjavik I sought out any source of inexpensive food in the streets around the hotel. There were no fast food chains nearby, so I was obliged to patronise an unexciting takeaway pizza parlour that boasted a stand-up bar where customers could eat if they so preferred . This meal set the (low) food standard for my visit, placing Reykjavik firmly at the bottom of my league table ranking European capitals in order of quality and availability of low-cost food. As compensation, back at the hotel I treated myself to a couple of somewhat expensive beers in the bar, assuring myself that I'd earned them.

The next day again dawned cold and cloudy, and after breakfast I walked the hundred metres or so over to Hallgrimskirkja, arguably Iceland's architectural masterpiece and a unique example of church design. The building is not, as it is sometimes erroneously labelled, a cathedral, but simply Iceland's most important Lutheran church. With a spire height of seventy- three metres it claims to be Iceland's tallest building and is hence visible from most parts of the city. Designed by a local architect, Gudjon Samuelsson, and built between 1945 and 1986, it is described as being of the Expressionist School, a catch-all category for certain public buildings erected in the early-to-mid – twentieth century whose designs resisted any existing method of classification such as Gothic, Norman, or Neo-Classical. The Sydney Opera House in Australia is perhaps the best-known example, along with certain buildings by architects such as Le Corbusier and, to a lesser extent, members of the Bauhaus School, all considered "Expressionists". The style is best summarised as being original and visionary, whilst at the same time reflecting elements of the natural world, all of which is found in abundance in the Hallgrimskirkja, Built in pale grey concrete, its Eastern end is perhaps the church's most remarkable feature, a corrugation of concrete, fifty or more metres broad at ground level, tapering upwards on both sides in graceful exponential curves to form the steeple, and topped by a steep-sided triangular belfry. The architect's intention was to evoke images of glaciers, lava flows, and possibly geysers.

Inside, as might be expected in a Lutheran church, there is little in the way of decoration, only tall slender columns reaching up to form gothic arches along either side of the nave. The windows, similarly tall and slender, are plain glass and there is little in the way of stained glass around. The church's crowning glory is, however, its pipe organ, a magnificent instrument weighing 25 tonnes and mounted in a wood-framed recess above the Eastern entrance. Built by the world-renowned German company Johannes Klais, who were builders of the organ in Birmingham's recently completed New Symphony Hall, the organ contains 5,275 pipes controlled by four manuals and 72 stops. Sadly I was unable to hear it being played, but I understand there is an international organ festival at the church every summer. The Hallgrimskirkja is, to my mind, an important building architecturally, musically, and ecclesiastically, showing that a "modern" concrete structure can be beautiful, whilst at the same time making a virtue out of the Lutheran principle of simplicity. In front of the church is a Statue of Lief Erikson, A Norwegian settler in Iceland who went on to sail westwards and become the first westerner to set foot on the North American continent in 1000AD, almost 500 years before Christopher Columbus arrived there.

Beset by the occasional snow flurry I walked the kilometre or so down to the harbour, known as the Old Port, to find only a single coastguard vessel tied up on the main part of the quay. I found long-disused railway tracks embedded in the tarmac, and a helpful display board on the history of the harbour confirmed there had once been a railway, which ceased operating as long-ago as 1928, making Iceland a railway (and, incidentally, tram)-free nation, a distinction it shares with only four others in Europe, San Marino, Malta, Cyprus and Andorra. At the time of my visit much of the fishing fleet was at sea, but in any case Reykjavik nowadays competes for this business with ports such as Grindavik, some fifty kilometres to the South. A few weather-beaten fishing vessels lay alongside the nearby fish quay, and it was here that I headed, having seen a flyer at the hotel advertising day-cruises devoted to whale-watching. Along the quay's Eastern pier I found three portakabins, each with a board outside offering such cruises, but all were deserted. I asked a youngish girl nearby when they were likely to be open, and was told that they would have closed once the last boat departed earlier in the day.

"You can see the whaling ships, though. Look at the end of the pier." She added, in perfect English but with a hint of an Icelandic accent.

I looked. At the end of the pier lay three large black vessels moored alongside each other, each about the size of an Isle of Wight ferry-boat, and each sporting a hefty harpoon gun on the foredeck above the prow. I couldn't help thinking that black was a highly appropriate colour for ships built to kill.

"They look menacing." I said, and added "Frightening even. Do they still hunt whales?"

"Yes." She replied. "I think it's disgusting. My friends think the same." She added. "But Parliament allows it."

"Do you eat whale meat?" I asked.

"Of course not. Never." She laughed. "Nobody young eats it. It is only for old people. Oh, and some tourists eat it in restaurants. Whale kebabs."

I assured her that even though I was a *bona fide* tourist I would definitely not be consuming anything whale-related during my stay, at which she smiled. Back on the harbour I ventured a little further westwards, only to be confronted by another whaler, this time high out of the water in dry dock, undergoing repairs as evidenced by the flashes of white light at several points where the hull was being welded. Beyond this I could see nothing further of interest and so turned inland towards the city centre. There I was delighted to find a reasonably-priced burger restaurant, a real find in a city where eating-out was proving to be very expensive. Most important of all, the menu contained no mention of whaleburgers. Suitably fortified, I left and walked through the narrow city centre streets, passing modern shop and office buildings interspersed with those of more traditional Nordic-design, reflecting the country's recent past as a Danish protectorate. These are characteristically clad in wood or corrugated steel, often painted in bright colours, and have pitched corrugated roofs often similarly brightly painted. I was reminded of the residential streets of Copenhagen, but sadly here there were far fewer cyclists to be seen.

Eventually I arrived at Tjornin, the Icelandic word for "Pond" and derived from the Norse word "Tjorn", as is the English word "Tarn". Tjornin is in fact a lake about half a kilometre in length and almost as broad, surprisingly perhaps located right inside the city centre. Locals refer to it as "the biggest bread soup in the world", it being popular place for residents to feed the local aquatic bird population. The skyline on the far side was dominated by Frikirkjan, "The Free Church of Reykjavik", its bright reflection distorted in the wind-rippled water. A white Nordic–style church, plain but elegant, and sporting a green-painted roof and spire, it was erected in 1899 by a "breakaway" group of disenchanted Lutherans following organisational problems in their church. I walked over to it along the path around the lake's perimeter, circumventing the occasional agglomeration of snow and Ice, and at one point disappointing a gaggle of ducks and geese that had gathered, hoping for food. After ten minutes or so I found myself at the church's green-painted arched entrance, and stepped inside to find a simple, uncluttered interior. Neat rows of white-painted pews on either side were interspersed with wooden columns supporting a wooden upper mezzanine, containing more pews. Daylight flooded in through the arched clear-glass windows along either side, and at the far end of the aisle an archway led through to the altar. The rather Spartan interior, typical of many Lutheran places of worship, briefly reminded me of the "Wee Free" church in Scotland, more correctly known as the Free Church of Scotland, which for doctrinal rather than organisational reasons split from the United Presbyterian Church of Scotland in 1900, and demonstrates a similar disdain for any unnecessary decoration inside its churches. From the church i continued my walk around the lake and into the adjoining park, joining a few hardy souls braving the bitterly cold wind as they jogged or walked their dogs. From there I hastened back to the warmth of the hotel, and popped out later to buy pizza at the takeaway.

Stepping outside the following morning it was evident that there had been a fresh fall of snow overnight, and with the leaden sky promising more to come, it seemed any lingering hope of seeing the Aurora Borealis that evening was rapidly fading. On this, my last day, I had decided to make the trip to the Blue Lagoon, a huge thermal bathing pool about 40 kilometres to the South, and after again finding difficulty in identifying any local bus route that went there, I settled for yet another "tour" service, this time starting from the BSI bus terminal, a windswept two-storey building on open land by the southern ring-road, thankfully not far from the hotel. The walk to the terminal presented yet another snow-and-ice obstacle course, but I arrived in good time for the 11am bus, and joined a large group of tourists from New York.

The journey of about an hour took us through more lava fields, consisting of little more than snow-sprinkled moss-covered outcrops of black basalt rock, with little undulating scenery to relieve the monotony. The first real sign of human activity came not from the Blue Lagoon, but from distant plumes of steam betraying the presence of the Svartsengi geothermal power station, situated less than a kilometre to the East of our destination. The power station uses geothermal hot water to drive its turbines, with excess water being piped across to fill the Blue Lagoon's outdoor bathing pool.

The lagoon's main building consists of a three-storey "L" – shaped building, flat-roofed, and constructed from glass, steel, and concrete. From the road it looks like nothing so much as a late twentieth-century local authority school, somewhat incongruously transplanted onto a lava-field. Inside the reception area I found a finely-tuned organisation dedicated to the noble art of making money from tourists, not something that sits well with me, but which seemed to delight my New York companions. In consequence I forewent the opportunity to sample most of the various pleasures on offer, and simply toured the place as best I could. Had I so wished, I could have paid the entrance fee, hired swimming trunks, a towel, and a bathrobe, bought a mudpack for my face and, after bathing, enjoyed lunch in the chic but very expensive restaurant. Surprisingly, I was permitted, fully-clothed, to go through to the Lagoon, even though I had no intention of bathing. As a result I was able to dip my hand in the 37 degrees water for a moment, just to say I'd done it. The water is high in minerals and algae, both of which are claimed to be good for the skin, and which allegedly help in the treatment of psoriasis, although I believe the jury's still out regarding this particular claim. The lagoon, around 200 metres wide and almost 100 metres across, is, as the name suggests, sky-blue, but in most parts the colour is half-obscured by mist, rising lazily from the hot water. As I watched, the New York group emerged from the changing rooms, deposited their bathrobes in the wooden poolside closets and gingerly slipped into the water to join those already swimming, floating, or simply standing around in waist-high water. The lagoon is encircled by precipitous lava deposits which form a craggy protective wall, giving the impression of a water-filled amphitheatre. Overhead, the grey sky hinted at more snow to come, and I was left wondering how much better this already spectacular scene would look under a clear blue sky, or, better still, at night, lit by the aurora borealis.

Back inside the building I located the cafe and drank an expensive beer at a table overlooking the lagoon, and then toured the shop, where I encountered the Blue Lagoon brand-name for the first time. On sale was a wide variety of "care" products, including Lava Scrub, made from particles of lava from the site, and currently 95 Euros a tube, and an algae and silica face-mask, made from the pool's algae and mud, for the same price. Considering myself to be in need of neither, but admitting that others may disagree, I turned instead to the fridge magnets and bought two, then headed off outside to explore the surroundings. About 300 metres to the east I could see a low-rise building in the lava field and set off to investigate, taking an uneven pathway between low moss-covered lava mounds. The sign outside the building said simply "Silica Hotel", and enquiries inside revealed that it is a 35-room establishment with its own geothermal pool, also fed by water from the power station. The helpful receptionist explained that they specialise in providing accommodation for those with skin problems, particularly psoriasis, but also cater for guests who simply wish to stay in the stunning location for a night or two. Outside, I decided to continue my walk as far as the road leading to the power station. It seemed somewhat surreal to find an industrial complex, shrouded in steam, in such remote and unforgiving terrain, and the site is certainly worthy of inspection by anyone seeking locations for the next James Bond film. Conscious of the time, I walked back along the lava obstacle course, with snow now falling, and in the Blue Lagoon car park I boarded my bus back to Reykjavik.

The following morning I caught the airport bus at the BSI terminal, and bade farewell to a fascinating and thought-provoking country. On the down-side, it is certainly an expensive place for a holiday, and the transport links are not particularly tourist-friendly, but I understand talks are currently well advanced on the construction of a tramway. The weather had been poor, although I accept that November is possibly not the best month to make the trip. The non- availability of reasonably-priced food had also been a major problem. On the plus side, however, there really is nowhere else like Iceland on the continent of Europe, and possibly in the world. In the short time I was there its natural wonders frequently gave me pause for thought about the planet's latent power, giving some perspective to the fragility of human existence. Whilst other European countries take pains to celebrate man's amazing achievements in art, science, and philosophy, Iceland simply reminds us that our enduring existence and well-being depends entirely on our planet's continuing benign disposition.

Chapter 18

Norway, Sweden, Denmark

For many years it seemed as if nothing changed in Norway. You could leave the country for three months, travel the world through coups d'etat, assassinations, famines, massacres, and tsunamis, and come home to find the only new thing in the newspapers was the crossword puzzle   **Jo Nesbo**

I love Sweden. The entire world should be like Sweden. They all like to drink and get naked, and the women are hot. I can't think of a better nation on the planet   **Drew Curtis**

Denmark is a small place. We all know each other   **Mads Mikkelsen**

Prostitutes seeking "business". Quisling execution. Viking links with my place of birth. Kon-Tiki boat. Hotel panic. Eight-kilometre British-designed combined road/rail bridge. Railway station that stores 3,500 bicycles every day. Carlsberg has 40% of the Russian beer market and an art gallery.

Scandinavia, the most northerly point of Europe other than a few remote parts of Russia, consists of three Nordic monarchies - Norway, Sweden, and Denmark. A fourth country, Finland, Scandinavia's immediate neighbour, is often inaccurately described as being part of Scandinavia, but is in fact simply a fellow-Nordic country. The region is known for its political stability, its predominately cool climate, its relatively sparse population, and its economic dependence on sea-related activities. Good travel connections between the three countries, unlike those of the Baltic States, led me to conclude that it made sense to visit all three in the same week, particularly given that the recent opening of budget-airline routes to the area, hitherto subject to airline and government-backed restrictive practices, had seen substantial falls in air fares. I decided on taking a round-trip, starting in Norway, and from there taking the train to Sweden and Denmark, from where I would return home.

On a chilly but bright late-spring evening I emerged from the arrivals hall at Torp Sandefjord Airport in Norway, an ex-military airfield that, in common with many others throughout the continent, had been adapted to civilian use to offer the likes of Ryanair and Easyjet as an alternative to the old-established international airports. Landing-fees at these "secondary" alternatives were considerably lower than those at the main airports, making them highly attractive to cost-conscious budget carriers. I particularly remember landing for the first time at Treviso, in Italy, the low-cost alternative to Venice's Marco Polo airport, and being surprised to see a squadron of Italian Air Force fighter Jets in hangars on the far side of the runway. There is, of course, a downside to these airports, as transport connections to and from the destination city-centre are not always convenient or speedy, and In the case of Torp Sandefjord I was obliged to embark on a 90-minute bus journey through uninspiring countryside to the centre of Oslo, around 110 kilometres to the North.

Norway, officially The Kingdom of Norway, has a population of just over five million, one-twelfth that of Great Britain, but is accommodated in a land area almost double the size. It has borders with Sweden, Finland, and Russia, and as much as a quarter of its land-mass lies within the Arctic Circle. A kingdom since 872AD, it has been ruled by more than 60 Monarchs and Earls. In the eighth and ninth centuries its inhabitants, the Vikings, sailed westwards to invade and settle in many neighbouring lands, including the British Isles and Iceland, and in the eleventh century AD Vikings were the first Europeans to set foot on the North-American continent. More recently, Norway attempted to remain neutral during both world wars, but with little success. In the First World War its merchant shipping fleet was effectively commandeered by the British, and during the Second World War the country was invaded by the Germans, forcing King Haakon and his family to flee to Rotherhithe in London. The debate still continues about the extent to which the Norwegian people collaborated with the Nazis during the war. In 1969 oil was discovered beneath the North Sea in Norwegian territorial waters and thus was created the country's largest single industry, that of oil and gas extraction, leading it to become the world's largest per capita producer of oil and gas other than the Middle-Eastern states. In consequence it nowadays enjoys the fourth highest income in the world per head of population. About a quarter of its income currently comes from oil and gas, but there are also thriving sea-food, mineral, and lumber business sectors. The huge taxation income from the oil industry led to the setting up of the Oil Fund, more formally known as the Government Pension Fund, the largest pension fund in the world, currently valued at around $900 billion. Its investment arm controls 8% of the world's stocks and shares, and it is the largest stock-owner in Europe. Norway, like Iceland, is a member of the European Economic Area, meaning that it enjoys the benefit of free trade with the European Union and in return allows free movement of EU citizens within its borders, but is not a full member of the Union.

Oslo, the capital, known as Kristiania and later Christiana in the period from 1624 to 1925, became the capital of Norway in 1814, and is currently home to just under a million souls in its urban area, slightly more than the population of Leicester, England. It is located at the north-eastern end of the Oslofjord, an inlet on the North Sea capable of taking ocean-going vessels, and sits astride the River Alna. Much of the surrounding countryside is composed of forests, hills, and lakes. As the country's largest port for both freight and passenger vessels, it Handles 6,000 ship movements annually, and sees some six million passengers come and go. Its six-line tramway network and similar-sized metro system provide rapid and efficient movement across the city. Oslo has recently been ranked the third most expensive city in the world, behind Singapore and Paris, and in December of each year it attracts the world's media spotlight when it plays host to the Nobel Peace Prize Ceremony. Prizes in the other disciplines – Chemistry, Physics, Literature, and Medicine – are presented in Stockholm, Sweden.

The airport bus deposited me at the central bus station, part of the railway station complex of buildings, and having made no prior hotel reservation I set off to look for suitable accommodation. A high-rise hotel nearby, with rooms set around a central atrium, proved acceptable, and I took a room on one of the higher floors which offered a panoramic view of the city and, most important, was free of traffic noise. After settling in and taking a shower, I took a walk around the block outside and found a cash machine where I obtained Norwegian Krone. Thus armed, and in need of sustenance, I searched for a McDonald's restaurant and was delighted to find one not far from the railway station.

McDonald's has had its critics over the years, but for me, when travelling, it has always been simply a restaurant where I could eat food of reliable quality at a reasonable price. However, for those, like me, who are careful with money, it is worth noting that the higher-priced "cheeseburgers", "whoppers", and other variations on the burger theme displayed temptingly in the photographs above the counter rarely include the simple "hamburger", which consists of a single burger in a bun with tomato and dill dressing. Cheaper by far than anything else on offer, the humble hamburger is normally relegated to the sidelines by being listed and priced only on the statutorily-required menu displayed on the wall at the end of the counter. Incidentally the cheapest McDonald's hamburger I ever found was in Clermont Ferrand, France, costing 49 Eurocents. Although that was some time ago, I have found that you can still expect to pay little more than one Euro in many European cities, and with very good coffee also costing a Euro, a highly acceptable meal of two hamburgers and a coffee can be had for around three Euros . In Oslo, with its extremely high cost of living, the bill came to more, but it was still, relatively speaking, a bargain. Suitably refreshed, I walked back to the hotel, and on the way encountered a couple of skimpily-dressed ladies loitering on the street corner, one of whom asked, in English – how did she know I was English?– if I was interested in doing business. I assured her that the only place I did business was in my office in England, which seemed to amuse both of them, and I walked on back to the hotel.

The following morning I descended in the glass lift in the atrium down to the ground floor, where I saw guests helping themselves to food from the extensive breakfast buffet on display. My own plan for breakfast was simple – return to McDonald's and repeat the previous night's meal, not necessarily the healthiest breakfast according to nutritionists, but pleasant enough. On my return to the hotel, however, I discovered to my horror that the buffet breakfast was in fact included in the room price, meaning that my walk to McDonald's had been entirely unnecessary. I had committed the traveller's cardinal sin of failing to establish if breakfast was included in the room price when I booked in. Back in my room I cursed my stupidity then got down to the serious business of consulting the street map provided by the hotel to plan the day ahead.

The first visit was to be to the Edvard Munch museum, where works by Norway's most famous artist are displayed. The collection of 1,200 paintings represents more than half of his entire output. Born in 1863 in Loten, at the time part of the United Kingdoms of Norway and Sweden, Munch was traumatised by the death of his mother from tuberculosis when he was five years old, and went on to suffer from bouts of depression and other psychological problems which he later blamed on his father, whom he described as "Obsessively religious". At the age of 18 he enrolled at the Royal School of Art in Oslo and began painting. Artistically, he became influenced by the movement known as German Expressionism, and lived in both Germany and Paris at various times. He died in 1944, during the occupation of his country by the Germans, and his funeral, orchestrated by the Nazis, suggested to some Norwegians that he had Nazi sympathies. His most famous work, "The Scream", exists in four versions, painted between 1893 and 1910, two in oils and two in pastels. Three are in Oslo museums, and the fourth was recently bought by a private collector for $120 million. Two were recently stolen, one from the Oslo National Gallery and one from the Munch museum, but both have since been recovered.

To reach the museum required a brief Metro ride to Toyen, followed by a short sunlit uphill walk through a small park alongside low-rise blocks of flats. The museum building itself, located at the top of the hill, is unexceptional, a single-storey glass, steel and concrete structure, with an open-air cafe on the paved piazza in front.

Munch, and Expressionism in general, are not everyone's cup of tea, but, as with many great artists, it is not so much a particular movement that defines them, but rather their changes in style over the years from youth to old-age. Some of Munch's work on display in the museum is far from meriting the catch-all "expressionist" label, particularly his earlier and later works, and it was fascinating to observe the chronological changes in style. Sadly, "The Scream" was out on loan, but I knew I would have a chance to see one of the two pastel versions in the National Gallery later in my stay. After buying a couple of fridge magnets in the shop I found a seat in the outdoor cafe in bright sunshine under scudding cumulus clouds, and drank an expensive but very welcome coffee. A hundred metres or so to the West lay the invitingly green expanse of the Botanical Gardens, but I decided against a visit as there were other more pressing attractions to view in the city.

Back on the Metro, I returned to Central Railway Station and took a walk to the National Gallery about a kilometre away, again running the gauntlet of the two ladies seeking "business" *en route*. The gallery, a three-storey flat-roofed brick-built construction dating from 1882, lies on a street corner and looks like nothing so much as a nineteenth century factory building. It contains a somewhat modest collection, including works by the likes of El Greco, Picasso, Renoir, Monet, and Cezanne, together with works by many Norwegian artists, but it is most memorable for its display of Munch pictures, including "The Scream", before which I stood for a good ten minutes or so in an attempt to understand what all the fuss was about. Greater minds than mine have attempted to unravel its mysteries, but to me it is simply the product of a troubled man expressing his state of mind in a medium he had mastered over many years. Other similarly-disturbed artists have used their art as a form of catharsis, with perhaps Vincent Van Gogh being the best example. A couple of years ago I visited Amsterdam, and in its Van Gogh museum toured an exhibition exploring the extraordinary similarities between the lifestyles and consequent art of Van Gogh and Munch. It taught me a great deal about both men, and was one of the most enlightening art exhibitions I have ever visited.

After buying the obligatory fridge magnet of "The Scream" in the modestly-appointed museum shop I left and continued along the road for half a kilometre or so towards the Royal Palace, a four-storey neoclassical pile, strikingly similar to Buckingham Palace in London, and set in elevated tree-filled parkland. The palace, currently occupied by the present King, Harald V, was vacated In April 1940, as a consequence of the German invasion during World War II, when the then King, Haakon VII, fled with his family and ministers to Tromso, seventeen hundred kilometres to the North. The seagoing leg of the journey was made aboard the British cruiser HMS Glasgow. The group took up residence for a short while in a log-cabin in the Malselvdalen valley, but in July of that year the entire Royal family and ministers boarded HMS Devonshire of the British Royal Navy and were evacuated to London, where the Norwegian Embassy in Palace Green, Kensington, became the seat of their government in exile. Broadcasts to the people of Norway were made regularly from Saint Olav's Norwegian Church in Rotherhithe, London, where the Royal Family were worshippers. They returned to Oslo in July 1945, aboard the British cruiser, HMS Norfolk. To show their gratitude, every December the Norwegian government donates a Norway Spruce tree to the British, which is erected in London's Trafalgar Square and appropriately decorated for Christmas.

I took the opportunity in bright sunshine to stroll around the Royal Palace Park, but forewent the opportunity to tour the palace. A walk along the tree-lined Johan's Gate followed, a boulevard taking me past the University to the gardens in front of the eclectic yellow-brick and grey granite Parliament building, opened in 1866 and known as the Stortinget. An unusual, if not to say unique design for a legislature, its nadir was reached in 1940 when it was used for a time during World War

II as barracks by the invading German army. From there I made my way eastwards along the seafront to the Akershus Fortress, a heterogeneous group of pantiled stone buildings dominating the promontory on the Eastern side of the port. Here I found a path leading upwards and took a seat on a park bench from which I enjoyed a panoramic view of the city. To my left the prow of a huge cruise liner obscured the prospect towards the North Sea, and directly ahead on the far side of the port I watched local ferries as they scurried back and forth, linking the city centre with settlements elsewhere on the shores of the Oslofjord, not to mention its forty or so islands. I lingered there In the fading afternoon sunshine, enjoying the peace and quiet that was only occasionally interrupted by the raucous cry of hooded crows as they gathered in the trees overhead. I was interested to note from my guidebook that the castle was the place where, on 24th October 1945, Vidkun Quisling, the Norwegian head of the "puppet" government installed by the Nazis in 1942, was executed for treason by an eight-man firing squad. The word "Quisling" has since entered the English language, meaning "Traitor" or "Collaborator". Ironically, Quisling's house, a huge villa in Oslo's leafy suburbs, is now a Holocaust museum.

On the way back to the hotel I called in at the railway station, as I'd previously spotted a supermarket on the concourse and needed food for a picnic dinner in my room. Fortunately I arrived there before 8pm, which I discovered is the legally-imposed deadline after which supermarkets were not allowed to sell alcoholic drinks. I purchased a few bottles of beer, hugely expensive compared with London prices, some cheese, potato salad, crisps, and almond cakes. Not exactly a feast fit for King Harald, but nevertheless a pleasant way to end what had been a very enjoyable day. As I dined in my room I channel-hopped and came across my favourite Clint Eastwood film, "Dirty Harry", transmitted in English with Norwegian subtitles. A perfect way to end the day!

I'd planned on leaving for Sweden the following afternoon, so was up bright and early as there was still more to see in Oslo. This time I took advantage of the sumptuous hotel breakfast, which I have to admit surpassed McDonald's in terms of quantity and quality, then deposited my luggage at reception and headed off to the bus station. Two museums had caught my eye when checking my guide book, the Viking Ship Museum and the Kon-Tiki museum, both located somewhat out of town on the Bigdoy peninsula along the North side of Oslofjord. No tram or metro line went near, but the number 30 bus conveniently took me to both, a pleasant journey of half an hour or so through the airy Oslo suburbs. On the way we passed the Norske Folkemuseum, visible from the bus, a plot of land containing ancient dwellings, mainly wooden, from various parts of the country that had been dismantled, transported, and reassembled on site. As the bus halted outside the entrance I was for a moment tempted to get off and pay the museum a visit, but decided there was not enough time for me to do it justice, and continued on to The Viking Ship Museum. I noticed it was not far from the Holocaust Museum, a huge country mansion and estate about a kilometre to the south that had been home to Vidkun Quisling, the Norwegian Nazi collaborator during World War II.

The Viking Ship Museum, completed in 1957, a bright airy building looking like a modern church, was of particular interest to me as I was born in the coastal area of Eastern England that had been a stronghold of the Viking invaders as early as the ninth century AD. My own home community bears a name ending in "by", the ancient Norse word for "village", and is located near a community whose name ends in "thorpe", the Norse word for "hamlet". I have long wondered if I have Viking blood in my veins! The museum houses two ships, both unearthed from clay burial mounds located south of Oslo, which had been used for the interment of important, albeit unknown, members of the Viking community. The Oseberg ship, dating from the ninth century, almost 22 metres ling and 5 metres broad, and with a mast some 10 metres high, was 90% complete when found. No archaeological preservation work was required as the wood, very dark oak, had been perfectly preserved in the clay. The ship is estimated to have been able to travel at a speed of ten knots, either under sail or being rowed by thirty of its crew of thirty-two men, meaning that a journey to the East coast of England could have taken as little as two-and-a-half days. The remains of the two women, the subjects of the interment, are displayed alongside, but sadly both grave mounds had been subject to the attention of grave robbers over the years, with the result that that no grave artefacts such as jewellery or precious metals have been discovered, and the two ladies' identities remain a mystery. The museum is a fascinating reminder that the Vikings were able to travel enormous distances in such boats, evidence of their expeditions having been found in places as far apart as Istanbul and Canada.

Back at the bus stop I caught the bus to its terminus at the Kon Tiki Museum, a small single-storey group of connected buildings erected in 1978 to house the Kon Tiki balsa-wood raft, built by Thor Heyerdahl . Born in Larvik, Norway. Heyerdahl was an adventurer and traveller, who became interested in proving that ancient civilisations had been able to travel long distances by sea using boats made from native materials. In particular, he believed that islands in Polynesia in the mid-Pacific Ocean had been colonised by South Americans from Peru, possibly as far back as the late stone-age. To achieve this, in 1947 he built a raft from balsa wood and other materials indigenous to South America, then sailed the 8,000 kilometres from Peru to the Tuamoto Islands. He later constructed a papyrus reed boat which he sailed from the West coast of Africa to Barbados. The voyages prompted much coverage in the press, and resulted in books and an Oscar-nominated film. Both vessels are to be found in the museum, together with much detail of his other anthropological researches.

From the museum I walked the short distance down to the shoreline in bright sunshine and took a seat on a bench facing out over the fjord towards the distant buildings of the city. Ships and ferry-boats of various sizes and types came and went, but all were dwarfed by the passage of the huge car-ferry bound for Kiel in Germany, heading purposefully towards the open sea as she began her 20-hour journey. Anglers, perched precariously on nearby rocks, cursed as the ship's substantial wash made its belated way to the shore and disturbed each man's chosen stretch of water. Once the boat was out of sight I boarded the bus and made my way back to the city centre, and after picking up my luggage from the hotel I crossed over to the railway station, bought food in the supermarket, and boarded the train for the four-hour journey southwards to Gothenburg, and later Malmo, in Sweden.

The train sped along the West side of the Oslofjord for a while, offering delightful sea views, with the green hills to the East brightly lit by the afternoon sunshine. Eventually the line veered inland and passed through widely scattered small towns and villages, set in a landscape of forests, farms and lakes. The rail border with Sweden, about two-thirds of the distance from Oslo and in a small village between two lakes, was passed at full speed and scarcely noticed. The port of Gothenburg eventually hove into view, Sweden's second-largest city with an urban population of 550,000 souls, approximately one-third as many as in the capital, Stockholm. From the train I caught glimpses of the city's major industry, shipping, evidenced by the numerous vessels moored in its harbour, the largest in Scandinavia. At the station I had a few minutes to spare before continuing on to Malmo, so

I stepped outside its main entrance to view the surroundings, finding only a small square with cafe tables, beyond which trams sounded their bells as they came and went.

Sweden is the third-largest member of the European Union by land area but has a population of only ten million, about the same as that of London in England. A constitutional monarchy, it lies outwith the Eurozone, retaining the Krona as its currency. It has thus far declined to join NATO owing to its long-standing status as a neutral nation. Its history is inevitably intertwined with that of its neighbours, Norway, Finland, and Denmark, for example at the end of the Napoleonic Wars in 1814 the Swedes became rulers of Norway, a situation that lasted until 1905. Sweden remained neutral during the Second World War, but was often obliged to make concessions to the Germans that were seen by some as violations of that neutrality.

Back inside Gothenburg station I located the platform for the train to Malmo, Sweden's third-largest city, located at the southern tip of the country, no more than thirty kilometres across the sea from Denmark. The three-hour train journey, as had been the case in Norway, passed through farmland, forests, and by small lakes, occasionally offering tantalising but all-too-brief sea views. It was dark by the time the train pulled into Malmo Station, and as I had no hotel reservation I immediately set off in search of the nearest hotel. The first attempt, requiring a walk across the nearby Rorsjokanalen, a city-centre canal, took me to a group of three hotels close by. At the first of these I was informed by the easy-on-the-eye blue-eyed blonde lady on reception that they had no rooms available, there being a conference of some sort taking place in the city. She doubted that I'd be successful elsewhere, but wished me luck. The two adjacent hotels proved similarly full, and, beginning to panic, I sought illuminated hotel signs on the tops of buildings further afield, and walked to each in turn, finally finding one with a room available.

Travelling without hotel reservations is, I must admit, always a bit of a gamble, but for me it's usually a risk worth taking. It means there is no potential loss of money paid in advance should the unexpected happen and the destination not be reached, and on the few occasions where I have necessarily slept overnight in a railway station waiting-room I have rarely found it intimidating. In this case, however, I was pleased to have avoided the inconvenience, and after I deposited my luggage in my room I walked the few hundred metres through windswept and largely deserted streets to Stortorget, the city's huge tree-lined old market square. There I found an outdoor cafe and considered my options for the following day over a beer. Malmo was not high on my agenda as a place to spend time, it being an important commercial centre but, it has to be said, something of a cultural desert at the time, although I believe things may have since improved. I was aware, however, that from Malmo it was only a short train-ride to Copenhagen, Denmark's capital, which promised much more in the way of diversion.

The following morning bright and early I made my way back to the central railway station, now revealed in the daylight as a handsome four-storey brick building with a pitched roof, sporting a campanile, something of a rarity in railway architecture. On the concourse I sought out the platform for the train to Denmark. Had I been in Malmo prior to July 2000 I would have been obliged to travel to Copenhagen across the Oresund Strait by ferryboat, a forty-minute dockside-to-dockside journey, which might be doubled when measured from city-centre to city centre. July 2000 saw the opening of the Oresund Bridge-Tunnel, Europe's longest combined road-and-rail bridge, linking Malmo with Copenhagen across the Oresund Strait via a combined bridge and tunnel. Designed by Ove Arup and

Partners of London, the bridge section of the crossing is eight kilometres in length, and feeds into a four-kilometre tunnel on the Denmark side. 36 million people used this crossing, whether by train or motor vehicle, in 2009. Only nine other bridge/tunnels exist in the world, and although there are several hundred road-rail bridges, there are few, if any, which also combine a bridge with a tunnel.

At the station I was directed to two isolated and separately accessed platforms on the far side specifically serving the trains to and from Copenhagen. There I purchased my ticket and went through a rudimentary customs check. I climbed aboard the half-full train, found a window seat, and soon we were easing out of the station and taking a somewhat circuitous route through the city suburbs. The line climbed steeply as we headed westwards up to bridge-level, some 60 metres above the sea, and suddenly we were out over the water, with views over the shipping lanes far below as we sped along. Overhead, the concrete road deck ran in parallel, its supporting posts casting flickering shadows through the train's windows. Then, as quickly as it had arrived, the glorious sea-vista disappeared from sight as we reached the man-made island of Peberholm about two-thirds of the way across, and we and the roadway plunged below ground into the tunnel that would take us to Denmark."Peberholm" means "Pepper Island" in Swedish, and was so named because of its proximity to the nearby natural island of Saltholm, "Salt Island" in Danish. The brakes were gently applied as we approached the only intermediate (and underground) station on the line, that for Copenhagen Kastrup Airport. Thirty-five minutes after leaving Malmo we were emerging from the tunnel and pulling into Copenhagen Central Railway Station.

As a footnote, the Oresund Bridge departure platform at Malmo Central station has since been made redundant following the boring of a tunnel underneath the station, principally to allow high-speed trains between Stockholm and Copenhagen to avoid the time-consuming need to run into the terminus and then reverse out. As a consequence the Malmo to Copenhagen trains now depart from new underground platforms accessible via escalators.

The Central station in Copenhagen, constructed in 1911, is a handsome three-storey elongated brick building with a pitched slate roof and interestingly muted gothic features. Its principal claim to fame is that every day 3,500 cyclists park their cycles in and around it, surely making it unique in the world. Cycling is a way of life in Denmark, as I was to discover during my stay, far more than in Amsterdam, the traditionally accepted world cycling capital.

Denmark, an absolute monarchy for almost 200 years up to 1849, and thereafter a constitutional monarchy, is a member of the European Union but has retained its own currency, the Krone. It was a founding member of both NATO and the United Nations. Between the ninth and eleventh centuries AD, Vikings originating from Denmark, along with those from Norway, invaded and colonised much of the continent of Europe and its surrounding islands, and at one time the Danish Vikings ruled much of the area that constitutes present-day England. Nowadays the country's only overseas territorial interests are in the autonomous countries of Greenland – population 56,000 – and the Faroe Islands – population 49,000 - which are subject to the Danish monarchy but largely self-governing. During World War I Denmark was able to maintain its neutrality, but in World War II it was occupied by the Germans between 1940 and 1945. The country is composed of 1,419 islands, supporting a population of just under six million souls, and is largely made up of flat agricultural land, the country as a whole having an average height above sea-level of just 31metres. The economy is heavily geared towards manufacturing, with its most important manufacturer Lego contributing around 5% of the country's gross domestic product. Food, including fish and pork products accounts for 19% of exports. Self-sufficient in energy, the country exports oil and gas. Its only land-border is with Germany, meaning that much of its export business to countries outside the European Union goes via the container port at Aarhus, 150 kilometres to the north-west of Copenhagen, the capital. Copenhagen itself straddles the two South-Western Islands of Zetland and Amager, and has an urban population of around 1.3 million, almost 25% of that of the country as a whole. Originally a Viking fishing village, it grew steadily over the centuries to become a major trading city, and by 1661 it had become the capital of the Joint Kingdoms of Denmark and Norway, a situation that lasted until the settlement that followed the Napoleonic Wars in 1814 when a new joint kingdom was established between Norway and Sweden, with "Joint" capitals of Oslo and Stockholm. Nowadays Copenhagen has a mixed economy, with no single product being dominant.

A short distance from the railway station I found a suitable hotel on Vesterbrogade, a four-storey building fronting onto the street, The helpful receptionist, who could have passed for the sister of the receptionist in Malmo, told me it had recently been modernised, and offered me a top-floor room overlooking a quiet central courtyard. After depositing my luggage I went outside, in bright sunshine and under scudding cumulus clouds to explore the area. There seemed no need to buy a travelcard, the city centre being compact with most places of interest easily accessible on foot. The only attraction that was any distance away appeared to be "The Little Mermaid", an inconsequential diminutive bronze statue located on a rock by the sea some two kilometres or so from the hotel, and inexplicably regarded as a "must-see" for tourists. Having seen photographs of it I decided that for me it was definitely a "mustn't see".

By now it was early-afternoon, and I was determined first of all to sample the city's most famous tourist attraction, the Tivoli Gardens. Opened in 1843, it is the second-oldest operating amusement park in the world, the oldest being Dyrehavsbakken, also in Denmark. Sadly, on arrival I found the place locked, with a notice stating that the season, from April to September had ended. Cursing my luck, I nevertheless strolled around the entire perimeter, a distance of around a kilometre and a half, peering through the fence like a disappointed child at the various funfair rides on offer. All the usual suspects were there – chairoplanes, roller-coasters, roundabouts, dodgems – and in the centre I could see a large lake, surrounded by parkland. Moored on the lake was a huge life-sized galleon, described as a "pirate ship" in my guide-book. I have had a morbid dislike of funfair rides ever since I was dared by friends to go on the Waltzer at a travelling fair in my home town at the tender age of twelve. At the conclusion of a terrifying few minutes the hot-dog I'd eaten earlier decided to make a return appearance. Even so, I was disappointed not to be able to take a walk inside and inspect the Tivoli's attractions close-up.

From there I crossed H C Andersen's boulevard – it's impossible to visit Denmark without coming across the storyteller's name everywhere – to visit the City Hall, one of Copenhagen's most attractive buildings. Set alongside a broad paved square, it is technically defined as being in the national romantic style, mediaeval in character but with hints of Art Nouveau. Seven stories high, and constructed from brick with a slate roof, it dominates the area, with its high steepled bell-tower visible from any elevated point in the city. On the far side of the square I could make out what appeared to be a campsite, and went over to investigate. Groups of placard-carrying hippies stood and chatted amongst multicoloured tents, whilst others sat around camping stoves and open fires on which food was cooking. Furniture had been brought from home, including bookshelves and, strangest of all, a purple sofa on which two protesters lounged, looking like nothing so much as a couple watching television in their living room. The protest, apparently named "Occupy Denmark" seemed to be inspired by the "Occupy Wall Street" movement that was taking place in New York at that time and concerned the banking crisis that was gripping the world at the time. Policemen looked on from a distance, evidently unwilling to do more than monitor the situation, and the scene, though busy, was entirely peaceful.

The guide-book mentioned that the City Hall was home to a rare horological masterpiece which I was determined to see, and inside the main entrance I was directed to a small room on the ground floor. Classified as an Astronomical Clock, the instrument stands in the middle of the room and is protected inside a glass cabinet around two metres square and half a metre deep, divided vertically into three sections. The clock was designed by Jens Olsen, a locksmith, born in Ribe, Denmark's oldest town, in 1872. At the age of 25 he travelled to Strasbourg and whilst there studied the astronomical clock in the cathedral. In 1902 he returned to Denmark to set up in business as a watchmaker, and decided to create his own astronomical clock. By the age of 60 he had completed its design and in 1943 was awarded funds to begin its construction. Two years later, with work well advanced, he died, never to see the completed instrument, which was finally set in motion in 1955 by King Frederick IX at a special ceremony. The clock contains over fifteen thousand components, and consists of eleven interconnected shining brass dials, each larger than the largest dinner-plate. Its complex mechanism indicates the local and solar time in Copenhagen, the time of day at any location on earth, and the time of sunrise and sunset in Copenhagen on every day of the year. A Gregorian calendar shows the day, date, month and year in perpetuity, together with phases of the moon and the day and date of Easter Sunday and other religious holidays for the next 2,500 years. The third section shows the star map over Copenhagen every night for the coming 25,000 years, together with the extent and duration of forthcoming solar and lunar eclipses, and planetary positions in orbit. It must be wound by hand every week, and is a wonderful fusion of science and art, reminiscent of gold artefacts from eighteenth-century France and Russia, whilst simultaneously evoking images of Charles Babbage's difference engine, a mechanical calculator constructed in the 1820s that was arguably the precursor of the world's first computer.

Outside, in late-afternoon sunlight, I reacquainted myself with the sights and cooking smells of the encampment in the square, and headed for a convenience store on the far side where I bought food for an evening picnic in my room. Back at the hotel I popped down to the bar, a bright and airy room themed in stainless steel and glass with green and white fittings, and seated myself on a bar-stool. Over a couple of Carlsberg beers I discussed the state of English and Danish football in our respective countries with the bartender, Frederik. He particularly wanted to talk about Jan Molby, arguably the best Danish player ever to join an English club, who played for Liverpool FC between 1984 and 1996. Molby had moved into football management at the end of his playing career, with limited success, and I was told he now appears on Danish Television as a pundit. We both agreed he was a top-class midfielder, as his 33 caps for the Danish International team will attest. As with most Danes, Frederik had almost perfect English, and for a moment I was reminded that I had spent this entire trip speaking in English without ever attempting, or more importantly, needing, to use even the most basic words such as "Please" and "Hello" in the local languages. The younger generation in Nordic countries nowadays seem almost to regard English as their mother tongue, and in my experience speak it more confidently than those who live in any other area of Europe. This may or may not be a matter of pride for we English, depending on your point of view.

The following morning was to be devoted to the Carlsberg legacy, but cultural rather than alcoholic. Carlsberg, currently the fourth-largest brewing company in the world and selling its products in 140 countries, was originally established in Copenhagen in 1847. Worldwide sales in 2016 were the equivalent of almost $10 billion, almost twice the value of the sales of Lego, the country's most successful manufacturing company. One example – there are many - of Carlsberg's dominance is the fact that it has a 40% share of the beer market in Russia. The company has a long history of sponsorship of sport and the arts, and it was the latter to which I was to turn my attention. Opposite the South-Eastern perimeter of the Tivoli Gardens, and consequently only a short walk from my hotel, lies NY Carlsberg Glyptotek, a dome-capped three-storey brick building whose 80-metre frontage has historicist and neo-classical references. Opened in 1897, it was built to house the collection of art and sculpture built up by Carl Jacobsen, the brewery's founder. Over the years the collection has increased in size to its current total of around ten thousand pieces of art, and whilst not as extensive as the country's National Gallery, which also contains much of interest, it is for me one of those galleries that contains a relatively small number of items, but many of very high quality.

The name of the gallery comes from the Greek word Glyphein, meaning "to carve". This relates to the fact that it was originally a collection of sculptures, and contains many important works such as "The Kiss" and "The Thinker", by Rodin, and "La Petite Danseuse de Quatorze Ans" ("The Fourteen Year-Old Dancer") by Degas. Whilst interesting to see these celebrated sculptures together in a single gallery, I was conscious that none of them is an original. "La Petite Danseuse", a wonderful bronze three-quarter life-size rendition of a young ballet dancer, adopting the fourth ballet position and clad in a fabric tutu, has been copied and recast at least 28 times since the original was first shown at the 1881 Impressionist exhibition in Paris. As for "The Kiss", there exist three versions, with the original located in the Musee Rodin in Paris. This particular version was produced by Rodin specifically to the order of Carl Jacobsen, the Gallery's founder, and a third version by Rodin is in London's Tate gallery. The original of "The Thinker" also has pride of place in the Musee Rodin in Paris, and there have been many copies made, including this one, which are spread throughout the world. All that said, it is a fascinating collection, and went some way to persuading me that sculpture, outwith the usual panoply of statues of kings, queens, and political dignitaries, is a worthy art form.

The reason for my visit, however, was to view the French Impressionist collection, spread over ten or so rooms and containing works by all the major artists of the period. Unlike many major galleries prominence is given to some of those lesser known, such as Berthe Morisot, the only female Impressionist of consequence, and Armand Guillaumin, a landscape artist much neglected in my opinion. The rooms containing works by Danish artists over the centuries merited the detour, as the French say, but the extensive collection of ancient Mediterranean statuary and artefacts left me somewhat cold. I finished my tour by taking a coffee in the glass-domed winter-garden amongst the palms and ponds, and left highly satisfied with my visit.

Outside, under scudding cumulus clouds, I turned south along H C Andersen's Boulevard towards the docks, about half a kilometre away. The road at this point is eight lanes wide, with a bicycle lane and three vehicle lanes each way, plus, of course the footpath on either side. I was amazed by the number of cyclists, far more than I'd ever seen in Amsterdam, commonly thought of as the cycling capital of Europe. A never-ending stream of cyclists came and went along the dedicated cycle lanes, physically separated from motor traffic by a raised kerbstone. At road junctions there were separate traffic lights for the cyclists, effectively giving the city two distinctive traffic management systems, one for cyclists and one for vehicles. I have nothing in the way of statistics to prove it, but I would wager that London's reluctance to separate cyclists and motor vehicles on its roads leads to many more deaths than in Copenhagen. A large proportion of the cycles were of the "sit up and beg" type, with full chainguards, hub gears and the inevitable metal basket suspended from the handlebars. Classic designs, they were reminiscent of the sturdy machines of my schooldays. The ladies' version varied only in that they had a plastic covering over the entire top half of the rear wheel on both sides to avert the possibility of a dress getting entangled in the spokes.

The harbour proved to be something of a disappointment. Effectively a canalised gap two hundred metres broad between two islands, there was little in the way of shipping to be seen, although I believe the passenger terminal for the Oslo ferry was lurking out of sight further towards the east. I was reminded of nothing so much as London's Docklands, with broad stretches of water overlooked by smart new housing and office developments. I did, however, take a walk around Stadsgraven, effectively a flooded area surrounding the old southern ramparts of the city, and now a pleasant lake and park, where children played amongst the trees whilst mothers gossiped on park benches. The waterfowl included many mute swans, Denmark's national bird, and I caught a glimpse of a rather splendid Green Woodpecker clinging to the bark of a tree.

I walked back over the bridge in yellowing afternoon sunlight and strolled down a granite-sett road alongside the narrow Frederiksholms Kanal, a haven of tranquillity so close to the city centre. Low rise dwellings on either side alternated with ancient brick commercial and government buildings, contrasting with the brightly-painted houseboats moored in the canal. Back in the city centre I took a seat at pavement cafe, ordered a beer – Carlsberg, of course – and watched the world go by. The cafe was located on a street corner by traffic lights and I was particularly interested to see many cycles sporting what were effectively sidecars, but attached to the front or rear of the machine. In one of these, three children, each no more than five years old casually chatted about this or that as their chauffeur, presumably their mother, waited for the traffic lights to change.

After a meal at my favourite burger restaurant that evening I went to bed early, as my flight was scheduled to leave at 9am the following day. The journey to the airport necessitated revisiting the Oresund Bridge railway line, but this time travelling only as far as the airport station. By lunchtime I was back in England, and contemplating the events of the past few days. I concluded that visiting Scandinavia had been an extremely pleasant experience – trouble free, relaxing, and educational. But I couldn't avoid the feeling that life there was just a little *too* relaxed and predictable for my taste, and concluded, not for the first time, that for travelling to be really memorable there must be the odd challenge along the way, or at the very least a light sprinkling of problems.

Chapter 19

Portugal

Portugal has a peaceful feel about it. I sit on the terrace overlooking the vineyard there and I feel cut off from the world. You need that sort of thing **Cliff Richard**

I love white Portugal wine better than Claret, Champagne, or Burgundy. I have a sad, vulgar appetite **Jonathan Swift**

Trans-Atlantic seaplanes. The world's best tram ride. Santa Justa free-standing lift. Another road/rail bridge. Capes on the floor at a wedding. Ships' propellers like Barbara Hepworth sculptures. Large sardines.

Portugal, Britain's longest-standing military ally, is the most Westerly country in continental Europe, bordered to the West and South by the Atlantic Ocean and to the East and North by Spain. Its border with Spain, 1,214 kilometres long, is the longest uninterrupted land border in Europe. Successively invaded since Prehistoric times by Celts, Romans, Germanic Tribes, Visigoths, Moors, and Christians, the country did not delineate its present borders until the middle of the fourteenth century, and in the following two centuries embarked on a period of exploration and empire-building known as the "Age of Discovery" that saw it establish colonies in Africa, South America, The Far East, and India. During this period the Cape of Good Hope was discovered, as were the sea route to India. and the land-mass of Brazil, giving rise to that country adopting Portuguese as its language. Today there are about 350 million Portuguese-speakers throughout the world. A monarchy until 1910, Portugal's revolution of that year followed the murder of the King, Dom Carlos, and his heir, Dom Luis Filipe and led to the establishment of a Republic.

The country was able to remain neutral during World War II, but after the war fought battles in many of its colonies that were seeking independence. Disquiet at home as a result of these military escapades led to the country's bloodless, so called "Carnation" revolution on 25th April 1974 when revolutionaries inserted carnation flowers into the muzzles of the soldiers' rifles as a symbol of peaceful defiance. In 1986 the country joined the European Economic Community, soon to become the European Union, and in 1999 Macau, its last overseas territory, was handed over to China. The country is a member of the Eurozone, meaning that its currency is the Euro, although at the time of our visit it still used the Escudo. It is principally a manufacturing economy, with almost 10% of its exports made up of car and petroleum products. Perhaps its best known export in the UK is fortified wine, better known as Port, produced in the River Douro valley near the second-largest city, Porto, three hundred kilometres to the north of the capital, Lisbon. Annual sales of Port have recently been around $500 million.

The visit to the country was relatively brief, meaning there was no time to travel to its second city, Porto or any of the popular holiday destinations to the south in the Algarve. My partner and I were therefore obliged to spend most of the time in Lisbon, the capital, a city lying at the mouth of the Tagus River and mainland Europe's westernmost capital, with an urban population of 2.7 million, similar to that of Birmingham in the UK, and the eleventh most populous city in the European Union. A Muslim city after invasion by Arabs and Berbers in the eighth century, it was, perhaps somewhat surprisingly attacked by the Norwegians on their way to the holy land in 1108, and eventually reverted to Christianity in 1147. The city's golden era was the sixteenth century, when it saw the departure of explorers such as Vasco da Gama to establish trade routes to India, South America, Africa, and the Far East. There followed a rapid growth in population and wealth, which was halted in 1755 when an earthquake, followed by a tsunami, reduced much of the city to rubble and killed 40,000 of its inhabitants. In World War II, as one of the few neutral ports on the continent, Lisbon assisted more than 200,000 refugees to flee from Nazi Germany. Since the war it has grown to be an important manufacturing and trading centre, producing 45% of Portugal's Gross Domestic Product. In recent years tourism has become an important part of the city's economy, with more than four million visitors arriving annually.

The airport, named Lisbon Humberto Delgado, has a somewhat unusual history. Opened In 1942, it provided land-bound connections for passengers that had disembarked from transatlantic seaplane flights at Cabo Ruivo Seaplane Base, three kilometres to the west on the Tagus River. A major road, Avenida Berlim, was built to connect the two sites. The seaplanes most commonly used on the flights from the USA were Boeing 314 "Dixie Clippers", operated by PanAm Airways, luxuriously fitted out with a separate dining room and bar area, and carrying 36 passengers in seats that could be converted into bunk beds. Cabo Ruivo finally closed in the 1950s when seaplane travel became obsolescent.

Outside the arrivals hall, in the mid-afternoon warmth of early spring, we sought out the service bus into the city, and were pleased to be told that the ticket we purchased gave us unlimited travel in Lisbon for the remainder of the day. On board, we settled back in air-conditioned comfort as we cruised along dusty streets, passing abandoned factories, areas of wasteland, then large commercial outlets, predominantly, it seemed, car and furniture showrooms. Half an hour or so later we arrived at Restauradores, a wide, tree-lined square in the city centre overlooked by handsome low-rise commercial buildings in a variety of styles and vintages. It was here that we first encountered the unique Lisbon mosaic pavement. The paving technique, which originated in 1842, consists of laying down small square pieces of stone known as calcadas, normally black or white, each around eight centimetres square, to produce attractive mosaic patterns covering pavements and other pedestrian areas. In the mid-twentieth century the practice was in danger of being abandoned due to a lack of suitably skilled workmen, and the prohibitive cost of its upkeep, but in 1986 the City Council set up a School of Pavers. where apprentices were trained to continue the work. An exclusively Portuguese art-form has therefore survived, visible everywhere in Lisbon and replicated in some ex-Portuguese colonies such as Macau in the Far East, and Rio de Janiero in Brazil.

We walked the short distance to the Hotel Monumental, located in a quiet road just off the square, and checked in. The middle-aged lady at the reception desk, it transpired, was from Goa, Portugal's one-time colony and nowadays an important tourist destination on India's West coast. Her parents may well have witnessed the invasion of Goa by the Indian Army in 1961, which ended 451 years of

Portuguese rule. She kindly showed us to our room, situated on the first floor overlooking the street, and after settling in we took a walk outside and crossed over the road to the crowded Rancho Grande Restaurant, a no-frills eaterie offering low-priced *table d'hote* meals at lunchtime, and, judging by the clientele, used as a canteen by local workers. The only entree on offer was baked cod with boiled potatoes and salad,, delicious and cheap but slightly reminiscent of school dinners.

Afterwards we went in search of a convenience store to get food for a picnic in the room later, and at the end of the road came across the Ascensor da Gloria, a funicular railway rising steeply through the streets and promising extensive views of the city from the top. Too good an opportunity to miss, we waited for the descending graffiti-covered railcar to arrive and joined a group of tourists for the ascent. Taking no more than two or three minutes, the vehicle climbed through a steep, narrow ravine between buildings to the road above. There we found as small tree-filled park, paved with calcadas, offering views over the pantiled roofs of the city towards the hills of the suburbs beyond. In the warmth of the afternoon sun we found a park-bench and enjoyed a few tranquil moments away from the hustle and bustle of the city streets below.

Determined to get maximum benefit from our "free" one-day travel passes, we consulted the guide book and found an interesting section on the number 28 tram route, informing us that it uses 1930s-vintage tramcars. It went on to say that the route threads its way through streets so narrow, and climbs hills so steep, that the city council has been unable to find any modern tram design that could cope with such exacting conditions, leading them to conclude that only the 1930s vehicles are capable of maintaining the service. A ride along the entire route would take us through many areas of the city rarely frequented by tourists, and the opportunity to do this in a vintage tram seemed too good to miss. A glance at the map showed the terminus to be about half a kilometre away, at Praca Martim Moniz, a broad square with fountains at either end and offering at its centre a number of open-air art exhibits. As we entered the square we spotted the tram waiting at its terminus on the far side, and hurried over to climb aboard. A single carriage, it looked every bit as old as its seventy or so years, non-streamlined and with advertising along the side beneath drop-down windows, most of which were open, allowing a cooling breeze to penetrate the crowded interior.

 A couple of minutes later the driver sounded the tram's bell to signal our departure, and soon we were rattling uphill along Rua Palma,, leading to Avenida Almitante Reis, a busy main thoroughfare, after which we made a sharp right turn taking us down Rua Maria Andrade, a narrow granite-sett side street lined with low-rise office buildings. The climb continued until we reached Rua Angelina Vidal, leading us into a residential area with shops and restaurants, outside one of which a group of men were playing backgammon. Here, some of the older buildings were clad in traditional Portuguese blue-patterned ceramic tiles, and sported first-floor balconies festooned with troughs containing all manner of house-plants. Shortly afterwards we entered a broader tree-lined street, the first since leaving the terminus, and, still climbing, stopped alongside the A Voz do Operario building on the left, a handsome white stone edifice with blue and yellow rendering. The name means "Voice of the Worker", it having been the headquarters of the then newly-established Cooperative movement in late nineteenth-century Lisbon. The movement eventually became an educational charity, of which this is the present-day head office, managing a network of schools for the poor throughout the city, and providing a wide range of services for disadvantaged children.

Suddenly we began a steep descent, with cars parked on either side of the road offering scant clearance for the tram to pass by, and we watched fascinated out of the open window as the driver inched us forward past particularly badly-parked vehicles, sometimes managing to avoid contact with only a few centimetres clearance. In Calcada de Sao Vicente it was almost possible for us to touch the wrought-iron railings of first-floor balconies by simply trailing our arms out of the tram window, and at the end the line turned sharply right past a cafe, which, we were informed by a fellow-passenger, was well-known over many years for its unlikely role in traffic management. Each day a man – apparently with no official status - would sit at a table just inside the cafe entrance, waiting for a tram to arrive. On hearing the sound of its bell he would spring from his seat, exit the cafe, and take on the role of a traffic policeman, stopping cars at the three-way junction ahead to allow the tram to proceed. He then returned to the anonymity of his cafe table to await the next arrival. Sadly, he was eventually rendered redundant when traffic lights were installed, but we were so impressed by the story, and indeed in need of a drink, that we decided to exit the tram at the next stop, walk back to the cafe, and have a beer at the very same table. Half an hour later we boarded the next tram and continued on our way, rattling along Escolas Gerais, a street so narrow it was scarcely wide enough for a car, never mind a tram. With tall buildings on either side, it is certain that its paved road surface has rarely if ever enjoyed the benefit of the sun's rays. Soon we emerged onto a broad thoroughfare from which we were able to glimpse the shimmering blue River Tagus beneath, and almost immediately began a steep descent which took us past Lisbon Cathedral. Something of an eclectic mix of architectural styles, due to the fact that it was heavily damaged in the earthquake of 1755, the Cathedral was thereafter rebuilt in a somewhat piecemeal fashion. We decided it did not merit the detour, as the French would say.

Descent continued through a commercial district, after which we entered Poiais da Sao Bento, a narrow residential street which saw the return of too-close-for-comfort first-floor balconies decorated with plants in tubs and troughs. Suddenly we emerged from the shadows into an open area alongside the huge Sao Bento Palace, the Assembleia da Republica, a white neoclassical pile, originally a monastery but now the seat of the Portuguese Parliament. At various times the building has been remodelled, with its neoclassical portico being added as recently as 1903. At its rear is the Prime-Minister's official residence, the Ten Downing Street of Lisbon, and the large open area in front is a favourite location for political demonstrations. Beyond, we entered a broad road that threaded through what was evidently a wealthy area of detached houses with well-maintained gardens, and finally arrived at a roundabout marking the end of the line. Not simply a means of getting from A to B, the 28 tram route is a means of sampling the many facets of life in Lisbon, and should be on the schedule of any visitor looking for more than just traditional tourist attractions. Naturally we remained on the tram, enjoying the return journey to Praca Martim Moniz square beneath a cloudless sky as the light began to fade.

South of the square lies a popular restaurant district, and we were looking forward to the opportunity to sample the city's best known dish, whole grilled sardines. Selecting a restaurant more or less at random, we took a seat outside and perused the menu, where the sardine prices were shown on a per fish basis. Based on the size of tinned sardines back home, we thought half a dozen or so each would be adequate, if expensive, for our needs. As we discussed desserts, a waiter emerged carrying the sardine order for a neighbouring table. From this it was evident that sardines in Portugal are the size of mackerel, and we rapidly decided that two each would be more than enough. We placed our order, along with a request for carafe of Vinho Verde, young white wine from the North of the country. it proved a delicious meal, the only slight drawback being that we were required to fillet each fish on the plate, whilst the poor creature's lifeless eyes gazed reprovingly up at us. For dessert we chose another Lisbon favourite, Pastel de Nata, a baked pastry tart filled with a custard-like mixture that usually includes egg-yolks, cream, butter, and cinnamon. Slightly reminiscent of an English custard tart, it is popular throughout the ex-Portuguese colonies, even in far distant Macao, now part of China.

The following day we had planned to take the train from the nearby Rossio station to Sintra, an attractive city on the edge of a National Park about half an hour from Lisbon. Rossio station, a four-storey stone building exuberantly decorated with sculpture, is curiously reminiscent of some of the palazzi fronting the Grand Canal in Venice. Its two street entrances are however, far from classically venetian in design, being inverted horseshoe-shaped, surrounded by intricately-carved stonework, and probably unique in railway (and much other) architecture. To our dismay we found the station was closed, a notice at the entrance informing us that long-term work was being undertaken in the tunnel a short way along the line. A rapid review of options resulted in a decision to walk the kilometre or so through the streets to the station at Cais do Sodre, down by the Tagus River, where we could get a train to Cascais, a small seaside town some thirty kilometres to the West and Lisbon's nearest "seaside" resort. A glance at the map showed us that Cascais has the distinction of being mainland Europe's most westerly town, and the guide-book mentioned that it has been a day-trip destination for the citizens of Lisbon ever since the line opened in 1928.

As we boarded the train at Cais do Sodre Station the sun emerged, and beneath clearing skies we set off along the North bank of the River Tagus, with views over choppy water to the industrialised South bank beyond. Soon we were passing under the April 25th suspension bridge, seventy metres above us, built in 1966 and connecting the North and South sides of the river. Its name commemorates the date on which the "Carnation Revolution" took place in 1974. Brown in colour, and over two kilometres in length, the structure resembles San Francisco's Golden Gate Bridge. It was originally simply a road bridge, but was converted to dual road-rail use in 1999 by the simple expedient of suspending railway tracks beneath the carriageway. For the first time in the country's history, trains were now able to run into central Lisbon from the South of the country. Previously, trains from, for example, the Algarve, terminated at Barreiro station on the South side of the Tagus, and passengers were obliged to complete their journeys by ferry across the river.

We decided we must take the train across at some stage of our visit, and shortly after leaving the bridge behind we approached the spectacular Monument of the Discoveries, a huge riverside carved monolith of concrete and rose-tinted stone, over fifty metres high, forty-six metres long, and twenty metres broad, celebrating Portugal's history of world exploration between the fifteenth and eighteenth centuries. Part of the structure is in the form of the prow of a sailing-ship, on which are carved 33 statues representing those who made Portugal so important in discovering new lands during the "Age of discovery". Explorers celebrated here include Ferdinand Magellan, the first person to circumnavigate the globe, Vasco da Gama, discoverer of the sea route to India, and Pedro Alvares Cabral, discoverer of Brazil. The monument stands in a broad square paved with calcadas, the ubiquitous mosaic stone, in the pattern of a compass and a world map. Opposite the monument lies Empire Square, an attractive formal garden beyond which lies the stone frontage and pantiled roof of the Jeronimos Monastery, 150 metres from end to end and dating from the sixteenth century.

Out in the suburbs, the line began to skirt sandy beaches, hugging the coastline all the way to Cascais, the terminus. Originally a small fishing village, Cascais, a community of some 200,000 souls grew rapidly as a seaside resort in the late nineteenth and early twentieth centuries when it became a favourite watering-hole for the Portuguese Royal family, thereafter attracting largely middle-class holidaymakers from Portugal and overseas. Much of the town was destroyed in the 1755 earthquake and tsunami, but it was slowly rebuilt, and in the Second World War Portugal's neutrality led to it playing host to the exiled Royal families of Spain, Italy, Hungary, and Bulgaria. Nowadays it remains a popular holiday destination, with temperatures similar to those on the Mediterranean, and its lack of high-rise hotels is attractive to many who prefer a relatively quiet vacation. Along the sea front are rocky coves and cliffs interwoven with a number of relatively small beaches, and close by there is also the inevitable harbour, nowadays converted into a marina.

Under a clear blue sky, and for the first time feeling the heat of the sun, we crossed over the road outside the station and skirted the roundabout opposite, heading for Avenue Valbom, a narrow granite-sett street boasting expensive shops, restaurants, and run-of-the-mill local businesses. At the far end we passed a bougainvillea-clad restaurant, and headed South towards the seafront along a road lined with tall palm trees, their fronds rustling in the gentle onshore breeze. A further left turn saw us threading our way through a pedestrian zone, past groups of brightly-clad holidaymakers dining at restaurant tables, and eventually we reached an elevated road along the seafront. At the far end of the road we found Praia da Rainha, a beach no more than fifty metres long, bounded on the landward side by rocks as high as a house. Nearby we spotted a convenience store and bought food and drink for a picnic, then descended to the beach, selected a couple of rocks comfortable enough to perch on, and ate our lunch in the warm sunshine, to the sound of waves gently breaking on the beach. Children splashed around noisily in the water, or made sandcastles, monitored unobtrusively by sunbathing parents. In such an idyllic location it was tempting to linger for the remainder of the afternoon, but we had more to do later in the day and somewhat reluctantly decided to head back to Lisbon. By now perspiring in the heat of the afternoon sun, we made our way to the station, and on the return train journey passed the Electricity Museum, a decommissioned power station overlooking the river. Deciding we must return later in the week to visit it, we returned to Cais do Sodre station where we took bus 736 to the Santa Justa Lift in the city centre.

The Santa Justa Lift, unique in Europe, is an open-air free-standing vertical lift connecting the top and bottom of a steep slope in the city centre. There are other "open-air" lifts elsewhere in Europe, most notably in Monte Carlo, but there the lift-shafts are carved out of solid rock in the cliff face and are not free-standing. Opened in 1902, The Santa Justa lift stands in the centre of a narrow *cul de sac* between buildings almost as high as itself, and is fabricated from steel latticework, similar in style, but not shape or height, to the Eiffel Tower in Paris. There is a hint of Art Nouveau about some of its decorative ironwork, hardly surprising given its turn-of-the-century date of construction. Inside the latticework a lift rises vertically from the lower street level to an open-air observation platform high above the surrounding rooftops, and from there a bridge-style walkway leads to nearby Carmo Square at the upper level. We joined the tourist throng at the ticket office and eventually found ourselves inside the polished-wood lift cabin, watching as the attendant first closed the noisy concertina lattice external gates, then the internal wooden doors, finally pressing the button to set the lift in motion. For a moment I was reminded of those rare occasions in my youth when I'd used the lift in an old-style department-store, and half-expected the attendant to call out "Third floor, ladies' underwear." In less than thirty seconds we were exiting at the top level and stepping out onto the viewing platform. At the far end a cast-iron spiral staircase led upwards to an open-air cafe, where we quickly found a table and ordered beer. Facing north, we looked out over pantiled roofs towards the Sao Jorge Castle, high on a hill on the horizon, but we might equally have chosen the view southwards over to the distant Tagus River to watch ferryboats criss-crossing the river. For an hour or so we relaxed in the fading light and watched the sun's last rays transform the distant castle into a fiery red citadel. In near-darkness we left along the top-level walkway and strolled downhill through the lamp-lit streets to the Rancho Grande restaurant.

We'd planned to spend part of the following day taking the train over the 25th April Bridge to the South side of the River Tagus, returning by ferry. The closure of Rossio Station, our intended starting-point, had resulted in a slight change of plan. We would now have to leave from Sete Rios, a somewhat isolated station in the North-Western suburbs, and it just so happened that one of Lisbon's finest art galleries was located nearby. To get there we first took the Metro to Rato Metro station and alighted at Campo Pequeno , then walked the hundred metres or so to the Calouste Gulbenkian Museum, a rather ugly, almost brutalist, "T"-shaped three-storey concrete and glass block in otherwise pleasant formal parkland. The museum was established in 1968 by the Calouste Gulbenkian Foundation, a charitable trust set up to administer the estate of Mr. Gulbenkian after his death. One of the world's richest people, Calouste Gulbenkian was a British businessman of Armenian parentage who made his money by developing much of the Middle East's oil reserves, and is credited with being the first person to have exploited Iraq's oil riches. Born in Constantinople, later Istanbul, in 1869, he studied Petroleum engineering at King's College London and took British Citizenship in 1902.

During his lifetime he amassed a huge and eclectic art collection, much of which he displayed to friends in his substantial four-storey town house on Avenue d'Iena in Paris. The Lisbon museum contains some six thousand works, of which a thousand are on display at any one time. Interestingly, several hundred of his works originally belonged to the Hermitage Museum in St. Petersburg, Russia. In 1930 Gulbenkian purchased them in a secret transaction when the Russian government were obliged to sell off parts of the Hermitage collection to stave off bankruptcy. The collection is extremely varied, covering ancient sculpture from the Egyptian, Greek, and Roman Civilisations, and European paintings and sculpture from the thirteenth century onwards, together with pottery and printed works. A pleasant group of Impressionist pictures includes one which particularly caught my eye, "The Break-up of the Ice" by Claude Monet, showing ice-floes on the River Seine at Vetheuil. Drama is rare in Monet's paintings, but this one provides a scene of high winds and bitter cold that is far removed from, for example, his idyllic pictures of his garden at Giverny. In general the museum is a collection well worth visiting for its consistently high quality, my only criticism being that it is rather too diverse.

From the Museum we took the bus to Sete Rios station, where, in bright sunshine occasionally tempered by wispy cirrus clouds, those traditional harbingers of an impending change in the weather, we boarded a southbound train. Soon after the journey began we passed under the white stonework of the Aguas Livres Aqueduct, its 35 gothic arches towering 65 metres above us and stretching away westwards across the adjacent Alcantara valley. Constructed in the 18th century, the Aqueduct brought an end to chronic water shortages in the city at the time, channelling water from canals located fifteen kilometres away. The train now entered a largely suburban area which gradually gave way to the heavily wooded western fringes of the city, whilst all the while running parallel to the North-South orbital motorway. Soon the line began to climb steadily as it approached the 25th April Bridge, and for the first time we caught a glimpse of the River Tagus in the distance. As with the Oresund combined road-rail bridge between Sweden and Denmark, the railway must align itself with the motorway just before the crossing commences, and is thereafter suspended underneath the carriageway of the bridge. The crossing, never less than spectacular, offered vistas to the left over the pantiled roofs of the city, whilst to the right the Tagus estuary shimmered in the sunshine, the air clear enough to allow us to discern beaches ten or more kilometres downriver. Approaching the South bank, we passed on the left the statue of Christ the King, an 82 metre-high pedestal topped by a huge statue of Christ, all on top of a 130 metre-high cliff and visible from virtually anywhere in Lisbon. In appearance it is much along the lines of the statue of Christ the Redeemer in Rio de Janeiro, Brazil. Shortly afterwards the train pulled into Pragal Station, and from there a bus took us eastwards to Cacilhas, a journey that can nowadays be made by a recently-installed light-railway.

Cacilhas is a small riverside community of six thousand souls, best known for its ferry service northwards across the river to Cais do Sodre, but at the time also the location of an important ship repair company, Lisnave Estaleiros Navais de Lisboa, To investigate further we took a short walk along the path leading from the bus station to the shipyard, wherein a couple of large merchant ships were undergoing noisy repair in dry dock. On the dockside stood two bronze propellers, glistening in the afternoon sun, each four or five metres in diameter, looking like nothing so much as a couple of huge Barbara Hepworth sculptures. Above and astride them a huge mobile crane, similar to those at the Harland and Woolf shipyard in Belfast, stood idle. We were not to know at the time that the yard had only a couple of more years to live, and that today it lies derelict, with the dry docks flooded and the mobile crane rusted to its tracks.

In need of sustenance, we walked over to the road opposite where we bought food and drink from a convenience store. In the warmth of the sun, pleasingly tempered by a gentle offshore breeze, we found a park-bench overlooking the impossibly blue River Tagus and ate our picnic, an experience sporadically enlivened by the comings and goings of river craft, and the antics of a mongrel dog retrieving sticks thrown into the water by its owner. As the ferryboat arrived we strolled over to the quayside and waited as its passengers disembarked. Once aboard and under way, we stood on deck in the ethereal yellow sunlight of late afternoon and simply enjoyed the view. This light, unique to southern Europe and beguiling in its beauty, attracted many of the Impressionist painters to the South of France in the late nineteenth century, each hoping to capture its elusive quality on canvas.

After twenty minutes or so we disembarked at the ferry terminal by Cais do Sodre station on the North side and took a three-leg Metro journey to Santa Apolonia Railway Station, three kilometres eastwards along the riverbank. At one time Lisbon's most important station, it was built in 1865 to facilitate the transfer of rail passengers from the European Continent to transatlantic ships moored alongside. Nowadays a shadow of its former self, serving only a few local destinations, it remains a handsome three-storey neoclassical building, fronting a single pitched train-shed over its half-dozen or so platforms. Inside it was eerily quiet, almost as if it were haunted by the ghosts of its heyday as the city's most important transport hub. From the station we walked half a kilometre or so uphill to the Water Museum, seeking more information on the Aguas Livras Aqueduct beneath which we'd passed earlier in the day, but we sadly arrived after closing time. A tram-ride took us part of the way back to the hotel, and we completed the journey on foot through a maze of narrow granite-sett streets .

The following morning we emerged from the hotel to find rain falling, and walked round the corner to the Gloria funicular railway which took us up to Rua Sao Pedro de Alcantarata. There, we caught the 758 bus to the National Museum of Natural History and Science, about two kilometres to the North-West and on the fringes of the city's Botanical Gardens. Much of the museum, a neoclassical stone edifice on a narrowish street, was closed due to building work, but we did manage to tour the preserved chemistry laboratory and lecture theatre, built in the mid-nineteenth century as part of the science faculty of Lisbon Polytechnic. In the mid-twentieth century we had both worked in laboratories, and were surprised to find that this laboratory from a century earlier was scarcely different from those in which we'd been employed. High-ceilinged, and with walls elegantly faced with delicate pink–flecked marble, the laboratory boasts half a dozen large workbenches in cherry wood, each with gas-taps along the centre, a reminder of the days when Bunsen burners were an essential component of chemistry education. Racks of chemicals in stoppered glass containers lined one wall, and on the bench opposite stood a glass-fronted fume cupboard, inside which stood a large hotplate on which chemical reactions that might emit noxious fumes would be carried out, the fumes being dispersed into the atmosphere outside by means of an extractor fan. Overhead, a mezzanine floor, edged by metal railings and supported by slender columns, exhibited laboratory equipment from the period. A door to the left led into the lecture theatre, a horseshoe-shaped raked amphitheatre with wooden seating, facing a lecturer's podium in front of which was a table somewhat similar to those used for autopsy lectures in medical schools.

From there we took the Metro to Cais do Sodre Railway Station down by the river and boarded the train to Belem, about five kilometres along the coastal line towards Cascais. At Belem we walked the short distance down the road in pouring rain to Museu da Electricidade on the banks of the Tagus River, a museum devoted to the energy industry and formerly known as the Tejo coal-fired power station, in its day the major provider of electricity to Lisbon. The conversion from electricity generating station to museum eerily anticipated the conversion of Bankside Power Station in London, which became the Tate Modern Gallery some ten years later. Museo da Electricidade, considered an industrial architectural masterpiece, is a huge complex of redbrick buildings, having hints of Art Nouveau and even Classicism in places, with a main turbine hall as large as Battersea Power Station in London. It opened in 1909, ceased operating in 1972, and in 1990 was reopened as a museum. Inside it is fully equipped and preserved just as it was when decommissioned. In the continuing rain we walked round the entire perimeter, a distance of a kilometre or more, before finding the poorly-signposted entrance. Inside, we walked through the cathedral-like structure of the turbine-hall past huge turbine-driven alternators and Babcock and Wilcox high pressure boilers, eventually reaching the dockside at the far end. There, boats would tie up to discharge their cargoes of imported coal and reload with coal-ash. Back inside we visited an exhibition which highlighted the often poor working conditions suffered by many who worked there.

The rain had ceased by the time we got back to the station, and there we caught the number 15 tram along the North bank of the Tagus as far as Praha do Commercio, "Commerce Square", a huge open space about two hundred metres square, surrounded by administrative buildings on three sides and with its open South side looking out over the river. Rebuilt after the 1755 earthquake and tsunami, the landside entrance to the square is through the Rua Augusta Arch, a triumphal stone archway some thirty metres high erected to celebrate the rebuilding of the city after the earthquake. From here we walked the hundred metres or so over to Rua da Prata to visit one of Lisbon's less celebrated attractions, the underground Roman ruins. During the rebuilding of the city after the earthquake, workmen discovered a maze of underground tunnels which, it transpired, were of Roman origin, dating from the first century BC, and to this day there are conflicting views as to their function. Subsequently covered over in the city's reconstruction, the tunnels remained hidden from view for more than two hundred years, but were recently opened to the public on a few selected days of the year. The decision to open them was not however, without its problems, as the only entrance is via a hinged steel trapdoor, resembling a square manhole cover, located between the tramlines and the pavement in Rua Prata. Here we joined a small queue and watched as the guide and his party emerged from the trapdoor, with a tram necessarily being held up whilst the process was completed. He then bade us follow him down the rickety steel steps into the floodlit tunnels, closing the hatchway behind us. Inside we found lengthy arched structures constructed from stone blocks, leading to side rooms and recesses. Normally flooded, the tunnels are cleared of water during the few days each year when they are open to the public. Only when back outside in the street did I realise how surreal the experience had been. Never before have I had the privilege of climbing down a manhole in a busy street whilst on holiday, an experience unlikely ever to be repeated!

The following day dawned cloudy and drizzly, and in the hope of finding better weather we took the decision to visit Coimbra, a landlocked city some 200 kilometres to the north of Lisbon and Portugal's ancient capital. A metro ride took us to Lisbon's brand new station, Lisboa Oriente, built to accommodate new high-speed international trains and opened in 1998. A magnificent lattice-steel, stone and glass construction, it nowadays handles 75 million passengers every year, just 25 million fewer than Britain's busiest station, London Waterloo. Located next to the city's biggest bus station it also incorporates a huge shopping mall, inside which we tracked down a hypermarket and bought food for the journey. On the breezy platform we boarded an Alfa Pendular train, similar to the Pendolino trains currently in use in Britain, and settled back for a journey taking a mere ninety minutes, at an average speed of 133 kilometres per hour. Free headphones were handed out by an attendant once the train moved noiselessly out of the station, enabling us to watch television on a screen suspended above the aisle if we so wished, and at the end of each carriage an illuminated sign indicated the speed in kilometres per hour throughout the journey. More commonly available nowadays, these innovations were considered revolutionary at the time. The route follows the valley of the River Tagus towards its source for the first thirty or so kilometres, then strikes out across unexceptional forested countryside, passing few communities of note. The city of Pombal, fifty kilometres from Coimbra, sports a twelfth-century hilltop castle visible from the train, but there is little else of note during the journey. We finally arrived at Coimbra "B" station, located about a kilometre outside the city-centre, and recently redeveloped to handle the new high-speed trains. This rather inconvenient arrangement means that the railway company has to run a shuttle service from Coimbra " B" to Coimbra "A", the station in the city centre.

The city, located on a hill by the broad Mondego River, is home to around 145,000 souls and was Portugal's capital from 1131 to 1255. Its university, originally established in 1290 in Lisbon, is the oldest in the Portuguese-speaking world. The student body currently numbers about 20,000, with the result that much of the city's economy is dependent on the University. From 1290 to 1559 it was Portugal's only University and again between 1759 and 1911.The city centre, a maze of tightly-knit streets, surrounds the elevated University campus, which was to be our first port of call. Composed of ten low-rise quadrangular buildings, in an area about five hundred metres square, it is compact but never claustrophobic. All pedestrian areas are attractively paved with black and white calcadas in abstract patterns, and in continuing rain we headed for the central courtyard, which boasts administrative and teaching buildings on three sides, one of which was the old Royal Palace, with the fourth side open and offering views of rolling hills to the south of the city. As we entered the square we noticed the doors of the University chapel, Sao Miguel, were open, and, ever inquisitive, stepped inside to find a wedding in progress. Many male guests were clad in the formal university attire of black capes and suits, and as the bride and groom turned away from the altar at the end of the ceremony, a number of guests removed their capes and lay them on the floor of the nave, providing an impromptu floor-covering for the newly-weds as they exited the church. I wondered at the time if we might adopt this tradition in the UK, perhaps laying down hoodies or tailcoats, depending on the predilections of the families involved.

The church dates from the early sixteenth century, and almost every square centimetre of its compact interior is baroqued with the usual Roman Catholic combination of gilt plasterwork, coloured frescoes, statues of Mary and Jesus, and coloured Corinthian columns. Never given to praising such decorative excesses at the best of times, I found this interior less palatable than any I can remember seeing. In an attempt to recover a sense of proportion, we walked down towards the open end of the courtyard and looked inside the Biblioteka Jaonina, the University library, dating from the mid-eighteenth century, a handsome neoclassical building on three floors. Here, baroque simply means "attractively decorated", with intricately carved wood the principal material for furniture and shelving, beneath tastefully painted ceilings, No longer in daily use by students, the library is principally a repository for some 200,000 rare books held in glass-fronted bookcases.

From there we visited the Great Hall of Acts, known as the Old Hall during the period from 1131 to 1255 when Coimbra was Portugal's capital and the building was part of the Royal palace. Originally the throne room, with predominantly red furnishings, it became the university's ceremonial centre, and is richly decorated with Portuguese ceramic tiles and life-sized portraits of ancient Kings. Its ceiling, emblazoned with more than two hundred rectangular panels painted by Jacinto Pereira da Costa in the mid-seventeenth century, is surely unique in the world, and whilst not rivalling that of the Sistine Chapel in the Vatican, is in its own way equally spectacular.

Back outside we walked in continuing rain through the narrow winding streets towards Coimbra "A" railway station, pausing along the way at a cafe in the ground floor of a mediaeval terrace for coffee and rather indifferent *palmiers*. At the station we caught the shuttle train to Coimbra "B" and there climbed aboard the train for Lisbon. As we travelled southwards the rain eased, leading to clear skies as we pulled in to Oriente station in Lisbon. That evening we dined on Chinese food, this time at a restaurant on the road along the top of the Gloria Funicular railway. The following morning we headed back to the airport and were back in a chilly Stansted in England by early afternoon.

Portugal's status as a sea, sun, and sand holiday destination is largely due to the popularity of the Algarve area to the south of the country, where it competes directly with Spain's Costa del Sol and Costa Blanca. The country has, however, much more to offer, particularly in and around Lisbon. It is one of the most attractive capital cities in Europe, and deserves recognition for its historic importance in the economic growth of the continent, and, indeed, the rest of the world. Above all, however, Lisbon is worth visiting if only to enjoy the delights of the number 28 tram, surely the world's best tram ride!

Chapter 20

Vatican City and Italy

Vatican City is a bit overrated in my opinion- no offence to the Vatican **Ed Stoppard**

If someone is gay and he searches for the lord and has goodwill, who am I to judge? **Pope Francis**

The Vatican is against surrogate mothers. Good thing they didn't have that rule when Jesus was born. **Elayne Boosler**

When (Pope) Benedict dies, he will have the pleasure of standing before whatever furious God he believes in, to answer for how it was that he knew for undeniable fact that one -- if not dozens -- of his priests repeatedly molested, abused and/or raped young children for decades, and he did nothing to stop it. How much does God believe the pope's argument that Vatican PR trumps paedophilia? Joe Ratzinger, 82, will soon find out. **Mark Morford**

Almost escorted out of the Vatican. Eur, the best place in Europe for Fascist architecture. Elastoplasts as change in shops. The School of Athens by Raphael and the Sistine Chapel restored. The shortest national railway in the world. Death of Mussolini.

The Vatican, more correctly known as Vatican City State, is a country located within the bounds of the city of Rome in Italy. Its area of 44 hectares and population of 1,000 souls makes it the smallest country in the world. It is an ecclesiastical state, ruled by the Bishop of Rome, otherwise known as the Pope."Vatican" derives from Vatican Hill, on which it stands. The hill is one of ten in Rome, but is not included in the group traditionally known as the "Seven Hills of Rome". The name possibly derives from an Etruscan settlement on the site, or from Vagitanus, a Roman god. The current city state has only been home to the Pope and his entourage since the fourteenth century, as prior to that they lived in the Lateran Palace on the other side of the River Tiber in Rome, interrupted by a period of 68 years when they moved to Avignon in France. The Vatican is part of the Holy See, from the Latin "sedes", "seat", an organisation governing Catholics throughout the world. Although an independent state, it has no diplomats, as this function is carried out by members of the Holy See located throughout the world.

1870 saw the unification of Italy's many principalities and kingdoms into a single republic, but a large tranche of land known as the Papal States resisted this process. Governed by the Holy See, and including the Vatican and the city of Rome, the Papal States stretched across central and northern parts of the Italian peninsula. As a result of their resistance, war was declared, and in that year the Italian army invaded and advanced on Rome. By 1871 the Papal States were no more, and the Papal Army was disbanded, but the problem of the future of the Holy See remained and became known as the "Roman Question". In the 1920s Pope Pius IX eventually renounced the bulk of the Papal States, and in 1929 signed the Lateran Treaty with Prime Minister Benito Mussolini, leader of Italy's National Fascist Party. This formally established the Vatican City as the sovereign territory of the

Holy See, leading to it becoming an independent state. It is defined as an Absolute Elective Monarchy, sometimes known as a non-hereditary monarchy, of which there are only two others in the world, Malaysia and Cambodia. During this period Italy was a constitutional monarchy, only becoming a republic following a referendum in 1946. The Vatican state remained *de jure*, if not *de facto*, neutral during World War II, and debate continues to this day regarding its relationship with Adolf Hitler's Nazis. Since then it has been militarily as well as economically dependent on Italy. It has no standing army, and its currency is the Euro, which it adopted when Italy joined the Eurozone in 2002. It has recently been given permission to mint its own Euro coins, up to a total value of one million Euros per year, but other than this there is no formal relationship with the European Union, it being considered a theocracy and therefore not eligible for membership.

A visit to the Vatican is usually just one part of a visit to Rome, or to the Lazio district generally, and so it was with me. I went in the mid 1990s, prior to Italy joining the Eurozone, and at a time when its economy had suffered from one economic crisis after another, as often as not resulting from, or contributing to, political corruption. My visit lasted five days, of which only one was devoted to the Vatican, and it is my intention in this narrative to concentrate on that, but I will also mention a couple of the lesser known attractions of the eternal city.

At the time of my visit the budget airlines were using Ciampino Airport, about fifteen kilometres from central Rome, and Europe's third-oldest airport in continuous use. It was opened in 1916, four years after Bucharest's Baneasa airport and three years after City Airport Bremen in Germany. It's interesting to note that I have used all three airports on my travels, and in each case the budget airlines had given them a new lease of life for short-haul flights following the building of larger international airports nearby. Other than its longevity, Ciampino has a further, rather more sombre claim to fame. On January 10th 1954 BOAC flight 781, a De Havilland Comet aircraft, one of the initial batch of the world's first commercial jet aeroplane, took off from Ciampino en route to London Heathrow. This particular Comet, of which there were by then eight in service, had been in revenue-earning service for less than two years. Twenty minutes into the flight it broke up over the Mediterranean with the loss of all on board. Seventy percent of the wreckage was recovered from the seabed and taken to England for scientific investigation, where the results were inconclusive. A further crash six months later led to the grounding of the entire Comet fleet and ultimately to major design changes in jet passenger aircraft that were subsequently incorporated in all modern planes. As a result of these two disasters, only around seventy Comets were ever sold to airlines, with the British aircraft industry taking many years to recover.

Ciampino was in fact Rome's main airport until 1960, often featuring in late 1950s Technicolor Hollywood and Italian films. I have an enduring image, resulting from prolonged exposure to such films in the early 1960s, of the beautiful heroine, always immaculately dressed in a smart two-piece and carrying a vanity case, emerging smiling into the sunlight from the door of what was often an Air France Caravelle jet airliner, and pausing at the top of the steps. There, she would wave excitedly to someone in the terminal, then descend to board the airside bus waiting alongside. It was always a mystery to me as to how she could actually identify the person she was waving to, given that the plane would normally be parked quite a distance from the terminal. Whilst not following this precise routine, I recommend watching Anita Eckberg's arrival at Ciampini Airport in Fellini's film "La Dolce Vita", a wonderful piece of nostalgia.

My arrival was, by comparison, unspectacular, and after buying Italian Lire at a bureau de change I exited the terminal under cloudy skies to track down the shuttle bus to Ciampino Citta railway station, ten minutes or so away, where I caught a graffiti-covered train to Rome's city-centre terminus, Stazione Termini. *En route,* I noticed that many of the line-side buildings and walls were similarly graffitised, and on the wall of a derelict railway building I noticed a fading message in white paint that had evidently been there for some time. It said, simply, "Si Divorcia" ("Yes to Divorce"). In fact it dated from before 1970, the year when divorce was legalised in Italy. The Roman Catholic Church up to that time had steadfastly opposed all political attempts at legalisation of divorce, and the difficulty of ridding oneself of an unwanted spouse in the absence of any legal way to do so was a frequent topic of drama and humour at the time, reaching its apotheosis in the 1961 film "Divorce Italian Style". I was reminded of the country's heated debates, reported in the press in the UK in the nineteen-sixties. It is a sobering thought that divorce has only been possible in Italy for forty-seven years. At the same time I concluded that Ferrovie dello Stato, the beleaguered nationalised Italian railway company, had accorded low priority to the removal of graffiti during the thirty or so years up to my visit.

Stazione Termini, Rome's principal railway station, is in part a monument to Benito Mussolini, Italy's dictator from 1922 to 1943. Originally opened in 1863, under the rule of the Holy See, the first rather pleasant neo-classical design was demolished in 1937, when work on a new modernist building to replace it began, its design approved by Benito Mussolini. Work was, however, suspended in 1943 when Mussoilni's Fascist government fell. Mussolini was arrested and imprisoned in an isolated jail in the Apennine Mountains, and was later rescued by German forces to become the leader of a grouping named The Italian Social Republic. His fate thereafter, whilst no longer relevant to Termini Station, is interesting simply because it was a seminal event in Italy's history, and relevant to my visit to Eur, a district of Rome, described later in this chapter.

On 25th April 1945, with allied troops advancing into northern Italy and the collapse of his country imminent, Mussolini and his mistress, Clara Petacci, along with her brother and a number of their supporters, set out by car for Switzerland, intending to board a plane there and escape to Spain. Two days later their convoy was stopped near the village of Dongo, on Lake Como, close to the Swiss border, by two anti-fascist partisans, members of the *Garibaldi* Brigade. The fleeing couple were quickly recognised by the local leader of the partisans, Urbano Lazzaro, and they and the others in the group was taken to Mezzegra, a tiny commune of one thousand souls, where they spent the night in the house of the De Maria family. The next day, 28th April, Mussolini and Petacci, together with her brother and most of their 15 fellow would-be escapees were taken outside and summarily shot dead. The shootings were conducted by a partisan leader who used the name *Colonnello Valerio*, but whose real identity remains unknown. At 3am the following day, any citizen of Milan who happened to be walking through Piazza Quindici Martiri, named in honour of 15 anti-Fascists that had recently been executed there by Mussolini's henchmen, would have seen a large van draw up in the square. He may have watched incredulously as the driver opened the doors at the rear of the van and offloaded fifteen human bodies, dumping them unceremoniously in the road before driving away. Anyone curious enough to examine this grisly delivery would have immediately recognised two of the bodies as those of their erstwhile dictator, Benito Mussolini, along with his mistress. By the end of the day their corpses, together with three of their entourage, had been suspended head-down from the roof of a nearby Esso petrol station.

The reconstruction of Termini station recommenced in 1947 in the modernist style, a huge steel, glass and concrete structure that is somewhat similar to many modern airport terminals. With a frontage of more than 200 metres, and covering 33 platforms, it is the second largest railway station in Europe after the Gare du Nord in Paris, France. Seen from inside, its roof, having no supporting columns, looks resembles a 200 metre-long wave. The name "Termini" does not refer to the fact that the station is, indeed, a terminus, but relates to the ancient baths ("Terme") of Diocletian, the ruins of which lie across the plaza. The station has been the location of many films over the years, including "Stazione Termini", also known as "The Indiscretion of an American Wife", released in 1953, in which Jennifer Jones plays a bored American wife in a liaison with an Italian gigolo, played by Montgomery Clift. From the station I walked the short distance to the hotel on Via Vicenza, pausing on the way to buy food and beer for dinner in my room, and checked in.

The following day, in pleasant sunshine, I bought a travel-card and took Metro line B from the station to Eur Palasport, about eight kilometres southwest of the city centre. The metro at the time had poor-quality signage at stations, to the extent that, for example, the station name-board on the wall opposite the platform at my destination had a couple of its letters missing, renaming it "Eur Pa sport", reminding me of the father's race that was a traditional event at school sports days in my youth.

Eur (pronounced Ay –ur) is not a district that many visitors to Rome have on their list of "must-sees". It boasts no ruins of ancient Rome, no renaissance art collections, and no beautiful cathedrals. It is, however, a unique and fascinating vignette of unfulfilled twentieth-century Roman ambition, a wonderful *melange* of the architecturally elegant and brutal, and a manifestation of the unrealised utopian dream of its creator, Benito Mussolini.

In the late 1930s, during Mussolini's time as leader, the decision was taken to hold the 1942 world's fair in Rome, and Eur, an undeveloped site of four square kilometres, was selected for this. Eur stands for Espozitione Universale Roma, and Mussolini planned to develop the site to create a new city centre for Rome once the Espozitione was over. Construction began in 1938, with the country's finest architects and town planners involved. The two principal architects, rivals in the city, were Marcello Piacentini, a proud proponent of traditional architecture, and Guiseppe Pagano, an unapologetic modernist. The resulting combination of reactionary and progressive styles would define Eur as unique. It was as if Canary Wharf in London, or, say, La Defense in Paris, had been designed by a partnership of Mies van der Rohe and John Nash. Sadly the outbreak of World War II saw the Espozitione cancelled, and the entire project was put on hold, half-built, in 1942. Construction restarted in the 1950s when the site was selected as part of Rome's forthcoming Olympic Games infrastructure in 1960.

Laid out in a grid pattern on either side of Via Christoforo Columbo, a broad central boulevard almost three kilometres long running from North-East to South-West, Eur boasts a plethora of low-rise office buildings that are unexceptional by today's standards. My initial reaction on arrival was to wonder why I'd come all this way simply to explore the Italian equivalent of, say, Milton Keynes, in England. It was only when I walked along the Boulevard that I began to appreciate the variety of architectural styles on offer within the huge open spaces on either side, each building looking almost as if it were part of an exhibition, which of course was the original intention of the Espozitione. Many seminal buildings of the twentieth century, such as the Lloyd's offices in the City of London, are partially hidden by otherwise mediocre structures, so may never be admired or, indeed, disliked, as they would if if they were free-standing. Eur's buildings are all free-standing and able to be judged accordingly. The most spectacular is Palazza della Civita Italiana, a seven-storey block, almost a cube, clad in white marble, in the New Classical or Fascist style. Known as the "Square Colosseum", it was intended by Mussolini to be a modern celebration of that Iconic ancient building. Standing atop a broad stairway, it dominates its tree-lined surroundings and is rightly considered one of the world's finest examples of Fascist architecture. Its unique feature is its nine identical Roman-style arches on each side, repeated on each of the seven floors and forming loggias, effectively walkways, in the space between them and the core of the building. On the ground floor, 28 of these arches protect statues, each 3 metres or so high and carved from Carrara marble, representing various occupations and philosophical ideas. One is simply named "The Right", and another, "Heroism", both essential elements of a fascist regime. Above the top floor is inscribed the text of a speech made by Mussolini in 1935 – "A Nation of Poets, of Artists, of Heroes, of Saints, of Thinkers, of Scientists, of Navigators, of Migrants". Nowadays the building acts as the headquarters for an Italian fashion company, something of a comedown from the heady days of the 1930s - from fascist to fashion in a mere eighty years.

Directly opposite Palazza della Civita Italiana is Palazzo dei Congressi, a huge low-rise theatre-cum-convention centre fronted by fourteen tall columns and topped in its centre by a fifty-metre cube. A strangely anachronistic mural ten metres or more high inside the entrance hall shows scenes from ancient Rome. Further along is the frankly outrageous Palazza delle Nazione Unite, a three-storey marble building constructed around the two-hundred metre perimeter of a circle, bisected by Via Christoforo Colombo, and boasting a columned frontage along its entire length. Just to the south of this, and more or less in the geographical centre of Eur, stands the Marconi Obelisk, almost fifty metres high and dedicated to the great inventor. Marconi was born in Bologna, but came to England at the age of 21 to raise funds to develop his invention of radio transmission and was effectively the creator of radio and, later, television broadcasting in England. The entire area of Eur is attractively surrounded by parkland and lakes, but lacks a sense of community and is largely devoid of residential accommodation and retail premises. The district represents a fascinating glimpse into the mind of Benito Mussolini, a man for whom modernism was to be welcomed, unlike his fellow-fascist and friend Adolf Hitler, who detested all modern art and architecture. Perhaps most important of all, it proves that Rome is not all about ancient ruins.

Prompted by the sight of Palazza della Civita Italiana, I decided to check out its ancient source of inspiration, the Colosseum, conveniently located on the way back to the city centre. I took the Metro to Pyramide, and outside the station was able to photograph that most unlikely of edifices to be found in this erstwhile capital of the western world, an Egyptian-style pyramid. Thirty-seven metres high, it hardly stands comparison with anything in Egypt, and rather than being the tomb of a pharaoh it is in fact the last resting place of Gaius Cestius, a middle-ranking Roman apparatchik of modest consequence who died in the first century BC. From there I took the number three tram onwards past Circus Maximus, the Roman chariot-racing stadium, built in the sixth century BC, and now a public park. Here the tram leaves the main road and proceeds through tree-lined parkland to a point opposite the Colosseum, my destination. I found a seat on a bench in the park overlooking this amazing amphitheatre and watched as trams, buses, and cars hurried by, their drivers probably inured to the building's status as a world icon.

Constructed in the first century AD, and known at the time as the Flavian Amphitheatre, the Colosseum could hold up to eighty thousand spectators. Thought of by many nowadays as simply a venue for gladiatorial contests, it in fact provided a wide range of entertainments, and was even occasionally flooded to enable mock naval battles to be presented. The name Colosseum may have been coined by the Romans because it was built near to a thirty metre-high statue of Emperor Nero, known at the time as "The Colossus of Nero", which in turn had been named after the Colossus of Rhodes, one of the ancient wonders of the world. The foundations of that statue still exist nearby. Many of the Colosseum's "backstage" facilities were located beneath the arena, including substantial numbers of caged enclosures housing the wild animals that were routinely killed in various forms of entertainment. There is no mention of bullfighting in any of the contemporary writings, but the current popularity of that "entertainment" in Spain and France may have its origins in the Colosseum. It is recorded that at the Colosseum's opening ceremony and games 9,000 animals were slaughtered. After the fall of the Roman Empire in the sixth century AD there were many different proposals over the years for its reuse, including converting it into a wool factory to provide work for prostitutes, using it for bullfights, or even turning it into a quarry.

I forewent the pleasure of a guided tour, and simply took a walk around the perimeter, a distance not far short of half a kilometre, before heading off to shops nearby to buy food for a picnic in my room that evening. At a rather run-down grocery store I paid with a five-thousand lire note (at the time the exchange-rate was around two thousand lire to one pound sterling) and I was due change of 100 lire. The lady told me they had no small change and offered me a couple of elastoplasts instead, which I duly accepted. At the time this was normal practice in Italian shops, and over the years I had been variously offered sweets, stamps, and telephone tokens whenever the shop had run out of 50 or 100 lire coins. To this day I wonder how these transactions were logged in the sales ledger.

The following morning, in pouring rain, I exited the hotel and heading for Vatican City, arguably the jewel in Rome's tourist crown. On the way I called in at the local bar and enjoyed a double espresso coffee, rarely available in England during those pre – Starbucks times, so an opportunity not to be missed. The bar's clientele, mainly men, appeared to be calling in on the way to work, taking the opportunity to glance through Corriere dello Sport, the daily football newspaper. For them, it seemed the only way to start the day was with an espresso, a cigarette, and an update on the fortunes of Lazio and Roma, the local football teams. In Lille, France, I found much the same thing in a working-class bar one morning, the difference being that some of the locals were already into their first *demi* (beer) of the day, and the newspaper was L'Equipe.

Suitably fortified by the best coffee I'd had for months, I checked the underground map to find that the metro transport authority had for some reason decided to give the Vatican a wide berth, with the nearest station, Ottaviano, more than half a kilometre away from St. Peter's Basilica. A short walk took me to the bus stop on Via Luigi Einaudi, where I caught the number 64 bus, crowded with commuters. As is usual in Rome, the journey was a battle through streets jammed with vehicles driven by unforgiving motorists, not made any easier by the incessant rain. Half an hour passed as we threaded our way westwards over the River Tiber, then suddenly we were opposite a ten metre-high brick wall, the Vatican's equivalent of a border fence. I was briefly reminded of the days when I used to drive past Holloway Jail in London on my way to work. A short walk around the corner and through a colonnade led me into the only unwalled part of the country, St. Peter's square, constructed in 1667.

Not geometrically a square, the piazza is in fact circular in shape, around 250 metres in diameter and paved with granite-setts. Colonnades, with a total of 284 columns, surround its southern and northern perimeters. The eastern perimeter is open, and a painted line on the road, similar to a "no parking" line but white rather than yellow, marks the country's border at this point. The magnificent edifice of St. Peter's Basilica stands opposite, and the view across the square will be familiar to those who have seen television footage of the Pope's weekly appearance at the window of his apartment overlooking the square, every Sunday at midday, when he blesses the crowd beneath. The facade of the basilica, almost fifty metres high, is classical in form, with Corinthian columns surmounted by a pediment. On the roof are statues of Christ, the Apostles, and John the Baptist, and behind this the huge dome dominates the structure. After taking refuge inside the colonnade to escape the continuing downpour, I rushed over to the entrance door of the basilica.

Constructed between 1506 and 1626, the basilica is built on land that, tradition maintains, was the burial site of St Peter, one of Christ's apostles and also the first Pope. The exact location of his mortal remains is claimed to be underneath the high altar. A complex of mausoleums does indeed lie beneath the altar, dating from AD130 to AD300, but of course no proof has ever been offered to the public that his bones are amongst those found there. No pope had ever permitted an exhaustive study of them, allegedly because a 1,000-year-old curse, attested by secret and apocalyptic documents, threatens anyone who disturbed the peace of Peter's tomb with the worst possible misfortune. The remains of four humans and several farm animals were found during excavations, but Pope Pius XII in 1950 admitted that none of the human bones could be proved to be those of St. Peter. Despite this, In 1968 Pope Paul VI claimed that nine bone fragments from the mausoleum were "identified as those of St. Peter in a way that we can consider convincing". Like most "relics" in the possession of the Roman Catholic Church these fragments have never been subject to any scientific analysis, and until this happens his words should be treated with scepticism. Nevertheless, as recently as three years ago, Pope Francis displayed the (unopened) casket purporting to contain these fragments to worshippers at the Basilica. From ancient writings it is likely that St Peter lived in Rome, and was possibly crucified there in the first century AD, but other than this there is no physical proof of any connection between him and the Basilica.

The building is believed to be the largest Christian church in the world, covering an area of 2.3 hectares, equivalent to three and a half football pitches. It supports what is believed to be the tallest dome in the world, at 136 metres, but not the largest by diameter. The dome has the added distinction of having been designed by Michaelangelo. Much of the carved stone-work inside is the work of Gian Lorenzo Bernini, arguably the greatest sculptor of the Baroque period, and, in the opinion of some, the greatest sculptor ever. I walked over to examine one of his pieces, Baldaccino, a 29 metre-high free-standing construction in bronze, claimed to be the largest piece of bronze art in the world, and was approached by a smartly-dressed man in a black suit.

"Excuse me sir. Are you English?"

"Er, yes. How can I help?"

"Please remove your hat."

I had worn my flat tweed hat that morning as protection from the rain, and hadn't given it a second thought on entering the Basilica.

"But it's soaking wet." I protested. "Too wet to put it into my pocket or bag. I prefer to keep it on my head."

"I must ask you to remove it sir. We have a dress-code in the Basilica."

At this he turned his jacket lapel over to reveal a concealed enamel badge, which I assumed was some sort of badge of authority. This was not going well.

"I really don't want to remove it. Look at that woman over there." I pointed to a lady nearby. "She's wearing a hat!"

"Sir, women are allowed to wear hats. Men are not. If you don't remove your hat I will have to escort you from the basilica. It is your choice."

There was just the slightest hint of menace in his voice. For a moment I contemplated suggesting that this was sexual discrimination and surely illegal, but common-sense prevailed and I did as I had been told. He turned and left without a further word. From that day to this I have never removed my hat in a Roman Catholic Church, simply in protest at such a bizarre convention.

I ended my tour of this magnificent building shortly afterwards and made my way out to the plaza, pulling my wet hat out of my coat pocket and restoring it to its rightful place on my head as the rain continued to fall. The next port of call was to be the Pio Clementine Museum and Sistine Chapel, both located to the North of the Plaza and Basilica. I walked around the north-western border wall, still forbiddingly more than ten metres high at this point, and located the queue outside the museum entrance in Viale Vaticano. Resisting the temptations of the souvenir stalls on the pavement outside, I waited in line and eventually entered, paid my entrance fee, and checked the plan provided by the lady on the cash desk. The museum is composed of almost forty different thematic collections spread over fifty-four rooms, and, as with the Hermitage in St. Petersburg, it requires much more than a day to do it justice. Some of it is rather esoteric, for example the Vatican Library and the Etruscan Room, and I was obliged to select highlights from the plan and ensure at least these were covered in my visit.

In any gallery or museum I normally head straight for the lift and go to the top floor, then work my way downwards, rather than having to climb endless staircases between floors. Here, however, I made an exception simply to climb the double-helix spiral staircase leading to the upper floor. Built in 1932, it replaced the previous staircase built in 1505 which was more a spiral ramp than a staircase, having been constructed to allow Pope Julius II to reach his upper-floor living quarters without leaving his horse-drawn carriage. The new staircase, intended only for pedestrians, is twenty metres or more in diameter at the top, with broad, shallow steps and an ornate solid metal banister. There is no central support of any kind, and the two intertwined helixes ensure that those climbing do not meet those descending.

At the top I headed for the far end of the first floor to visit the Raphael Rooms, home to the frescoes of Raphael Sanzio da Urbino, who was born in 1483 and died suddenly at the age of 37 after what was rumoured to have been a tempestuous night of love-making. He, Michaelangelo, and Leonardo da Vinci are considered the trinity of great masters of the Renaissance period, and all have works on display in the Vatican. At the same time that Michaelangelo was creating his frescoes in the Sistine Chapel, Raphael was commissioned by Pope Julius II, he of the horse-drawn carriage to his first-floor quarters, to paint frescoes on the walls of what was intended to be the Papal library. There are four rooms, each containing four frescoes, mainly constructed in the form of semicircles, some of which are as large as five metres high and almost eight metres across. Above each are ceiling frescoes. Subjects covered included historical events, religious matters, and my particular favourite, "The School of Athens". This remarkable work, painted between 1509 and 1511, was an attempt to portray twenty-one philosophers who had been members of the philosophic fraternity in Greece during the pre-Christian period, the so-called "School of Athens", who are portrayed, more or less life-size, as if discussing elements of philosophy amongst themselves inside a courtyard. Raphael of course had scant knowledge of their facial appearances, other than being able to view the few busts that had survived, and only Plato, Socrates, Aristotle, Pythagoras, Euclid, Ptolemy, and Diogenes can be identified with any degree of confidence. The almost-hidden figure in the left foreground is believed to be Raphael himself. It is an astonishing piece of work, and experts to this day dispute the identities of many of the figures, and find hidden meanings everywhere. It is, possibly mischievously, located opposite "La Disputa" (Theology), and other than "The Last Supper" in Milan, by Leonardo da Vinci, it is arguably the most famous fresco in the world, all the more remarkable considering that its creator was only 28 years old when it was completed. As with most fresco artists, he did, of course, have assistants who helped with the artwork.

From there I headed back down the spiral staircase to the sixteen rooms of the Pinacoteca, the Museum's art gallery. Built in 1931 as an annexe to the main museum building, it contains art collections amassed by successive Popes since 1775. In particular it is the home of one of only sixteen oil paintings in existence that are generally accepted as being by Leonardo da Vinci, although there are another half-dozen or so oils attributed to him but whose provenance is disputed by experts. His most famous painting is, of course, the Mona Lisa, in the Louvre museum in Paris, and here in the Vatican there is a lesser-known work, St. Jerome in the Wilderness. Probably painted around 1480, it is a part-finished portrait of St Jerome, clad in what looks like a toga, squatting on a rock beside a recumbent lion. Not a particularly inspirational piece of art, a metre high by three-quarters of a metre wide, and largely brown in colour, it nevertheless was a welcome addition to my ongoing attempts to "tick off" all sixteen of Leonardo's oil paintings. The Pinacoteca rooms contain a high concentration of important pre-nineteenth century art, a collection which was stolen by Napoleon during the Napoleonic Wars but was returned when he was defeated in 1815.

I made my way back to the main building and exited into the elongated Belvedere Courtyard. Thankful that the rain had ceased, I took a seat for a moment under clearing skies before heading off to the Sistine Chapel at the southern end of the Museum. Built between 1473 and 1481, the chapel has a decidedly plain and unspectacular exterior, being a simple rectangular brick building with a pitched pantiled roof and little in the way of external decoration. It is nowadays used for various Papal special occasions, but its main function is as a venue for the Conclave of the College of Cardinals each time a new Pope is elected. The winner requires the backing of two-thirds of the 200 Cardinals present, and there may be several rounds of voting before a clear victor is found. The result of each round is communicated to the world via a chimney on the apex of the roof. If black smoke emerges then that particular round of voting has been inconclusive, and if white smoke then a new Pope has been elected and the message "Habemus Papam" (We have a Pope) is transmitted to the estimated 1.2 billion Catholics around the world, amongst whom I certainly do not count myself.

Joining the inevitable queue of tourists eager to view the Michaelangelo frescoes inside, I shuffled slowly forward as the numbers allowed to enter at any one time were regulated to match, more or less, the numbers leaving. Finally stepping inside, with my cap firmly lodged in my pocket, and subject to stern warnings that photography was not permitted, I was immediately struck by how much smaller it seemed than I'd expected. At just 13 metres wide by 40 metres long and twenty metres high, the building allows no external light other than through the few small clerestory windows located just beneath ceiling level. As a result, my immediate feeling was one of disappointment, given the fact that the chapel is regarded as the Vatican's greatest treasure. In one corner of the room the most recent spate of restoration work, started in 1980 and in its final stages at the time of my visit, was evidenced by aluminium scaffolding which I later discovered made use of the slots in the wall that had supported Michaelangelo's wooden scaffolding when he originally created the frescoes between 1508 and 1541. Over a period of 450 years or so his artwork had been seriously affected by the presence of candle wax, smoke, vehicle exhaust pollution, heat, humidity, dust and bacteria.

None of this deterioration was now evident in the sparkling and glorious colours of the restored areas, and In particular the fresco on the far (altar) wall depicting the last judgement. Almost thirteen metres square, it was painted by Michaelangelo over a period of five years, contains over 300 mostly nude figures, and, as is normal in the many "Last Judgement" frescoes in Roman Catholic Churches throughout the world, shows the good ascending to heaven and the bad descending to hell. As a subject for discussion by the philosophers depicted in "The Athens School" it would rightly arouse heated debate, and not a little derision, but as a piece of art it is arguably unsurpassed in the world, needing much more time to study than was available on my visit. One character in particular, "The Damned Soul Alone", a naked man with a horrified expression being dragged down towards the River Styx, is a wonderful cameo amongst so many. The ceiling frescoes are dominated by "The Creation of Adam", showing a naked Adam reclining on a Hillside and a fully-clothed God in the sky, both with arms outstretched and forefingers almost touching.

By now it was getting late and I exited the chapel, mightily impressed, and walked back round the border wall in bright sunshine, having no need to wear my hat, back to St. Peters Basilica. In my earlier visit there had been a long queue for the lift to the dome, but this time there was no problem and shortly afterwards I found myself up on the gallery around the perimeter of the dome's base, looking down from on high at the tourists and worshippers milling around on the mosaic floor far below. On the far side of the gallery I located the exit door and was delighted to be able to step outside onto the basilica roof, where I was able to take panoramic photographs of Rome. One particular part of The Vatican caught my eye, however. Just inside the border wall to the South I could see railway trucks and a small station, and I later made enquiries as to its function. Apparently a railway connection was first suggested to Pope Gregory XVI in the 1830s, and he is reputed to have responded in French "Chemin de Fer? Chemin d'Enfer!" ("Iron road? Road to hell!") We may safely assume he was not a railway enthusiast. It was not until 1929 that construction of the railway began, and the station was finally opened in 1934. Known as the Holy See Railway, it was principally used for the delivery of (duty-free) goods to the Vatican, but became the departure point for the first time to a passenger train when Pope John XXIII used it for a pilgrimage to Assisi. The smallest national rail system in the world, with a track length of 300 metres, it is administered by Italian State Railways and since 2015 the visitor may now enjoy an excursion each Saturday from this station to the Papal Palace of Castel Gandolpho some thirty miles away.

At the end of a busy but highly rewarding day I caught the number 64 bus back to the hotel. Just around the corner I found an inexpensive pizza restaurant where I was able to watch my order – pepperoni - being prepared and cooked. Accompanied by a couple of Peroni beers, it was a meal fit for a king – or even a Pope.

The Vatican is certainly a contender for the accolade "The greatest show on earth" but is not, in my view, quite as magnificent as Venice. It contains some of the world's finest art and architecture, but has none of Venice's wonderful topography or daily dynamism. The Vatican is, for me, a glorious but rather sterile commemoration of man's ability to achieve the sublime, whereas Venice has managed over the years to create and preserve the sublime whilst remaining a living, fallible city.

During the following couple of days I visited other tourist attractions in Rome including The Forum, the ancient political centre of the city dating from the fifth century BC, the Spanish Steps, location of the house of John Keats, poet, and the Trevi Fountain, immortalised in films such as "La Dolce Vita", "Roman Holiday" and "Three Coins in the Fountain". None of these merits a detailed description here, but there was one other attraction that does. The Pantheon, visited the next day in pleasant sunshine, required a somewhat circuitous journey on a number 70 bus followed by a ten-minute walk, but, as I expected, it merited the detour, as the French say. Built around 126 AD, and originally a temple dedicated to a Roman god, it was converted into a church in the seventh century. It has a circular floor plan, fronted by a rectangular portico supported by tall grey granite columns. The building's crowning glory, almost literally, is its dome, forty three metres in diameter and made from 5,000 tons of concrete. It remains today as the world's largest unreinforced concrete dome. Its portico-and-dome structure has been copied countless times throughout the ages in many parts of the world.

I stepped inside to find a large, lofty circular space, surely a unique shape for a church currently in use, and pleasantly devoid of any baroque decoration. Various sculptured figures are placed in niches at floor level, most of which did not detain me for long, but with one exception. On the left, surrounded by a large crowd of tourists, I found the tomb of Raphael, the artist and creator of "The School of Athens" fresco in the Vatican, who was a mere 37 years old at his death in 1520. To his right is the tomb of his Fiancee, Maria Bibbiena, who died before they could marry. I suppose you could say that I was paying my respects.

 The visit proved yet again that Italy will always be close to my heart, for a myriad of reasons. Foremost of these is its wonderful history, with the Roman Empire even influencing my daily life back home when I regularly cycled along Ermine Street, the local Roman Road. There is so much that is beautiful in the country, both man-made, such as St. Peter's Basilica, and natural, from the Alps in the North to the Island of Sicily in the south, not to mention Stromboli, the volcanic island which erupts molten lava every twenty minutes or so. Add to this the elegance of the Milanese, the pleasure of sitting by a harbour in a cooling breeze drinking wine as the sun goes down, the taste of fresh-made pasta, and, of course, Venice, "La Serenissima", and it is difficult to find another European country that is Italy's equal.

Chapter 21

San Marino, Italy

Welcome to Bologna on Capital Gold for England versus San Marino with Tennent's Pilsener, brewed with Czechoslovakian Yeast for that extra pilsner taste and England are one down **Jonathan Pearce**

Bologna is the best city in Italy for food and has the least number of tourists. With its mediaeval beauty it has it all **Mario Batali**

Bologna is famous for producing Popes, painters, and sausage **Lord Byron**

The Barbie museum. Cassini astronomical instrument. The only double throne in the world. Thoughts of Jack Vettriano. Death of Ayrton Senna. More cars than people.

In my younger days my fiancée and I used to drink at a particular pub where we knew the landlord, Mike, and his wife, Anne. It was the early sixties, and the Costas in Spain were beginning to open up as package holiday centres, but at the time a favourite sea, sun, and sand destination for the British was Rimini, on Italy's Adriatic coast. Mike and Anne spent a week there, and on their return showed us their holiday snaps. Anne looked pretty good on the beach in her bikini, but Mike, a large man, photographed badly. In some of the photos he looked like nothing so much as a pink beached whale as he sprawled on the sand. Nevertheless, my Fiancée and I were duly impressed and vowed to visit Rimini as soon as we could. Sadly, we never made it together. Thirty-odd years and a divorce later my new partner and I had the opportunity to spend a few nights with friends in Bologna, central Italy, about 120 kilometres from Rimini. It was too good an opportunity to miss, and on consulting the map I found that Rimini was a mere twenty kilometres from San Marino, one of the countries on my "to do" list.

And so it was that we found ourselves exiting Bologna Guglielmo Marconi Airport on a balmy summer's evening and catching the bus for the twenty-minute journey to the city centre. The airport is named after the inventor of radio communication, who was born in Bologna and later settled in England to develop the invention that transformed the world.

Bologna is Italy's seventh-largest city with a population of a million, similar to that of Birmingham in England, and is the capital of the Emilia Romagna region of northern Italy. Situated on a flat plain at the foot of the Apennine Mountains, near to the confluence of the Reno and Savena rivers, it is an important centre of commerce, and is the location of what is claimed to be the world's oldest University, established in 1088. It was here that the word "University" was originally coined, being derived from the institution's full title in Latin, "Universitas Magistrorum et Scholarium", translated as "Community of Teachers and Scholars". Until the unification of Italy in 1870 Bologna was a major city of the Papal States, which occupied a swathe of what is now central and northern Italy, and was ruled from the Vatican by the Pope. After the Papal States were defeated by the Italian army in 1871 the city became part of the Kingdom of Italy, which was later to become a republic following a referendum to abolish the Monarchy in 1946. Much of Bologna's historic city centre was destroyed during World War II by Allied air-raids in 1943, following the downfall of Benito Mussolini, the country's Fascist dictator. After the war the city became a centre of communist activity, and continues to be largely left-leaning politically. Originally a walled city, only part of the mediaeval wall survives, together with twelve of the ancient city gates, but the route of the wall, around six kilometres long, may still be traced around the perimeter of the city centre.

We exited the airport bus at Centrale Railway Station, just outside the northern section of the city wall, and took a number 38 bus to our friends' apartment on Via Caduti della Via Fani, about a kilometre away. The six-storey apartment block had retail shops on the ground floor and overlooked Parco Don Bosco, a pleasant wooded park, which we looked forward to exploring in the coming days. On arrival our hosts offered us food, beer, and conversation, all of which were most welcome, but eventually the day's exertions caught up with us and we headed for bed. The following morning, fortified by brioches purchased from the bakery on the ground floor of the apartment block, we stepped outside in bright sunshine and took the bus to the railway station where we bought travel-cards. Thus armed, we took a number 27 bus to Piazza Maggiore, the city's central square, a broad, slate-grey and magenta flagstone-paved area surrounded by mediaeval buildings of brick and stone. Dominant on its south side is the San Petronia Basilica, dating from 1390 and claimed to be the largest brick-built church in the world at 132 metres long and 66 metres wide, giving it a floor area equivalent to a large football pitch. It is somewhat unusually aligned North-South, with the north side facing the square, and is certainly not a handsome building from that angle. The facade was originally simply a plain brick wall from ground level to the apex of the pitched roof, but an attempt was made in the sixteenth century to improve it by cladding it with carved white marble. This was abandoned, possibly on grounds of cost, when the marble had reached one-third of the way up the building, thereby leaving two thirds of the undecorated brickwork still exposed. The resulting "part-finished" appearance is, to say the least, disappointing.

The interior of the basilica is typical of its date, with gothic arches atop the ten columns that support the roof, but there is little in the way of outstanding artwork amongst its niches and chapels. It does, however, contain an historically important item called a Meridian Line, normally described as a scientific instrument, and dating from the seventeenth century. Its presence in the building is somewhat ironic, for at the time the church was unwilling to accept any scientific proposal that could be seen as running counter to religious dogma. This antipathy arguably reached its zenith when Galileo Galilei, the greatest scientist of his day, appeared twice before the Inquisition of the Catholic Church to explain why his scientific investigations had led him to believe that the Earth orbited the Sun, in direct conflict with the church's contention that the Sun orbited the Earth. At his second appearance before the Inquisition in 1633, he was found guilty of heresy and sentenced to house arrest for the remainder of his life.

In 1656, only fourteen years after Galileo's death in captivity, Giovanni Domenico Cassini, at the time Professor of Astronomy at Bologna University, was permitted by the church to install his Meridian Line inside the San Petronia Basilica. The "instrument" was simply a strip of metal, originally iron but replaced with brass in 1775, sixty-eight metres long, and inlaid into the stone floor of the church on a slight diagonal along one side of the nave. Twenty-seven metres above it, in the south-facing church wall, an angled narrow hole, was drilled, which acted much like the pinhole in a pinhole camera and projected an image of the sun onto the brass strip below. From the position of the image on the strip on any particular day it was possible to determine the precise time of midday, and the position of the image along the length of the strip could also be used to determine the date. The Meridian Line was also used by Cassini to calculate the exact length of a year, and with it he made further attempts to prove that the earth orbits the sun. The church, in its turn, found the meridian line useful in determining the dates of forthcoming liturgical days. Other similar Meridian lines exist throughout the world, often, but not always, installed in churches. One of the best-known, but shorter, is in the Cathedral in Florence. The open-air Meridian Line at Greenwich in London, popular with tourists, serves a different purpose, having no "pinhole camera", and merely locates the position of the line of zero-degrees longitude. As a postscript it is interesting to note that some years later Cassini was to discover four of Saturn's moons during his observations of the heavens. In recognition of this, the space probe launched in 1997 that has sent back remarkable pictures of the planet Saturn, its rings, and moons, was named by NASA as the Cassini probe in his honour. I have yet to see posthumous recognition of his greatness by the church.

The piazza outside the basilica was somewhat unaccommodating to visitors in that there was no public seating of any kind, so it seemed we would be obliged to squat on the steps leading to its entrance in order to plan the remainder of the day. On the opposite side, however, the sunlit tables of a busy cafe beckoned, and there we enjoyed coffee whilst watching the world go by. It is a sobering thought that this was at a time when there were few if any mobile phones, no electronic tablets, and certainly no selfie sticks, meaning that people in cafes were obliged to talk to each other, and tourists took photographs of buildings, rather than of themselves.

Next on our itinerary was the Canal Window. Not on the usual tourist trail in the city, this curiosity is located in Via Piella, about half a kilometre to the North of the basilica. The walk took us along some of the city's forty kilometres of colonnades, which provide pedestrians with shelter from the sun's rays throughout the city centre and beyond. *En route* we passed the San Pietro Cathedral, a seventeenth century pantiled baroque construction in brick, with few distinguishing features save for a rather plain campanile, seventy metres high, which is visible throughout the city. Along the way we passed the Celtic Druid Bar, reminding us that there are few cities in Europe without an Irish pub nowadays. The roman-arched colonnades continued as we entered Via Piella, a one-way street scarcely wide enough for a bus to pass through, which eventually narrowed even more at Porta Govese, one of the twelfth-century city wall's arched gateways. On the left hand side, thirty or so metres further on, and between two shops, we found an unremarkable stuccoed wall. Its only feature was what appeared to be a small wooden hatch at head height, about half a metre square, with a handle to its left-hand side. Opening the hatch revealed the unexpected sight of a narrow canal running between the somewhat ramshackle backs of four-storey houses on either side. I learned later that the waterway is known as Canale delle Moline ("Mill Canal"). No more than five metres wide, and open to the sky, its water runs into a culvert beneath the pavement on which we stood. Bologna's history is inextricably linked to its sixty kilometres of canals, many wholly underground, which were essential to the city's commercial activities between the thirteenth and nineteenth centuries. As a major textile producer at the time, the canals were constructed to drive water-wheels connected to domestic spinning and weaving equipment, especially for the production of silk, as well as supplying domestic water and driving commercial flour mills. The canals were in part fed by an underground Roman aqueduct, eighteen kilometres long and eighteen metres below ground level, bringing water from the foothills of the Apennine mountains to the West of the city.

We continued our walk as far as the railway station, where we boarded a number 30 bus to the erstwhile religious community of San Michele in Bosco, translated as "Saint Michael in the Woods". Consisting of a conjoined church and monastery, it stands on a wooded hill not far south of the city centre. The church is unremarkable, a pantiled brick construction with roman arches. The monastery, no longer in use as such, is attached to the church, and consists of three large courtyards, one circular and two square, linked by the three –storey terraced brick buildings that surround them. Much of the monastery is out of bounds to visitors, due to its use as an orthopaedic hospital. We paused at the top of the steps leading up to the church to enjoy the view northwards over the roofs of the city, uncluttered by modern buildings of any sort. From there, the city's unique mediaeval towers were particularly prominent. During the twelfth and thirteenth centuries up to 100 of these were built, some reaching as high as 100 metres, and each around 10 metres square in plan. To this day their function is unclear, but it is suggested they were simply a way for local dignitaries to demonstrate their wealth by building higher than their neighbour's tower. Most were able to be climbed using internal staircases, possibly making them useful as military look-out posts, but this fails to explain why there were so many. Over the years the number declined, to the point where now there are only two remaining, unsurprisingly referred to as "The Two Towers". They stand next to each other in the city centre, with the largest, the Asinelli Tower, measuring just under 100 metres high. It is claimed that the architect of the ill-fated twin towers in New York, Minoru Yamasaki, was inspired by the two towers in Bologna.

On the right-hand side of the top floor of the old monastery we entered a corridor, the only part of the building open to the public. Named the Cannocciale di Bologna, it runs along the entire 160-metre length of the building. Cannociale means "telescope" in Italian. At the corridor's northern end is a window, some two metres high and a metre or so wide, giving a fine view over the city, with the Asinelli Tower prominent some 1500 metres away. We were advised by a visitor, somewhat mysteriously, to walk the 160 metres to the other end of the corridor and look back towards the window. To our surprise, from there the Asinelli Tower appeared to fill much of the window, giving the illusion that we were looking at it through a very long telescope. Apparently there have been many proposed scientific explanations for this phenomenon, but it remains something of a mystery. Outside, in the easing heat of the sun, we perched on the Cathedral steps again and continued enjoying the view, this time free from optical illusions, until the bus arrived. Back at the flat, over dinner, we found that our hosts had no explanation either. Perhaps San Michele in Bosco is haunted!

The following morning saw us up bright and early to get the train to Rimini, the seaside resort 120 kilometres distant on the Adriatic coast. We called in at the convenience store on the ground floor of the block of flats to buy food for the train journey, and as so often happened in pre-Euro Italy, the lady shop assistant apologised, told us she was out of 100 lira coins, and as "change" offered first a couple of Gettonis, metal tokens which could be used instead of coins in a public telephone, or, as an alternative, postage stamps to the value of our change, both of which we rejected, Her final offer was a handful of boiled sweets, which we accepted. At the station we boarded the train and were delighted to find an empty compartment. Carriages with compartments, almost unknown nowadays, were common at the time, each compartment seating six or eight people in a relatively confined space. In them, complete strangers would feel free to strike up a conversation, and occasionally there may have been a romantic encounter. Today's "open" carriages have to some extent eliminated this interaction between fellow-travellers, which of course some may regard as a blessing. On this occasion we had the place to ourselves, and as we waited to depart, I noticed that the window could be opened by grasping a handle at the top and sliding the glass downwards, in the way that a car window slides open. Most continental railway carriages in the post-war years had this facility, designed to enable personal luggage to be loaded directly into the compartment from the platform, thus avoiding the need to carry it along the carriage's corridor. I stood by the window, slid it half-way down, and leaned out to watch the activity up and down the platform. A simple pleasure, nowadays denied to all save those travelling in a few trains running in ex-Soviet countries.

The journey took us through an unremarkable agricultural region, dotted with ancient farmhouses, and the first stop was the town of Imola, a small community of some 70,000 souls which was until 2006 the home of the Formula One San Marino Grand Prix. The circuit, located on the south side of town, and not visible from the train, was chosen as being the nearest to San Marino in 1981, and continued to host the race until 2006, when Belgium acquired that particular slot in the Formula One calendar. Imola will be forever remembered by enthusiasts as the place where 34-years-old three-time world champion Ayrton Senna was killed in an appalling accident in the 1994 Grand Prix. The accident prompted huge changes in attitudes towards safety in Formula One racing, making it the relatively injury-free sport that it is today.

Before long we were entering the Rimini suburbs, and, after crossing the canal, the train, brakes screeching, juddered to a halt inside the station. A seaside city of 150,000 souls on the Adriatic Sea, Rimini's principal source of income is from tourism. To this end it boasts over a thousand hotels, ranged along fifteen kilometres of broad sandy beaches. Planning rules have meant that it is not a "High-Rise" waterfront and most hotels are around eight storeys or fewer in height, usually surrounded by spacious areas of open land.

Outside the railway station we crossed the plane-tree lined road in warm sunshine, located the bus stop for the number 72 bus to San Marino, and joined the lengthy queue of tourists awaiting its arrival. Once aboard, we settled back in air-conditioned comfort, and as we drew away we were subjected to a short and unintelligible tannoy announcement in Italian by the driver, who then switched on the radio and entertained us with the Italian equivalent of Radio Two for the entire journey. I have no particular objection to "easy listening" music generally, but it is much more difficult to appreciate when you know none of the songs and only have basic Italian. Out in the suburbs we rode through leafy lanes past pleasant pantiled detached houses draped in bougainvillea and wisteria, the colours of their blooms intensified in the bright sunshine. At the city boundary we passed under the Autostrada Adriatica, a 750 kilometre motorway linking Bologna with Italy's south coast, and were suddenly out in the countryside on a dual carriageway, Commercial premises of one sort or another came and went as we approached the San Marino border, marked with what appeared to be a pre-European Union customs building with its associated vehicle holding area, now unused. On the same site, somewhat incongruously, we sped by large numbers of garden ornaments, ranging from small gnomes to two-metre tall copies of Michaelangelo's "David", all on sale outside a roadside shop. Soon we were driving through suburban streets, climbing all the while as the bus negotiated several hairpin bends before arriving at the high stone walls of our destination, Guaita Tower, the ancient fortress of San Marino. Constructed atop Monte Titano at a height of 740 metres, the fortress stands on the edge of a precipice giving spectacular views over the surrounding plains, with the beaches of Rimini visible through the distant haze.

The Republic of San Marino is the world's oldest republic and Europe's third-smallest State after Vatican City and Monaco. With an area of 61 square kilometres it is home to some 33,000 souls, similar to the population of the town of Morecambe, in Lancashire, England. The republic contains eight municipalities, the largest of which is Serravalle, and the capital is The City of San Marino. The name derives from Marinus, a Croatian stonemason, later sanctified as Saint Marinus, who established a monastery on Monte Titano in 301 AD. The country claims to be both the world's oldest currently existing sovereign state and constitutional republic, although both claims have been disputed from time to time. A thriving economy built around finance, industry, and tourism makes it the tenth most wealthy country in the world based on gross domestic product per head of population, and it is the only country in the world with more vehicles than people. It is not a member of the European Union, although, like The Vatican, it uses the Euro as currency, and has permission to mint its own Euro coins. San Marino is ruled by an elected "Grand and General Council" and there are two heads of state, known as the Captains-Regent, who together serve a six-month term, a practice derived from the political structure of ancient Rome. Citizens are known as the Sammarinese.

At the coach station, in warm sunshine moderated by a gentle mountain breeze, we walked through the archway in the castellated city wall and headed up a gently-sloping traffic-free narrow lane past the inevitable souvenir shops and cafes towards Palazzo Pubblico, San Marino's seat of government. A four storey grey stone building, with a frontage of no more than twenty-five metres and perhaps thirty-five metres high, it features gothic-arched windows, a three-arch colonnade, and a squat square tower on its castellated roof. The building is arguably the world's smallest legislative chamber. Outside the entrance stood three sword-carrying military guards, in dark blue tunics and magenta trousers, and the entire scene was heavily reminiscent of the stage set of some middle-European light opera by such as Strauss or Offenbach. We took a seat on the wall along the open side of the adjacent square, and enjoyed the breathtaking view over verdant rolling hills dotted with farms and small communities. San Marino certainly, as the French say, merits the detour. At the far end of the piazza we followed yet another narrow lane, thronged with tourists, and arrived at San Marino Cathedral. Neoclassical in design, with its entrance guarded by six tall Corinthian columns, it was constructed in 1836 on the site of an erstwhile seventh-century edifice. Inside it is relatively uncluttered, unlike many a Roman Catholic Church, and it contains a red-upholstered gilded throne which is surely unique. Intended for the two heads of state, the Captains-Regent, it is necessarily double the width of a normal throne, making it more of an elegant park bench than a throne. The cathedral has a reliquary dating from 1586 which purports to contain body parts from the country's founder, Saint Marinus of Croatia.

On the way back to the bus stop we happened on something never seen before in our many years of travelling. Amongst the souvenir shops inside the fortress wall, we came upon the "Barbie Museum". Unable to resist, we entered expectantly, and inside we found a display of several hundred Barbie Dolls, all different, sporting a huge variety of costumes including formal wear, casual wear, and, of course, wedding dresses. A veritable riot of colour, most were in their original boxes, and many were labelled with information about the date when they were issued, together with an indication of numbers sold, and comments about fashion trends during the relevant era. Rarities were given particular prominence, and a separate small section was devoted to Barbie's decidedly unflamboyant boyfriend Ken. I understand that recently a record auction price of £9,000 was paid for a single Barbie Doll. We exited, feeling both enlightened and slightly discomfited by this glimpse into one of the lesser-known backwaters of Western culture, and headed to the bus station and travelled back to Rimini.

It was mid-afternoon when the bus drew up in the forecourt of Rimini railway station. We had time to spare, so crossed the railway using the pedestrian underpass and walked a kilometre or so along the tree-lined Viale Principe Amadeo to the beach, past well-maintained low-rise blocks of flats and the occasional detached private house, some old and some new. On arrival at the beach, we took a seat on a park bench and in the heat of the afternoon sun drank delicious peach-flavoured iced tea fresh from the chilled cabinet of a convenience store nearby. Surprisingly, perhaps, there were few people about, and we were enjoying the tranquil scene when a phalanx of noisy wedding cars arrived and parked nearby. Out of them emerged the bride and groom and a number of exuberant wedding guests, all formally dressed. Amidst much jollity they headed for the beach, and we watched as the wedding photographer went about his business, taking pictures of the group against a background of golden sand, the glistening blue Adriatic Sea, and a cirrus-flecked sky. I was reminded of the seaside paintings of Jack Vettriano, the Scottish artist, which show formal activities taking place on a beach much like this. "The Singing Butler" was one of his works that particularly came to mind. The episode seemed to confirm that Rimini is nowadays decidedly middle-class, much like Le Touquet in France, and certainly nothing like many of the resorts on the Costas in Spain that eventually took the lion's share of the UK package-holiday business. My mind went back forty years to that evening in the pub when Mike had proudly shown us his holiday snaps from Rimini. Little did he realise that he was part of the very beginning of the package- holiday revolution in the UK, with Rimini and other Italian resorts becoming major destinations at the time. Over the years, Rimini seems to have done rather well for itself despite losing this business, and appears to have moved up-market in consequence. Nowadays it could almost be described as Genteel.

The journey back to Bologna was uneventful, and we enjoyed a couple more of days in and around the city. Not one of Italy's popular tourist destinations, Bologna is nevertheless about as authentic an Italian experience as it's possible to find. More relaxed than Rome or Milan, prettier than Naples, and cheaper – much cheaper - than Venice, it has much in its favour. And, of course, a day at the seaside is little more than an hour's train ride away in Rimini!

Chapter 22

Malta

Malta is the only country in the world where the local delicacy is the bread   **Alan Coren**

Malta is a sod of a place   **David Niven**

Street of brothels. A Papal Bull. US Sixth-Fleet aircraft carrier. Vintage buses. Currency embarrassment. The History of Mr. Polly. Two ferries.

It had been my ambition to visit Malta ever since my childhood days as a stamp collector. Maltese postage stamps were much more exotic than those from most of the rest of Europe in that they were larger and contained images of interesting landmarks, which invariably gave an air of eastern mystery to the country. At the time Malta was a British colony, and the presence of the Queen's image on each stamp gave them a rather reassuring colonial appearance. Such stamps, along with those from many other countries, evoked dreams of visiting exotic places, and I'm sure my love of travelling dates back to these times. In the event it would take me until 2008 to make the journey to Malta, and then only by courtesy of one of the budget airlines that had emerged in the latter part of the twentieth century.

The country, correctly known as the Republic of Malta, is an archipelago of three small islands situated in the Mediterranean Sea, about a hundred kilometres south of the Italian island of Sicily. Its land area of 316 square kilometres makes it the tenth-smallest independent country in the world, about half the size of the UK's Isle of Man. Its population of some 450,000, similar to that of Cardiff in Wales, makes it by contrast one of the world's most densely populated countries. The capital, Valetta, is the second-smallest national capital in the European Union, with an area of 0.8 square kilometres, just over twice that of Vatican City. The country became a member of the European Union in 2004 and adopted the Euro as its currency in 2008. In the period up to 1972 the currency had been the Maltese Pound, which then became the Maltese Lira until it was superseded by the Euro. Malta's strategically-important marine location, close to major Mediterranean trade-routes, has led to it being invaded and captured by at least nine different nations since Roman times. In 1814, at the end of the Napoleonic Wars, the Treaty of Paris ceded the country from the French to the British, who ruled it until its independence in 1964.

Malta played no active part in the First World War, other than as a refuge for wounded soldiers, but its strategic location inevitably led to it being a target for the Axis powers in the Second World War, when its proximity to Sicily led to it being heavily bombed by the German and Italian air forces during a series of three sieges between 1940 and 1942. During the war it was used as a naval base for allied surface and submarine vessels, and was a vital listening post, intercepting enemy messages which were then relayed to the Enigma team at Bletchley Park in England for decoding. Benito Mussolini, the Italian dictator, made plans to invade the country in 1940, but withdrew the plan on the advice of his military tacticians and instead launched a campaign aimed at destroying the British naval fleet based there, an action which produced no clear victory for either side. Airborne attacks on the island and its naval base escalated on the arrival in Sicily of German air squadrons, with 2,500 tonnes of high explosive being dropped in the first four months of the siege, leading to two-thirds of Valetta's population fleeing to the countryside. The air-raids eventually ceased in April 1941 when Adolf Hitler decided to concentrate on fighting on other fronts, and for a brief period from June the British were able to recommence offensive air operations from Maltese airfields against Axis naval convoys sailing through the Mediterranean. Air raids by the Germans restarted after a few months and continued until July 1943. Three-years of bombardment had seen 30,000 buildings damaged and the loss of 55 warships, including 38 submarines. 21,000 people lost their lives, of which, surprisingly perhaps, only 1,300 were civilians. The bravery of the inhabitants led in 1942 to the island being awarded the George Cross Medal, the civilian equivalent of Britain's highest award for gallantry, the Victoria Cross, by the British monarch King George VI. An image of the medal is to this day incorporated in the national flag and the medal itself is displayed in the War Museum..

The country is made up of of three islands, Malta, Gozo, and Comino, none of which rises more than 253 metres above sea-level. Comino is the smallest at only 3.5 square kilometres, and is uninhabited save for one hotel. Gozo is larger at 67 square kilometres and is the northernmost of the three, with a population of 31,000, most of whom live in the town of Rabat. Malta itself is the largest island, with an area of around 250 square kilometres, and is the location of the capital, Valletta, on its East coast, together with the country's largest city, Birkikara. Principal sources of revenue for the island include port transhipment activities at Marsaxslokk Harbour on the Island's southeastern coast, together with electronic and textile manufacturing. Tourism sees 1.6 million visitors arriving annually, and is nowadays a vital part of the economy.

Valletta occupies a peninsula between two harbours on the East coast, and serves as a port for both merchant and naval shipping. Its narrow streets, many scarcely wide enough to allow a vehicle to pass, are laid out on a grid system, and are lined with terraced dwellings up to five stories high, an arrangement that is reminiscent of the residential city-centre streets of Naples in Italy. The periphery of the city, by contrast, allows spectacular views of the surrounding communities and the Mediterranean beyond. There is a small amount of parkland located at the point at which the peninsula joins the mainland, but other than this Valletta consists of buildings and little else.

My budget airline flight to the Island in March 2008 passed off without incident, and I entered the arrivals hall at the airport, still locally referred to as Luqa airport, a reference to the Second World War when, as Luqa military base, it had been the Allies' major airfield throughout the conflict. I immediately headed for the nearest foreign exchange dealership.

"I'd like to buy Maltese Pounds please." I said, confidently. The man looked at me quizzically.

"I believe we may have some souvenir sets, sir. I will check for you."

"I'm not looking for souvenirs. " I said, bemused." I just want money to spend. "

"The pound is no longer used here, sir. Not since 1972. It was replaced by the lira."

"Then I'll have lira." I said, interrupting him. "What's the exchange-rate?"

"I can't sell you Lira."

"Whyever not?"

"Since three months ago we have been using the Euro in Malta." He said, with growing impatience.

"Would you like to buy Euros?"

I ruefully confessed that I would, and completed the transaction. The moral of this vignette is simple. Never travel in ignorance of the currency in use at your destination, as it may result in your looking a complete idiot. Ten years later I can still scarcely believe that this happened, following so many decades of travelling.

I was heading for Sliema, a community a couple of kilometres to the west of Valletta, and took the local TD2 bus from the airport, a stopping service that took twice as long as the express service, and was less frequent, drawbacks which were far outweighed by the fact that it cost a fraction of the price. After a short wait the bus arrived, and in pleasant evening sunshine I climbed aboard and bought my ticket from the driver. It was here I discovered one of the many minor effects that a change of currency can have in a community. The price for a flat-rate ticket prior to the introduction of the Euro had been 20 lira cents, the equivalent of 47 Eurocents on the day the currency change – over took place. It would have been understandable if the bus company had decided to round this up to 50 eurocents, for convenience, but it seemed that they had been persuaded by their political masters that this would be an inflationary move, so they confirmed the ongoing ticket price of 47 Eurocents. As a result, bus drivers were obliged to carry huge stocks of 1 Eurocent coins to enable them to give change to the inevitable large number of passengers who would be tendering fifty-Eurocent coins. My particular driver had discovered that the rubber moulding along the base of his driver's side window was shaped such that it allowed him to line-up perhaps twenty or more one-cent coins on their edges along it, thus avoiding constant searching through his money-tray every time a fifty-Eurocent coin was tendered by a passenger.

I accepted my ticket and the three eurocents change and took a seat behind the driver for the hour-long drive to the coast road in Sliema. As we exited the airport I was somewhat surprised to find that the Maltese drive on the left, a reminder of colonial times. The journey was otherwise unexceptional, and on arrival at the coast road I disembarked and walked the short distance to my rather modest hotel, a building with splendid but expensive sea-view rooms, but which offered "economy" rooms at the rear at an extremely reasonable rate. I opted for one of these, and took the lift to my room on the fourth floor, where, as promised, the window offered an uninterrupted vista of the brick wall opposite. After checking the television for any channels in English, and, as is so often the case, finding only BBC World Service and CNN, I went outside and took a walk around the block, in a vain search for a convenience store to buy food. Adjacent to the hotel I found a cafe whose outdoor tables looked out across the road to the Mediterranean beyond, and I took a seat amongst the few customers already there and ordered a beer. There I sat, in quiet contemplation, listening to the waves gently lapping the rocky seafront, a soporific sound occasionally interrupted by the urgent cries of squabbling gulls or the passage of a noisy motor scooter. As the sun set, the light over the distant ocean changed imperceptibly from yellow to orange and finally to a vivid red. For no obvious reason my mind went back to Mr Polly, the protagonist of "The History of Mr. Polly" the novel by HG Wells, a book I had very much enjoyed reading as a set text at school many years ago. Towards the end of the book our hero is seated outside the Potwell Inn, a village pub somewhere in England, where he has finally found contentment in life. His companion, the landlady, sits beside him as they gaze across the fields at the setting sun.

"Sometimes I think I live for sunsets." Said Mr. Polly.

"I don't see that it does you any good always looking at sunsets like you do." Said the landlady.

"Nor me. But I do. Sunsets are things I was made to like."

"They don't help you." She said, thoughtfully.

"Who cares?" he said. "Whenever there's signs of a good sunset, and I'm not too busy, I'll come and sit out here."

They said no more, but sat on in the warm twilight, until at last they could scarcely distinguish each other's faces. They were not so much thinking, as lost in a smooth, still, quiet of the mind.

Mr Polly and I have a lot in common, I thought, as I finished my beer.

The following morning I ate a breakfast of bacon and fried eggs, washed down with indifferent coffee, in the almost empty hotel dining room, then headed out to the bus stop. On the way I passed Sliema Point Battery, a low stone fort with a rectangular tower built by the British in 1876 as part of the island's defences. Its military history is scarcely remembered nowadays, given that it is now occupied by a large restaurant. At the bus-stop I awaited the arrival of one of the country's vintage single-decker buses to take me to Valletta, the capital. At the time of my visit all buses were owner-operated, more or less similar to the way taxis are organised in any city, but with routes issued to drivers on a rotation basis to enable each driver to operate on the most profitable routes for a specific number of days in each month. As a result of this "owner-driver" system, many of the vehicles were of vintage status. Mostly dating from the 1950s, they sported curved windscreens, with much of the bodywork decorated with chromium-plated trim, most noticeably in the hub-caps. Painted canary-yellow, with white roofs and a broad red stripe along the full length, they proudly bore the names of long-gone manufacturers such as Leyland, BMC, Ford Thames, Opel, and AEC. Inside, the driver's area would be personalised, with brightly-coloured decorations that included religious icons, football memorabilia, and photographs of family members. A bench seat installed lengthwise opposite the driver allowed its occupants the dubious pleasure of watching him as he went about his business. Sadly these vehicles were withdrawn from service in 2011 when the British company Arriva took control of the country's buses, but 90 of the best examples were preserved and may still be seen on special tourist services. I was anxious to use one whenever possible during my visit, sometimes leading me to ignore the arrival of two or three modern vehicles on a particular route in the hope that the next would be of the vintage variety. No single bus route used vintage vehicles exclusively, so it was always a lottery as to whether one would turn up.

This time I was lucky at the second attempt, and managed to find room on the bench seat at the front. The journey was pleasant enough in the morning sunshine, taking in the coast road and offering views of the glistening Mediterranean. We quickly reached Marsamxett harbour, on the North side of the Valletta peninsula, and passed the Sliema ferry terminal, from which boats cross the harbour to the North coast of the capital, skirting Manoel Island on the way. The boat trip takes only about ten minutes, avoiding a road journey of about six kilometres, so I made a note to sample it in the next couple of days. The bus proceeded inland for a while, then skirted the Msida yacht marina, before finally taking the main road into Valetta and stopping at the bus station, necessarily located outside the city walls as the streets inside are too narrow to cope with frequent bus traffic. Valletta is in any case so small that a walk from one end to the other takes no more than twenty minutes.

The busy bus station, entirely in the open air and with no shelter available, somewhat bizarrely reminded me of the camel caravanserai in Giza, Egypt, a transport hub seemingly disorganised but obviously with underlying order to the cognoscenti. At the somewhat makeshift office I sought a map of bus routes and timetables of the principal services, but was greeted with a shrug of the shoulders by the man in charge. The best he could do was to point to the destinations listed on each of the many bus stops. As it was, I had no intention of travelling further that day, but checked a few of the stops and made notes, particularly regarding the bus to Cirkewwa, the ferry terminal for the trip to the islanf of Gozo. After checking out the ornate Triton Fountain, a landmark in Valletta but sadly not working on the day, I walked over to the City Gate, a simple rectangular stone structure some 12 metres high and 15 or so metres wide, with a rectangular road entrance in the middle and similar but smaller pedestrian entrances on either side. Built in 1965, and described as being in the Italian Rationalist style, It had no architectural merit whatsoever and I was delighted to learn that it has since been demolished, but sadly replaced by what some say is an equally meritless structure. It leads to Republic Street, the nearest thing Valletta has to a High Street, which runs West-East all the way along the peninsula, mostly on a downward slope. My first call, not far inside the city wall, was to the National Museum of Fine Arts, which I understand has recently closed in preparation for its reopening elsewhere. Much of its content was work by unremarkable local artists, although I was intrigued to find that in the past they had had an exhibition by Emvin Cremona, the country's foremost postage stamp designer and undoubtedly the artist responsible for some of the stamps in my boyhood collection. Sadly, there was little of note on display, other than a small but nevertheless attractive watercolour of Valletta and its harbour by JMW Turner.

From there I walked the short distance to the St John Co-Cathedral, Valletta's principal place of worship. The term Co-Cathedral refers to the fact that the Bishop is also the leader of St Paul's cathedral in Mdina, the original capital of Malta. A Roman Catholic church, it stands back from St John Street, just off Republic Street, and was constructed in the sixteenth century in the Mannerist style, a heavily pared – down version of classical architecture with just a couple of Doric columns either side of the roman-arched doorway and a small pediment above at the top of two pilasters. On either side of the building are bell-towers, with the bells visible from the road. Inside, the church is undoubtedly unique, as a result of it being built by the Order of Knights of the Hospital of Saint John of Jerusalem, also known as the Knights Hospitalier, a mediaeval Catholic military order linked to the crusades to capture the holy land in the eleventh and twelfth centuries. As its military power waned thereafter, the order became principally a religious and humanitarian organisation. Malta became its last major territory, calling itself the Sovereign Military Order of Malta, but it retains a presence in many countries throughout the world, with a direct link in the UK through the St. John's Ambulance Association.

The interior, as I expected, is oppressive in its baroque flamboyance, in stark contrast to the building's plain exterior. The principal attraction, located in the oratory, is Caravaggio's painting titled "The Beheading of St. John the Evangelist", his largest-ever work, about four metres by five metres, and the only one of his paintings that he signed. The signature is to be found, somewhat bizarrely, beneath the blood flowing from St. John's half-severed neck. It is a remarkable piece of art, and definitely, as the French say, merits the detour. The cathedral has one other point of interest, the unique collection of marble tombstones in the floor of the nave, marking the burial sites of some of the more important members of the Knights Hospitalier. Many of these are intricately carved, and inlaid with coloured stones that add to the already hugely colourful interior of the building. In the adjacent museum there are a few tapestries designed by Peter Paul Rubens, which did not detain me for long.

Back outside in the sunshine I continued my walk along Republic Street, and at the rear of one of its buildings I found, praise be, a branch of Marks and Spencer, wherein I purchased half a bottle of Rioja, being careful to ensure it had a screw cap, and a couple of sandwiches, to be consumed later. In this part of the city the rigid grid-pattern of streets is at its most unforgiving, with few if any curves visible either in the layout or the buildings themselves. Streets are little more than flagstone-paved canyons, lined by terraced houses three or four-storeys high, built from ochre-coloured stone, with little or no open areas visible other than beside public buildings. Many of these homes have stone balconies that project over the street, supporting what is effectively an extra room constructed from metal, almost invariably painted green, with windows. Valletta's streets have much in common with Naples, I thought, or parts of the number 28 tram route in Lisbon. Buses manage to penetrate the peninsula, but only along the much wider perimeter road. Otherwise, cars and walking are the only means of getting about, with the roads just about wide enough to allow vehicles to pass by those that are parked.

I continued on towards the end of the peninsula and called in at St. Paul's Pro-Cathedral, Malta's Anglican cathedral, called a "pro cathedral" because it is actually one of three that are for some reason attached to the Diocese of Gibraltar. A neo-classical stone structure with a sixty-metre spire which dominates Valetta's roofscape, it was completed in 1844 and suffered damage in the war, a souvenir of which has pride of place inside. A light-blue Royal Air Force ensign, tattered and ridden with bullet-holes, hangs on the wall beside one of the aisles. Now protected by glass, it was rescued from RAF Luqa, the airfield at which allied planes were stationed during the war, and which is now the international airport. The flag remains a powerful reminder of the sacrifice of those killed defending the Island, and in 2002 underwent meticulous conservation treatment. The interior of the cathedral is otherwise unremarkable, and outside, in warm sunshine, I perched on the wall beneath its Ionic columns to eat my sandwiches and drink my Rioja.

That done, I retraced my steps as far as Strait Street, a slightly dilapidated flagstone-paved alleyway rather than a street, and largely pedestrian-only, running parallel to Republic Street for more than 300 metres. At its eastern end balconies on either side almost connect overhead, whilst Further West it opens out somewhat as a one-way street for cars. Few visible clues survive regarding its notorious past as the red-light district of the city during Valletta's military heyday, which dates back as far as the sixteenth century during the years of the Knights of Malta. The street was particularly busy in the nineteenth century when the harbour played host to substantial numbers of British warships. Prostitutes found rich pickings in the bars, music halls, and brothels that opened up to entertain visiting sailors. In the twentieth century an attempt was made to reduce the burgeoning incidence of sexually transmitted diseases when the girls were given metal tags as proof that they had successfully passed their most recent medical examination. Violence was not unknown, particularly when NATO units visited in the 1950s and 1960s, providing an excuse for regular punch-ups between American Sixth-Fleet sailors and French, Italian, and British personnel. By 1970, however, the area was in decline, and Strait Street gradually reverted to being a slightly unpleasant and decaying backwater. Bar owners transferred their businesses to St. Julian's, North of Valletta, which is nowadays the happening destination in Malta for those who like clubbing. As for the prostitutes, history doesn't record their fate.

I continued westward towards City gate and turned south near the city wall to visit one of the few green areas of the city, the Upper Barrakka Gardens. No more than 100 metres square, the gardens provided welcome respite from the bustle of the city streets. Constructed on the top level of the fortifications, they overlook the Grand Harbour to the South. As I walked through the entrance gate I was delighted to spot a couple of Painted Lady butterflies, the first sign of wildlife I'd yet encountered in Malta, if you discount the ubiquitous gulls. The gardens were built in the seventeenth century to provide a recreational area for the Knights of Malta. Two parallel rows of stone arches some twelve metres high run along the side overlooking the harbour. These were originally roofed to provide shade, but the roof disappeared in the eighteenth century, one theory being that the French took it to use as firewood when they invaded in the siege of 1798.The gardens boast oleanders and geraniums, interspersed with cypress and palm trees. Dotted around are numerous plaques celebrating various Maltese worthies, together with a bust of Winston Churchill presented to him by the people of Malta in 1955. An inscription beneath states "To you half the world owes its freedom, its survival, and justice is its triumph."

Alongside the arches I took a seat on one of the wooden benches thoughtfully provided, and relaxed in the warm afternoon sun, taking advantage of the opportunity to finish the half-bottle of Rioja I'd purchased earlier. The view from the arches was spectacular, with the Grand harbour far below shimmering in the vivid Mediterranean light. Beyond, on the South side of the harbour, I could make out the narrow serpentine streets of Birgu, a fortified city that is home to only 2600 souls and is somewhat bizarrely twinned with Saint-Tropez in France. To my right a Destroyer from the USA sixth fleet was tied up at the dockside, apparently receiving provisions from the delivery trucks alongside. Without warning, I heard the sound of an aircraft engine and watched as a seaplane rose from the water far below and flew seawards till out of sight. Minutes later I spotted the ferry from Birgu beginning its crossing of the harbour, and made a note to use it at some time during my stay. As the shadows began to lengthen I somewhat reluctantly headed for the nearby bus station, and found a vintage bus to Sliema on the stand and ready to depart. Back at the hotel I ate pizza and drank beer at the bar next door, happy to have spent such a pleasant first day in the only country in the world that boasts a medal for heroism.

The following day I planned to visit Gozo, the second largest island in the archipelago, a journey requiring me to take the bus to Cirkewwa, a natural harbour at the North end of the main Island, and from there board a ferry to Mgart on Gozo. Unsure if there were any buses direct from Sliema, I travelled to the Valletta bus station and made enquiries there, to be told the Cirkewwa bus Number 42 was due to leave in about twenty minutes. Taking a seat on the wall of the still-dry Triton Fountain, in warm sunshine and under a clear blue sky, I awaited its arrival, and was disappointed to find it was a modern bus. With only a half-hourly service, and a longish journey ahead, I decided I had no time to wait for the next one in the hope it would be a vintage model. Once aboard I settled back in my seat and watched as we threaded our way through busy streets for the first half-hour or so, only entering open countryside once we'd passed through Mosta, thirteen kilometres and numerous stops into the journey. Most of my travelling companions were local people, going about their daily business, but towards the rear I heard distinct American accents, reassurance that tourist dollars were boosting the economy in this decidedly off-peak time of year.

Mosta, a town of some 20,000 inhabitants, is famous for its huge circular domed church, which was bombed by the Luftwaffe in 1942 whilst a service was taking place. The building was clearly visible from the bus. The 500-kilogram high-explosive bomb pierced the dome and landed on the floor, but failed to explode, so avoiding the deaths of the 300-strong congregation, who naturally considered the event to be a miracle rather than a rare failure of Nazi technology. A bomb disposal unit from the Royal Engineers made the ordnance safe and it was taken to the sea nearby to be exploded. I could report no miracles in the remainder of the journey, which passed alongside fields, olive groves, and woodland, and on the way skirted the pretty blue-sea bays of Xemxija and Mellieha. The final leg took us through rocky, sparsely populated scrubland to the even more sparsely populated port of Cirkewwa. I was surprised to find that it was little more than a large car park with a couple of portakabins, one of which was the ticket office, although I understand it has since been improved with more suitable passenger facilities added. I purchased a ticket and awaited the arrival of the boat, visible in the distant heat-haze as it passed Comino Island. On board, I took a seat on deck to watch as cars were loaded, then sat back in the heat of the midday sun as the vessel slowly made its way across the flat-calm waters separating the two islands.

Mgarr, my destination, turned out to be a small but busy port, with houses, shops, and offices alongside a marina, in sharp contrast to the almost-deserted Cirkewwa. Outside the ferry terminal I located the number 301 bus to Victoria, the capital, and was delighted to find that it was a vintage model, resplendent in the Gozo livery of Grey with a red stripe along its length. The five-minute journey took me to the almost deserted bus station in Victoria, from where I set out to walk to the Citadel, the central fortified area of the city, about half a kilometre to the North. On the way I passed a shop from which came the irresistible smell of baking, so I entered and asked the lady assistant to recommend a snack. She unhesitatingly replied "Pastizz" and pointed to a number of pastie-like concoctions on the shelf beneath the counter. I happily bought two, one containing ricotta cheese and the other mushy peas.

"Speciality of Malta." She said, smiling.

To accompany them I chose a bottle of peach-flavoured iced tea, always a favourite of mine when picnicking outdoors in the heat of a typical Mediterranean day. I continued my walk along Republic Street and turned right to climb to the citadel entrance. The huge fortified structure, about 200 metres square, built of sand-coloured stone, dominates the city from its elevated position. Not simply a military base, it at one time housed an entire community, and its narrow flagstone-paved lanes within the walls are testament to this. Once inside, I located the cathedral and walked up the broad flight of thirty or so steps to its entrance. Baroque inside and out, it was built in the early eighteenth century following the destruction of the previous building in an earthquake. Inside it is typically Roman Catholic, and could regrettably be described as a symphony in pink, with drapes in that most unreligious of colours suspended from the arches above each of the side chapels, and huge pink pilasters forming part of the building's inner walls. Some may say it's more like a boudoir than a cathedral, but I couldn't possibly comment. The building does, however possess a redeeming feature, in the form of a *trompe l'oeuil* "dome", painted on a flat ceiling above the nave and from below looking for all the world like a genuine decorated dome, similar to that at Sant' Ignacio in Rome.

Outside, I walked the few yards over to the Cathedral museum, where I found a somewhat uninspiring collection of papal memorabilia, but with one interesting exception. The building was only granted cathedral status in 1864 when Pope Pius IX determined that the Diocese of Gozo and Camino should be independent of that in Valletta. The decision was communicated in the form of a Papal Bull, a parchment document about forty centimetres square written in Latin and issued by the Holy See as the papal equivalent of a royal decree or charter. The origin of the name can be traced back to the days when such documents were authenticated by the attachment via hemp-cord of a lead seal, known as a bulla. Nowadays authentication is usually by means of a red-ink stamp, although on documents of great solemnity or importance the Bulla is still used. I was delighted to discover that this particular bull was on display in the museum, it being the first I had ever seen.

Outside, in the heat of the afternoon I took a walk along the ramparts, enjoying glorious vistas over the city below. Beyond the outskirts I saw a verdant rolling landscape interspersed with cypress trees and, to the East, olive groves. The island of Comino dominated the sparkling blue Mediterranean waters to the south, and to the north, far beyond the horizon, I could imagine the Island of Sicily basking in the afternoon sunshine. A slight breeze sprang up as I perched on a couple of dislodged masonry stones and ate my two pastizzi, followed by the thirst-quenching iced-tea, which was still slightly chilled despite the day's heat. During such tranquil moments, occasionally experienced by me in Mediterranean countries, I have found that a simple pleasure somehow encapsulates the joy of travelling, if only for a few brief moments. Such experiences, mundane in themselves, can be almost epiphanic at the time, and invariably linger on in the mind long after visits to museums and suchlike have faded from memory. Even now, as I write, I find myself recalling the otherwise unexceptional experience of the Gozo picnic with exceptional clarity, experiencing once more the feeling of deep pleasure that it evoked.

I walked back to the bus station past the usual souvenir shops and stopped to buy a fridge magnet, my souvenir of choice on such visits, before catching the bus back to the port. This time the sea was slightly choppier due to the freshening breeze, but the crossing was uneventful, and I was delighted on reaching Cirkewwa to find a vintage bus waiting for passengers. It was on route 222 which, as it transpired, went direct to Sliema rather than Valletta. Had I been able to obtain better route information at the start of the holiday I realised I could have taken this bus from a stop close to the hotel that morning without going into Valletta. The return journey of seventy-five minutes, taking in communities on the North-east side of the island, was delightful, running as it did along the coast for much of the way, but this was somewhat countered by the fact that the bus's suspension had been designed some fifty years previously and was less than forgiving on bumpy roads. Arriving back at the hotel at dusk, I headed for a desperately needed comfortable seat at the cafe next door and relaxed after a most enjoyable day.

The following day, which was to be my last on this fascinating island, I decided to travel to Valletta by ferry rather than the usual bus, and walked the half-kilometre or so along the coast road to the ferry terminal, where I took a seat outside the ticket office amongst tourists and locals to await the boat's arrival. Another warm day was in prospect as I boarded the ferry for the ten-minute journey across the bay, skirting Manoel Island *en route* as we headed towards the ochre-coloured northern city walls and jumbled skyline of Valletta. On arrival at the capital, right by the fortress wall, the crew enacted the docking procedure with the consummate ease born of routine, and I and the twenty or so other passengers disembarked to walk up the hill to St Mark Street. From here I headed for the bus station as I was interested to follow the route of the old Malta Railway, a single line of only 11 kilometres from Valletta to Mdina, the ancient capital, which operated from 1883 to 1931. It would be a chance both to see more of rural Malta, and perhaps view the remains of an important part of the island's British colonial history. I sought advice from the man in the office at the bus station and was told the number 56 bus would be suitable.

The journey began near the sites of Valletta and Floriana railway stations, long-since disused, both of which were located in underground tunnels when the line was in operation. All trace of the line's remains soon disappeared from view as the bus trundled through busy suburban streets and industrial estates, but once out in the countryside the railway route became more evident in the form of a few long-disused embankments and bridges. It soon became apparent, however, that the line could only be explored properly by car, and I was obliged to change my plan, deciding that a stop at somewhere rural might be a rather pleasant alternative. The opportunity arose as we approached a small community on the Southern outskirts of the town of Attard. Here I exited the bus, finding myself at a road junction, and about fifty metres down a side-road I found a cluster of buildings set amidst cypresses and palm trees, purporting to be a "craft village" where pottery, jewellery, glassware and the like were on sale. A brief visit to each outlet failed to persuade my hand to trouble my pocket, but the sight of a cafe at the far end, complete with visitors enjoying drinks at the tables outside, attracted my interest. Here I ordered a beer and in the heat of the midday sun watched people come and go, my attention being occasionally diverted by a couple of argumentative starlings picking up food scraps from the floor. The cafe was attached to a shop that sold ceramics, and after finishing my beer I popped inside to see what was on offer. Amongst the items on sale I was astonished to find several flat circular ceramic place-mats bearing the coats of arms of major football clubs, including Manchester United. I must confess that the juxtaposition of an English football team logo alongside artistically-designed and beautifully-decorated tableware did not receive my unalloyed aesthetic approval. Needless to say, I forewent the pleasure of acquiring the piece, and made my way back to bus stop to catch the next bus back to Valletta.

Whilst in the Upper Barrakka Gardens in Valletta two days previously I had noticed a ferry-boat crossing the Grand Harbour, and was determined to discover more about it. I walked from the bus station to the gardens, but found that the route down to the ferry terminal at Lascaris was something of an obstacle course involving narrow streets and stairways, which I eventually and perspiringly negotiated successfully. Interestingly, this vertical descent of 58 metres is nowadays covered in about 25 seconds by means of a free-standing lift of that height, built in 2014, its function similar to the free-standing Santa Justa lift in Lisbon, Portugal. I located the ferry terminal, purchased a ticket, and set off on what in effect was a pleasant mini-cruise of some three kilometres on a flat-calm sea, enjoying spectacular views of both Valletta and Birgu, my destination. The US sixth-fleet destroyer, still tied up alongside the Valletta waterfront, dominated the view sternwards, whilst the streets of Birgu drew ever closer ahead. Birgu is a tiny city of some 2,600 souls, and lies on the North side of a gradually-narrowing inlet perhaps a kilometre in length. It is an ancient port with three-storey dockside stone buildings along much of the inlet, but boasted very little in the way of commercial shipping activity at the time of my visit. It has, however, developed a large marina, providing moorings for a huge number of private yachts. Narrow streets rise steeply from the dockside road, and many of the ochre-coloured stone homes and offices sport enclosed balconies, roman-arched windows and doors, and flat roofs that in many cases support a recently added room or two. Much of the architecture has an unmistakable Moorish quality.

I walked up to the open space known as Victory Square, located not far from the ferry terminal, and found it surrounded by what appeared to be ancient three- and four-storey buildings. I later discovered that, far from being ancient, all the square's houses and commercial premises date from the post-war period, as the area had to be rebuilt following its destruction by the German and Italian air-forces during World-War II. A 40 metre-high clock tower in the middle of the square was demolished in one of these air-raids, and the clock hands are today on display in a nearby church, with the clock mechanism stored elsewhere nearby in the hope that one day the tower will be rebuilt. I spent a pleasant half-hour or so outside a bar in the square enjoying a beer and watching the world go by, to the noisy accompaniment of what seemed to be a particularly tense game of backgammon at a nearby table. The only other diversion was the sight of a bright-eyed brown lizard scuttling along at my feet and disappearing round the corner as quickly as it had appeared.

Eventually, and somewhat reluctantly, I made my way back to the ferry and enjoyed the spectacular crossing back to Valletta. There, I avoided the 58-metre climb by taking the 133 bus from the stop outside the ferry terminal to the bus station, where I changed onto a number 13 vintage bus, and enjoyed the journey through busy streets in fading light back to the hotel. The following morning I caught the bus to the airport and had an uneventful flight home.

It had been an all-too brief visit to this fascinating country, and I vowed to return, wondering if next time I might take the ferry to Valletta from Pozzallo in Sicily, thereby enjoying a four-hour Mediterranean cruise. Malta is typically Mediterranean, but with a unique history and culture, and I was conscious that there was much more to see and do there. I understand that the Island of Comino merits a day trip, and much more waits to be discovered in the communities around Valletta and in the old capital, Mdina. I hope to see you again soon, Malta!

Chapter 23

Belarus

My homeland of Belarus is an unlikely place for an Internet revolution. The country, controlled by authoritarian President Alexander Lukashenko since 1994, was once described by Condoleeza Rice as 'the last outpost of tyranny in Europe.' **Evgeny Morozov**

Belarus is stuck in the past. Before you. Belarus has no enemies, and now we have enemies everywhere...Belarus today is a pariah country. **Alexander Kozulin**

If, in Soviet times, we had Stalinism, in Belarus today we have Lukashenkoism **Anatoly Lebedko**

It's better to be a dictator than to be gay **Alexander Lukashenko**

Hotel with strip club and casino. A prostitute's proposal. Cyrillic script problems. Lack of tourist information. Penalty fare on the train. Marvellous Stalinist architecture. The cleanest city I've seen. Popeye and Olive Oyl.

Belarus....where should I start with the great Belarus adventure? As the last communist dictatorship in Europe, and one of only three remaining in the world – the others being North Korea and Cuba - Belarus has for many years been the only country in Europe that actively discouraged visitors, by means of the most onerous visa regime in the entire continent. As a consequence it received few visitors from the West, resulting in there being little or no tourism infrastructure. In recent years Russia, its neighbour and most important international partner, has gradually opened its borders, albeit whilst retaining visa requirements, with the result that, for example, St. Petersburg is now one of the most westernised tourist destinations in Europe. In 2005, Ukraine, another neighbour, abolished visa requirements for visitors from the European Union, a rather bizarre consequence of it having hosted the Eurovision Song Contest, when visa requirements were temporarily suspended for the two-week period before and after the contest. Soon after this it permanently abolished visa requirements for European Union citizens. Poland and the Baltic States became visa-free when they joined the European Union, leaving Belarus as an isolated and uncompromising exception amongst the old Soviet Union countries bordering the European Union, when it continued to insist that visitors could only enter if in possession of a visa.

My Belarus visa enquiries began around 2010, when I made my first visit to the country's embassy in London. I was told that I would need a letter of introduction from a Belarus company before they would even consider issuing a visa. I said that I had no past or present contact with any Belarus company, so this would not be possible, but the official said he may be able to obtain such a letter on my behalf at a cost of about £130. Add to this the cost of the visa, which I believe was £80 at the time, and I would have had to spend £210 before even setting foot in the country. Once there I would be required to register my presence with the local police, and there were further complications should I wish to arrive by train from, say, Lithuania or Poland. A second equally unsatisfactory visit to the embassy took place in 2014, and at that point I decided simply to wait in the hope things might change.

In June 2017 my attention was drawn to an article in a newspaper stating that a tour operator, Regent Travel, was now offering visa-free tours to Belarus, and I phoned them immediately. I was delighted to hear that the country had recently lifted visa requirements for visits of five days or fewer. The company had a tour scheduled to depart within a week or so, unfortunately inconvenient for me, but as a compromise they offered to book flights, hotel, and transfers on my behalf for a solo visit to Minsk, the capital, at a date that was acceptable. Such an arrangement meant I would be free to explore the city at will, and thus I was able to persuade myself that this was not a formal guided tour, something I've always tried to avoid when travelling. At last I would now be able to set foot in Belarus, the 49th and final country to be visited as part of my plan to visit every European nation.

And so it was that I found myself at London Gatwick Airport's South Terminal, checking in for the three-hour flight by the Belarus national airline, Belavia, to Minsk, the capital, aboard one of their recently-acquired narrow-bodied Brazilian Embraer E195 jets. I was disappointed to find that the company had recently retired its fleet of vintage Russian Tupolev Tu134A aircraft that had been used on the London service since 1973 and were a legendary product of the post-war Russian aircraft industry. The all-female cabin crew, smartly clad in grey two-piece suits with matching grey and pink chiffon scarves, went about their pre-flight duties, including the distribution of boiled sweets to each passenger, a procedure that I thought had been abandoned years ago by most western airlines. In theory the physical action of sucking a sweet improves the ear's ability to respond to changes in cabin pressure during take-off and landing, but the efficacy of this is, I believe, doubtful to say the least. It did, however, prompt pleasant memories of the halcyon days of flying in the pre-budget airline era. Such memories were further evoked when we were served a hot meal of chicken with vegetables, accompanied by fruit juice and followed by good coffee. No alcoholic drinks were available throughout the flight, and the crew made no attempt to sell duty-free goods to the passengers, a practice which met with my unconditional approval.

Two hours or so into the flight I was handed a landing card, consisting of two identical closely-typed A6-sized forms on an A5-sized piece of paper. It had been many years since I had completed one of these, and I was confused about a couple of the boxes to be completed. I called a stewardess, who reached over and withdrew the in-flight magazine from the pocket in front of my seat and opened it at a page showing an example of a correctly completed document. I did the best I could, but was obliged to make a couple of crossings-out, leading to a niggling worry that it might be rejected at the airport immigration-desk.

As we entered Belarus airspace the clouds below gave way to clear skies, revealing a sunlit landscape of fields and forests stretching to the distant horizon. A faultless landing produced a round of applause from my fellow-passengers and I made my way nervously to immigration. The uniformed officer took her time as she carefully examined every detail of the landing cards, my passport, and a letter from my travel insurer confirming my cover. After what seemed an eternity she eventually stamped all three and bade me continue on my way. Gleefully, almost vaingloriously, I strolled through customs and from there found myself in the recently-modernised glass, steel, and concrete arrivals hall. I quickly spotted my name on a tablet held up by Vladimir, my driver for the journey to the hotel, and shook his hand. For a moment my mind went back to pre-electronic days when anyone meeting an arrival at an airport would hold up a piece of cardboard bearing the arriver's name written in felt-tip pen. I remembered one particular occasion when I spotted a little boy, perhaps five years old, holding up a piece of cardboard on which was written, simply, "Daddy".

The hour-long drive to the city was something of a revelation. I expected a journey through run-down suburbs with dismal soviet-style tenement blocks on all sides. The reality couldn't have been more different. The airport itself is surrounded by immaculately manicured lawns that wouldn't be out of place on a golf-course. On the right-hand side of the exit road we passed half a dozen vintage passenger aircraft, lined up as museum exhibits, including such legendary Soviet airliners as the Tupolev 134 and the Ilyushin IL76, both stalwarts of the Russian Aeroflot fleet in the post-war communist years. The motorway beyond ran first through silver birch woodland, then past picket-fenced villages with brightly-coloured wood-clad cottages bathed in afternoon sunshine, before skirting lush green fields and hay meadows. Grass verges were litter-free and as well-kept as the airport lawns, and whilst there was plenty of traffic the road was not excessively busy. The journey did, however give me occasional cause for concern as Vladimir made phone calls as we sped along, even at one point resorting to texting. We were soon entering the airy outer suburbs of the city, whose well-spaced high-rise blocks sported a variety of architectural styles and details, suggesting that the city planners were determined to avoid conformity, in contrast to the usual "straight-up-and-down" structures common in the West.

The hotel, a conventional thirteen-storey building, was originally constructed to house participants in the 1980 Summer Olympic Games, nominally held in Moscow but farmed out to various venues elsewhere in the Soviet Union. Dinamo Stadium in Minsk was selected as the location for the early rounds of the Olympic football competition, as was the Republican Stadium in Kiev, Ukraine. Since that time the building has served as a traditional city-centre hotel, and now found itself welcoming tourists from the West following the easing of visa requirements. After checking in I made my way up to my room on the tenth floor, a pleasant enough space with the usual amenities. The view from my window northwards was spectacular, an uncluttered landscape of parkland interspersed with modern high-rise buildings, with a glimpse of woodland and fields in the far distance.

My doubts about Minsk as a tourist destination were already beginning to dispel as I unpacked, and were further diminished when I explored the hotel's neighbourhood and found a bar with tables outside, adjacent to a convenience store where I could buy food for a picnic in my room later. For this I needed local currency, the ruble, divided into 100 kopecs, and I returned to the lobby to change fifty US dollars, which I'd been told were more widely acceptable than pounds sterling, The exchange rate was approximately two rubles to the dollar, or 2.5 to the pound. Thus armed, I visited the shop and on my way back stopped off at the cafe, where I found a table outside and ordered half a litre of beer costing less than two pounds. In the warm evening sunshine I watched the world go by, smugly satisfied that I'd finally made it to Belarus. Alongside the cafe was a broad, litter-free pavement, and beyond that a busy six-lane boulevard, where I was disappointed not to spot a single communist-era Lada, Moskvitch, or Trabant car. As I sat enjoying my beer the people of Minsk strolled by, many in family groups, reminding me of evenings spent at pavement cafes in such cities as Madrid and Marseilles during the summertime. In the fading light I ordered another beer and noticed that the couple at the adjacent table were in animated discussion, which eventually led to the man departing. The lady, dark-haired, thirty-something with deep blue eyes and a pretty face, came over to my table unbidden and introduced herself as Inga. I introduced myself and told her I was English but had no Russian. She said that was OK as she spoke some English, and informed me she was from Minsk and had two daughters. I mentioned that I was staying at the hotel, and she smiled broadly

"We go to your room?" she asked, brightly.

"Why?" I replied. "I'm enjoying my beer here."

"We make love." She said, seductively. "All night!" She added, as a bonus. "One hundred dollars...."

As if to prove her credentials she opened her leather jacket and displayed her ample wares, scantily covered by a white lace blouse.

"But I'm a poor English tourist." I said. "I don't have a hundred dollars to spare."

She frowned, paused for a moment, then responded

"OK Mr. David. Seventy dollars. And that's my best price. You will enjoy!" she added, reassuringly.

"I'm afraid not." I replied." I told you, I'm poor."

She considered this for a while but eventually must have decided she was wasting her time.

"OK. I go. You give me five dollars?" she added, as an afterthought.

"No." I said. "But it was nice meeting you."

At that she was gone. My first opportunity to socialise with a local Belarusian had failed. I felt somewhat disappointed that the conversation had been so brief, but pleased that the encounter had ended amicably enough. I was already beginning to warm to this city, a place I'd feared visiting for so many years.

Belarus, formerly known by its Russian name, Byelorussia, and previously as White Russia, has a turbulent history. Landlocked, and about the same size as Great Britain, it has a population of some ten million souls. No part of the country is more than 350 metres above sea level, and 40% of its landmass is covered by forest. It has a substantial agricultural economy that sits alongside its well-developed manufacturing industries. The country has, through the centuries, been part of Lithuania, Poland, and Russia, but declared itself as an independent republic in 1918 after 120 years of Russian Tsarist rule. The German invasion during World War II led to the deaths of an estimated three million of its citizens and the devastation of its economy in a programme of ethnic cleansing. After the war it became known as the Belarus Soviet Socialist Republic, and was rebuilt under the control of the Soviet Union, whose influence continues to this day. In 1990 the country declared itself to be a sovereign state and changed its name to the Republic of Belarus, and in 1994 Alexander Lukashenko was elected president, a position he still holds 23 years later. His authoritarian style has led him to be described as the last Communist dictator in Europe. In an attempt to show the European Union that Belarus was in fact a modern democracy, in 2010 he held a presidential election, later declared unsafe by outside agencies such as Amnesty International . Mr. Lukashenko received almost 80% of the votes cast, and five of the candidates who stood against him were subsequently arrested, tortured, and jailed. As a result, the country's present political status precludes it from joining the European Union. More recently, there have been signs that Mr. Lukashenko may be considering easing the strict regime by which the country is controlled, but for this to occur would require the wholehearted approval of Russia.

Minsk is the capital city and home to just over two million souls, about twice the number in Birmingham, England, and representing about 20% of the country's population. Bisected by the Svislach River, it is largely flat, with just a few small hills in the suburbs. The current layout of the city owes itself to the events of World War II following the invasion of Belarus by the Germans in 1941. Its population at the time, just 300,000, declined as the Nazis pursued an ethnic cleansing programme, but the infrastructure remained reasonably undamaged. The infrastructure problems arose later in 1944 when the Russians arrived to take back control from the Germans. During the ensuing fighting 80% of the city's housing was destroyed, along with large parts of its industrial base and transport facilities. By the end of the war the population had fallen from 300,000 to just 50,000. Under Russian control after the war the city centre was rebuilt in the Stalinist-style, with grandiose modern and neo-classical public buildings interspersed with handsome six-storey office blocks lining wide plane-tree lined boulevards. Much of the land was given over to parks, and a substantial bus and trolley-bus network was established, together with an underground railway. This huge rebuilding exercise means that few buildings in the city date back more than seventy years. About 40% of the city's workforce is employed in the manufacturing sector, making tractors, trucks, vans, and electrical goods.

The following morning I had breakfast in the hotel dining-room, enjoying cheese, ham, toast and tomatoes, washed down with good coffee, whilst noting that few of my fellow diners were tourists. Thus refreshed, I sought information from the lady in reception about the procedure for travelling around the city. She told me that there was no such thing as a day travel pass covering buses, metro, trams, and trolley-buses, meaning that I must purchase individual tickets for each journey. Financially this was not a major problem given that a single-trip ticket cost around 60 kopecs, or around 25p in sterling. Sadly, however, there were no maps available showing bus, tram, and trolley-bus routes, but I was advised that the number 1 bus, which stopped conveniently right outside the hotel, would take me to the city centre and railway station. Fortunately I had with me a map of the metro that I had downloaded from the internet, giving station names in Cyrillic and Latin script, which I thought would be helpful.

Cyrillic script is a constant problem for travellers in some countries in Eastern Europe, particularly when it comes to reading place names when using the train or bus. Translation is a two-stage process. Each letter must be converted to its Latin equivalent – for example, "c" in Cyrillic is equivalent to "s" in Latin, "H" in Cyrillic is "En" in Latin, and "Y" in Cyrillic is "u" in Latin. It is helpful to carry a list showing Cyrillic/Latin alphabet phonetic pronunciation simply to make an attempt at translation as this sometimes helps in identifying a place name. For example, Moscow is written in Cyrillic as "Mockba". Knowing that "c" is pronounced "s", and "b" is pronounced "v", the word may be read as "Moscva" which is recognisable as Moscow. There are many pitfalls, however, and other than learning Russian as a language there is no easy solution to the problem. Having studied science at University I'm reasonably familiar with the Greek alphabet, much of which is similar to Cyrillic, so this is helpful, but often when travelling to a particular destination by train or metro I find it easier to memorise the first few letters simply as a pattern of shapes which should be recognisable on the station name-board on arrival. In countries such as Russia that have a well-established tourist industry it's not such a problem, because much is written in both Cyrillic and Latin, but Belarus had not yet reached this point. Fortunately numbers are the same in both scripts.

I walked across from the hotel to the bus stop and awaited the arrival of the Number 1 bus. The bus-shelter contained no details of services using that particular stop, no maps of any sort, and no identification name. Fortunately I had a reasonable street map of the city centre and knew where I was heading. When the bus duly arrived I entered at the front and tapped on the glass partition separating the driver from his passengers. He in turn slid back a small hatch in the partition and through this I offered cash. He took it, selected change and a ticket and handed them to me. I then validated the ticket in the adjacent machine and found a seat. The process was much the same as I had encountered on Estonian trams. Making use of my street map, which helpfully showed drawings of important landmarks, I travelled as far as the main crossroads in the city centre, near to which lay the National Museum of Art, an imposing neoclassical structure somewhat out of kilter architecturally with a city that had largely been destroyed during the war. Inside the museum I found a small shop selling guide books, all in Cyrillic, together with a few fridge magnets and, strangely, postcards. This would be my first-ever trip abroad where no postcards were on sale in the few souvenir shops in the city, and I concluded that in this electronic age perhaps no one sends postcards anymore, a sobering thought for the world's post offices. The gallery proved to be adequate regarding art from Belarus and Russia, but otherwise there was little of interest. Its contents were looted by the Nazis when they invaded in 1941, and have never been recovered. Mark Chagall, a Belarusian born in Vitebsk, is rightly celebrated in the museum as the country's most famous artist and the last survivor of the European Modernist School, living until 1985. He spent much of his life in France, but also worked in Russia and the United States, being responsible for creating the huge stained-glass window named "Peace" in the United Nations building in New York. He also was responsible for designing the ceiling of the Paris Opera House.

Opposite the gallery I noticed a steel pipe, about ten centimetres in diameter and wrapped in heat insulating material, emerging vertically from the pavement surface to a height of about two metres and then running horizontally at this height for the full length of the block, branching at various points towards the various buildings on that side of the road. Similar pipe networks exist in parts of Berlin, and were once common in many ex-Communist cities. Known as "District Heating", the pipe network provides communal heating from a central source, often a large boiler-house or power station, to blocks of flats and offices throughout a specific area of the city. Such systems are particularly common in places that suffer from extreme cold in winter, and each year, usually in April, the heating is turned off for the summer. In Berlin the insulation is brightly coloured, giving it something of the air of an art installation, but in Minsk it is a workmanlike off-white colour.

In bright, warm sunshine I strolled past the Central Park to the Belarus Central house of the Army Officers, a rather homely-sounding title that belies the grandeur of the building. A six-storey grey stone edifice, with a frontage of 100 metres or so, it dominates, almost subjugates, the surrounding parkland and streets. The dominance is further emphasised by the presence in front of a forbidding black stone plinth, five metres high, supporting a menacing decommissioned Russian T34 tank, a design dating from 1941 and still in use in various parts of the world. The building's architectural style may be described as modern with hints of neoclassicism, and I can think of few architecturally similar structures in the west, other than the Pentagon military headquarters in the United States. I found a bench amongst the plane trees in the park opposite and watched a couple of hooded crows arguing over a piece of bread. I was pleased that they were eventually able to settle their differences without resorting to the use of the T34 tank.

From there I crossed the road via the underpass, litter-free like the rest of the city, and emerged on the far side to view the Trade Union Palace of Culture, a pure classical building much like the Parthenon in Athens, supported by sixty Corinthian columns and with pediments at either end incorporating Elgin Marble-like sculptures. Entirely white, with the exception of its pantiled roof, it seemed somehow entirely out of place in a communist dictatorship, but is nevertheless a very attractive feature of the city. Somewhat incongruously, it nowadays plays host to two popular nightclubs. Opposite, in the centre of Octyabrskaya Square, a huge paved space, stands The Palace of the Republic, an entertainment and cultural centre, constructed over a 25-year period and completed in 2001. Delays in the construction process were attributed to the fall of the Soviet Union in the 1990s. Some fifty square-section unadorned columns, twenty metres or more high, support this imposing grey stone edifice, inside which there are two large concert-halls, a cinema, and cafes.

Having experienced these four splendid examples of monumental Soviet extravagance I decided to seek contrast in the suburbs, and the nearby Kastryckaja metro station on line 1 seemed ideal for this. The method of entry to the system was, to say the least, unusual, if not unique. At the ticket office in the far corner of the entrance hall I handed over the usual 60 kopecs. No ticket was issued, but I was given a circular piece of red plastic, resembling nothing so much as a tiddlywink. A helpful man indicated that it must be dropped into the slot in the barrier, which then opened up and allowed me through. Much has been written about the grandiose metro systems in St. Petersburg and Moscow, but the Minsk system is far more workmanlike and functional. Little in the way of chandeliers or artworks grace its platforms, and the trains are best described as adequate, but it is perfectly satisfactory in every way and whisked me through eight Cyrillic-named stations to the end of the line at Urucca. There I took a seat in a garden area overlooked by handsome ten-storey apartment blocks and marvelled at the utter cleanliness of the place. There was simply not a piece of litter to be seen.

Back at Kastryckaja station I took a walk northwards to what may be described as the old town, an area of narrow streets bordered on one side by the Svislach River and on the other by Pieramozcau Prospekt, a main highway into the city and the road on which my hotel was located. The principal attraction here was the Cathedral of the Holy Spirit, the national cathedral of the Belarusian Orthodox Church. I took a seat in the broad paved area opposite to view this delightful twin-towered church with its attached monastery buildings, its white walls and green roof standing proud against a blue sky flecked with cumulus clouds. In the unrelenting heat of the sun I was delighted to hear the bells begin calling the faithful to prayer. After a couple of solo notes a carillon played a complex range of tunes as worshippers arrived for the service, and for fifteen minutes or so I enjoyed what amounted to an outdoor concert.

As the carillon fell silent I walked across to the church entrance and stepped inside, finding space by the inner door to observe proceedings. As is normal in orthodox churches there were no seats, so worshippers remained standing as the service progressed. There was no preacher yet in evidence, but church music was playing and the congregation, mainly women with heads covered, frequently crossed themselves as they waited. A few latecomers bowed or curtseyed as they entered, with one middle-aged lady devoutly sinking to her knees. As they stood waiting, a door in the screen behind the altar opened and the priest emerged, along with three or four of his colleagues, all clad in highly ornate robes. He spoke to the assembled congregation whilst swinging his golden incense-burner back and forth. After a while he handed the burner to one of the colleagues who, accompanied by the others, carried it to every corner of the room, swinging it as he went, whilst the recorded choral music continued. Eventually the group returned to the altar area where a few more words were spoken by the priest, after which they returned through the door whence they had come.

I made my way back to the outer entrance, passing something similar to a betting-shop counter in the foyer, around which congregation members had gathered and where money and pieces of paper were changing hands. I presumed this was the Orthodox version of the Anglican collection plate. Outside, a pleasant breeze had sprung up and I headed to a restaurant nearby for a well-earned beer and my first authentic Belarusian meal, starting with a rather thin Borscht soup which was followed by Draniki, a form of potato, pork and onion pancake. The young waiter, who had excellent English, recommended Krynica beer, brewed in Belarus, a dark beer not unlike brown ale, and after sampling it I was happy to agree with him. Opposite the restaurant stands a wonderful bronze statue, possibly the best I've ever seen, a life-size representation of a vintage open carriage pulled by two horses, similar to the real-life horse-drawn carriages you might find in the tourist areas of many European city centres. Cast in bronze, the statue certainly seemed to be popular with the tourists, many of whom delightedly climbed into the carriage to have their photographs taken. Completely lifelike, with the two horses appearing slightly distracted, just as they might be in real-life, it could almost be mistaken for the real thing in the dark.

The journey back to the hotel was not without its problems. Pieramozcau Prospekt is an extremely busy six-lane boulevard with only occasional crossing points, and my hotel was about a kilometre away on the opposite side. There were only a couple of crossing points, one at road level and one as an underpass. I chose the latter, requiring a deep descent down many steps, and the equivalent climb on the opposite side. Somewhat tiring after a hard day, it was nevertheless an interesting experience in that the underpass was yet again immaculately clean and graffiti-free with no trace of any antisocial behaviour ever having take place there. It was becoming clear that the city's cleanliness rivalled that found nowadays only in North Korea, Japan, and perhaps Singapore. Back at the hotel, I happened for the first time to notice two adjacent doors at the far end of the lobby that were decorated with gold and silver ornamentation. One was labelled "Strip Club" with an entrance price of 50 rubles, and the other simply said "Casino". I resisted the twin temptations and made my way up to my room.

The following day after Breakfast I set out in pursuit of one of my principal objectives in this visit, that of taking a journey by train, a simple enough pleasure, but one which could present complications, given that I had no specific destination in mind, and that all written train information was likely to be exclusively in Cyrillic characters. In addition to this, I had learned of a guided bus tour to a couple of tourist destinations taking place later in the week which I rather liked the sound of. I normally avoid organised groups when travelling, but in the case of Belarus I was prepared to make an exception as there was no easy way to get to these places by public transport. The lady in reception at the hotel helpfully phoned through to the tour operator, who said I must present myself at their office in central Minsk to make payment. Thus armed with directions, I took the bus as far the railway station.

Opposite the station is City Gate, not in this case a traditional gate in a city wall. But instead a pair of classic Stalinist residential tower blocks, one on either side of Vulica Kirava, a narrow street. The two blocks, highly ornamented stone edifices, dominate the area and are arguably the city's best reminder of its Communist heritage. Those who have seen the Palace of Culture and Science in Warsaw, Poland, will recognise the grandiose style, known as Stalinist Empire, or simply Socialist Classicism. The style was popularised in USSR countries during Stalin's era as Communist dictator from 1933 to his death in 1953, and was particularly common in those cities that were in greatest need of new housing following heavy war damage. Arguably the finest example is Hotel Ukraina in Moscow, 26 stories high and an iconic landmark in that city. The two City Gate blocks in Minsk are, by contrast, only around 12 stories high, but in the context of their location are equally imposing, and are an important example of Soviet architectural heritage.

The instructions I'd received suggested the tour office was at the rear of a nearby block of flats, but after failing to track it down I asked a couple of young girls who thankfully had good English and directed me to the right place. The office building stands opposite Minsk Dinamo Stadium, the Belarusian equivalent of Wembley Stadium in England, which was undergoing a complete rebuild as witnessed by the cranes towering over the part-demolished terraces. As the home of two football clubs, F C Minsk and Dinamo Minsk, in addition to the Belarusian national football team, the stadium had recently had its capacity reduced to a mere 34,000 spectators following the closure of part of the terracing for safety reasons. Back in 1980 it had hosted the preliminary-round football matches of the Moscow Olympics, an event that saw the construction of my hotel to accommodate teams and spectators.

In the tour operator's office I took a seat at the desk of Natasha, an attractive blue-eyed blonde, who entered my passport details into the computer, then printed two copies of an A4-sized two-page contract which detailed the tour programme the following day. Both copies were rubber-stamped and handed to me to sign, one of which I handed back along with the appropriate payment in US dollars. Natasha marked the departure location on my map, and I was told I must be there before 9am the next morning. I had never previously been required to sign a formal contract of any sort when travelling, let alone when booking a guided tour, making this a "first", one of many I would experience in Belarus.

In my quest to sample the Belarus railway network I made my way back to the recently modernised railway station, a somewhat underwhelming synthesis of concrete and steel. There, I first checked the electronic departure board for a possible destination, but as it was in Cyrillic script I quickly concluded that I must make enquiries at one of the ticket windows, so sought out the one with the shortest queue. Sadly, the lady at this window had no English, nor did any of her colleagues, so she was unable to help. It was then that I noticed a tourist information sign, which directed me upstairs to a cavernous and packed waiting room overlooking the platforms. In the centre of the room a rather forbidding uniformed lady stood behind what appeared to be the information desk, but unfortunately she also had no English. There were no leaflets, maps, or timetables of any sort by her desk, so I was obliged to return to the ticket hall and join another queue. This time I was lucky – the lady at the ticket window picked up her phone, called a colleague, and passed the phone to me through the window. The person on the line had good English, and she suggested I go to Zaslauje, about half an hour away, and gave me platform details and departure times which I hurriedly scribbled down. I handed the phone back to the ticket lady who listened to her colleague's instruction and issued what I thought was a return ticket to Zaslauje. As I was to discover later, it was in fact a one-way ticket, costing 1 Ruble 50 Kopeks, equivalent to about 60 pence. It is undoubtedly the cheapest fare in Europe for what amounted to half an hour's train journey.

Thus armed with my precious ticket, I made my way along the 300 metre – long platform which was occupied by an inter-city train to Moscow, composed of the familiar blue carriages with curtained windows that commonly make up eastern European international trains. For me, these trains have always evoked the romance of long-distance travel, and, to my shame, I have used them far too little over the years. At the far end of the platform, on an adjoining line, stood my train, its streamlined red carriages glinting in the bright afternoon sun. I discovered later that it had only recently been purchased from a Swiss manufacturer, and was of a type that can nowadays be seen at any major railway station in Europe. Its clean, uncluttered profile contrasted sharply with the unashamedly functional design of the Moscow train alongside. I took a seat on the platform bench to await the arrival of the driver, and watched the trolley-buses come and go in the square outside the station, overlooked by the City Gate tower-blocks. It was a scene, I thought, that hadn't changed much since the post-war days of Joseph Stalin, save for one important difference. On the far side I could just make out the unmistakable golden arches logo of a McDonald's burger restaurant. Eventually the train doors opened, and I stepped inside, delighted to be embarking upon my first-ever journey on a Belarus train. Exactly on time, we accelerated out of the platform and passed quickly through the suburbs. Soon we were travelling along the main line towards Vilnius in Lithuania, through lush green countryside interspersed with the inevitable stretches of silver-birch woodland.

Zaslauje, the final stop for our train, is little more than a village, and is located on a busy main line. To my horror I found that passengers leaving the station are required to access the adjacent road by the simple expedient of stepping across the tracks, as there is no footbridge or subway. As I was checking to be sure there were no trains approaching before crossing the line, a middle-aged man, somehow guessing that I was a tourist, approached me and said "museum". He beckoned me to follow him down a narrow dirt-track between brightly painted wooden cottages, and at the end of the lane led me to the yard of a cluster of ancient unpainted wooden farm buildings. At the entrance an elderly lady greeted us and directed us to the first of three buildings, which appeared to be some sort of living accommodation for workers, reminiscent of the "flop-houses" of Victorian London. The remainder of the museum consisted of a flour mill on three floors which used traditional granite millstones, driven by a diesel engine from Poland dating from 1900 according to the manufacturer's nameplate. The building was identical to that of a traditional windmill, but without the wooden sails. In a separate building I was shown a fully-equipped blacksmith's shop, containing an anvil, tools, and a fire with bellows. This particularly interested me, being the son of a blacksmith, and I imagined that my father would have worked in a similar place in his youth. Adjacent to the forge was a barn providing storage space for flour and corn. No English was spoken throughout the tour, but it was nevertheless an informative glimpse of Belarus village life from, I suspect, not too long ago. Afterwards I toured the village, finding nothing remarkable other than an attractive Orthodox Belarusian church at the top of a hill, overlooking what might be described as the village pond, alongside a children's play area. I concluded that the community was remarkably similar to many English villages, the only difference being that the corrugated-roofed cottages were decidedly eastern European in appearance.

The walk back to the railway station in the heat of the afternoon sun gave me cause to ponder on the day's events. I had managed to penetrate deep into the countryside of the last communist dictatorship in Europe, and by accident had come across a delightful museum that I was sure doesn't appear in any tour guide. I thought of my father, working as a blacksmith all those years ago, and wondered what he would have said if he'd been told his son would one day be visiting a blacksmith's shop, much like his own, in Belarus in Eastern Europe. I also thought of the years I'd spent waiting for the relaxation of the Belarus visa rules that finally enabled me to make an entirely unplanned visit to this pleasant little village. An unpredictable series of events had brought me there, and the experience simply proved why independent travelling is so life-affirming – you never know what's round the next corner!

Back at the station I crossed over to my train and climbed aboard. As we sped towards Minsk the ticket inspector arrived and told me there was a problem with my ticket. There was little to discuss, as she had no English, but I guessed it was a one-way ticket rather than a return ticket as I'd specified in the phone call at Minsk station. By use of hand-signals she managed to inform me that I would have to pay a penalty fare of two rubles, or about 80p in sterling, taking the cost of the return journey to around £1.40, which I was more than happy to pay. On arrival in Minsk I decided it was time to take a trolley-bus ride, as I'd last travelled on a trolleybus more than 40 years previously in Walsall, England. Nowadays a rather unfashionable method of transport, trolleybuses are extinct in the UK and an endangered species in much of continental Europe. The stop outside the station seemed the ideal place to start, so I waited for the next one to arrive, paid the driver the 60 kopec fare, and settled back for the journey. After twenty minutes or so of travel we were in the suburbs, and I exited at the next stop, crossed over the road and boarded another trolley-bus heading back to the station. Five minutes later we halted in between stops on a busy road, and the driver signified that he could proceed no further as there had been a road accident up ahead. Apparently the trolley-bus was unable to swerve around the two cars involved. Passengers were invited to proceed on foot to the next stop, about a kilometre away, resulting in a long walk in the heat of the afternoon sun. Some way along the road another trolley-bus line joined ours, so I and my fellow passengers were able to continue our journey from the next stop without much delay. There are those who would say that had we been on a bus the hold-up would not have occurred, as the driver would have been able to circumvent the scene of the accident. In response I would simply point out that the trolley bus is much quieter and more environmentally friendly than anything fitted with an internal combustion engine.

The final visit of the day was to Caliuskinsau Park and Botanical Gardens, requiring a metro ride on line 1, followed by a short walk from the metro station to the entrance gate. The park itself was unlike any I've seen in England, being so densely packed with huge trees that in many areas light struggled to reach the ground. More like an urban forest than a park, it reminded me of tales from childhood such as Little Red Riding Hood or Babes in the Wood, where the hero or heroine is obliged to walk in fear through a dark and forbidding forest. As an immaculately clean public space, however, it was delightful, criss-crossed by paths and full of the sound of birdsong. At the far end I found the Children's Railway, not the usual miniature railway usually found in parks, but a fully functioning railway about a kilometre long with a station at either end. Such installations, common in Eastern Europe, are used as extracurricular educational facilities aimed at training schoolchildren for a career on the national railway system. The first was opened in Gorky Park, Moscow, in 1932, and there are currently sixteen in operation, exclusively in Communist or ex-Communist countries. Nowadays they mainly serve as tourist attractions but continue to be operated by teenagers. The narrow-gauge Minsk railway possesses two large diesel locomotives and two trains each of six blue carriages, with each carriage capable of carrying around 15 passengers. Sadly it wasn't in operation on this particular day, but the spotless locomotives and carriages were parked in the station ready for action. After taking the obligatory photograph I headed back to the Metro and returned to the hotel.

The following morning I was up bright and early to get to the old town to catch the bus for the tour that I'd arranged the previous day. The weather was showing signs of deteriorating, and there was a slight chill in the air following a violent thunderstorm during the night, but the sun was shining as I took a seat on the bench by the cathedral to await the arrival of the coach. Others in the group arrived sporadically, and eventually we were about fifteen in total. The vehicle duly arrived and Olga, our guide, a pretty young lady clad in a blue-striped Breton shirt and blue jeans, welcomed us aboard with the news that we would be away until around 7pm as the distance to be travelled was around 270 kilometres. She confirmed we would be visiting tourist sites at Mir and Nesvizh, and informed us that "Mir" in Russian means either "Peace" or "World". "Mir" was also the name of the old Russian orbiting space station launched in 1986, which was declared obsolete in 1999 and "de-orbited", that is to say deliberately sent out of orbit to burn up in the earth's atmosphere over the South Pacific. Hoping not to meet a similar fate, I settled back in my seat as we set off through the suburbs, soon passing fields, forests, and villages as we took the E30 motorway south-westwards in the general direction of the Polish border. Mir, a small village of some 2,500 souls, lies just off the motorway about 100 kilometres from Minsk, and on arrival there we drove through the immaculately-maintained village streets to the sixteenth-century castle.

The village of Mir has an interesting history as one of the ten Belarusian fiefdoms of the Radziwill family. The family also owned dozens of villages in Ukraine, Poland, and Lithuania, including Nesvizh, which we were to visit later, and for hundreds of years were considered the equivalent of royalty in the region. Anyone who remembers the Kennedy presidency in the USA may have heard of Stanislas Radziwill, who was married to Caroline Lee Bouvier, younger sister of Jacqueline Kennedy. It is difficult to exaggerate the family's influence and connections throughout Europe and North America even today.

The village dates back to the fourteenth century, and its turbulent history is inextricably linked to that of the region over many centuries of invasion and war, culminating in the arrival of the Germans in 1941, an invasion that led to the murder of 2,400 Jews, about half the population, from which it has never fully recovered. The outlines of the streets that were destroyed by the Nazis can still be seen on Google Earth images to the North-East of the castle, our destination. The castle, part of which is nowadays a hotel, is a UNESCO world Heritage Site. Originally built in the Belarus gothic style, it was rebuilt many times after falling into disrepair, culminating in it being severely damaged during the Napoleonic period and finally being completely restored over a sixteen-year period starting in 1922. Further restoration work took place as recently as 1983, and it was opened to the public in 2010. The building, which stands by a large man-made lake, is constructed in brick on a stone foundation, with pantiled roofs. There are five circular towers, one at each corner and one over the entrance gate, each topped by a conic roof with mansard windows. Brickwork surrounding mullion window and door frames is rendered in white plaster, giving the whole a strangely Tudor appearance. Inside, we walked across the courtyard, a surface of uneven stones laid in concrete that required care to negotiate, and entered the living quarters where we were asked to don blue plastic covers over our shoes to avert damage to the beautifully polished wooden flooring.

In its later days the castle was used as a home by its owner Mikhail Svyatopolk – Mirsky and the rooms reflect this use, giving it the air of a somewhat grandiose stately home, with a large ballroom, sumptuous dining rooms, and various retiring rooms and bedrooms. Every room boasted a porcelain heating stove, better known as a masonry heater. Such stoves were common in large houses in most of the former USSR countries, and can be seen at their best in the Catherine Palace in Tsarskoye Selo (Pushkin) near St Petersburg. Normally built into the corner of a room, they can be as much as two metres square and often reach from floor to ceiling, sometimes three or four metres high. Performing essentially the same function as the western fireplace, they are covered in decorative porcelain tiles, some depicting the family coat of arms, and use wood as fuel, with the internal fire-grate located just above floor level. Those in Mir were particularly fine examples, sporting very high quality tiles which in some cases made them the focal point of otherwise nondescript spaces. Paintings of family members filled the walls of each room, together with tapestries, an art-form that has never been able to rouse my enthusiasm. At the end of the tour we were taken to a restaurant in the basement where we ate a lunch of chicken and vegetables, accompanied by Krynica beer. The two men who shared my table, one Dutch and the other German, ensured my undying envy by announcing that the previous day they'd taken the train to Vitebsk, not far from the Russian border. A 600-kilometre round trip had cost twenty rubles first-class, equivalent to around eight pounds sterling. At that moment I vowed to return to Belarus simply to take advantage of these wonderfully cheap rail fares.

Outside we visited a small chapel built in the castle grounds, then walked along the lakeside under darkening skies back to the bus. I noticed for the first time a couple of middle-aged female fellow-passengers, one of whom had removed her coat to reveal a large tattoo on her bulky upper arm exactly like the ship's anchor that Popeye the Sailor Man sports in the cartoon series. From that moment I would think of her as Popeye and her friend as Olive Oyl.

The journey to Nesvizh, handily located about twenty miles from Mir on the other side of the E30 motorway, passed without incident. A community of some 14,000 souls, and, like Mir, at one time owned by the Radziwill family, it claims to date from the thirteenth century, but recent research suggests it was established in 1447. As with Mir, Nesvizh has a turbulent history, having been occupied at one time or another by Poland, Germany, Russia, France, and Lithuania. Our visit centred on the castle, a World Heritage site, located on the eastern fringes of the city by a small lake. Before visiting the castle we were invited to view Corpus Christi, believed to be one of Europe's earliest Jesuit churches and a reminder that the Russian Orthodox Church has no monopoly regarding religious worship in Belarus, where 25% of the population are Catholic. The building, a traditional white-rendered stone edifice with a dome, was commissioned by Prince Nicholas Radziwill in the sixteenth century and is currently under restoration, requiring us to walk across duckboards between scaffolding poles to reach the main door. As with most Roman Catholic churches, the interior is decorated with extravagant but largely uninspiring murals on almost every surface, but for me the most interesting items were the very unusual stained glass windows consisting of simple rectangular coloured squares that bizarrely echoed the neoplasticism style of the twentieth-century artist Piet Mondrian. The church contains the mortal remains of 72 members of the Radziwill family, which, fortunately, we didn't get to see. Other than this, there was little of note, and we exited to make the short walk to the castle entrance, passing a parade of souvenir stalls outside the main gate. The road leads over a moat that is fed from the adjoining lake, and the low black cast-iron fence on either side was festooned with locked padlocks, many heart-shaped and some painted pink, presumably left by couples keen to demonstrate their undying love for each other. I'd first come across this practice about ten years previously on the railings by the road leading to the Roman bridge in Cordoba, Spain. If only we could discover how many of these relationships have endured!

The castle is much larger than that at Mir, and the internal courtyard is similarly paved with uneven stones that make walking a somewhat unpredictable business. Again, like Mir, it is more a stately home than a castle, but having said that it is surrounded by a brick castle-style wall. The building stands within landscaped parkland and is essentially a group of pantiled five-storey buildings gathered around the courtyard, with a couple of high domed towers that guard the front and rear entrances. The stonework is rendered in ochre plaster, and is reminiscent of the buildings in Siena, Italy. Inside the courtyard the castle looks like a rather grand city-centre square, and nowadays it sees use as an open-air concert venue from time to time. Our guide, Ivan, a retired government translator with excellent English, invited us into the reception area and asked us to don the obligatory blue plastic overshoes for our visit. His knowledge of the history of the place was astonishing, providing never-ending stories of the triumphs and disasters of what seemed like the entire Radziwill family. One story amongst many was the tale of Catherine Radziwill, who flew to South Africa in the 1890s to stalk Cecil Rhodes, the British colony's Prime Minister and founder of Rhodesia. Her attempts at developing a sexual relationship with him sadly failed, on account of the fact that he was gay.

The tour turned out to be much like the Mir tour, and by the time we exited the castle the rain had arrived, sporadic at first but heavier as we reached the bus pick-up point. On board the bus, I took a seat behind Popeye and Olive Oyl and settled down for the return journey. As we headed along country lanes towards the motorway I was surprised to see visibility fall outside, as if we were driving through fog. Suddenly we encountered a rainstorm so severe that water began seeping in through the roof of the bus. In many years of travelling I have never seen a rainstorm like it, and I have the greatest admiration for our driver who managed to navigate his way through it with no bad consequences. Eventually we left the storm behind, and by seven o'clock were back at the old town in Minsk. It was time for a Krynica beer, taken in an almost empty Chinese restaurant opposite the Cathedral of the Holy Spirit. Thus refreshed, I walked the kilometre or so back to the hotel in showery rain and a biting northerly wind.

The next morning I checked out of the hotel at 9am and soon afterwards my taxi to the airport arrived. My final slightly anxious moments at the airport passed uneventfully as I checked in and passed through security – in total my passport was thoroughly examined four times – and once at the gate I treated myself to a Burger King cheese-burger and coffee – cheap at five rubles, around £2.00. The snack served as an *entree* for the meal later on the plane.

A final problem arose at Gatwick airport, making me for a while doubt my own mental capacity. The captain's announcements on the plane had been largely in Belarusian, with only the occasional brief attempt at hurried English. As a result I couldn't say whether or not he'd advised passengers to set their watches back, but in any case I failed to do it. When I arrived at Gatwick railway station my watch told me that the time was after 4:30pm, the start of the peak period for fares. Needing to top up my Oyster card with cash to allow for this, I went over to the information desk and asked the man to point out the Oyster card top-up machines, which he duly did. I mentioned that I needed to top up as I didn't have sufficient credit for the peak period. He looked at me quizzically and remarked that the peak period didn't start for quite a while. Puzzled, I topped up my card at the machine and went over to the train indicator to see when the next train to Clapham Junction was to depart. I was shocked to see it timed at 14:54. I immediately assumed that the indicator was faulty, and I was about to return to the information desk when I suddenly realised that it was in fact just after 2:30pm rather than 4:30pm, well before peak fare time. Somewhat chastened, I went down onto the platform and caught the 2:54pm to Clapham Junction.

There is so much to say about my Belarus odyssey. It has pride of place in being chronologically the last of the 49 countries that I needed to visit to complete the set. For perhaps ten years I had monitored the travel pages of the press and internet to see if the President, Mr Lukashenko, was considering relaxing his country's onerous travel restrictions, and I must admit I still remained somewhat sceptical right up to the moment when I landed at Minsk airport. The country had, however, been a revelation. I'd imagined a European version of North Korea, expecting to find a strong police presence on the streets, a cowed population, and a personality cult that manifested itself in pictures and statues of the president dominating public buildings and squares. Instead I found a clean, modern, outward-looking capital city, Minsk, with broad tree-lined boulevards and attractive parks, boasting the finest concentration of spectacular post-war architecture to be found anywhere in Europe. Elsewhere on the continent there are, of course, pockets of such architecture. Eur, the area near Rome created in the 1930s under dictator Benito Mussolini, is similar, but covers a tiny area compared with Minsk, and of course Moscow has its share of grandiose soviet-era buildings but these are scattered widely across that huge city. The city of Minsk is living proof that there were positive aspects of the post-war Communist era, outweighed as they were by that system's many calamitous failings. In the surrounding countryside a largely agricultural economy seems to have liberated itself from the yoke of communist collectivisation, but has not yet attained the levels of food productivity current in the West. Politically, the people, and in particular the president, seem to be Ideologically torn between continuing the hitherto close relationship with their post-war masters in Moscow, or developing a new relationship with the unashamedly capitalist European Union. The easing of visa requirements, for which I am eternally grateful, is to me a sign that the country is at least willing to put aside some of its communist ideals in order develop the tourist industry, a potentially lucrative source of business and foreign exchange. My message to Mr Lukashenko is that he leads a fascinating country that is ripe for tourist development, and I simply hope he will continue to make it easier for visitors to come and enjoy it.

Chapter 24

Turkey

The military consider themselves the real owners of this country [Turkey] because they are ready to give their lives to save us. But I would like to be governed, not saved. I want to be saved from the people who want to save me

Mehmet Dülger

Turkey is a European country, an Asian country, a Middle Eastern country, a Balkan country, a Caucasian country, a neighbour to Africa, a Black Sea country, a Caspian Sea country, all of these

Ahmet Davutoglu

Dancing bear. 100 kilos of gold, and the 4th-largest diamond in the world. United Nations blue berets. Travel via Beirut. Train 23 hours late. Currency exchange problem. Airline strike. No coffee in the country. Coup 6 months later. Public transport incomprehensible.

Turkey, officially The Republic of Turkey, may truly be described as an enigma, due in large part to its many profound constitutional and geographical contradictions. A fervently secular state in obedience to its twentieth-century founder Mustafa Kemal Ataturk, it perversely has a tenacious Moslem culture. It is a strong parliamentary democracy, but three military coups and two military interventions since 1960 have seen parliamentary rule overturned for periods of time. Educationally and philosophically a nation aligned with the mores of Western Europe, it pays more than lip service to its Middle-Eastern neighbours in these matters. Economically and spiritually sophisticated in Ankara, its capital, and Istanbul, its largest city, the country includes vast swathes of sparsely inhabited land that have for centuries been worked by peasants, and continue to be so. Geographically Turkey lies astride both Europe and Asia, although for me it will always be a European country. A dispute with Greece over which of them should legitimately rule the Island of Cyprus has been raging since 1950 and seems no more likely to be resolved today than it was almost seventy years ago. Occasional attempts by Turkey to be considered for membership of the European Union have foundered at the first hurdle as Greece is a European Union member and claims sovereignty over that island. Turkey's somewhat chequered recent democratic history and alleged human rights violations have not, of course, helped its cause. Despite these contradictions, the country remains a fascinating melting-pot of faiths and cultures, with a resilient and motivated populace. It remains one of the most fascinating parts of Europe, and for me is only bettered as a travel destination by Italy and France. My first visit took place as long ago as 1980, when I was returning home after a couple of months working in Sanaa, capital of Yemen, then known as North Yemen.

My route home from Sanaa took me first to Nicosia, capital of Cyprus, where I was to finish my report over a period of a week or so. As is still the case, the island was divided at the time, with the southern side under Greek control and Turkey ruling the North. The two sectors were separated by a United Nations – controlled no man's land running East-West across the entire island and which caused Nicosia to be divided into three zones, Turkish, United Nations, and Greek. I was staying in the Greek zone, but was intrigued to find out if it might be possible to cross over to the Turkish side. There was certainly no official route through for civilians, but after studying the map I and a colleague located a military crossing and decided to give it a try. Late one afternoon we drove over to Markos Drakos Avenue in the West of the city, one of the closed roads which crossed no man's land, thereby linking the Greek and Turkish sectors. We pulled up at the guard-house on the Greek side and I wound the window down to ask the Greek guard if we could proceed. A brief shrug of the shoulders suggested we could try, and the barrier was raised, allowing us through into battle-scarred no-man's land.

Almost immediately we came upon the Ledra Palace Hotel, a pleasant stone building of five stories with balconied windows and high Moorish arches guarding its entrance. Built in 1949, The Ledra Palace was at one time Nicosia's most prestigious hotel, boasting 200 bedrooms and regularly playing host to visiting heads of government. The years of fighting between the Greeks and Turks from 1963 to 1974 had, however, taken their toll, as the hotel had been considered a strategically important target by both sides and had frequently come under fire. Following the signing of the truce in 1974 it found itself marooned in no man's land and was eventually acquired to accommodate the men of the Sector 2 United Nations Roulement Regiment, who have continued to occupy it ever since. Aa we drove past it there were just a few UN soldiers hanging around, and the building itself looked extremely down-at-heel, the stonework being severely pock-marked as a result of eleven years of artillery bombardment. We drove on unchecked and soon arrived at the Turkish guard-house on the North side of no man's land. I wound the window down and asked the bearded guard if we could go through. "No." He replied, simply, a gold tooth glinting as he spoke. We executed a three-point turn and retraced our route along the potholed road back to the Greek guard-house.

"No luck?" said the guard, raising the barrier.

"No."

"Did you offer money?" he asked, smiling.

"No." I replied, wondering if he was joking.

"Sometimes it works." He assured me. "Bring dollars next time." He added, and saluted.

And so ended my first attempt to enter the Turkish Republic of Northern Cyprus. Thirty-three years later, in 2013, I finally made it by walking through from the Greek to the Turkish side via a newly-opened pedestrian checkpoint grudgingly set up along Ledra Street in the city centre by the two protagonists. I describe this in another chapter of this book.

After finishing my work in Nicosia I decided to make my way home to England via Istanbul in Turkey, where I wanted to spend a few days of my annual holiday. The flying distance between Nicosia and Istanbul is about 750 kilometres, no more than a couple of hours by plane, and it seemed logical to fly there from Larnaca, the international airport on the Greek side of Cyprus, south of Nicosia. However I reckoned without the stand-off between the two countries which meant there were no flights from Larnaca to Turkey, just as there were no flights from Greece to Ercan, the airport on the Turkish side of the island. It was clear that I would have to travel via a third country, and a glance at the map suggested Beirut, the capital of Lebanon, as a possible candidate, a mere 250 kilometres away. I managed to book a three-legged itinerary that would take me to Beirut, and from there to Ankara, Turkey's capital, using Middle-Eastern Airlines, and finally from Ankara to Istanbul by Turkish Airlines. It occurred to me that this detour almost doubled the distance to be flown, but it seemed there was no alternative.

The following morning I presented myself at Larnaca International airport for the morning flight to Beirut. Larnaca had for many years been a British military installation, but in 1974 found itself pressed into service as a civilian airport when the Turkish invasion meant that Nicosia airport, up to then the major airport in the country, was forced to close. Today, Nicosia airport's decaying buildings still stand derelict within United-Nations-controlled no-man's land, its departure hall occupied only by pigeons, and its hoardings outside carrying faded posters advertising flights by BEA and BOAC, two airline names that coincidentally disappeared in 1974 when British Airways was created. Larnaca was to become the Island's major airport on the Greek side, and today it handles more than six million passengers annually.

The flight to Beirut was uneventful until the pilot banked the plane in preparation for his final approach. It was then that I saw for the first time the devastation that five years of civil war had brought to a once-beautiful coastal city, in its heyday known as the Paris of the Middle-East. Down below I could see whole areas in ruins, and as the landing gear clunked into place we flew by the Holiday Inn hotel, thirty stories high and, though still standing, damaged almost beyond repair by years of artillery fire. As the highest building in the city, and thus strategically vital, It had been the site of some of the fiercest fighting as the various factions fought for control. It is said that much of the Holiday Inn crockery and cutlery, not to mention fixtures and furniture, may be found in present-day homes in Beirut. The civil war was to continue for a further ten years, by which time much of this great city would be all-but destroyed, but even today the Holiday Inn still towers proudly over the city centre, the subject of a continuing debate between its joint-owners as to whether to renovate or demolish it.

Fortunately there was no military action on the day I arrived, and indeed the airport appeared to be operating as near to normal as is possible in a war zone. It had recently undergone renovation following damage from shelling in 1977 and was in reasonable condition considering the state of much of the rest of the city. As I walked across the tarmac I was understandably nervous, however, being conscious of the fact that hostilities could recommence at any moment. Once inside the terminal I headed for the transit lounge and bought myself a Turkish coffee, a drink that has been a favourite of mine whenever I've found myself in the Middle East. It's made by adding coffee grounds, sugar, and water to a small metal pot with a long handle and heating the mixture until it begins to boil, then allowing it to simmer for a short while. From my table in the cafe I watched my fellow passengers come and go, amongst whom were a number of unarmed blue-beret United Nations personnel, not, by the look of it on duty but, presumably like myself, in transit. They may have been involved in a recent UN deployment near the country's southern border, responding to an Israeli invasion. My flight to Ankara was eventually called, and I boarded the plane, somewhat relieved to be leaving, but regretting that I'd had no time to visit the city and see how its citizens were managing to live amid the chaos. As we flew by the Holiday Inn I remembered my encounter with the Ledra Palace hotel in Nicosia only two days previously. Both buildings, heavily battle-scarred as a result of recent fierce fighting, bore witness to the value of United Nations military intervention in such circumstances. Since then I have visited Kosovo, in the Balkans, where a substantial United Nations presence continues to keep the peace after fifteen months of warfare in the late 1990s. *Plus ca change, plus c'est la meme chose....*

As we headed North over the Mediterranean I settled back in my seat, secure in the knowledge that at least there was no civil war in Turkey, and looked forward to my final flight of the day, from Ankara to Istanbul. At Ankara airport I headed for the government-run *bureau de change* to buy Turkish Lire using US dollars, there being no privately-run bureaux de change. At the time the country was in severe economic difficulties, and had found it necessary to introduce stringent foreign exchange controls designed to prevent citizens from buying strong foreign currencies such as US Dollars or Pounds Sterling. Anxious not to buy too much of a currency that in consequence would have little value elsewhere in the world, I communicated my worries to the government official who blithely told me that it was not a problem. All I needed to do, he said, was to retain the documentation he would supply with the currency, and present this at the airport *bureau de change* on leaving the country, and any lire I had left over would be converted back to dollars. Reassured, I changed perhaps a hundred more dollars than I thought strictly necessary, in case of emergencies, and carefully stowed away the form he and his colleague had signed. I then headed for the Turkish Airlines domestic departure area for my flight to Istanbul.

The area was strangely quiet, with just a few people scattered around amidst a sea of empty seats, and none of the check-in desks was occupied. Worried, I eventually found an English-speaking official who informed me that Turkish Airlines were on strike and all flights, including mine, were cancelled. This was not good news given that it was late-afternoon and I was still 450 kilometres from my destination, Istanbul. I resigned myself to seeking a hotel in Ankara for the night, and trying again at the airport the following day, but my informant said there was no indication the strike would be over by then. In any case, I was aware that Ankara, although an interesting capital city, was a pale substitute for Istanbul when it came to tourist attractions. I decided to investigate taking the train, and, for once ignoring my self-imposed rule to always travel by service bus, I flagged down a taxi and was driven to Ankara railway station.

Ankara station is a handsome art deco building built in 1937 from brown stone and grandly fronted by a colonnade supported by six high columns. Inside I found it served a mere six platforms, two of which were for local trains, surely making it one of the smallest capital-city railway stations in the world. I checked the timetable and noted there was an overnight non-sleeping car train to Istanbul, exotically named the Anatolia Express, leaving at 10pm, and decided to take it. Over at the ticket office the ticket clerk made it clear he had no English, so I tried French, which produced a similar response, but my third attempt, using my very basic German, was successful. At the time much of the German automotive industry was staffed by expatriate Turkish workers, and I presumed that for many Turks, German was the preferred second language. As I handed over the cash for the ticket I thought that perhaps the extra Turkish Lire I had been persuaded to buy earlier may have been a wise move after all.

I bought a kebab at a nearby stall, together with some provisions for the journey, and found a seat in the crowded waiting room on platform 1, its smeared windows providing an uninterrupted if murky view over the platforms. My fellow-travellers, about a hundred in number, mainly single men and family groups, many of whom were clad in loose-fitting Middle-Eastern-style dress, sat quietly chatting amongst themselves as the yellow light of the evening sun, already diminished by the grime-covered windows, was further attenuated by the cigarette-smoke haze inside. As I sat reading, the door swung open and two soldiers carrying automatic weapons entered, causing immediate cessation of all conversation as they marched in step between the ranks of seated passengers. Evidently satisfied with their inspection, they left as quickly as they'd arrived, but reappeared twice more in the next hour or so. On the third visit they stopped to interrogate a middle-aged man who, ashen-faced, was requested to accompany them as they left. He didn't return. This brief vignette of Turkish life in 1980 was one of those otherwise unremarkable events that have for no logical reason remained ingrained in my memory ever since.

Later, as I glanced out of the window, I spotted a train arriving at the platform on the far side. It was only 8:45 pm and my train wasn't due to leave until 10pm, but I was slightly anxious that it could be the Anatolia Express. If so, there was surely no harm in climbing aboard even though it wasn't due to leave for an hour or so. I gathered up my luggage, crossed over to the platform, asked someone at the train's open window if it was bound for Istanbul and received a nod in response. I spotted a vacant seat in the open carriage, and on my way to claiming it squeezed past a couple of itinerant food and drink sellers who left the train almost immediately afterwards. No sooner had I I settled into the seat than the train lurched forward and began to pick up speed. In a mild panic I said "Istanbul?" to the lady opposite and she nodded. I discussed this experience with a barman in Istanbul a couple of days later who said the train might simply have for some reason left one hour early, but he suggested that the more likely explanation was that it was the previous day's train running twenty-three hours late.

The journey took about nine hours to complete, during which I slept fitfully, but I was eventually awoken at around 6am by the screeching of brakes as the train pulled into Haydarpasa station in Istanbul, which I believe has the distinction of being Asia's westernmost railway terminus. I had finally arrived at my destination, more than twenty hours after leaving Nicosia. Had there been no dispute between Greece and Turkey over the island of Cyprus, my journey time would have been about ninety minutes.

Istanbul – named from an originally Greek phrase meaning "in the city" - is undoubtedly one of the world's great cities, partly because it is strategically important geographically, being situated on either side of the narrow Bosphorus strait that allows marine access to the Mediterranean for those countries to the North that have major merchant and naval ports on the Black Sea. The most important of these is, of course, Russia. The city's population currently stands at slightly over fourteen million souls, the eighth largest in the world. That part of Istanbul on the West side of the Bosphorus is deemed to lie in Europe, whilst that on the East side is considered to be in Asia. Originally founded by the Greeks as Byzantium in 660BC, the city became the eastern capital of the Roman Empire in 330AD and was renamed Constantinople in honour of Emperor Constantine. In the fifteenth century Constantinople was conquered by the Ottomans and became the capital city of the Ottoman Empire, which at its height controlled much of south-eastern and central Europe, together with northern Africa and parts of the Middle-East, resulting in the city becoming an Islamic stronghold. By the outbreak of World War I the Ottoman Empire was in decline, resulting in Turkey being occupied by British, French, and Italian forces, and after the war, in 1923, a Republican movement, led by Mustafa Kemal Ataturk, the country's founding father, succeeded in creating the Republic of Turkey, a secular state. Although the capital was unofficially known as Istanbul as far back as the eighteenth century, it only became the official name in 1928 when Turkey adopted the Latin alphabet. The country took little part in World War II, other than allying itself with the Allies in the final few months, and in the post-war period suffered from successive military coups in 1960, 1971, and, six months after my visit, in 1980. Political instability resurfaced following a further attempted coup in 2016, which was defeated.

Haydarpasha station in Istanbul is an imposing six-storey sandstone building, originally constructed in 1909 as the Western terminus of the Baghdad and Hejaz railway, a line that ran for 2,500 kilometres. It also became the terminus of the Trans-Asia Express, which used a line 3,000 kilometres long linking Istanbul with Tehran in Iran, in a rail journey that lasted eight days. Situated at the water's edge on the eastern side of the Bosphorus Strait, the station presents newly-arrived passengers with a breathtaking view over the water towards the distant palaces, mosques, and minarets on the far side. The panorama is arguably the most spectacular vista from the steps of a railway station entrance anywhere in the world, with the possible exception of that from Santa Lucia station by the Grand Canal in Venice. In the years up to 1973, it was from this quayside that passengers wishing to continue their journey westward through Europe were obliged to take a ten-minute ferry-boat journey over to the western bank of the Bosphorus, a journey occasionally delayed mid-stream to give right of way to merchant ships, and, sometimes, Russian warships, on their way to or from the Black Sea. On the far side passengers would make their way to the city's Sirkeci station to continue their journey by train. All this changed in 1973 on completion of the first Bosphorus Bridge, a road suspension bridge 1,560 metres in length and not unlike the much longer Humber Bridge in England. As a consequence the ferry services from the quayside at Haydarpasha were severely curtailed as passengers opted to cross the bridge by taxi or bus.

In the slight chill of early morning, and somewhat bleary-eyed, I considered the available options and for once chose the most expensive, a taxi, to get me to my hotel. The ensuing journey of about eight kilometres provided spectacular views over the glittering waters of the Bosphorus and the skyline beyond. The hotel, an unremarkable twenty-storey concrete tower-block, seemed somehow incongruous amidst the surrounding minarets and pantiled roofs. At reception I was somewhat disappointed to be informed that I'd have to wait until 11am to get access to my room, so I headed over to the bar, as by now I was in dire need of caffeine in the form of a strong Turkish coffee. I'd promised myself many times over the years that when I finally made it to Turkey I would be able taste Turkish coffee in its country of origin, in the way one might, for example, wish to sample an espresso coffee during a visit to Milan. Sadly, I was to be disappointed. The barman explained that the country was experiencing severe economic difficulties and as a consequence had been unable to import coffee beans. He therefore regretted that he could only offer instant coffee to guests. Deeply disappointed, but in need of caffeine from whatever source, I ordered a large Nescafe and took a seat at a table. There I spent much of the following three hours or so making plans using my guide-book to the city. As I write this I am reminded that my visit to Istanbul was at a time before the internet was invented, and mobile telephone networks were still in their infancy. Nowadays it is all too evident that travellers seem to depend heavily on electronic media for their travel information requirements, but I am gratified to have noted during my recent travels that guidebooks continue to be used by many.

At 11am I presented myself at reception and was given a Yale-style metal key, a somewhat cumbersome item when compared with today's plastic cards, and took the lift to the twelfth-floor. The view from my room over the rooftops of Istanbul was stunning, and irresistibly beckoned me to explore. According to my map the best place to start was Taksim Square, located only a couple of hundred metres south of the hotel, and Istanbul's equivalent of London's Trafalgar Square, but without the fountains and plethora of statuary. To get there required a walk through Taksim Gezi Park, a small but welcome area of greenery in a city not renowned for its municipal parks. On the far side of the park I could see that a large crowd had gathered around the square and there appeared to be some sort of ceremony taking place. A glimpse of uniforms confirmed that it was a military occasion, with lines of armed soldiers standing stiffly to attention as they were inspected by an officer. Little did I realise that in less than six months' time this very same square would play host to tanks as a military coup took control of the country, costing hundreds of lives.

A word may be appropriate at this point regarding public transport in Istanbul at the time of my visit. In the post-war period the city boasted substantial tram and trolleybus systems, but these were scrapped in the mid to late 1960s, as they were in many UK cities, because they were deemed to cause traffic jams in the narrow streets. There was no underground system, so on my arrival in 1980 there were only three land-based methods of getting about the city. Taxis were numerous, but expensive. Buses were cheaper, but route information was not easily available. And then there were the Dolmus, an inexpensive taxi –style system which is still in use today. Dolmus drivers wait for customers at a particular pick-up spot and don't set off until they have a full complement of passengers heading to the same approximate destination. Nowadays the vehicle is likely to be a minibus, but in 1980 many were battered old gas-guzzling American cars from the nineteen fifties and sixties, bearing such iconic names as Chevrolet, Dodge, and Plymouth. It was marvellous to see these old warhorses, many built just after the Second World War, plying their trade, often carrying seven or eight passengers in what must have been extreme discomfort. It is to my eternal regret that I didn't use one on this particular visit, simply because the identification of destinations and routes seemed to require knowledge of the city which I didn't possess. As a result, the bus was my favoured form of transport, but written information on routes and times was hard to come by, so I spent much of my time simply noting details of useful bus routes in the hope of using them at some stage during my stay. As it transpired, I did a lot of walking, which after all is good for the heart and soul. As a postscript to the Dolmus story, I believe some of the vintage cars still operate in the city, but are now only available for private hire by tourists.

From Taksim Square i headed south and downhill towards the Bosphorus, first on a busy main road lined with cafes, convenience stores and kebab restaurants, then later through a warren of narrow residential back-streets. Navigation was necessarily largely by the sun, it being mid-morning by now and the sky cloudless, but I also knew that as long as I was descending I must be nearing the sea. As luck would have it I emerged into the open area just north of the Galata bridge, a flimsy-looking floating metal structure, less than 500 metres long, linking the northern and southern banks of the Golden Horn, a major inlet of the Bosphorus. The quayside at the bridge's northern end proved to be the terminus for numerous cross-Bosphorus ferry boats of all shapes and sizes, each steadily filling up with passengers as I watched. On the quayside were one or two stand-up cafes, and around them itinerant traders sold snacks from baskets. Most interesting of all were the fish stalls, where fish purchased by the owners from some of the dozens of anglers fishing from the bridge and quayside were fried and sold to the waiting passengers. I drank a Nescafe at one of the stand-up stalls, but forewent the opportunity to sample the fried fish, as I'd been advised against it by the receptionist at the hotel on the grounds that the waters around the bridge were heavily polluted. I will forever remember the sights, sounds, and smells of this busy community at Galata Bridge, which sadly was largely swept away with the building of a new bridge in 1994, an uninspiring concrete-and-steel structure that now carries both cars and trams across the Golden Horn. A few anglers are still to be seen on the bridge, fishing for their supper, but the life and soul of the area has been largely lost.

From there I walked the kilometre or so northwards along the shore of the busy Bosphorus to the Dolmabahce Palace. Opened in 1856, this rather elaborate grey stone building, an eclectic, some might say overwhelming, mixture of neoclassical, baroque, and rococo styles was commissioned by Sultan Abdulmecid I as his preferred home following his decision to move from the Topkapi Palace, previously the home of the Ottoman rulers for centuries. Covering 4.5 hectares, and with 285 rooms, the palace has an attractive frontage more than 200 metres long facing the Bosphorus, but its principal claim to fame is that its construction was one of the reasons for the ultimate downfall of the Ottoman Empire. Building costs totalled five million gold lira, equivalent to 35 tonnes of gold, resulting in the empire defaulting on its public debt in 1875 and eventually succumbing to financial control by other European powers. As a result the empire became known as "The sick man of Europe" and Turkey eventually became a republic. I strolled around the beautifully laid-out gardens in the afternoon sun, but at the time the building was not open to the public so I was unable to investigate the interior. I compromised by finding a seat near the quay leading to the Bosphorus, the seaborne entrance for the Sultan and guests, from which I could enjoy watching the always-fascinating parade of shipping. Over on the Asian side I could make out the outline of Hydarpasa railway station, where I had arrived in the city some twelve hours previously.

From there I walked back to the hotel, conscious that the previous night's less than ideal sleep pattern was beginning to catch up with me. The route took me by Besiktas Stadium, the home of the football club of that name, and onwards along Kadirgalar Street, on the North side of which was a pleasant wooded area. About half way along the street I was startled to see a shabbily-dressed man heading towards me carrying a tambour-style drum and stick, and holding a leather leash which was attached to the muzzle of a huge brown bear obediently ambling along on all fours beside him. As he drew alongside me he stopped, instructed the animal to rise onto its hind legs, and began beating the drum, at which point the creature, now standing taller than its owner, "danced". The stick was used to "persuade" the animal to contort itself in various ways, and as the show went on a number of onlookers gathered round, probably as astonished as I was by the spectacle. After a couple of minutes the show ended, at which point we all scurried away, ignoring the man's plea for money. After this impromptu piece of street theatre I took a short uphill walk through what was almost scrubland back to the hotel. Reluctant to pay the cost of dinner in the hotel's restaurant, I found a nearby cafe where I dined on Doner Kebab with chilli sauce and salad, washed down by a couple of glasses of Efes beer, a meal fit for a King, or even a Sultan.

The following morning I obtained information on bus routes from the hotel reception and returned by bus to Galata Bridge, from where I walked the half-kilometre or so to Sirkeci station, Istanbul's European-side railway terminus. I was initially disappointed to find a modest group of buildings fronting no more than six platforms, all of which were in the open-air. Sirkeci was the original terminus of the Orient Express international train that began running from Paris to Constantinople, in 1889. Prior to this, as far back as 1883, various trains had carried the Orient Express name but had required passengers to change at one or more intermediate station. The route and termini of the train changed many times over the ensuing years, with Istanbul ceasing to be the eastern terminus in 1977, three years before my visit. The train's heyday was undoubtedly the 1930s, when it offered luxurious sleeping-car and dining facilities that have featured in more than a dozen romantic films over the years. In a somewhat depressing finale, the last train known as the Orient-Express (with a hyphen) ran on December 10th 2009, between Strasbourg and Vienna. The main station building, described as being in the European-Orientalist style, has some architectural merit, but nowadays it is difficult to imagine it ever having played host to the rich and famous.

This brief visit to Sirkeci was a prelude to the day's main objective, a visit to the nearby Topkapi Palace, located high on a promontory overlooking the Bosphorus and Golden Horn. It required a somewhat circuitous climb through pleasant parkland in warm sunshine to get to the entrance on the South -West side. Construction of The palace began in 1459, and it was to become the home of the Ottoman emperors and the administrative centre of the Empire for almost four hundred years. It remained the seat of power until the Dolmabahce palace was built for Sultan Abdulmejid in 1856, but thereafter retained some administrative functions until, in 1924, following the fall of the empire, it was converted into a museum. The name "Topkapi" refers to one of the entry gates, translated as "Cannon's Gate". The building consists of four linked courtyards, each performing a different function, and is more than half a kilometre long and three hundred metres wide, requiring a full day's visit if it is to be explored thoroughly. I had less time available and wanted to concentrate on the main attractions, so headed over first to the harem, located between the first and second courtyards.

At its entrance is the Harem Treasury, where financial and legal records were maintained, managed by the Chief Harem eunuch. All males working in the Harem were required to be castrated, but history does not record if they had particularly high-pitched voices as a result. The harem housed a large number of concubines, many of them slave-women captured during military campaigns, together with the sultan's wives, usually much fewer in number. In total there are more than 100 rooms, the area also providing living quarters for other personnel essential to the smooth running of the palace. The harem was administered by the Sultan's mother, herself previously the wife or concubine of the Sultan's father. The eunuchs' quarters were adjacent to, but separated from, those of the concubines and wives, and the extensive apartments of the Queen Mother were situated nearby. The Sultan himself lived in the fourth courtyard, where many administrative rooms of state are to be found. Of these, I was particularly taken by the circumcision room, a space decorated with Islamic-style ceramic tiles wherein royal princes received the "snip" in accordance with tradition during a short ceremony. In a later visit to Turkey I witnessed a communal circumcision ceremony in the open air, where the young victims, dressed in military band-style uniforms, were seated on the perimeter of a revolving contraption, much like a fairground roundabout, bringing each boy in turn in front of the circumciser who did what was required then moved on to the next. The Topkapi circumcision room was by contrast a much more intimate location, occupying an area about five metres square with a low upholstered bench along the wall beneath the windows.

I was by now in need of light relief from all things biological so headed for the Conqueror's Pavilion, also known as Fatih Kosku, an area on the south side of the third courtyard raised on a terrace above the surrounding gardens, beneath which is a colonnaded walkway. Here are exhibited some of the priceless artefacts acquired by the Ottoman dynasty over a period of almost five hundred years.

There are four rooms, the first of which did not detain me for long, being largely given over to Islamic items, but in room two I came across a largish crowd admiring the Topkapi Dagger, a priceless gold-handled curved weapon 35 centimetres long in a gold scabbard, decorated with diamonds. The handle bears three huge Colombian emeralds, each perfect and measuring some three centimetres by two. The dagger's popularity is undoubtedly due in part to the fact that the 1964 film "Topkapi" dealt with a fictional attempt to steal it, but it is also simply a stunning example of Ottoman art. From there I moved on to the third room where I found another large group of visitors, this time surrounding an illuminated glass case built into the wall. It displays the Spoonmaker's Diamond, believed to be the fourth-largest diamond of its kind in the world at 86 carats. Set in silver and surrounded by 49 smaller diamonds. the stone's provenance is shrouded in mystery, in common with many of the world's exceptionally large diamonds. Its name originates from a probably apocryphal story that it was bought in 1669 by a jeweller who specialised in making decorative spoons. He assured the seller that it was glass, and handed over three spoons as payment. In nearby free-standing cases were two candlesticks, each a metre long, studded with diamonds, and each made from 48 kilograms of solid gold. Never before, or since, have I gazed on almost 100 kilograms of gold at one time. Finally, in this room, as if to emphasise the surreal nature of much of this amazing building, I came across a reliquary purporting to contain bones from the right forearm and hand of John the Baptist. Its importance as a relic is deemed to be all the greater because John was believed to have baptised Jesus with this, his right hand. However, similar reliquaries exist in Serbia, Montenegro, and Romania, leading to the inescapable conclusion that John the Baptist had four right arms.

I had been recommended to visit the area of authentic Ottoman town-houses dating from the eighteenth and nineteenth - century which is located around Cancurtaran Street, about 300 metres south of the palace. The street runs alongside the railway which, in its heyday, brought passengers from Paris to Sirkeci station on the Orient Express, but, sadly, is now principally a commuter line. A run-down area of the city, it was however showing signs of being renovated when I visited, as it contains a high concentrations of original four –storey wooden houses, many unpainted and looking decidedly down-at heel in their blackened-grey wood-plank cladding. Most were jettied, a process whereby the upper floors overhang the street, similar to the design of half-timbered Tudor houses still to be found in areas of England. Many of them appeared structurally unsound, particularly around the upper floors, but the area provided a glimpse of how a working-class area of the city would have looked in the heyday of the Ottoman Empire. I believe that in recent years there has been a concerted effort to preserve and renovate as many of these homes as possible.

About a couple of hundred metres inland I came across the Blue Mosque, one of Istanbul's iconic buildings, its domes and minarets being visible from most parts of the city. In general I find mosque interiors particularly uninteresting as they can never be repositories of fine art, given that any artistic representation of the human form is forbidden in the Moslem faith. For those who are aficionados of patterned ceramic tiles and calligraphic representations of verses from the Quran, mosque interiors are undoubtedly fascinating, but I do not count myself among them. Architecturally, however, I find Mosques more interesting, and the Blue Mosque, so-called because its interior is lined with predominantly blue tiles, is certainly an architectural masterpiece. Created in the early part of the seventeenth century, it consists of a fifty metre-square mosque adjacent to a similar-sized courtyard. The building itself supports thirteen domes or half-domes, and the colonnade around the perimeter of the courtyard boasts a further thirty smaller domes. As I made my way to the entrance I was waylaid by a young lad, no more than twelve years old, in T-shirt and jeans, who was selling shelled pistachio nuts, one of my favourite snacks, at a small stall. I bargained with him briefly before agreeing to what he determinedly assured me was his best price. He carefully weighed out the nuts and presented them to me in a paper cone fabricated from a torn-out page of the Istanbul telephone directory. I have to say I approved both his entrepreneurship and commitment to recycling.

Along the wall leading to the entrance to the mosque a number of worshippers were washing hands and face using the open-air taps provided. I forewent this opportunity for ablutions, and after removing my shoes, illogically anxious that I was seeing them for the last time, I crossed the threshold and stepped onto the red carpet that covered the entirety of the floor inside. A few worshippers were already arriving, even though the mid-afternoon call to prayer had not yet sounded. As I'd expected, the interior was an imposing huge multi-domed space, but otherwise there was little to catch the eye. The thousands of predominantly blue handmade ceramic tiles that cover most of the interior walls were certainly attractive, but the displays of calligraphy did not excite my interest. I exited, somewhat coincidentally as the muezzin began the call to prayer, regained my shoes, and walked over to the adjacent gardens to view the building's domes and six elegant fluted minarets. History relates that the six minarets caused uproar when they were built, because the only other mosque in the world with six minarets at that time was the Ka'aba Mosque in Mecca, Islam's holiest place. The problem was swiftly resolved when Sultan Ahmed paid for a seventh minaret to be added to the Ka'aba Mosque, thus restoring its superiority. I came away from the Blue Mosque suitably impressed by it as a handsome building, but underwhelmed by the interior.

The Islamic problem with images inside mosques is never more evident than inside the Hagia Sophia museum, which I visited briefly, situated as it is only about 100 metres or so from the Blue Mosque. Architecturally similar to a mosque, it was constructed in 537AD as a Christian Eastern Orthodox Cathedral, and as such was decorated with mosaic images of Christ and other bible characters. When the Ottomans overran the city in 1453 the Cathedral was converted to a mosque and the Christian imagery was concealed under layers of plaster. In 1928 the building became a museum and in the course of renovation the plaster was removed, revealing the ancient Christian images for the first time in almost five hundred years. Unfortunately there is now a movement afoot to reconvert Hagia Sophia back to a Mosque, which, if it happened, would presumably result in the mosaics being plastered over once more, or, even worse, destroyed. After a brief tour of the museum I headed back across the Galata Bridge and caught a bus back to the Hotel, to find there was still no Turkish coffee to be had in the bar.

The following day was to be my last full day in the city, and I consulted my guide-book over breakfast to check the attractions I had yet to visit. Foremost amongst these was the Grand Bazaar, located on the southern side of the Galata Bridge, not far from the Blue Mosque. I caught the bus at the stop just down the road from the hotel and found a seat immediately behind the driver from which I could view our progress. Drivers in this most hectic of cities were as usual both unforgiving and relentless, appearing to see any obstacle in the road ahead as a personal challenge to be overcome at all costs. We wove our way through snarled-up road junctions, past Dolmus gas-guzzlers waiting for business and badly parked vehicles delivering to local businesses. Occasionally a horse and cart, and in one case a donkey cart, joined the relentless parade of vehicles of every make and age, although I failed to spot a single bicycle during the entire journey. On the far side of the Galata Bridge I worked my way on foot through narrow streets past retail shops of every description and eventually arrived at the Nuruosmaniye gate at the eastern end of the Grand Bazaar. Ignoring the two itinerant carpet-sellers advancing purposefully as I arrived, I passed through into the huge covered market and paused, bemused by the labyrinth before me.

The Grand Bazaar was first created in the mid-fifteenth century when Constantinople, as it was then known, became the capital of the Ottoman Empire. Whilst it originally traded in such things as fabrics and foodstuffs, it rather bizarrely also boasted a section devoted exclusively to the buying and selling of slaves. As with all covered markets – I was reminded of the one in Riga, Latvia – the stalls spilled out beyond the covered area to encompass many of the surrounding streets. The total area of the market under cover is some 22,000 square metres, equivalent to the size of about three football pitches, and it is claimed to be the most visited tourist attraction in the world at 91million visitors per year, but this is somewhat debatable. Publicity material states that it contains 4,000 shops, many organised into specialist areas such as spices, carpets, gold, jewellery, and clothing. To me it was at first bewildering, given that the prospect of getting lost inside seemed real enough, but after a while I simply abandoned any thought of navigating to this or that area and simply enjoyed my journey through the sights, sounds, and smells of this unique location. I occasionally passed stalls where serious bargaining was in progress, often involving American tourists and hand-knotted carpets, but my own purchases were restricted to buying 250 grams if shelled pistachio nuts from a stall offering an impossibly huge range of nuts and dried fruit. It was easy to imagine that the colourful, noisy, atmosphere and entrepreneurial energy may have changed little since the height of the Ottoman Empire. I lingered longer than I had expected to, but eventually headed back in warm sunshine through the narrow streets to the Galata Bridge and enjoyed a glass of Nescafe at one of the fish stalls.

From there I crossed over Tersane Street and entered Karakoy station, the terminus of an underground funicular railway a mere 1500 metres long which climbs steeply up to Beyoglu, a hilltop area in the city centre. Two trains operate the line, one descending as the other ascends, and there is a passing loop at the half-way point. Both trains are hauled by means of steel cabling located between the rails. I was interested to travel on this railway for many reasons, foremost of which was the fact that it is the second-oldest underground railway in the world. The oldest, London's Metropolitan Railway, opened to the public in October 1863 and linked Paddington Station to Farringdon Street in the City of London. A little known fact connected to the Metropolitan line is that Londoners seeking entertainment in the years between 1863 and 1868 were able to travel on it to Farringdon Street and from there walk to nearby Newgate Prison where they could watch public hangings. It is reported that crowds at these executions could exceed 100,000 in the case of the most notorious murderers, and many of these observers would arrive by underground. Public hangings were finally abolished in England in 1868. The link with Istanbul, though unconnected with public hangings, is nevertheless significant. In 1869 Sultan Abdulaziz, ruler of the Ottoman Empire at the time, became aware of the six-year success of the Metropolitan Railway Company in London and invited its management to survey the Karakoy to Beyoglu route with the object of building an underground railway linking the two. A company was created to handle the contract, named Metropolitan Railway (Constantinople), and the line was opened in January 1875, remaining Istanbul's only underground railway until 1989 when the first of the new Metro lines was opened. It is interesting to speculate as to whether the share certificates for the Istanbul company are still to be found in the archives of London Underground Ltd, the eventual successor to the Metropolitan Railway.

Karakoy station proved to be a bright and airy building. I waited on the platform, able to see the full length of the line climbing through the tunnel and offering a glimpse of the top station, Beyoglu. The two modern electric trains, running on guided pneumatic tyres, were at the point in the tunnel where the line divides into two, allowing the one ascending to pass the one descending. When the line was opened it was driven by steam and there were two wooden carriages to each train, one carrying people and the other livestock. The "people" carriage was divided into four sections, with first and second-class halves each further divided into men and women compartments.

The journey to the top, taking all of ninety seconds, was uneventful, and soon I and my fellow-passengers were exiting into the busy street high above the city at Beyoglu. I had decided to take the opportunity to visit the Galata Tower, about half a kilometre away, one of the city's major landmarks. Any panoramic photograph of the Istanbul skyline will almost certainly include this cylindrical tower with a conical roof dominating the surrounding rooftops and indeed the entire city. The short walk downhill, beneath a clear blue sky, was a pleasant enough stroll along narrow streets lined with the usual mixture of shops, kebab restaurants and souvenir stalls. I arrived at a broad flagstoned square on the right, at the centre of which stood the the tower. 67 metres high, and almost 17 metres in diameter at the base, the building is partially surrounded by trees, and its substantial stone construction bears witness to its original purpose of defending the Galata Bridge area of the city from enemy attack. From the eighteenth century onwards it was deemed more useful as a look-out post for fires, reflecting the fact that Istanbul had more than its fair share of serious fires during the Ottoman period and thereafter, with practically every major building being partly or wholly destroyed at one time or another. Indeed, the Galata Bridge over the Golden Horn, which I crossed several times during this visit, was later destroyed by fire in 1992. I forwent the opportunity to climb the tower, at the top of which I understand there to be a restaurant and nightclub, and instead headed back to the hotel on foot via Taksim Square, somewhat relieved to find no trace of the military there. I returned to the restaurant just down the road from the hotel, and ate a well-deserved doner kebab accompanied by Efes beer.

The following day, my intended day of departure, I was delighted to discover that the Turkish Airlines strike was over, so took a taxi to the airport. At about the half-way point along the motorway the traffic was beginning to back up, and I became slightly anxious that I might miss my flight, my worries not alleviated by the *sotto voce* cursing of my driver. Fortunately the delay was brief, as its cause was soon evident. Coming towards us, travelling the wrong way down the outside lane of a three-lane motorway, was a little old man riding a donkey cart.

At the airport I tracked down the government foreign exchange desk, as I needed to change my surplus lire back into dollars, as instructed by the man at the desk in Ankara. He'd told me to hand over the lire, along with the form that had been duly signed by him and his colleague, and had assured me that this would ensure the return of the fifty or so dollars-worth of lire I hadn't spent during my stay.

The official at the counter examined the form, scratched his head, and looked at me over the top of his reading glasses.

"I cannot change lira. Sorry."

"Why not?"

"This form only signed by two colleagues. Must have three signatures."

^But there were only two people in the office at Ankara. That's why there are only two signatures."

"Sorry sir. This is the law. Perhaps their colleague was not there because of the strike. I am sorry but I cannot help you."

And so it was that I took home Turkish lira notes that I wouldn't be able to exchange in England, and which would lose 90% of their value in the coming few years. I still have the notes, and optimistically wonder if they have any value to numismatists.

This visit to Turkey had been an eye-opener in many ways, making me aware of the country's complex history and political idiosyncracies. Mustafa Kemal Ataturk, the founder of a republic that is now 96 years old, was determined that it should be secular, and this is still the case, although the clamour to become a Moslem state is getting ever louder. Few women covered their heads in public when I was there, but nowadays large numbers seem to wear headscarves. At the time I was in Istanbul there were numerous signs that the country was in less than perfect health, with foreign exchange problems, an airline strike, raw material importation problems, and a decaying infrastructure, It wasn't a complete surprise to me when a military coup took place only six months later. But despite its political and economic traumas, I found Istanbul a vibrant, fascinating, busy city, and it certainly ranks amongst my top five European cities to visit. It is unique in the continent of Europe and we should treasure it for that.

Chapter 25

The United Kingdom

England is a nation of shopkeepers **Napoleon Bonaparte**

We have always found the Irish a bit odd. They refuse to be English **Winston Churchill**

Oats – a grain which in England is generally given to horses, but which in Scotland supports the people **Samuel Johnson**

England is the most class-ridden country under the sun. It is a land of snobbery and privilege ruled largely by the old and silly **George Orwell**

Where Napoleon failed, I shall succeed. I shall land on the shores of Britain **Adolf Hitler**

Stone from the Great Wall of China. Meeting with Frank Dickens, the artist who drew Bristow. Knickers in St. Paul's Cathedral. Mozart rehearsal in church. Pie and Mash restaurant. Warship guns trained on motorway service station. The ship launch that went wrong. The oldest object in the world.

The United Kingdom, more correctly known as The United Kingdom of Great Britain and Northern Ireland, and hereinafter referred to as the UK, is a sovereign state dating from 1707 and is located off the North coast of continental Europe. Within it, England, Wales, Scotland, and Northern Ireland are commonly referred to as countries, but are not sovereign states, and therefore fall outwith the accepted definition of a country. The name "Great Britain", which is also used from time to time, refers to the island occupied by England, Scotland, and Wales, but excludes Northern Ireland, which is located on the adjacent island of Ireland and has no land border with the other three. Great Britain is made up of a single island of 210,000 square kilometres surrounded by some 800 smaller offshore islands, resulting in a coastline that may be between 12,000 and 18,000 kilometres long depending on the method of measurement. Great Britain's population is approximately 61 million souls, which by definition excludes the almost two million who live in Northern Ireland. The UK's capital, London, is situated in England, and there are additional devolved capital cities in Wales, Scotland, and Northern Ireland. London is also regarded as being England's capital, although there are those who argue that from a historical perspective the City of Westminster, located within London's borders, is England's true capital.

In the nineteenth century the UK controlled an empire that stretched around the globe, and which at its peak consisted of around 100 countries, including such huge land areas as India, Canada, and Australasia. In many of these nations the UK's influence is still evident in the form of their indigenous language, culture, politics, and sport, and as a consequence English is the third most widely spoken mother tongue in the world after Mandarin and Spanish. It is also the second language in 55 non English-speaking nations, and the UK's most powerfully political ally, the United States of America, is also English-speaking, due to the fact that the original settlers in that country spoke English. In the twentieth century the size of the empire fell sharply as its member-states achieved independence, and during this time the UK was part of the victorious group of allies in two world wars. In 1973 the country joined the European Economic Community, later to become the European Union, but has recently decided to leave that organisation.

I find it difficult to write about the UK as if I were a visitor, given that it has been my home for most of my life. Were I a Frenchman living in Paris, for example, I would find it easy to describe a holiday visiting one or more of the many tourist destinations in the UK, but my own exploration of this country tends to be in the form of days out or, at most, weekends away. Should I find that I have a longer period free from work I usually take the opportunity to go to continental Europe, simply because there is much yet to explore there. Living close to London, however, gives me the opportunity to make a day-trip to the capital whenever the fancy takes me, and in this chapter I thought I might describe a recent day-out in that most cosmopolitan and fascinating of all European cities.

My trip began as usual with a walk in bright sunshine to my nearest station, located on the suburban railway network known as London Overground. There I topped up my Oyster card with cash at the automatic machine in the station. Somewhat similar to the *Decouverte* card in Paris, the Oyster card is a stored-value piece of plastic, available to visitors as well as residents, that allows me to travel by train, tram, bus, and underground throughout London. It is a highly convenient, not to say inexpensive, way of getting around the capital. I boarded the train and settled back as it ambled through the leafy suburbs of North London, eventually reaching Queen's Park station where I exited and crossed the platform to catch the already-approaching Bakerloo Line underground train. At this point the underground line is very much above-ground, but soon afterwards it dives beneath the surface as it heads towards the city centre. My destination was Trafalgar Square, requiring me to leave the train at Charing Cross Station and walk the short distance along the subway to its exit at the edge of the square.

Trafalgar Square, a broad open space in the heart of the capital, has long been London's venue for political protest and rallies, being large enough at 100 metres square to hold crowds of many tens of thousands. At its centre is Nelson's Column, a structure 47 metres high and topped by a 5 metre-high statue of one of the country's naval heroes, Vice Admiral Horatio Nelson. It was he who commanded the victorious English fleet against Napoleon Bonaparte of France at the battle of Trafalgar in 1805, and he died, aged 57, on board his ship after being hit by a sniper's bullet during the battle. Some of the British survivors, in need of medical attention, were taken to Gibraltar, the nearest major port, and a few of those that later died were buried in the Gibraltar graveyard which I visited some years ago.

On the North side of the square lies the National Gallery, a classic Neoclassical building (if that is not an oxymoron) constructed in grey stone, and fronted by three porticos, the two outermost each supported by four columns, and the centre one by eight columns. Founded in 1824, it has available for display more than 2,000 paintings, covering art from the thirteenth century to the end of Impressionism in the early twentieth century. I make a point of popping into the National Gallery

Whenever I'm near Trafalgar Square, often just to view the magnificent collection of Impressionist works, which is conveniently reached by taking the right-hand doorway at the top of the stairs in the entrance-hall. On this particular occasion I headed for the group of works by Claude Monet, and in particular a favourite of mine entitled "Gare Saint Lazare", a smallish oil-painting he created in 1877 showing the interior of one of the major railway stations in Paris.

Having rented a studio near the station, Monet had become fascinated by its steamy, smoky interior, and resolved to capture the scene on several canvasses under varied light conditions and from different vantage points. On some mornings he would arrive at the station with his easel, paints, and several stretched canvasses, intending to work on more than one on that particular day. As a result, he faced the problem of carrying them home despite the fact that the paint had not necessarily dried. One of his ingenious solutions to the problem was to pierce tiny holes In the four corners of each canvas which matched exactly the location of four thin nails, point outwards, that he had hammered into the corners of his easel. As he prepared to return home at the end of the day he would slip one of the canvasses onto the four nails, followed by four small cork spacers, one for each nail, and a second canvas could therefore be slipped on top of the first with no possibility of the two coming into contact. The process could be repeated with more canvasses if appropriate. Monet eventually produced twelve works, each showing the station interior from different viewpoints and at different times of day, and close examination of the example in the National Gallery reveals the pinholes clearly visible in each of the four corners of the canvas. Such a superficially unimportant detail, probably unnoticed by most of those who view the painting, is hugely significant in the history of art. It was the Impressionists who were among the first artists to make the decision to work in the open air, rather than in a studio, as they strove to capture everyday life on canvas. Their predecessors had, for the most part, created religious, still-life, and portrait paintings within the confines of a studio. The decision to work outside presented many practical difficulties, of which that encountered by Monet at Gare Saint Lazare is a typical example.

On the East side of Trafalgar Square I called into the church of St. Martin in the Fields, an older Neoclassical building dating from 1726 with a columned portico and a spire 59 metres high, six metres higher than Nelson's Column. It was here in 1816 that John Constable, the artist, married Maria Bicknell in a ceremony sparsely attended due to the bride's family's opposition to the union. Constable's most famous work "The Hay Wain" is, by some strange quirk of fate, today on display in the National Gallery not much more than 50 metres from the church. As is often the case at St. Martin in the Fields, a concert was planned for that evening and the orchestra, crammed into the space between the front row of pews and the altar, were in rehearsal. The sound of the sublime second movement of Mozart's Symphony number 39 filled the church, occasionally halting in mid-bar when the conductor heard something that displeased him. I found myself wishing I could attend the concert proper later in the day.

Following this rather pleasant interlude I reluctantly departed and walked the short distance to the Strand, a main road running East-West across the city, where I waited at the bus stop to catch the number nine heritage Routemaster service as far as Aldwych. The red double-decker Routemaster buses, instantly recognisable with their open platforms at the rear and their fare-collecting bus conductors inside, operated almost all of London's bus services from 1956, with the last vehicles being taken out of service in2005. Ideal for jumping on and off in between stops when stuck in heavy traffic, many Londoners mourned their passing and there was much delight when it was announced that two routes would continue to use them. One of these was the number nine route, which I intended to take. When the bus duly arrived I climbed aboard and offered my Oyster card to the conductor, who scanned it with his hand-held electronic caed-reader, a far cry from the days when he would issue a paper ticket in return for cash by turning the handle of his aluminium ticked machine. I mentioned to him that the service seemed rarely to be full and he agreed, saying he was sure it wasn't paying its way. Sadly, it was withdrawn in 2014, but the other heritage route, number 15, continues to operate between the Tower of London and Trafalgar Square.

At Aldwych I headed east along Fleet Street, once the location of the offices of most of Britain's national newspapers, and sought out one of my old haunts, Ye Olde Cheshire Cheese pub, almost hidden in an alleyway on the North side. Dating back to the period following the great fire of London in 1666, the Cheshire Cheese was a popular watering hole for newspaper employees during the nineteenth and twentieth centuries, and over the years attracted its fair share of literary characters, with Charles Dickens, Alfred Lord Tennyson, Sir Arthur Conan Doyle, and PG Wodehouse reputed to have been regular drinkers there at one time or another. I ordered a beer at the bar and took a seat in the gloomy and sparsely populated interior. In the years before the newspaper industry moved away from the area the pub would already have been busy at this mid-morning hour, and my mind returned to the time thirty years earlier when I worked just round the corner in Little New Street.

At the time I was a great admirer of a cartoon artist by the name of Frank Dickens, who drew the daily "Bristow" comic strip for the Evening Standard, a London newspaper headquartered in Fleet Street. Bristow was a world-weary clerk who worked in an office in the city and the strip chronicled his daily attempts to find humour in his hum-drum existence. On that particular day I had been highly amused by the previous day's cartoon and resolved to buy the original. I telephoned Frank Dickens at his office, and he assured me he had the artwork by his desk, so we agreed to meet in Ye Olde Cheshire Cheese to complete the transaction. At 11am prompt I arrived, spotted him at the bar, and introduced myself, After concluding our business I offered to buy him a drink, which he eagerly accepted, and he of course offered to get the next round. For the following couple of hours he regaled me with tales of drinking sessions at various bars in the city with various Fleet Street characters, some known to me, others not. One story in particular concerned a late-night party he'd attended in the West End, not much more than a mile or so from his flat in the Barbican centre. Details of the journey home from this heavy drinking session would forever remain a mystery to him, as he woke up the following morning alone in a hotel room about 100 metres from his flat. To that day he had no idea why or how he got there. After more stories and drinks I eventually told him I had to get back to my office and left him just as he was ordering another pint. I was undoubtedly unfit for work for the remainder of the afternoon, and spent the time keeping out of the way of my colleagues until going-home time.

On this day some thirty years later I restricted my drinking to what is euphemistically labelled a "swift half" and went on my way. Incidentally, just around the corner from the pub is Doctor Johnson's house, a splendid four storey town house that is open to the public. It was he who published the first English dictionary in 1755. I visited the house whilst working in Little New Street and was amazed to find therein a block of stone taken from the Great Wall of China. There must be few people that pass along nearby Fleet Street who are aware that they are so close to part of the Great Wall of China.

From the Cheshire Cheese I continued along Fleet Street as far as St. Paul's Cathedral. In years gone by I would not have hesitated to call into this magnificent building, created by Sir Christopher Wren in 1697 after the previous cathedral had been destroyed in the Great Fire of London. However the Cathedral authorities recently saw fit to begin charging an entrance fee, and at that point my interest in the interior waned. My first-ever visit to the Cathedral was in the 1960s when I stayed for a few days at the flat of a London-based girlfriend. One day I expressed an interest in visiting the Cathedral, so the following morning saw us touring the building and climbing the stairs to the whispering gallery, a circular walkway around the base of the dome. Once there I persuaded my girlfriend to accompany me in the climb right up to the top of the dome and beyond if possible. Together with a few other brave souls we clambered up the somewhat rickety staircase located in the space between the interior and exterior skins of the dome, and eventually emerged blinking into the daylight as we reached the lantern perched on the dome's top. Here we took time out to rest after the climb and take in the breathtaking views over the city.

We were not finished climbing, however. Inside the lantern a vertical steel ladder, with twenty or so rungs, led upwards into the Golden Ball, the highest part of the cathedral other than the golden cross that surmounts it. Only one person at a time could climb this ladder, and he or she would be expected to spend no more than a few seconds at the top, perhaps take a brief look at the view of London through the slits in the ball, and then climb down to make way for the next in the group. Being a chivalrous type, I bade one of the ladies present, an attractive twenty-something, to go first, and she smiled her acceptance of the offer and began the climb. As she approached the top I looked upwards and found myself gazing up the inside of her loose skirt, thus discovering that she was wearing white lace knickers. Chivalry eventually reasserted itself, and when she descended I moved to help her step off the ladder. I insisted that her equally attractive female companion should be next in line for the climb, and this time was able to establish that the knickers were of blue cotton. Sadly my girlfriend had by now taken stock of the situation, and somewhat forcefully insisted I go next. When I descended she muttered that she had done the climb before and didn't want to repeat it, and suggested, or rather demanded, that we should return to the whispering gallery. A consequence of this experience is that whenever I happen to see the golden ball atop St. Paul's Cathedral, from whatever vantage point in London, I immediately think of ladies' underwear. This association of ideas was not, I suspect, the original intention of Sir Christopher Wren, nor of the current dean and Chapter of the Cathedral.

From the cathedral I walked southwards towards the river, with the intention of crossing to the opposite bank using the pedestrian-only Millennium Bridge. The bridge, as the name suggests, was opened in June 2000, with much ceremony and publicity, but suddenly closed two days later after it was found to be "wobbling" alarmingly. The closure lasted for two years, during which time the structure was strengthened, but by then it was already known as the "Wobbly Bridge" and continues to be referred to as such by many Londoners. Buffeted by a freshening wind, I made my way over it to Tate Modern, London's principal home of modern art, located right by the bridge. Built in 1947 as an electricity generating station known as Bankside Power-Station, it was designed by Sir Giles Gilbert Scott, whose only architectural achievement of any merit throughout a long and somewhat undistinguished career was Liverpool's Anglican Cathedral. The power station, constructed from 4.2 million bricks, was an immense and unprepossessing building, towering over the river bank like a twentieth-century fortress, It had little or no architectural merit, except possibly in the eyes of industrial design fetishists. Two hundred metres in length, and forty metres high, the building supported a central square brick chimney whose top is almost 100 metres above ground level. In the austere post-war years there was little demand for elegance in industrial buildings, and in that regard Scott succeeded magnificently. Electricity generation on the site ceased in 1981 and the empty building's future lay in the balance for many years until permission was granted to convert it into the UK's national modern art gallery. After huge internal structural alterations, but with minimal external changes, it opened its doors to the public as Tate Modern in 2000.

Inside, its magnificent turbine hall, which rises to the full height of the building, is used to house temporary art installations, and alongside this the five floors of galleries and exhibition spaces, recently extended, offer a wonderful collection of twentieth-century art, in my view only bettered by that in New York's Museum of Modern Art. To me, no visit to London is complete without a visit to Tate Modern, many of whose works were created during my lifetime. I find much that is mysterious, and often incomprehensible, in modern art, but also much that is fascinating in terms of the way the various schools and movements that came and went during the twentieth century reflected political, social, and cultural life at the time. For me, twentieth century history is incomplete without an understanding of those artists prominent at the time. Many of the works demand more than just a casual glance to understand the artist's intentions, and I rarely have the time or inclination to study any particular work in detail, but nevertheless I find much that is provocative and instructive in the works on show in that vast building. Man's inhumanity to man was never more manifest than in the tumultuous century that has just passed, but I find reassurance in the fact that at the same time there lived great artists who sought to express themselves peaceably and with integrity. In short, Tate Modern serves to renew my faith in the essential goodness of human nature. My visit this time was necessarily brief as I was on something of a tight schedule, but I nevertheless found time to view yet again works of the likes of Picasso, Braque, Giacometti, Dali, and Magritte. I continue to struggle when it comes to understanding Mark Rothko and Jackson Pollock, but have not yet given up on them.

From Tate Modern, in bright sunshine, I took the Thames River Bus to Greenwich, a mini-cruise, if you will, eastwards along the River Thames, making full use of my Oyster card. The River Bus service has become something of a commuter facility in London in recent years, allowing passengers to travel between any of 29 piers on the river stretching from Hampton Court in the West to Woolwich Arsenal in the East. The journey to Greenwich was scheduled to take about fifty minutes, including a stop at the Pier of the Tower of London. The first tourist sight *en route* was HMS Belfast, a light cruiser battleship once of the Royal Navy, now moored on the south side of the river as a museum ship and open to visitors, many of whom were visible wandering around on deck. I remembered visiting her soon after she arrived in London in 1971. During the previous 33 years she had attacked enemy shipping in various parts of the world, and one incident among many took place in December 1943 when she played a key role in the sinking of the German warship Scharnhorst, killing 1,932 members of the crew of that vessel. At the time of my visit in 1971 I found that none of the many information notices on the ship mentioned death or killing, despite the fact that this was the sole reason for her existence. As I sailed by on the River Bus I wondered if, forty years later, there continues to be an embargo on the use of the word "death" on HMS Belfast. Incidentally, I am informed that a naval enthusiast, presumably with too much time on his or her hands, has calculated that the guns on the starboard side, pointing menacingly in an approximately North-Westerly direction, and at 45 degrees elevation, would, if they were ever fired, result in the destruction of the London Gateway service area on the M1 motorway 13 miles away.

Tower Bridge soon followed, on this day sadly mistakenly referred to as London Bridge by a group of American tourists seated behind me. Built in 1894, its specification at the time required that the carriageway could be raised to allow the passage of tall sailing ships through to the Pool of London, a stretch of the riverbank where goods were loaded and unloaded. As a result, a high-level walkway was installed, connecting the two 65 metre-high towers of the bridge, and accessed by means of staircases attached to each tower, thus allowing pedestrians to cross when the carriageway was raised. For some reason the walkway soon became a night-time haunt of prostitutes, leading to it being closed in 1910. History does not record whether prospective clients, having climbed the staircase, were in any fit state to perform when they arrived at the top.

The river broadens out on the eastern side of the bridge, giving views of the renovated dockland area that is interspersed with more venerable industrial and residential buildings. As we approached Greenwich we passed Burrell's Wharf on the north bank of the river, nothing more than a muddy stretch of land sloping upwards from the water's edge towards the buildings and road behind. It has, however, a place in history as the site where the SS Great Eastern, the largest iron steamship in the world at the time, was built in the 1850s. The ship's designer, Isambard Kingdom Brunel, one of Britain's greatest engineers, was determined that it should be built on the Thames, but could find no dry-dock large enough to take her length of 211 metres. As a result he made the bold, some say foolhardy, decision to build her "sideways-on" to the river at Burrell's wharf. The project was beset by technical and financial problems from the start, and on the day of the "sideways" launch in 1857 she resolutely refused to slide into the river. Two months later the launch finally occurred on a particularly high tide, and subsequent fitting-out of the vessel meant that her maiden voyage was delayed until September 1859, by which time Brunel's health had deteriorated and he died shortly afterwards at the age of 53. It is likely that the stress brought on by the project was a major contributory factor to his death. Great Eastern was a commercial failure and ended her days in the 1880s as a floating advertising hoarding on the River Mersey at Liverpool, promoting the John Lewis Partnership department store. One of her masts was acquired by Liverpool Football Club and can be seen today in use as a flagpole at the Kop end of the Anfield football ground. Great Eastern was sent to a scrapyard on the Mersey in 1889, thirty years after her maiden voyage, and Burrell's wharf saw no further shipbuilding activity.

Opposite the wharf, on the south side of the river, the River Bus slowed and tied up at my destination, Greenwich. There is so much to see in Greenwich that a full day may easily be spent there, but as time was short I decided on this occasion to concentrate my attention on the Royal Observatory. I headed up the steepish hill through Greenwich Park, a pleasant stretch of greenery covering more than 70 hectares, passing families picnicking on the grass whilst enjoying the view over the river towards the skyscrapers of Docklands beyond, and groups of young people half-heartedly played ball games nearby. Others, some with dogs in tow, strolled amongst the trees. At the top of the hill I came upon the Greenwich Meridian line, a metal strip embedded in the pavement outside the Royal Observatory. Hordes of visitors were queuing to have their photographs taken standing astride the line which purportedly marks the location of zero degrees longitude. Those standing astride it can claim to have a foot in each hemisphere of the earth. However the line's position has recently been checked for accuracy astronomically, with the result that the correct location of the Meridian is currently 2.3 metres west of the metal strip.

The observatory, constructed to enable astronomical observations, consists of an eclectic group of buildings, mainly constructed from brick, with the tallest some five stories high. Most were built in 1675 on the site of Greenwich Castle, where King Henry VIII kept his mistresses back in the sixteenth century. The highest building in the complex is surmounted by the Time Ball, a red sphere of some two metres diameter pierced by a vertical pole around six metres high. The ball, which is able to move freely up and down the pole, is normally held in a raised position at the top, but at 1pm each day it is allowed to drop, and after a short while is raised back to the top. This procedure is nowadays purely symbolic, but when installed in 1833 the ball drop allowed ships' masters down on the river to set their clocks as they prepared to set sail. The determination of longitude at sea in those days required the presence of an accurate timepiece on board ship, without which navigation would have been impossible.

Sadly I arrived too late to witness that day's drop, but in any case was more interested in visiting the museum. In particular I wanted to see – and touch – the Gibeon Meteorite. A meteorite is an object, principally made of iron, which would normally be found in the vast emptiness of space but which, serendipitously, has wandered close to the Earth and has been captured by the Earth's gravity, eventually falling to earth. In space, such objects are known simply as meteors, and at various times of the year the earth passes through clouds of these particles on its journey around the sun. These are visible at night as "meteor showers", pieces of rock often no larger than a grain of sand that glow as they burn up whilst passing through the atmosphere. Those that don't burn up, and therefore land on the earth's surface, are known as meteorites. A study suggests that between 18,000 and 84,000 meteorites weighing more than ten grams land on the earth every year, whilst another suggests the aggregate weight of meteorites falling to earth every year can be as much as 78,000 tons, most of which would be dust-sized particles. The Gibeon Meteorite is exceptional in many ways. It fell near the town of Gibeon in Namibia in prehistoric times, shattering into hundreds of fragments, many of which have been recovered. Its estimated total weight is 27,000 kilograms, and the fragment in the museum weighs a few tens of kilos. It dates from 4.5 billion years ago, the period when the solar system was being formed, and looks much like a solidified piece of slag from a steel furnace, but is in fact composed of 90% iron and about 7% nickel. Around 50 centimetres by 30 centimetres by 20 centimetres, it is on display inside the museum, and visitors are invited to touch "The oldest object on earth". I did as was asked, touching it for a few lingering moments, then continued on my tour of the museum.

By now quite hungry, I made for Greenwich town centre, pausing for a few minutes to view the stalls at the very good indoor market, before heading to the place where I knew I would eat well and cheaply. In business since 1890, Goddards of Greenwich is a traditional "Pie and Mash" and "Jellied Eel" establishment. As recently as fifty years ago such places could be found on most high streets in the Greater London area, but nowadays there are only a few still trading. Originating in Victorian times, they served cheap meals to the working-classes, offering little in the way of variety or sophistication, but much in the way of nourishment. Pies were originally filled with eel, but later contained minced mutton or beef, and were served with mashed potato and what was known as "liquor", not an alcoholic product but a simple parsley sauce, pale green in colour. As an alternative, customers could have jellied eels, a dish consisting of eels chopped into pieces around an inch long and boiled in a spiced stock. Eels are highly gelatinous, and in consequence so was the stock. Three or four pieces of the cooked eel were placed in a serving-bowl, the stock was poured over and as it set it became a clear jelly. The eels and jelly were then eaten together. In the nineteenth century eels were so numerous in the Thames that they were almost considered vermin, and thousands were caught daily in nets and taken to Billingsgate Fish Market to be sold. It is somewhat chastening to realise that they were so numerous because they were highly resistant to the many diseases to be found in the heavily-polluted Thames at the time. In addition to this traditionally limited savoury menu, there were hot puddings such as apple crumble or bread and butter pudding with custard.

The restaurant offers the traditional menu at low cost, and food is served at the counter in a space that is very basic, with white walls half-tiled in green, and rudimentary wooden tables and chairs. I collected a plate of pie, mash, and liquor, together with a cup of tea, and found an empty table by the window. From overheard snippets of conversation at adjacent tables it seemed that many of my fellow-diners were middle-class, something of a change from the clientele of even fifty years previously. I would suggest, perhaps charitably, that like me they were simply interested to sample what had been the staple food for Londoners for 100 years and more. After finishing my pie and mash I returned to the counter and ordered jellied eels, which I found to have the flavour and texture of sea-caught fish.

From the restaurant I walked the short distance to a small circular brick building topped by a glass dome down by the river, the entrance to the Greenwich Foot Tunnel, a pedestrian and cycle tunnel joining the North and South banks of the river and emerging in what is known as the Isle of Dogs on the North side. Opened in 1902, it was originally constructed to allow workers living on the south side of the river to commute to the nearby London Docks on the north side, but nowadays it is principally a means whereby anyone wishing to cross the river, often for leisure purposes, may do so quickly and free of charge. At either end users may choose to take the lift, or use the 100-step spiral staircase to reach the tunnel 15 metres below. I opted for the stairs, and set off along the 370 metre-long tunnel, the wall of which is lined with more than 200,000 white brick-sized tiles. The centre line of the combined path and cycleway is marked by a white line, and there is appropriate signage advising cyclists to keep to the left, but this instruction was ignored by many of those who sped by as I walked along. Children seemed to be particularly fascinated by the acoustic reverberation produced by their excited shouting. At the far end I opted to take the spacious lift to the surface rather than climb the stairs, and found myself sharing it with three or four cyclists and several other walkers. The attendant turned away others who were waiting, announced that he was closing the doors, and a short time later I emerged at ground level. Before me lay Island Gardens Park, a small grassy area dotted with trees which overlooks the river, on the far side of which I could see the sunlit buildings of Greenwich.

From there it was a short walk to Island Gardens Station, one of the stations on the Docklands Light Railway, a rail system established in 1987 as part of the redevelopment of Docklands, an area of East London that had gone into decline when London's docks failed to modernise in the 1960s. Over the years the amount of business steadily declined as ships began to use container ports elsewhere in the UK, and by 1980 the scene was one of desolation, with derelict warehouses, rusting dockside cranes, and disused ship berths. Ironically this industrial wasteland, covering an area of 22 square kilometres, was located in a city that had in recent years suffered a severe lack of land available for building. As a result the London Docklands Development Corporation was established to regenerate the area, and today it is a vital and vibrant part of London's business community, particularly in the provision of banking and financial services. Its high-rise commercial and residential buildings of steel, glass, and concrete are visible on the skyline from many elevated parts of the city. A development of this magnitude required the creation of adequate infrastructure, and in pursuit of this the railway was built, with 39 kilometres of track serving 45 stations. It was recently extended outside the docklands area via a tunnel to Lewisham on the South side of the river. Trains are driverless, with the result that the front passenger seat provides uninterrupted views forward, and I quickly installed myself in this prized position when the train arrived. My destination, about 30 minutes and 11 stops away, was Royal Victoria Station, necessitating an elevated journey through a maze of modern commercial and residential buildings, most of which possessed little or no architectural merit. At Royal Victoria I exited the station, crossed the road, and walked the short distance to the Emirates Air Line.

No flying takes place at the somewhat pretentiously named Emirates Air Line. Its only connection with the airline industry is that it is sponsored by Emirates, the Dubai-based airline and the largest in the Middle-East. The Air Line is, in fact, simply a gondola lift, sometimes incorrectly referred to as a cable car, which crosses the Thames over a distance of some 1.2 kilometres. Gondolas, each carrying half a dozen or so passengers, are suspended from continuously-running cables, and climb to a height of 90 metres as they cross the river. My Oyster card gave immediate access to the platform, where I waited a few seconds for the next gondola to arrive, and jumped in as it moved alongside. The ride provided spectacular views on all sides, enabling me to see westwards as far as Tower Bridge and beyond, whilst to the East I was able to make out the M25 motorway bridge at Dartford 15 kilometres distant. Southwards, the Royal Observatory at Greenwich was visible, with the time ball raised in anticipation of the next day's drop. I found the journey-time of just ten minutes insufficient to do justice to the views available, whether by eye or camera, but I would still recommend the Emirates Air Line as the most spectacular way of crossing of the Thames in London. At the end I stepped smartly out of the gondola, and, conscious that it was getting late, quickly walked the 200 metres or so to North Greenwich Pier. There I took the River Bus to Embankment, from where I made my way back home.

Dr Samuel Johnson, he who kept a block of stone from the Great Wall of China in his house near Fleet Street, once said to his biographer James Boswell "When a man is tired of London he is tired of life; for there is in London all that life can afford." He's right. There is so much to do and see in this great city that I find it difficult to imagine ever being tired of the place. I regularly do what I did in this particular case – simply take off for the day with no particular destination in mind, and go where the fancy takes me. I have my favourite places of course, such as the National Gallery and Tate Modern, but these are never essential parts of any day out. I feel blessed that this sometimes chaotic but always fascinating metropolis is on my doorstep, and always look forward to the next visit.

Chapter 26

Cyprus and the Turkish Republic of Northern Cyprus

The EU initially decided to end the isolation of Turkish Cyprus, to balance the accession of Cyprus. But the EU has not carried through on its promise. **Ali Babacan**

Turkey will be in Cyprus forever **Recep Tayyip Erdogan**

No man's land. Spotted preparing to take photographs of the border. The old airport occupied only by pigeons. Scavenger pelicans. A Haircut. A visa for a non-country. United Nations soldiers. Made it to the Turkish side 30 years after my first attempt.

In my chapter on Turkey I referred to my first visit to Cyprus some thirty years ago, and in particular my failed attempt at the time to penetrate through from the Greek side to the Turkish sector of this divided island, a division that was the result of it being invaded by Turkey in 1974. Following the invasion, Cyprus was partitioned, with a buffer zone being set up between the Turkish-controlled North and the Greek-controlled South, administered and defended by United Nations forces. The capital, Nicosia, straddles this buffer zone, with the result that the city's northern inhabitants live in the Turkish sector, whilst those in the south inhabit the Greek sector, and the buffer zone is uninhabited. At the time of my original visit there were no legitimate means whereby an ordinary citizen could cross the buffer zone, which extends the full length of the island from East to West.

Following the invasion, Turkey named the Turkish-occupied zone in the North "The Turkish Republic of Northern Cyprus", but failed to persuade the international community to accept it as a bona fide country. As a result, Turkey is the only nation in the world that recognises The Turkish Republic of Northern Cyprus as a country. One result of its "non-country" status is that there are no direct flights from anywhere in the world other than Turkey to its principal airport at Ercan. Those seeking to fly there are obliged to travel via a Turkish airport, usually Istanbul, where they must change planes. In consequence, budget airlines may only fly direct to airports in the island's Greek sector, one of which is at Paphos, a coastal city and holiday resort some 150 kilometres South-West of the capital, Nicosia, and my destination on this occasion. The Greek part of the island, known as the Republic of Cyprus, became a member of the European Union in 2004 and adopted the Euro as its currency in 2008. It has *de jure* control over the entire island, but is currently unable to exercise that control over the Turkish sector.

On my arrival at Paphos airport, a nondescript steel, glass, and concrete construction, I made my way to the bus stop outside and caught the bus to Karavella bus station, located in the north of the city, a somewhat windswept open area with a single portakabin-style office. From there I walked the four hundred metres or so alongside the busy B7 road to the hotel, requiring me to negotiate a narrow pot-holed pavement in much the same way that soldiers might negotiate a minefield. From there I turned right onto Archbishop Makarios Avenue, named after the one-time President of the country and its leader for most of the period between 1960 and 1977, a time of civil war and encompassing the invasion of the island by Turkey. Celebrated as a hero throughout the Greek sector of the island, Archbishop Makarios is particularly honoured in Paphos, having been born in a village nearby. The city itself is relatively small. Being home to 32,000 souls, but this number increases dramatically during the summer season as it is a major holiday destination, seeing around one million tourist arrivals per year. There is a small fishing port, and local farms grow tobacco, bananas, and grapes.

I checked into the small, family-run hotel, a white two-storey pantiled detached building with red-shuttered windows and, at the rear, a pleasant flag-stoned courtyard surrounding half-a dozen palm-trees. Choosing a first-floor room overlooking the courtyard, I deposited my luggage inside and headed out to a nearby convenience store where I bought cheese, tomatoes, nachos, biscuits, and a half-bottle of red wine with a screw cap, ingredients for a picnic in my room later. On my return I popped into the small hotel bar, empty save for the *patron* behind the counter and a couple of his cronies perched on bar stools. There I bought a bottle of Keo beer, found a chair outside in the courtyard, and took my ease beneath the palm trees. As night fell, black clouds began to gather overhead, and before long a loud thunderclap heralded the arrival of a storm of biblical proportions, sending me scurrying back to my room, where I settled back to watch the television and eat my picnic meal. Through the window I could see the palm-fronds swaying violently in the wind, and hear torrential rain pounding the flagstones below, but the storm eventually abated and slipped away southwards, leaving peace and quiet in its wake.

On grounds of cost I decided against having the hotel breakfast the following morning, and settled for a couple of cups of coffee in the bar before heading back to the bus station to check bus times to Nicosia, the capital. The pavement alongside the B7 road was even more hazardous than before, as it now sported puddles of indeterminate depth following the previous night's thunderstorm, and in consequence I spent most of the time walking in the road. At the bus station I was delighted to find a restored single-decker red and green Bedford bus parked outside, a rare survivor of the thousands that used to serve the island's communities during the second half of the twentieth century. The vehicle has railings around its roof which served to hold in place heavy items of luggage, including livestock, which were too bulky to be carried inside, thus leading to its popular nickname "The Chicken Bus". Such buses were phased out when the European Union introduced a directive on emission controls across the 28 member states, an order which also led to the withdrawal of Malta's delightful vintage buses and the iconic Routemaster double-deckers in London. Whilst appreciating the environmental benefits of this decision, I feel a tinge of regret at the loss of such wonderful workhorses. This particular "Chicken Bus" was preserved as a heritage item and available for hire for weddings and similar functions.

At the office I obtained timetable information for my planned journey to Nicosia the following day and then boarded a number 618 bus, bound for Kato Bus Station by the harbour, a journey of about ten minutes and downhill most of the way. Beneath scudding clouds and chilled by a relentless autumnal onshore wind I took a walk along the harbour-side in the direction of the castle, a square stone fortress of little architectural merit, built some time after the Ottomans invaded the island in 1570. Along the way I passed by a restaurant, now closed for the winter, where thirty years previously I was enjoying an alfresco meal with work colleagues when suddenly I was forced to defend my food from the rapacious beaks of two hungry pelicans who were roaming around the seafront intent on stealing from diners' plates. The manager at the time explained that Paphos is a stopover point on the birds' migration route, making it the avian equivalent of a motorway service area.

The castle had little of interest to recommend it, confirming my view that castles are like waterfalls – when you've seen one you've seen them all. I walked back and tarried a while in the little group of souvenir shops opposite the bus station, where I bought a fridge magnet. There were few tourists about, it being chilly and out-of-season, and I was reminded of seaside visits in my childhood at similar times of the year when closed shops, empty restaurants and dismal bars conspired with chilly, often rainy, weather and near-deserted streets to guarantee that the most optimistic of visitors would find little to be cheerful about. One of my favourite films, "The Punch and Judy Man", a black-and-white movie starring that flawed genius Tony Hancock, captures beautifully this end-of-season English seaside atmosphere.

By now I was in need of breakfast, and in the area behind the seafront I happened upon Lidas Street, where I spotted the welcoming frontage of the Papantoniou Supermarket, its open doors offering sanctuary from the dreary world outside. As I wandered around the shelves, selecting food to eat in my room that night, I was unsurprised to hear English voices amongst many of my fellow-customers, confirming that Paphos has a large British expatriate community. After paying at the till I decided to check out the store's cafe, where I found a notice offering a full English breakfast for just two Euros forty-nine cents. Incredulous, I asked for more detail, and was informed by the lady serving that it included a fried egg, bacon, two hash browns, mushrooms, and baked beans, together with two slices of toast and butter. As if this were not enough, she added almost as an afterthought that the price included unlimited coffee. Worried that she might change her mind, I quickly handed over two Euros and fifty cents and generously told her to keep the change. Taking a seat by the window, I waited with eager anticipation whilst the meal was being prepared, and a few minutes later I was tucking into one of the best meals I've ever had on my travels, although it has to be said that my culinary bar has never been set particularly high. Afterwards I lingered over a second cup of coffee, then a third. I concluded that such a meal, devoid as it was of exotic trimmings, pretentious presentation, and, worst of all, "drizzling", could not, for me, have been bettered in the finest restaurant in Cyprus. Heartened and refreshed, I left the supermarket and headed for one of the few seafront bars that were open. Inside, I took a seat by the window with a view over the calm waters of the harbour, beyond which were the decidedly turbulent waters of the Mediterranean. A few tourists came and went, well wrapped-up against the chill wind, and I ordered a beer.

Afterwards I caught the bus back up the hill, and as I walked to the hotel I paused at the open door of a small barber's shop. The owner, a stocky man with dark hair, greying at the temples, and a greying moustache, leapt from his seat, smiled a gold-toothed smile and in English bade me enter. After quickly checking the price-list on display I walked in. I've found, when travelling, that it's worth keeping an eye open for barber's shops in the vicinity of the hotel, as it's often possible to get a perfectly acceptable haircut costing as little as half the price back home. As he fastened the cape around me the owner introduced himself as Theo. I told him I was David.

"You on holiday Mister David?"

I told him yes, but added that I was here principally to visit the Turkish sector.

"You can do it in Nicosia. Ledras Street." He said, helpfully, scissors clicking as he spoke.

"I know. Is it easy?"

"I don't know. I never went. I won't go until those Turks leave. It is my country. They stole my Uncle's house near Famagusta. Bloody Turkish family living there now. My uncle had to leave everything behind"

"I'm sorry to hear it." I said, aware that this was an entirely inadequate response given that the Turkish invasion was clearly still the cause of deep resentment.

"Will Cyprus ever be one country again?" I asked, hesitantly. "Surely it would be good for business." I added, optimistically.

"One day it will." He said, darkly, in a tone that betrayed revenge rather than reconciliation.

We went on to discuss less contentious matters such as the large British expatriate community in Paphos, which he considered good for business, and, of course, we talked football. After half an hour or so I emerged into the street much better informed about the community than when I entered, and, I hoped, much better groomed.

That evening I bought a doner kebab at a takeaway shop nearby and consumed it at the stand-up table outside on the pavement. Next door to it was a bar lit by multi-coloured neon lighting and fitted out in black and chromium. It was not normally my kind of establishment, but a television on the far wall was showing live football, so I entered, ordered a beer, and took a seat on a bar stool to watch the game. Later, back at the hotel I ordered a Cafe Americano at the bar and took it into the moonlit courtyard, where I chatted to a fellow Englishman who regaled me with a litany of problems resulting from his recent separation from his wife. Any problems I might have had soon seemed paltry by comparison, and I retired to my room shortly afterwards.

The following morning I made my way to the bus station, bought a ticket for the 11am intercity bus to Nicosia, and took a seat in the shelter to await its arrival. Far from being a "Chicken Bus", the vehicle which arrived was a comfortable modern air-conditioned touring coach. As we threaded our way through the suburbs of the city I happened to notice a Debenhams Department Store, not something I'd expected to find in Cyprus. Soon we were out in the countryside, heading along the A6 coast road, with views to the South of the sparkling Mediterranean under a clear blue sky, and on the landward side fields and woodland which gave way to the peaks of the Troodos Mountains in the distance. I believe Mount Olympus, at almost 2,000 metres high the highest point of this mountain range, is sometimes snow-capped in winter. As we approached Limassol, the principal sea, sun, and sand destination in Cyprus, I could see on the horizon Akrotiri, the British military base, the sea glistening beyond it. I was fortunate enough to visit Akrotiri on a previous visit, and remember it principally for its idiosyncratic domestic architecture. The married quarters for servicemen were for the most part copies of 1930s semi-detached houses that could be found throughout suburban London, and seemed strangely out of place in a Mediterranean environment.

After skirting Limassol we turned northwards along the A1 motorway through hilly terrain and soon were negotiating the busy suburbs of Nicosia, our destination. As it transpired, the main bus station in Solomou Square was only about 100 metres from my hotel, where I took a first-floor room principally on the basis that it had a balcony. Once installed, I took a seat on the balcony and watched the world go by, enjoying a glass of red wine from the bottle I'd bought in the supermarket in Paphos. Directly beneath my room was the hotel car park, small, and triangular in shape. This less than ideal configuration meant that parking was something of a lottery for the hotel guests. Those arriving simply parked wherever they could find space, whether or not it meant impeding the exit of vehicles already there. I watched as a driver who found himself blocked-in was obliged to go to the hotel's reception desk and eventually return, accompanied by the owner of the offending car, who then moved it to allow him to leave. The incoming driver of course immediately took the space vacated. This entertaining game of musical cars, rather than musical chairs, was repeated several times as I watched, seemingly considered an occupational hazard by drivers, who betrayed no animosity regarding the inconvenience caused.

The following morning, as a chill breeze blew in from the direction of the Troodos mountains, I again took a seat on the balcony and ate a breakfast of peach-flavoured iced tea and a couple of croissants I'd bought the night before. It was Sunday, nominally a day of rest, but I had a busy schedule ahead of me, it being the day when I would finally attempt to visit the Turkish Republic of Northern Cyprus. Success would mean the realisation of an ambition going back thirty years or so, to the time when I'd first attempted and failed to cross into the North via the road in Nicosia's western suburbs that led past the Ledra Palace Hotel in no man's land.

This time I headed for Ledras Street, about half a kilometre to the East, which, despite the similar name, has no connection to the aforementioned Ledra Hotel. Ledras street is largely pedestrianised and may be considered the principal downtown shopping street of the Greek sector of Nicosia, similar in status, although not in size, to Oxford Street in London. Of its half-kilometre length, the southernmost 350 metres are located in the Greek sector, 50 metres are in no man's land, and the northernmost 100 metres are in the Turkish sector. I paused on the way for a much-needed coffee at a cafe on the corner of Vasiliou Voulgaroktonou and was surprised to see dozens of young Filipino women congregating nearby. I discovered later that there is a well-established expatriate Filipino community in Nicosia, many of whom act as housekeepers for wealthy Cypriots and some of the country's 40,000-strong Russian community. The Filipinos traditionally don't work on Sundays and take the opportunity to socialise with their fellow expatriates, for some reason choosing this particular area of the city as their regular meeting-place. The fact that it was close to a Roman Catholic Church nearby may also have been a factor. Incidentally, I believe there is even a Russian-language radio station on the island.

As I sat outside the cafe, a man emerged from within, wheeling what looked like a battered and rusty hostess trolley, which he parked on the pavement, thereby obliging pedestrians to step into the busy road should they wish to pass. He then returned inside and emerged with a rather frayed electrical extension cable which was presumably connected to a socket inside the cafe. This he plugged into a box at the end of the trolley. From the box emerged a bicycle-style chain that engaged with cogs attached to several spits running the length of the upper part of the trolley. In the tray beneath the spits he placed pieces of charcoal and lit them with the assistance of liberal squirts from a tin of lighter-fuel. A colleague eventually emerged from the cafe carrying a plate piled high with kebab meat and vegetables which were then threaded onto the spits. Finally, the man threw a switch on the side of the box, causing the chain to start moving, and the spits to slowly rotate. In a matter of twenty minutes or so I had witnessed the creation of a street-barbecue, albeit by a process which probably contravened many health and safety regulations, but which nevertheless produced delicious-looking lunch-time food for the customers.

I strolled the short distance from there to Ledras Street and began my walk northwards along this busy pedestrian thoroughfare, crammed with shops and cafes, in search of the border with the Turkish Republic of Northern Cyprus. I eventually came upon a sculpture named "The "Resolution", consisting of a number of aluminium rods, each around three metres long, emerging upwards at angles from a circular stone base. I understand it is intended to represent a protest against human rights violations, and has the universal declaration of human rights written in Greek in its base. To its right a number of people queued at a windowed wooden checkpoint, and I joined them, eventually offering my passport to the uniformed lady inside. She scanned it and bade me walk on, and suddenly I was walking through no man's land, but was prevented from viewing this mysterious area by the tall hoardings on either side. Up ahead, on the left, stood the Turkish checkpoint, and I joined the queue. At the window my passport was carefully scanned by the uniformed immigration officer, who explained that I needed a visa, a requirement of which I had been unaware. I was about to turn back when he said, matter-of-fact,

"I give you visa. One moment please."

So saying, he reached for a blank printed form, somewhat smaller than an A5 sheet of paper, on which he entered my passport details, afterwards rubber-stamping it.

"Keep this with your passport." He said, sharply, as he handed it over. "Valid 90 days. You can use any number of times. Welcome to the Turkish Republic of Northern Cyprus." He added, smiling, and waved me through.

I learned later that the "Visa" was supplied on a separate sheet of paper for good reason. The Turkish Republic of Northern Cyprus is not recognised as a nation by any country in the world other than Turkey. Any written or stamped entry in a passport by a "non-country" is deemed by the rest of the world to be a defacement of the document, and automatically renders it void. The Turkish authorities are thankfully conscious of this and have instructed their border force accordingly, thus avoiding the possibility of making large numbers of passports unusable.

This was indeed a moment to savour. Thirty years or so after I'd first attempted to enter the Turkish sector of Cyprus from the Greek side, I'd finally made it. Of course, during the intervening years I could at any time have visited the Turkish side simply by flying from London to Istanbul, where I would have been obliged to change planes to get an internal flight to Ercan, the Northern Cyprus airport, but somehow the Ledras Street route seemed a much more satisfying way of achieving this long-held ambition. Feeling rather smug, I set off to explore Turkish Nicosia in the company of other tourists, and not unexpectedly almost immediately encountered a small bazaar, in which I was first offered a fez, then a Manchester United Wayne Rooney shirt, and In a nearby shop I found shelves laden with boxes of multicoloured Turkish Delight, one of which I purchased as a gift to take home. All prices were shown in Euros and Turkish Lire, but it seemed that the bulk of transactions took place in Euros. By now it was almost midday, and as the sun shone down from a clear blue sky I moved on through the narrow streets towards St. Sofia Cathedral, currently known as Selimeye Mosque. Elegantly constructed in light-brown stone, and dating from the thirteenth century, the Mosque boasts two tall, slender minarets that are visible from almost all elevated vantage points in Nicosia. Its history to some extent mirrors that of Hagia Sofia in Istanbul, in that it was originally erected as a Greek Orthodox Christian Church, but became a mosque when Cyprus fell under the control of the Ottoman Empire in the sixteenth century. As a result of its conversion from its Christian origins, it is one of the few mosques in the world that boasts flying buttresses. I glanced briefly around its majestic interior before heading for the much more interesting Buyuk Han, close by.

Buyuk Han is a caravanserai, which translates as "roadside inn", a place where travellers could spend the night in the days of animal transport. The word is derived from the Persian "karvan", a group of traders or pilgrims, and "seray", a building with enclosed courtyards. Buyuk Han is a typical example, dating from 1572, which rather bizarrely became the main prison in Nicosia from 1892 to 1903 under British rule. A stone building, two storeys high and around 50 metres square, it surrounds an airy quadrangle in which stands a small circular domed mosque. The inner walls are cloistered on both levels, their roman-style arches lending a pleasing symmetry to the view from ground-level. For a time in the 1950s the building saw use as a rather run-down refuge for poor families, but in the 1990s it was restored and is now arts centre. I wandered around, finding much of interest artistically, but nothing that might persuade my hand to trouble my pocket. By now the heat of the sun persuaded me to find a bar, and in the broad street outside I found a suitably empty table outside a cafe and ordered a beer.

The lady brought me a bottle of Efes Turkish beer, without offering any alternative, and for a moment I'd been tempted to ask if she had Keo, the rather pleasant Greek beer which I'd been drinking thus far on this trip. I decided such a request might be impolitic in the circumstances. To accompany the beer I ordered shish kebab and rice, which was delicious, then sat for a while drinking Turkish coffee whilst watching the tourists come and go. I paid for my meal in Euros, which seemed somewhat ironic given that this small corner of a "nation", unrecognised as such by almost the entire world, is governed by Turkey, a country that has consistently failed to meet the European Union's criteria for membership.

Much that I could see prompted memories of times spent under a hot sun in pavement cafes on the bustling, dusty streets of Istanbul, and when I heard the call to prayer by the muezzin at Selimeye Mosque this served only to emphasise the similarity. For a moment I thought of those living in both sectors of this divided city, now able to sample the other's way of life by the simple expedient of crossing at the Ledras street checkpoint whenever they chose. There are those who may regard it as a small step on the road to reunification, but to the pragmatists that day is still probably many years away.

Somewhat reluctantly I returned to the checkpoint and walked south through the Greek sector past busy shops and restaurants. Half way along I bought a coffee in McDonald's, a bargain at 1 Euro 50 Cents, and took a seat at a table outside. I was surprised to see a couple of uniformed United

Nations soldiers stroll by, recognisable by their blue berets, and asked them if they would be prepared to let me take their photograph. After a short discussion they declined and walked on. This brief encounter reminded me that UN peace-keeping operations are often potentially dangerous, as had been the case in both Lebanon and Kosovo when I visited those countries. Cyprus, by contrast, is a peaceful island with a developed economy, and would surely be seen by UN personnel as one of their organisation's more desirable postings. A few minutes later I also moved on, intent on visiting the Venue Cafe, situated on the sixth floor of Debenhams department store a little further down the road.

The store, owned by the well-know British retail chain, was typical of its fellow outlets in the UK, laid out on six floors, helpfully connected by escalators, and offering clothing, household goods, and the like. I made straight for the busy cafe on the sixth floor, from which, I had been told, it was possible to take panoramic photographs of the city, including much of the Turkish sector. I was not to be disappointed, and on my arrival set to work quickly with my camera, mindful of the fact that I didn't actually intend to buy food or drink. Visible from the North-facing window was the whole of Turkish Nicosia, dominated by the Selimeye Mosque, and beyond that a hinterland of rolling hills leading to the Kyrenia Mountains, clearly visible under a brilliant blue sky about 15 kilometres away. In the foothills of the mountains the Turkish Cypriots have created an enormous representation of their flag, a red crescent moon and single red star on a white background with red horizontal stripes above and below. Measuring approximately 800 x 300 metres, it is painted on bare rock on the hillside, and attracts the eye from any elevated position in Nicosia in much the same way that the "Hollywood" sign does in Los Angeles. Alongside it is painted an additional crescent and star of similar width and height, this time in white, above the words "Ne Mutlu Turkum Diyene. K. Ataturk", the first four words of which translate as "How happy is the one who says he is a Turk.", a motto of the Turkish Republic. "K Ataturk" refers to Kemal Ataturk, the founder of modern-day Turkey. The red and white flag is illuminated at night, no doubt intended as a constant reminder to those living in the Greek sector of Turkey's territorial claim. I quickly took photographs whilst trying my best not to disturb *bona fide* customers at the tables, and then returned to Ledras Street. Recently I discovered that Debenham's closed the store in 2015 and the premises were subsequently acquired by H and M Clothing, who sadly decided to close the cafe when they moved into the building, with the result that the sixth floor is no longer accessible to the general public.

I continued walking southwards then turned left and entered the Shakolas Tower, one of Nicosia's tallest buildings, rising to 11 storeys. The Greek authorities had recently authorised the opening of an observation room, so I paid the fee and took the lift to the top floor. The room offers a 360-degree panorama of the entire city and surroundings, and contains audio-visual presentations of events in the city's recent history. From its windows I caught tantalising glimpses of predominantly green no man's land, an area more or less untouched by man since the Turkish invasion in 1974. I recently listened to a radio programme in which the presenter, who had special permission to enter the no man's land area, spoke of finding an unlocked house inside which were the remains of the meal abandoned by the family as they fled the area in 1974. Nearby, the reporter described a car showroom where unsold vehicles from 1974 are still to be found, coated in dust, and untouched more than forty years after the invasion. Not for the first time I wondered if some budding entrepreneur might persuade the Greeks, the Turks, and, most important, the United Nations, to grant permission for organised groups to tour this remarkable time-capsule.

By now it was late-afternoon and there was a slight chill in the air as I made my way back to the hotel. The Filipino ladies had left, presumably to resume their housekeeping duties, and once back in my room I took up position on my balcony to consume a picnic meal and watch the world go by. It was a relaxing end to what had been a busy but very enjoyable day, and I had the added bonus of now being in possession of a visa, duly stamped, allowing entry to one of the world's few non-countries, the Turkish Republic of Northern Cyprus. Incidentally, it shares this status with six other "countries" around the world, namely Taiwan, Kosovo, Palestine, North Korea, Armenia, and Israel, each of which is not recognised by at least one current United Nations member.

The following morning, as I breakfasted on my balcony, I noticed police activity in the nearby main road, with traffic being held up. I rushed outside and spotted a gaggle of press photographers outside the Classic Hotel, just around the corner. They sprang into life at the arrival of a short motorcade, and I was told that one of those exiting the leading vehicle was the President of Cyprus, presumably arriving from the Cyprus Parliament building, located no more than a couple of hundred metres down the road. I took photographs and went on my way, heading back towards the Ledras Street checkpoint, but on this occasion, instead of continuing through to the Turkish side I took the last turning on the right, Nikokleous Street, which would in theory allow me to shadow the route of the southern border of no man's land eastwards. At the end I turned left, towards the border, but found that street blocked off by a wall, beyond which stood a blue-and-white-striped wooden guardhouse with horizontal slit-holes, giving the United Nations occupants a clear view of me as I paused to take a photograph. I hurriedly abandoned thoughts of photography thereafter and turned right along a road running parallel to the border, but some 50 metres or so south of it. I was unsurprised to find similar barriers constructed from piled-up blue and white oil-drums, or concreted breeze-blocks, blocking streets that had once led North to what is now the Turkish side. *En route* I passed the occasional business, one such being a workshop where men were making cane seats for chairs, but in general the area was quiet enough to remind me of a walk through the streets of a village. Private houses were interspersed with the occasional shop or bar, and entire streets running West-East adjacent to the border were inaccessible. For a city with an urban population of 310,000 souls, it seemed strange to walk through its centre and hear little more than birdsong.

After perhaps half a kilometre I came across the Pancyprian Gymnasium, a strangely out-of-place neoclassical stone building and Nicosia's oldest-established school, which once numbered amongst its teaching staff the writer Lawrence Durrell, and amongst its pupils Achbishop Makarios, the first president of Cyprus. His statue in white marble stands in front of the entrance to the nearby Archbishop's Palace, a large and elegant two-storey pantiled building, its outer walls cloistered with roman arches on both levels. Whilst the palace itself is not open to the public, it does however contain within its grounds the National Struggle Museum, which I was particularly keen to visit. The museum is dedicated to the period from 1955 to 1960 when the Island was fighting a war of independence against its colonial masters, the British. The exhibits were much as you'd expect from a guerrilla war – armaments, photographs of prisoner-of-war camps, letters, and details of notable incidents. The most emotionally troubling room is located on the second floor and displays black-and-white photographs and names of each of the hundreds of Cypriots who died in the struggle. In the middle of this room a wooden bar hangs from the ceiling, from which three nooses are suspended. It is claimed these were the actual nooses used by the British to hang nine Cypriot prisoners who were sentenced to death after being captured during the conflict. There is a similar room in Dubrovnik in Croatia showing photographs of all those killed in the siege of that city by the

Yugoslav People's Army during 1991. The British signed the declaration of independence in 1959, but the troubles continued thereafter partly due to the subsequent arrangements made between the Turks and Greeks. Archbishop Makarios was the first Cyprus president following independence and ruled until 1977.

From the museum I made my way back to the Ledras Street crossing and returned to the cafe on the Turkish side for beer and a kebab. I contemplated the possibility of walking along the no man's land border on the Turkish side but decided against it as I'd already been spotted wielding a camera on the Greek side and my presence had undoubtedly been noted. In any case the heat of the afternoon sun persuaded me to linger at the cafe, and I took the opportunity to chat to the lady who served me regarding the opening of the crossing. Business had never been better, she confirmed, but stopped short of agreeing with me when I suggested it would be even better should the island be reunified.

"We are proud people. It is our land. We fought for it."

"But business...?"

" My business is OK as it is. I don't need more."

"You like earning Euros here?"

"Of course. But Turkish Lire just as good."

"You have children?" I asked, cautiously.

"Yes. Two boys. "

"Do you want them to have a better future? Perhaps in the European Union? Earning Euros?"

"They can go there to work if they wish. Money is good there. They will send me Euros. My brother works in Stuttgart. He has good job. But he will always be Turkish Cypriot. So will my boys."

With that she turned away to serve a group of tourists. Half an hour later I finished my beer, paid my bill in Euros, and returned down Ledras Street, which was by now almost deserted. Soon I was back on my hotel balcony watching the inevitable game of musical cars in the car park down below, and pondering the Turkish-Greek conundrum that blights this delightful corner of the Mediterranean. As with the dysfunctional car-park, I concluded that there appeared to be no short-term solution to the island's problem, and those who live there, just like the hotel staff, would simply have to make the best of the situation. I was reminded of my visit to Belarus, another delightful country, whose people would I'm sure benefit enormously if only they, and their politicians, could be persuaded to abandon decades of dogma.

The following day I headed to the bus station, from where I returned to Paphos, spending my final night in the idiosyncratic hotel before catching a flight the following morning back to London. As my plane headed out over the Mediterranean I wondered when I would return. Of one thing I was sure, that the Island would still be divided, which I find dispiriting. Cyprus is, I believe, an example of that old adage that the whole could be so much greater than the sum of its parts.

THE END

Copyright David Birkett 2/11/2017

Printed in Great Britain
by Amazon